Earth Summit 2002
A New Deal

Edited by Felix Dodds
with Toby Middleton

Earthscan Publications Ltd
London • Sterling, VA

This book is dedicated to the Memory of Michael McCoy, the first Northern Co-Chair of the United Nations Commission on Sustainable Development NGO Steering Committee. A generous American, a friend and supporter of the global NGO Movement, and a tireless fighter for a more just and humane world for all

Revised edition first published in the UK and USA in 2001
by Earthscan Publications Ltd

Reprinted 2002

First edition 2000

A catalogue record for this book is available from the British Library

ISBN 1 85383 867 5

Typesetting by PCS Mapping & DTP, Newcastle upon Tyne
Printed and bound in the UK by Creative Print and Design Wales, Ebbw Vale
Cover design by Declan Buckley

For a full list of publications please contact:
Earthscan Publications Ltd
120 Pentonville Road, London, N1 9JN, UK
Tel: +44 (0)20 7278 0433
Fax: +44 (0)20 7278 1142
Email: earthinfo@earthscan.co.uk
http://www.earthscan.co.uk

22883 Quicksilver Drive, Sterling, VA 20166-2012, USA

Earthscan is an editorially independent subsidiary of Kogan Page Ltd and publishes in association with WWF-UK and the International Institute for Environment and Development

This book is printed on elemental chlorine-free paper

Contents

PART I: ROADBLOCKS TO IMPLEMENTING AGENDA 21 AND HOW TO OVERCOME THEM

PART II: A NEW CHARTER

PART III: OVERRIDING CONCERNS

List of Figures, Tables and Boxes

FIGURES

TABLES

BOXES

List of Contributors

Cletus A Avoka is the Minister for Environment, Science and Technology of Ghana. He is Member of Parliament for Bawku West in the upper east region of Ghana. Until his appointment to this ministry in November 1998, he was the Minister for Lands and Forestry. Formerly he held a number of positions in the public service of the country. He is a lawyer by profession.

Stephen Bass, Director of Programmes, IIED, is an environmental planner and forester with 18 years of experience working principally in Western Asia, the Caribbean and Southern Africa. He has specialized in the assessment, formulation and monitoring of participatory natural resource and forest policy, starting with work on national conservation strategies and similar processes. He also has considerable experience in institutional development in forestry and environment. At present he is working on sustainability assessment in forestry, and on developing and assessing market-based instruments, notably forest certification. As IIED's Director of Programmes he is responsible for strategic programme development, research planning and quality control.

Stephen is also Associate Departmental Lecturer, Oxford Forestry Institute, Associate Researcher at the European Forestry Institute, and Affiliated Associate, Island Resources Foundation. Previously, he worked as Southern Africa Programme Manager for IUCN and as Warren Weaver Fellow.

Barbara J Bramble is Vice-President for National Wildlife Federation's Strategic Programmes Initiative, which develops new projects to confront the conservation challenges of the 21st century. Formerly, she founded and directed for 16 years NWF's international division, which concentrates on ensuring that global economic forces are harnessed for the benefit of wildlife, natural resources and people. Barbara Bramble helped organize the International NGO Forum, the largest NGO conference at the Earth Summit at Rio in 1992; and she has worked with NGOs from many countries on joint campaigns, such as World Bank and WTO reform and pesticide safeguards.

Before joining NWF, Barbara Bramble served as legal adviser to the Council on Environmental Quality, in the Executive Office of the US President, and as an environmental lawyer representing national and local conservation groups in cases involving energy, land use and pollution. She received her JD from George Washington University, and a BA in History from George Mason University.

Jeb Brugman is the founding Secretary General of the International Council for Local Environmental Initiatives (ICLEI). He has a 16-year career in the local government sector, focusing primarily on municipal efforts to address major regional and global issues, including the environment, military conflict and human rights. He conceived and launched the Local Agenda 21 initiative in 1990.

Gro Harlem Brundtland is Director-General of the World Health Organization. A qualified medical doctor specializing in child and public health, she was also former Minister of the Environment and Prime Minister of Norway. Dr Brundtland chaired the World Commission on Environment and Development that led to the United Nations Earth Summit in Rio de Janeiro, 1992. She authored the seminal work *Our Common Future: Report of the World Commission on Environment and Development* in 1987.

Margaret Brusasco-Mackenzie is Vice-Chair of UNED-UK. She was, for many years, head of International Affairs and Trade and Environment in the Environmental Directorate General of the European Commission. Latterly she was adviser for the follow-up to the Rio Summit. She has taken part in many international environmental negotiations and has contributed to several books and written articles on international environmental policy. She has degrees in Law from University London, Kings College, and Yale University.

Nitin Desai is United Nations Undersecretary-General for Economic and Social Affairs. He was formerly a consultant for Tata Economic Consultancy Services and lecturer in economics at the universities of Southampton and Liverpool. He has been a member of the Commonwealth Secretariat Expert Group on Climate Change and the Board of the Stockholm Environment Institute. From 1985 to 1987 he served as Senior Economic Adviser for the World Commission on Environment and Development (WCED, known as the Brundtland Commission). From 1990 to 1993 he was Deputy Secretary-General of the United Nations Conference on Environment and Development (UNCED), with responsibility for coordinating the work of the UNCED Secretariat related to the development of Agenda 21. In March 1997, Secretary-General Kofi Annan appointed Nitin Desai to coordinate, and subsequently head, the consolidation of the three UN economic and social departments. The consolidated department provides substantive support to the normative, analytical, statistical and relevant technical cooperation processes of the UN on the economic and social side. He is also the Convenor of the Executive Committee on Economic and Social Affairs, which brings together the heads of all the UN Secretariat entities directly concerned with economic, environmental and social issues.

Felix Dodds is Executive Director of the United Nations Environment and Development Forum (UNED Forum). He is also Co-Chair of the United Nations Commission on Sustainable Development (CSD) NGO Steering Committee. He has been active in all of the CSD meetings and coordinated the NGO lobbying teams for the Habitat II and the Earth Summit II conferences. His previous books have been *The Way Forward: Beyond Agenda 21* (Earthscan, 1997) and *Into the 21st Century: An Agenda for Political Realignment* (Green Print, 1988). He is a member of Green Globe that advises the UK Foreign Secretary and Environment Minister on sustainable development. He also sits on the Board of Greenwich Environmental Management Services Ltd (GEMS) which advises small- and medium-sized businesses.

Victoria Elias is Deputy Director of the Centre for Environment and Sustainable Development 'ECO-Accord' (Russia). She graduated from Moscow Lomonossov State University as a biologist. For a number of years Victoria was involved in research on aquatic ecology and water toxicology. She also teaches biology and ecology to students. Since 1989 Victoria Elias has been active in the environmental NGO movement in Russia and abroad. Victoria is a member of several national and international NGOs, as a regional representative for the Newly Independent States (NIS) and central and eastern Europe (CEE) at the CSD NGO Steering Committee and Management Committee. She has chaired the Coordination Board for pan-European ECO-Forum since 1999. Issues of public participation and freshwater management and conservation in the context of sustainable development are the main areas of Victoria's interest in her activities and research.

Pieter van der Gaag is Executive Director of ANPED, the Northern Alliance for Sustainability. Within ANPED he coordinates the corporate accountability and responsibility programme. The programme brings together a broad coalition of non-government organizations working on achieving corporate accountability. He currently serves as NGO contact point for the OECD Working Party on the Review of the Guidelines for Multinational Enterprises, and serves on the steering group for the CSD Review of Voluntary Initiatives and Agreements.

Rosalie Gardiner is Policy Coordinator at UNED Forum and currently working on the preparations for Earth Summit 2002 in Johannesburg in September 2002. Inspired and motivated by the vital need for sustainable development globally, she has undertaken research on a whole range of issues, such as the tourism industry, finance, HIV/AIDs, freshwater and marine and coastal management, as well as examined different decision-making processes used to assist progress towards sustainable development. Rosalie specialized in Environmental Economics and Management (BSc) at York University and went on to complete a Master of Research in Ecosystems Analysis and Governance at the University of Warwick, UK.

Winston Gereluk represents the Public Services International (PSI) on matters relating to the CSD, and environmental issues generally. The PSI is an international trade secretariat for public-sector trade unions, and such represents millions of public employees around the world. Winston has participated in delegations and the production of literature on behalf of the International Confederation of Free Trade Unions at the last five sessions of the CSD, and is a member of Greenpeace. He is employed by the Alberta Union of Provincial Employees, an affiliate of the National Union of Public and General Employees in Canada. He also instructs and develops industrial relations courses for Athabasca University in Canada.

Herbert Girardet, a UN Global 500 Award recipient, is author of *The Gaia Atlas of Cities* (1992) and *Earthrise* (1992) and other environmental books. He also works as a TV producer, mainly on environmental documentaries. Currently he is series editor on a six-part international TV series – *The People's Planet*. He is visiting professor at Middlesex University, London, and Chairman of the Schumacher Society, UK.

John Gummer was the longest-serving Secretary of State for the Environment the UK has ever had; a member of the Queen's Privy Council for the last 14 years, he was first elected as a Member of Parliament in 1970. He became the Chairman of the Conservative party at a very young age and went on to 16 years of top-level ministerial experience. While at MAFF he chaired the

European Council of Agriculture Ministers during the negotiations for the GATT round, and represented EU ministers in Chicago during the final stages of the trade negotiations. Following the conferences on climate change in Berlin and Geneva the Secretary-General of the United Nations selected him for a Committee of Distinguished Persons advising on Habitat II (UN Conference on Human Settlements). In 1996 he was elected Chairman of the Environment Committee of the OECD by his fellow ministers. Since then, in an unprecedented cross-party gesture, the Labour government took him as part of the UK's delegation to the Earth Summit II United Nations Special Session and subsequently to the Kyoto and Buenos Aries Climate Change Conferences.

Since leaving office John Gummer has been appointed Chairman of the International Commission on Sustainable Consumption, Chairman of the Marine Stewardship Council, and chosen as a member of the select Track II diplomatic group to advise the Chinese government on climate change. He has set up, and now runs, Sancroft International, an environmental consultancy working with governments, international organizations and blue-chip companies around the world.

Minu Hemmati is a psychologist by profession, having specialized in environmental and social psychology and women's studies. Since 1998, Minu has been working as an independent project coordinator with UNED Forum in the area of women and sustainable development (www.uned-uk.org). She has attended the Habitat II Conference in 1996, all CSD inter-sessional meetings and sessions since 1997, Earth Summit II, and CSW meetings. Minu has been elected Northern Co-Facilitator of the CSD NGO Women's Caucus for the period May 1999–April 2001.

Maximo 'Juni' Kalaw is the Executive Director of the Earth Council. A graduate in both Economics and Management, he has held a number of high-level posts, including Director of the Bank of Asia and of the Bankasia Finance Corporation. Previously President of such NGOs as the Green Forum Philippines, the Haribon Foundation and the Philippine Institute of Alternative Futures, Juni is now working with the Earth Council in drafting the Earth Charter. He was the Co-Chair of the International NGO Forum at the Earth Summit in 1992, and subsequently the Executive Director of the Earth Summit II International Secretariat. Widely published in the field of sustainable development, Juni has also been recognized by a number of awards for his work.

Rob Lake is Director of Policy at Traidcraft. The charity arm of Traidcraft works at a policy level on fair and ethical trade that benefits the developing world; on corporate accountability and social responsibility and corporate governance; on social reporting and accounting; and on socially responsible investment. The organization also carries out practical small-business development initiatives in developing countries. Before coming to Traidcraft, Rob Lake worked at the Royal Society for the Protection of Birds (RSPB) and at Friends of the Earth (FoE) on international environment and development policy, EU environmental issues and local-level environmental initiatives.

Warren (Chip) Lindner is currently an adviser to the LEAD (Leadership for Environment and Development) programme. Chip served for three years as Executive Secretary of the World Commission on Environment and

Development (the Brundtland Commission), which in 1987 published the landmark report *Our Common Future*. In April 1988 he created the Centre for our Common Future on which he served as Executive Director until its closure in 1995. During this period he also served as international coordinator of the 1992 Global Forum held in Rio de Janeiro at the time of the first Earth Summit. From June 1996 until the end of 1998 Chip served as senior adviser on North–South issues to the Chairman and Executive Secretary of the 12th World AIDS Conference. Recently, he was presented by the president of Brazil with the Order of the Southern Cross, the highest civilian award granted by the government of Brazil.

Jürgen Maier is Director of the German NGO Forum Environment & Development, a network of about 60 NGOs formed after the Earth Summit to coordinate the Rio follow-up among German NGOs: Climate Convention, Biodiversity Convention, Desertification Convention, CSD, WTO, FAO and other relevant fora. He has held this position since 1996. Previously he worked as Secretary General of the German Asia Foundation and International Secretary of the German Green Party.

Frans de Man as international secretary of a Dutch left-wing ecological party called PPR, Frans de Man got to know the field of international politics and development cooperation during the 1980s. In 1990 he became consultant in tourism planning, first for national and regional governments in The Netherlands, later for the Dutch Nature Friends. In 1987 he initiated the Retour Foundation to stimulate positive developments in tourism and to fight negative aspects. As consultant for Retour he worked on sustainable tourism projects in Tanzania, Cameroon, Ecuador and Costa Rica from 1994 onwards. He developed the Dutch branch of ECPAT (the fight against child sex tourism) and acted as adviser to this international organization. He advises the Dutch government on multistakeholder processes in tourism resulting from the Agreement on Sustainable Development with Costa Rica. Since April 1999 he is the northern Co-Chair of the NGO Tourism Caucus and participates in the Steering Committee of the UN Working Group on Sustainable Tourism. The latest project he developed is the Holiday Mirror, a website reflecting the opinions of local inhabitants of tourism destinations on tourism and tourists.

Laurie Michaelis is the Director of Research for the Oxford Commission on Sustainable Consumption, which is developing an action plan on sustainable consumption for Earth Summit 3. Laurie has a PhD in energy studies, on wood use and the potential for alternative fuels in Kenya. He has worked as a volunteer in development organizations, as a school teacher and as an energy technology analyst. From 1992 to 1999 Laurie worked for the OECD, initially focusing on energy, transport and climate change but most recently leading programmes on eco-efficiency and resource efficiency.

Toby Middleton is International Communications Coordinator for UNED Forum's Towards Earth Summit 2002 project. He is manger of the project's website www.earthsummit2002.org and the Roadmap to 2002 website. He is editor of the project's online newsletter, Network 2002 (global circulation of over 30,000 organisations).

Toby co-ordinated the UK national one-day preparatory conferences to the 1999 Seattle WTO Ministerial. He has participated and chaired meetings at several international UN meetings, representing UNED Forum and has been a member of the UK Government Delegation, including several sessions of the UNCSD and UNEP's Governing Council and global meetings of UNEP's National Committees. Toby represented UNED UK on the UK Multi-lateral Agreement on Investments Coalition from 1998 to 1999.

Toby has worked with the OUTREACH team, producing daily newsletters at these international events, culminating as editor of OUTREACH at the London WHO Environment and Health Conference in 1999. He has worked with the UN CSD NGO Steering Committee, establishing and coordinating the activities of the NGO Tourism Caucus at the 7th Session of the UNCSD.

Derek Osborn is the Chairman of the UK Round Table on Sustainable Development. He also chairs the United Nations Environment and Development Committee in the UK (UNED-UK), and the trustees of the International Institute of Environment and Development. He is a non-executive Director of Severn Trent Plc, and Chairman of its environment committee. As a senior environmentalist he advises governments, international bodies, voluntary bodies and business on long-term environmental and sustainable development issues. In 1997 he was the Co-Chairman of the negotiations for the Special Session of the UN General Assembly (sometimes known as Earth Summit II), five years after the 1992 Earth Summit in Rio.

Deike Peters is Director of Environmental Programmes at the Institute for Transportation and Development Policy (ITDP), an international research and advocacy NGO dedicated to promoting sustainable transportation. She originally came to New York from her native Germany for a one-year student exchange. Deike now holds MSc degrees in International Affairs and Urban Planning from Columbia University and is currently a PhD candidate in Urban Planning and Policy Development at Rutgers University. Her dissertation investigates the complex role of transport infrastructures and policies in shaping European economic development and integration.

Jagjit Plahe worked as a Researcher for the Multilateral Development Initiatives Programme of Eco News Africa, which is an African development NGO. She now works as an independent researcher on trade and human rights issues. She is also the Southern Coordinator of the NGO Task Force on Business and Industry.

Nina Rao is Head of the Department of Tourism, College of Vocational Studies, University of Delhi, since 1978, and has pioneered tourism studies courses at other universities and through the Open University system. She is on the Planning Board of EQUATIONS, an NGO dealing with tourism policy, development and impacts, which is currently engaged in an extensive study on domestic tourism in India and preparing for a national workshop on tourism's impacts on women. She is involved in reformulating the North–South tourism dialogue and updating the mission statement for the Asian network, and is closely associated with GATTS issues and the debate on biodiversity understanding in India, towards developing a people's plan for safeguarding biodiversity. She is also Co-Chair for the NGO Tourism Caucus, CSD-7, and author of two books on Ladakh and the Western Himalayas, published by Roli Books, Hong Kong.

Lucien Royer is the Health, Safety and Environment Officer for both the International Confederation of Free Trade Unions (ICFTU) and the Trade Union Advisory Committee to the OECD (TUAC). He coordinates programmes throughout the world and represents trade unions at the United Nations, OECD, and other international bodies with respect to health, safety and environment. Originally from Western Canada, he was involved in environmental litigation and environmental law reform, and was a founding member of the Canadian Environmental Network. He formed part of the Canadian government delegation at Bergen in 1990 and at Rio in 1992.

Andrew Simms is currently the head of the global economy programme at the think tank the New Economics Foundation (NEF), and an adviser to Christian Aid, the overseas development agency. In the past he studied at the London School of Economics, and worked in politics and for a range of development and environment organizations. In particular, he has been part of campaigns on: debt relief, climate change, food security and genetically modified food, and corporate accountability. He is currently working to highlight the vacuum of regulation in the global economy, and the contradictions between the 'business as usual' approach and meeting the need for social and environmental well-being.

Simon Upton has been an MP in the New Zealand parliament representing the National party since 1981, when he won selection as the National party candidate for the Waikato electorate, aged 23. He was educated at Southwell School and St Paul's Collegiate in Hamilton. Subsequently, he took degrees in English and Law from the University of Auckland, and has an MLitt in political philosophy from Oxford University. He is also a Rhodes scholar. Between 1990 and 1999 he was Minister for the Environment and from 1996 to 1999 Associate Minister of Foreign Affairs. In this capacity he chaired the 7th Session of the CSD. He has a website where he discusses a range of environmental and CSD issues. The address is: www.arcadia.co.nz. Simon Upton has long-established interests in music, literature and political philosophy, as well as geology and botany. He is a keen skier, and an enthusiastic gardener on his Ngaruawahia property. He is currently Spokesperson for Foreign Affairs, Culture and Heritage, and Superannuation. He was appointed to the Privy Council in 1999.

Foreword: From Rio to Earth Summit 2002

Klaus Töpfer

When I attended the Earth Summit in 1992 I did so as the German environment minister. The Rio Summit, I believe, was a milestone in awakening the world to the need to work together for the sake of our planet and the future generations that will live here.

As I prepared to leave Germany, I don't think I, or for that matter any of us then arriving in Brazil, realized how important the summit would be. While writing this Foreword I reflected on what has been achieved due to the Rio Summit. The outcomes include:

- Agenda 21;
- The Framework Convention on Climate Change;
- The Convention on Biodiversity;
- The Rio Declaration;
- The Forest Principles.

These were all agreed to at Rio; this by itself would have been an enormous achievement, but this was not all that came out of the summit. There was agreement for the negotiation of a desertification convention; a conference on straddling and highly migratory fish stocks; the development of indicators on sustainable development; the creation of sustainable development strategies; and the setting up of a new commission within the Economic and Social Council of the UN. This itself has ensured the monitoring and implementation of much of Agenda 21, and the development of work programmes in areas such as consumption and production, education, tourism and forest biodiversity through the Intergovernmental Panel, and then Forum, on Forests.

Perhaps one of the most interesting developments since Rio has been the impact of the chapters of Agenda 21 on major groups. In particular, the chapter on local authorities has been catalytic to making Agenda 21 a real document at the local level where there are now over 2000 LA21s.

As executive director of UNEP and the Centre for Human Settlements, I am enormously aware of the impact that cities have on our environment. The LA21 process has been, and will continue to be, an opportunity for local stakeholders to talk and agree on how they can make their local communities more sustainable. It has helped break down mistrust between different stakeholders and has focused on the future.

As we start the preparations for the Earth Summit in 2002, 10 years from Rio and 30 years from Stockholm, most of the world's problems are still getting worse. The difference between the last two summits and 2002 is that we now know a lot more and we have started to turn the tide. In 2002 we need to address the environmental security issues such as freshwater, fisheries and food security and environmental refugees.

If there is to be success in 2002, then one thing is clear: there will need to be additional funds from developed countries to enable developing countries to grow sustainably. Aid flows have for the first time since 1991 started to move in the right direction – not much, but it is now going in the right direction. The campaign by Jubilee 2000 for debt cancellation is to be congratulated and will have an impact on financing development. This isn't enough by itself and we do need to look for 'new and additional funds'. I commend the work of UNDP in broadening the debate on this topic.

We need to set targets and dates that are realistic to deliver the change that is needed. There will also need to be a debate on the international machinery to achieve what we want, and 2002 will be significant in setting out the direction.

This book is produced by UNEP's national committee in the UK and has drawn in some of the key people who are working to make 2002 a significant event. I welcome the call for a 'New Deal' and UNEP will play its part. In 2002 we will be bringing out the next issue of the *Global Environment Outlook* report (GEO-2002), which will ensure that the environmental data is there for governments to make the decisions that need to be made.

I hope that all of you who read this book will join in the preparations for Earth Summit 2002.

Introduction

Derek Osborn

At the beginning of this millennial year 2000, many people in the world can still feel the warmth and energy generated by the first Earth Summit in Rio in 1992. Its inspiration glows on our backs, and its vision spurs us forward to complete the tasks it set and to meet the challenges of the new millennium. Now, as we look forward, the tenth anniversary of Rio in 2002 is looming up as one of the first big opportunities of the 21st century.

This book is a timely wake-up call – a bugle summoning support from around the world to prepare for a new Earth Summit in 2002. Anyone who has been involved with international processes will know how long it takes to prepare for major international events, and to build the public and political momentum to ensure worthwhile results. The time for action is now.

The Earth Summit at Rio in 1992 was a major advance for the cause of sustainable development throughout the world. World leaders signed two major international conventions on climate change and biodiversity. The Rio Declaration on Environment and Development proclaimed 27 principles to guide sustainable development. A comprehensive programme of action for implementing sustainable development throughout the world (Agenda 21) was adopted, together with a set of principles to guide the sustainable management of forests. A basis for providing new and additional resources to the countries of the South to assist them in the transition to more sustainable patterns of development was also agreed upon.

The energy generated by the Rio process is still one of the most powerful driving and integrating forces in the global sustainable development agenda. However, progress since then has been patchy. In some parts of the world, on some issues and in some sectors of society, the principles of Agenda 21 and its conventions have helped significantly to strengthen and guide the drive towards more sustainable patterns of development. But the developed countries failed to deliver on their promises to provide more assistance to the developing countries to promote sustainable development. Political and public attention has seeped away. On some issues, in some countries, events are still moving in the wrong direction.

The review of achievements, five years after Rio at the Special Session of the UN General Assembly in 1997, might have been the occasion for facing up to the failures since Rio, and for renewing and strengthening the commitments made at Rio. But in the event, there was insufficient preparation and public attention to generate the political will for stronger commitments. With a few significant exceptions, the main conclusions of the special session did not go much beyond reasserting the objectives of Agenda 21.

The tenth anniversary of Rio in 2002 will be the biggest opportunity for a comprehensive effort to push forward the sustainable development agenda throughout the world that is likely to arise for at least the next ten years. The year 2002 could, and should, be more like 1992 in Rio and less like 1997 in New York. It could be made the occasion for a big push forward. It is an opportunity not to be missed.

We all know that there is a mass of unfinished business in the sustainable development agenda. The environment is deteriorating. The pressures of population and unsustainable consumption are increasing. The natural world and biodiversity are suffering. Poverty is endemic. Inequalities between and within countries are growing more acute. Globalization is opening up the whole world to the free market. But proper guidance or regulation of this market to protect the environment and social goods is lagging behind. 2002 is a prime opportunity for a new generation of active champions to seize hold of the sustainable development agenda and push it forward vigorously.

In this book a number of the leading players from around the world present their views of the opportunities and challenges which 2002 represents on many of the key issues. We in UNED hope that their contributions at this early stage will help to focus the debate as the preparations for 2002 move ahead this year.

The United Nations Environment and Development Forum (UNED Forum) is a multistakeholder body, which draws together representatives from local government, business and trade unions, scientists and the academic community, non-governmental organizations in the environment and development fields, groups representing women and youth, and many other bodies concerned with promoting sustainable development in the world. It is in close touch with similar organizations and groupings in both the developed and developing world. This year UNED has established an international advisory board to facilitate and promote the participation of major groups throughout the world in international discussions and negotiations on sustainable development issues.

Over the past two years, UNED has been canvassing opinion around the world and assembling views about the tenth anniversary of Rio and what it could achieve. More and more people are getting drawn into this consultation, and a consensus on what is wanted from 2002 is still evolving. But there is a wide measure of agreement crystallizing around the following key objectives:

- a revitalized and integrated UN system for sustainable development;
- a new deal on finance – enabling a deal on sustainable development;
- an integration of trade and sustainable development;
- a clearer understanding of how governments should move forward nationally in implementing Agenda 21;
- a new charter which could lay the foundations for countries to frame their sustainable development policies;
- a review of the work of the present set of Rio conventions – looking at overlaps, gaps and obstacles;
- a set of new regional or even global conventions;
- a set of policy recommendations for the environmental security issues that face us;
- a set of agreed indicators for sustainable development;
- a clear set of commitments to implement agreed action by the UN, governments and major groups.

The challenge is now to create the mechanisms to enable this to happen.

Preface to the Revised Edition

Felix Dodds

This revised edition of *Earth Summit 2002* has been updated with two new chapters on freshwater (Chapter 23) and energy (Chapter 24). It is being completed after the first preparatory meeting for the Johannesburg Earth Summit 2002.

Although the first preparatory meeting was organizational, already thoughts are starting to coalesce around some interesting thematic areas for Earth Summit 2002 to address.

INTERNATIONAL INSTITUTIONAL GOVERNANCE

Institutional governance was a non-issue for the Special Session of the UN General Assembly (UNGASS, commonly known as Earth Summit II or Rio +5) convened in 1997 to review the Rio Earth Summit. It has become increasingly clear that, as they are presently configured, the multi-lateral institutions are unable to address sustainable development.

In February 2001, the United Nations Environment Programme (UNEP) Governing Council agreed to set up a Ministerial working group to look at environmental governance issues. This UNEP initiative is to be welcomed as a clear attempt to open themselves up for review.

The discussion may address the issue of the need for a World Environment Organization. A number of studies by, among others, the German Advisory Council on Global Change (WBGU), the Yale Dialogues, the Royal Institute of International Affairs and the Leadership for Environment and Development (LEAD) programme have already looked at this. Chapter 25 of this book also addresses some of the options for international governance structures.

One issue that the UNEP initiative will not look at is the future of the UN Commission on Sustainable Development (CSD). The position of the CSD in the UN structure, its effectiveness and, if it is to have a future, what its work programme might look like, are just some of the questions being asked.

Perhaps the most difficult issue to look at is whether Earth Summit 2002 will offer a chance to review the economic governance architecture and relationship to sustainable development. The Global Environmental Facility (GEF) has started a process to look at its future in this area but what about the World Bank, International Monetary Fund (IMF) and World Trade Organization (WTO)?

CONVENTIONS

There are six Rio conventions and protocols that should be reviewed in relation to Earth Summit 2002:

1   Cartagena Protocol on Biosafety, under the Convention on Biological Diversity (CBD) (3 ratifications out of the 50 required for entry into force).
2   The Kyoto Protocol, under the UN Framework Convention on Climate Change (UNFCCC) (23 ratifications out of the 55 required).
3   UN Convention to Combat Desertification (requires funding).
4   Agreement on Conservation and Management of Straddling Fish Stocks and Highly Migratory Fish Stocks, under the UN Convention on the Law of the Sea (UNCLOS) (27 ratifications out of the 30 required, EU countries still to ratify).
5   Rotterdam Convention on the Prior Informed Consent Procedure for Certain Hazardous Chemicals and Pesticides in International Trade (13 ratifications out of the 50 required).
6   Stockholm Convention on Persistent Organic Pollutants (to be adopted, 50 countries needed to ratify).

One key challenge for governments is to be able to come to the summit in 2002 having ratified these conventions and adequately funded them.

INTERNATIONAL DEVELOPMENT TARGETS

Earth Summit 2002 should help to set in motion the work programmes to enable the international development targets (IDTs) to be realized. In many cases this should include setting incremental targets for 2005 and 2010. The IDTs that should be reviewed include:

•   *Education:* To narrow the gender gap in primary and secondary education by 2005, and ensure that by 2015 all children complete a full course of primay education.

- *Environment:* To reverse the loss of environmental resources by 2015.
- *Health:* To reduce infant mortality by 66 per cent and maternal mortality by 75 per cent by 2015, and ensure access for all to primary reproductive health service by 2015.
- *HIV/AIDS:* To halt, and begin to reverse the spread of, HIV/AIDS by 2015. To reduce by 25 per cent the rate of HIV infection in people aged 15–24 in most affected countries before the year 2005, and globally before 2010. At least 90 per cent of young men and women must have access to HIV-preventative information by 2005 and 95 per cent by 2010.
- *Poverty:* To halve by 2015 the proportion of people globally (currently 22 per cent) whose income is less than US$1/day.
- *Sustainable development:* National strategies for sustainable development to be completed by 2002 and implemented by 2005.
- *Water:* To halve by 2015 the proportion of people who do not have access to safe drinking water (currently 20 per cent).

SECTORAL/CROSS SECTORAL ISSUES

Whatever the issues are for Earth Summit 2002, the approach should be a sectoral one looking at the cross sectoral issues though a sectoral lens. Taking water as an example, what has been the impact of globalization? What finance is required? What would appropriate gender mainstreaming look like? What technology transfer, capacity building and governance structures need to be in place? This approach should enable us to identify who is going to do what, by when and how.

STAKEHOLDERS

The approach for Earth Summit 2002 is to engage the stakeholders throughout the preparatory process. This makes it the most innovative approach to developing global policy agreements. UNED Forum has produced a report to help identify how stakeholders might be more creatively engaged in the preparatory process for 2002 and generally at the international level. This can be found at www.earthsummit2002.org/msp.

Earth Summit 2002 should be seen as a landmark event, but we should also be thinking about where we hope to be in 2003, 4, 5, 6 ... to infinity, and beyond. The forthcoming summit needs to be seen as the starting block to set this all in motion.

Part I

Roadblocks to Implementing Agenda 21 and How to Overcome Them

Roadblocks to Agenda 21:
A Government Perspective

Simon Upton

Agenda 21 was motivated by perceptions of a deteriorating world environment and the need for humankind to clean up its act. However, like all compromises engineered by the UN system, and despite the best efforts of the able people involved, Agenda 21 is a version of everything. It means all things to all people and hides a maze of differing judgements and aspirations.

For the developing world, as the initial chapters of Agenda 21 make quite clear, the priority remains economic development and the alleviation of poverty and its worst manifestations – hunger, disease, illiteracy. For the developed world the priorities are rather different. There, poverty is not really much of an issue, except at the margins. The developed world has the time to look at what it is doing to its natural surroundings, its environment, and to feel an overriding sense of concern about it. Of course, these are crude generalizations. Many in the developing world feel very strongly indeed about their environment. Many in the developed world hardly give a toss.

However, the broad picture is, I think, valid. The approach of the developing world was: 'You, developed countries, are worried about the state of the global environment. You want us to take action. However, our perception is that you have basically created this state of affairs through your own excesses. Furthermore, our priorities are limited to the basic needs of survival. So if you want us to take part in your global drive, you must give us the resources to do so, and you cannot expect us to do anything which interferes in any major way with our drive for economic development.' Their interlocutors in the developed world argued along the following lines: 'The indications are that the global environment is deteriorating, and deteriorating all the quicker because of runaway resource use and development in an increasing number of countries. There are growing global problems of climate change, loss of biodiversity, pressures on freshwater, marine pollution, hazardous waste accumulation and so on. These and other problems are reflected at the regional and local level. We must all play our part together in changing the way we do things, for our individual good, and for the good of the planet. Development that isn't community based – wherever it takes place – is doomed and self-defeating.'

Again, this is a broad generalization. There are many in the developing world taking action on the environment without waiting for help from outside. There are many in the developed world prepared to take a lead on environmental action without any guarantees that others will follow suit.

But to my mind these are pretty much the fundamental differences of view that make Agenda 21 less a blueprint for action, with all that denotes in terms of acknowledged roles, planning and sequencing, and more a challenging proposition, one that still requires a *modus operandi*.

It is still needed. I am no expert on every facet of the state of the world environment. I have a particular concern about the atmosphere and the toxic by-products of modern industrial processes. If I follow indications given by science-based bodies like the IPCC, UN agencies like UNEP and the FAO and non-governmental think tanks like the World Resources Institute then we continue to face challenges in a number of other areas. Global population is increasing fairly rapidly, especially in developing countries and in urban environments, where problems of waste and pollution are intensifying. Food production may be able to keep pace, but distribution isn't, to the same degree. There are increasing problems getting access to clean, safe freshwater. Energy use is rising, and with it the production of carbon dioxide, the major greenhouse gas contributing to global warming and climate change. We may be cutting down on the use of ozone-depleting substances but the ozone layer remains in a fragile state: continued vigilance is required. We are overloading the global nitrogen cycle, and this plus unsustainable agricultural practices is leading to soil degradation. Acid rain is a growing problem in Asia. On the biodiversity side, the global forests estate continues to shrink. Bioinvaders are a particular menace. The state of the world's oceans is cause for real concern, with habitats, especially reefs, and fish stocks under extreme stress.

Broad conclusions that can be drawn from all this are as follows: changes in natural ecosystems are occurring on a larger scale than ever before. There are important changes occurring in the global systems and cycles that underpin ecosystem functioning. And the threats to biodiversity are severe, both in terms of extinction of species, and loss of habitats.

The fact is that we have been aware of these and other problems for some considerable time. And it is not as though we have done nothing about them. We have at least made an effort at the international level to organize ourselves, in fora and under legal conventions. The problem I think is that very often we get bogged down in process and the substance gets lost.

I was aware of this especially when I was facing, with some trepidation, the prospect of chairing the 7th Session of the United Nations Commission on Sustainable Development (CSD-7) in April 1999. The CSD had the reputation of being a turgid talk-shop, which resulted in nothing of substance and devoted its attentions to the painful word-smithing of negotiated texts. I was gratified to find that many of my fellow ministers were quite of my mind, and like me wanted to see the CSD change its ways and become once again a body capable of providing real direction to the effort in favour of sustainable development.

One of the key subjects we had to deal with was Oceans and Seas. The complex tangle of bodies and instruments coming under the UNCLOS umbrella gives the impression of a minutely regulated resource. So it may be, but for all that we have not yet succeeded in managing it sustainably.

I am not sure that the New York environment is a good one for discussion and decision-making on sustainable development. In New York it must compete for attention with so many other issues better suited to that environment. It is hard to take climate change seriously if you have not experienced life on an island atoll 3 metres above sea level where you are prey to any big wave. It is hard to get steamed up about the ozone layer unless you live, as I do, in a country where UVB exposure is a major cause of cancer. And poverty has no meaning if you have not made your home and livelihood, if you can call it that, on a rubbish heap without clean water to drink or wash and no hope of anything better. Though there may be no alternative to New York and its processes, we need to remind ourselves constantly of the reality about which we appear to talk so knowledgeably. We need to dig Agenda 21 out of the morass of bureaucractic process, diplomatic verbiage, and the mental trenches laid down on the battlefield of geopolitical debate.

We need to put Agenda 21 back on the road again. But we also need to get our bearings. One of the main problems we face in this regard is that we have no clear idea of exactly what we are aiming for. What is the paradigm of sustainable development? Does one exist, and is it useful to try to define it? Or should we instead agree to focus our efforts on four or five priority areas?

The core of the problem is what and how people produce and consume. This is a very difficult issue, because it impinges on the fundamental tenets of economic development, of aspirations that everyone has for a better life through increased economic means, and of the freedom and flexibility to explore and try things out. The challenge for us, and it is increasingly one of life and death, is to find ways of exploiting our natural and physical environment in ways that conserve its capacity for exploitation in the future.

At the bottom, we're involved in substituting natural capital with intellectual capital. We can no longer depend on seemingly inexhaustible supplies of virtually anything, and we are having to find ways of using resources more efficiently, both in terms of the benefits we draw from them and the degree to which we render them unfit for future use. What we don't know enough about is the extent to which the intellectual capital can be substituted for the natural capital. So managing the risks inherent in that process of substitution becomes critical. Facing a major challenge such as climate change, for example, some claim that the future growth in intellectual capital – manifested, for example, in climate-friendly technologies – will take care of any risks. However, set against the magnitude of the risks involved and the long time frames required to reduce concentration levels of greenhouse gases, sole reliance on the white knight of intellectual capital is a deficient risk-management strategy. There is a need to take precautionary action.

The tools we have to meet this challenge globally are not all that well developed. International relations up to this century have evolved largely to meet the needs of individual states in terms of the acquisition – or the prevention of acquisition – of territory, hegemony, trade rights and so on. This reflects a basic grab for resources and power. The idea that there might be something for every country to gain from international exchange, and that there should be economic stability to allow them a chance to gain it, is relatively recent. It is reflected in the Bretton Woods instruments and later in the GATT. One prime motivation was the need to find ways of reducing the sort of tensions that led to World War II, of setting the whole world on a path to economic development and prosperity that, it was hoped, would minimize the chances of a nuclear Armageddon. The idea was to provide a global framework for economic development and, through the UN, for political security that would allow every country to pursue unmolested its sovereign interests in getting richer without impinging upon the freedom of others to do the same.

The idea that the rest of the world should be interested in what other countries do internally, except in terms of military build-ups and other possible threats to security, is also of recent origin. The interest in, and opposition to, ideological systems of government that favoured aggressive proselytism and acquisition of territory and power gradually extended to human rights abuses – one of the strongest generators, along with starvation and poverty, of political instability. The envelope of enlightened self-interest was being pushed further and further.

It is, however, quite a step from there to a willingness to recognize that the rest of the world might have a legitimate interest in the way individual countries pursue their sovereign interests in the economic activity that was the hope and focus of the post-war settlement. There are still many countries, and they include the world's most powerful country as well as many developing countries, where there is an unwillingness to recognize that the rest of the world could have a legitimate interest in these ostensibly internal matters.

The sense of feeling one's way into the future is reflected in the current state of action. It is in some ways counterintuitive to begin with action on ozone, because it represents one of the few likely success stories; but it stands in useful contrast. Since the entry into force of the 1987 Montreal Protocol on Substances that Deplete the Ozone Layer, there has been an estimated 70 per cent cut in consumption of ozone-depleting substances, and it is hoped that with the full implementation of the Protocol and its adjustments and amendments, the ozone layer will recover by 2050. It is predicted that in so doing, 20 million cases of skin cancer will have been avoided, along with other serious damage to human and animal health and terrestrial and aquatic ecosystems.

In climate change the picture is very different. The developed country parties in Annex 1 to the 1992 UN Framework Convention on Climate Change may well meet their non-binding commitment to reduce their greenhouse gas emissions to 1990 levels by the year 2000 – in aggregate, if not individually. But the first steps in effective binding action must await the entry into force of the 1997 Kyoto Protocol and the first commitment period of 2008–2012.

Parties to the UNFCCC have not yet worked out what long-term concentration level of gases is safe, and therefore what transition path they should follow towards a global envelope covering the needs of all. Many developing countries strongly resist the prospect of having to take action in future, but so do many in the developed world. There is a variety of reasons for this, as I have outlined earlier. Climate change is fraught with uncertainties. Greenhouse gas reduction involves no clear future benefit – the benefit would be damage avoided rather than any net increase in wealth or well-being; it involves actual and ongoing costs – except for those quick enough to position themselves to advantage. It will affect all important areas of economic activity.

In respect of biodiversity, we have rather a mixed bag. Prior to the 1992 Convention on Biological Diversity (CBD) there was already a number of multilateral environment agreements (MEAs) which addressed problems of species loss and the need for conservation at both the regional and global levels. These instruments have had some success but at best can only be considered work in progress. The CBD involves an attempt to draw the various strands of species and habitats into a composite global whole. However, a problem of the CBD has been in defining what it should do that will make a difference, and then knuckling down to do it. The highest priority for a majority of parties to the CBD was the negotiation of a Protocol on Biosafety; this gradually turned into something of an inquisition against the products of biotechnology in general. Talks were initially stalled in February 1999 when agreement on the text of the Protocol was not forthcoming and the First Extraordinary Meeting of the Conference of the Parties of the CBD was suspended. The Protocol was finally adopted in January 2000.[1] Meanwhile, though the CBD has initiated work programmes in various areas, it has yet to make any real difference to the continued global loss of biodiversity.

The pressing need for remedial action in respect of the marine environment was one of the most important issues before CSD-7. The problem here is not that there is not a coherent legal framework – there is, provided by the UN Convention on the Law of the Sea – or a lack of attention to particular issues and risks. Rather, the problem is that there is no overall oversight of the management of the world's oceans and the effects that it is having. The problem was illustrated graphically for a number of fellow CSD members during my visits to the major continents by the chart in Figure 1.1.

Note the complexity of the system that has been built up over the decades to provide an overall management framework to deal with the two key problems: pressure from the exploitation of living marine resources and marine pollution, including land-based sources. It is further illustrated by the fact that when it came time for the UN system to publish a report on the state of the world's oceans and their management prior to CSD-7, the various agencies concerned were hard put to coordinate their efforts to do so.

This system has not dealt with the problem of overfishing which remains a major international environmental problem. The activities of subsidized industrial fleets from the world's richest countries distort the global resource balance away from the needs of developing countries often dependent on small-scale fisheries. In the long run, we face the prospect of an environmental disaster and threats to peace and security.

In terms of pollutants, wastes and other hazardous materials, various instruments have been or are in the process of being developed based on the broad principles of safety, environmentally sound management and the control of transboundary movements. In

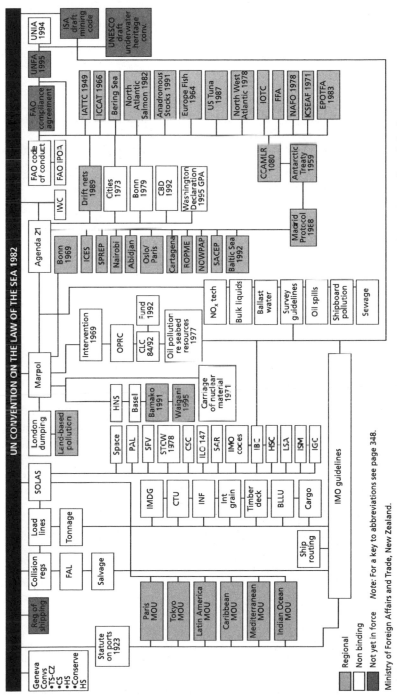

Figure 1.1 *Framework of the UN Convention on the Law of the Sea shows lack of provision for global ocean management*

Ministry of Foreign Affairs and Trade, New Zealand.

Note: For a key to abbreviations see page 348.

addition to the 1989 Basel Convention on the Control of the Transboundary Movements of Hazardous Wastes and Their Disposal, attention has focused on:

* marine pollution from ships;
* land-based sources of marine pollution, which account for some 80 per cent of marine pollution and degradation;
* the handling of dangerous chemicals (the 1998 Prior Informed Consent Convention);
* long-lived chemical pollutants (the Persistent Organic Pollutants Convention negotiations); and
* nuclear safety.

Land-based sources of marine pollution are a particularly pressing problem, but the Global Programme of Action addressing them has lost momentum. The Basel Convention may well have complicated its task with the 1995 amendment, yet to come into force, banning trade in hazardous wastes between OECD countries and non-OECD countries. This does not seem to be a useful or productive distinction to make in terms of promoting the environmentally sound management of hazardous wastes.

The Basel ban amendment illustrates the need to develop and disseminate the basic understandings and principles underlying the integration of economic development and environmental protection. In addition to the CSD, work and debate is going on in other international bodies and fora. The OECD is devoting increased attention to the core issues of sustainable development. Debate in the WTO's Committee on Trade and Environment continues, with no resolution in sight to the question of the relationship between MEAs, the use of trade measures to enforce environmental protection requirements, and the responsible free-trade ethic of the WTO. The Intergovernmental Forum on Forests (IFF) is also worth mentioning as an example of an approach to promoting sustainable management practices in a high-profile economic sector of environmental significance. There is ongoing debate in the IFF about the need or otherwise for a binding global convention on forests.

However, let's not confuse activity with effective action. On climate change we are taking the first tentative steps in the dark. Our action to eliminate ozone-depleting substances may be producing results, but we may have reckoned without atmospheric global warming and its capacity to offset the gains of such action by thinning out the stratospheric ozone layer. We continue to lose species and habitats. We do not even know how many, nor how important they may be. We are fishing out the world's oceans, and progressively destroying the marine habitat through the wastes and pollutants we dump on land or in the sea. These are reflections of the fact that we have yet to find and live by the paradigm of sustainable development.

What are the obstacles to more effective action? Firstly, it is the nature of environment issues that we are so often trying to stop and then repair, if possible, environmental degradation caused by the unsustainable use of natural and physical resources. There is a strong perception of costs, but the benefits are often not perceived as appropriable, or near enough at hand to weigh in the balance against the economic cost.

Secondly, we are usually talking about risks and uncertainties rather than certainties. Climate change is the classic case: it would all be so easy if there was scientific certainty about the impacts and effects of anthropogenic greenhouse gas emissions, but there is no certainty.

These can be seen as good arguments on narrow economic or commercial grounds to discount the value of present action. And this is especially so when the counter-driver may not so much be greed for more but the need to relieve basic poverty.

Third is the tendency to exaggerate the costs of action. I mean this not only in the sense of overestimating these costs, but also in the sense of actually influencing developments so that the costs are inflated beyond what is essential.

Fourthly, the lack of capacity – particularly in many developing countries – is a real limitation on the ability to participate positively and fully in international action on the environment. This is often exacerbated by weak or undeveloped systems of resource governance, where once again the priority may be food for survival or other basic needs. Good governance and improved capacity to balance the needs of the environment and development will not in themselves feed, house or clothe people. But they may prevent further deterioration of their plight.

The fifth obstacle is the perennial problem of poor communication. Thinking and policy is still too compartmentalized along distinct environmental and economic lines. Too often governments fail to achieve a whole-of-country-interest approach and this is carried through to the international sphere.

The problem is strongly exacerbated by deep-seated distrust and suspicion between countries of the North and the South. This can at times seem like a convenient device to avoid the need for action on the part of so-called developing countries that are really nothing of the sort. But there is also, despite funds such as the Global Environment Facility (GEF), a perception of failure to live up to expectations of wealth transfer. Given the outlook for international aid transfers, we must find ways of doing so that better fit a world where government is shrinking itself so that the forces of commerce, industry and civil society, more widely, can expand.

What can we do to overcome the roadblocks to Agenda 21 – or pull it out of the mire – and thus arrest the degradation of the global environment and implement the paradigm of sustainable development?

There is no simple answer. A new, ponderous piece of international bureaucracy in the form of a world environment authority or organization is not the answer. We are hardly engaged on the road to sustainable development, and until we have made a lot more real progress such proposals only seem to me to divert attention from the real issues.

The need is to continue the hard slog. Work must continue on the various components of an overall system that will, in time, be fittingly capped by an authority or an organization capable of sustaining the momentum towards sustainable development. There is undoubtedly a need for improved networking among existing institutions. There may be a need for improved mandates, although one should not underestimate the political difficulties of winning agreement to these in the UN system.

Clearly, improved communication must be a big part of the answer. We achieved, at times anyway in the CSD, something approaching a real dialogue, enough to whet the appetite of a number of fellow ministers who were as frustrated as I was with the rigid and stupefying routines that had made the CSD for many a complete non-event. We can also work in other fora to engage the interest of other relevant sectors where there is an obvious disjunction between the environment and other concerns.

A key objective in working on improving communication will be to advance understanding of the link between the environment and development. There are gaps in knowledge and techniques in many sectors about how to manage and develop resources in a sustainable way. Many of these can be overcome by the sharing of information in or through specialized fora. The CSD can and should articulate further the vision of sustainable development adumbrated in Agenda 21, as it progresses through its treatment of sectors and themes.

There is now a strong focus on sustainable development in the OECD and we can expect that organization to devote a good part of its analytical skills to the issue. Will the WTO follow the aspirations of retired head Renato Ruggiero and do the same? The WTO is criticized by non-governmental organizations (NGOs) in particular for being devoted to free trade to the exclusion of all other concerns. Leaving aside for the moment the environmental benefits of free trade objectives such as the elimination of agricultural and fishing subsidies, the WTO itself has had a bad press. A WTO agreement such as the Sanitary and Phytosanitary Agreement is in fact a basic instrument of international environmental protection.

The link needs to be understood and acted on in capitals first and foremost: officials often seem to argue inconsistently in the WTO and environmental fora. There is widespread suspicion that all the talk about the environment is simply aimed at finding new ways of protecting the rich economies from the growing competition coming out of the developing world. If there is to be any hope of major advances in winning global acceptance of a paradigm of sustainable development, we cannot afford the damage caused by ill-judged attempts to load questionable environmental issues on to the WTO agenda. The precautionary principle, which should be restricted to major instances or threats of environmental degradation, may not survive attempts to make it a pretext for any action that is not sustainable under the WTO agreements.

That problem may, in part, be overcome by improved resource governance in countries that lack it. Well-directed, environmentally integrated development assistance will continue to be of importance. I also look forward to a rapid development of the capacity of the GEF to offer capacity-building assistance not just to make basic assessments, but also to allow countries to build up their participation in the response to global environmental problems. New Zealand has pushed for this in the GEF, particularly with regard to its South Pacific neighbours, and has also assisted directly through New Zealand Overseas Development Aid (NZODA), for example with climate change adaptation. More needs to be done to ensure that the big development institutions such as the World Bank integrate sustainability criteria within their development assistance.

I cannot overstate the importance of science, which is the lynch pin. We owe what we know already about the degradation of our natural and physical resources to science. Is it too much to hope that one day science will develop a generally agreed picture, in sufficiently useful detail, of the state of the world environment? Some countries, including New Zealand, have made a start with their own environments. We are also pushing for such a scheme for the globally vital Antarctic environment. UNEP is developing elements of a global scheme through its work.

Building on its solid track record to date, the law can play an important role in ensuring that sustainable development is the new foundation of cooperation in the international community, rather than the cause of terminal strife. This is by way of sound, fair, rules-based systems that promote responsible environmental management and leave less and less room for irresponsibility. I said earlier that I thought that the tools of environmental remediation and sustainable development were not yet well developed. Perhaps the exception is the Montreal Protocol, where there is a broadly coherent framework including an effective interface between science and policy, realistic commitments with flexibility as

Box 1.1 Multilateral and Regional Treaties and other Instruments in the International Law of the Sea

Seabed

United Nations Implementing Agreement 1994: Agreement setting out a regime for the exploitation of the resources of the deep seabed beyond national jurisdiction, under the auspices of the International Seabed Authority (ISA).

ISA Draft Mining Code (to be developed): When completed, the code will set out regulations for the sustainable exploitation of polymetallic nodules on the deep seabed.

UNESCO Draft Underwater Cultural Heritage (to be developed): When completed, the convention will prescribe a regime for the protection of underwater cultural heritage.

Fisheries

United Nations Fish Stocks Agreement 1995: Agreement for the implementation of the provisions of UNCLOS relating to highly migratory and straddling fish stocks, setting out principles for cooperation, management and enforcement of fisheries management measures.

FAO Compliance Agreement 1993: Agreement to promote compliance with international conservation and management measures by fishing vessels on the high seas.

FAO Code of Conduct 1995: A non-binding voluntary code for responsible fisheries, setting out principles for fisheries management, fishing operations, aquaculture development, integration of fisheries into coastal area management, post-harvest practices and trade and fisheries research.

FAO International Plans of Action 1998: Voluntary plans of action for the reduction of incidental catch of seabirds and sharks in longline fisheries.

IATTC 1949: Convention for the Establishment of an Inter-American Tropical Tuna Commission to manage the tuna and billfish fisheries off the coast of Central America.

ICCAT 1966: International Convention for the Conservation of Atlantic Tuna, establishing a commission to manage the tuna fisheries of the Atlantic Ocean.

Bering Sea 1953: Agreement establishing a commission for the preservation of the halibut fishery of the Northern Pacific Ocean and the Bering Sea.

Bering Sea Doughnut Hole: Agreement governing the management of marine living resources in the high seas area surrounding the North Pole.

North Atlantic Salmon 1982: Agreement for the conservation of salmon in the North Atlantic, establishing the North Atlantic Salmon Conservation Organization and prohibiting high seas salmon fishing in the North Atlantic.

Anadromous Stocks 1991: Agreement between US, Japan, Canada and Russia prohibiting the fishing of anadromous species on the high seas of the North Pacific unless the parties otherwise agree, and implementing procedures for the reduction of incidental catch of anadromous stocks.

European Fisheries Convention 1964: Agreement recognizing the extension of coastal state fisheries jurisdiction to 12 nautical miles.

US Tuna Treaty 1987: Agreement between the US and several South Pacific states for the provision of access to South Pacific tuna fisheries in return for the payment of access fees.

North-West Atlantic 1978: Agreement to manage the fisheries of the North-West Atlantic.

IOTC: Agreement establishing the FAO Indian Ocean Tuna Commission for the management of tuna stocks in the Indian Ocean.

FFA: Agreement between FAO South Pacific Forum Fisheries Agency states to establish a fisheries agency to assist in the management of tuna and other highly migratory fish stocks in the Southern Pacific Ocean. The governing body, the Forum Fisheries Committee, adopts and sets minimum terms and conditions for access to South Pacific fisheries waters.

NAFO 1978: Agreement establishing the North-West Atlantic Fisheries Organization for the purposes of the optimum utilization, rational management and conservation of the fisheries of the North-West Atlantic.

ICSEAF 1971: Agreement establishing the International Commission for the South-East Atlantic Fisheries for the purposes of managing fish stocks in the Atlantic Ocean of the southern coasts of Africa.

EPOTFA 1983: Agreement for the management of the tuna fishery in the Eastern Pacific Ocean off the coast of South America.

CCAMLR: Agreement establishing the Commission for the Conservation of Antarctic Marine Living Resources, which regulates fishing within the waters surrounding the Antarctic.

Drift Nets 1989: Convention prohibiting fishing with long drift nets in the South Pacific.

IWRC 1946: Convention establishing the International Whaling Commission for the proper conservation of whale stocks for the purposes of the orderly development of the whaling industry. Has established a moratorium on all commercial whaling.

Protection of the Environment

Agenda 21: Non-binding declaration setting out principles for global and regional action for sustainable development and protection of the environment.

Regional Environmental Programmes: Regional environmental organizations with responsibility for the preservation of the marine environment:

- *SPREP:* Convention for the Protection of the Natural Resources and Environment of the South Pacific Region
- *Nairobi:* Nairobi Convention for the Protection, Management and Development of the Marine and Coastal Environment of the Eastern African Region
- *Abidjan:* Convention for Cooperation in the Protection and Development of the Marine and Coastal Environment of the West and Central African Region
- *Oslo/Paris:* Oslo/Paris Convention on Protection of the Marine Environment of the North-East Atlantic
- *Cartagena:* Convention for the Protection and Development of the Marine Environment of the Wider Caribbean Region
- *ROPME:* Regional Organization for the Protection of the Marine Environment, which relates to the Middle East
- *NOWPAP:* North-West Pacific Action Plan
- *SACEP:* South Asian Cooperative Environment Programme
- *Baltic Sea:* Convention on the Protection of the Marine Environment of the Baltic Sea Area

CITES: Convention on the International Trade of Endangered Species of Wild Fauna and Flora, which establishes a trade certification scheme in order to regulate, or prohibit, trade in endangered species.

Bonn: Convention on the Conservation of Migratory Species of Wild Animals which provides that states shall cooperate to protect endangered migratory species which occur within their jurisdiction.

CBD: Convention on Biological Diversity, which provides that states shall cooperate for the conservation and sustainable use of biological diversity.

Washington Declaration: Washington Declaration on the Protection of the Marine Environment from Land-Based Activities which recognizes the United Nations Global Programme of Action to address marine degradation from land-based activities.

Antarctic Treaty and Madrid Protocol: The Antarctic Treaty 1957 provides a consultative system in respect of the various interests in Antarctica. The Madrid Protocol on Environmental Protection 1991 extends protection to the Antarctic environment and related ecosystems.

Marine Pollution

MARPOL 1973/78: International Convention for the Prevention of Pollution from Ships, which provides for binding regulations governing the prevention of pollution by oil and other hazardous substances.

Intervention 1969: International convention relating to intervention on the high seas in the case of oil pollution casualties, providing that parties may take such measures as may be necessary to prevent, mitigate or eliminate the effects of oil pollution following a collision on the high seas.

CLC 84/92: International Convention on Civil Liability for Oil Pollution Damage which makes the shipowner liable for any pollution damage caused by oil which has escaped or been discharged from a ship.

Fund Convention: International Convention on the Establishment of an International Fund for Compensation for Oil Pollution Damage. The convention creates the International Oil Pollution Compensation Fund to provide compensation for pollution damage and to refund governments the cost of measures taken to prevent or minimize pollution damage.

Oil Pollution Regarding Seabed Resources 1977: Convention on Civil Liability for Oil Pollution Damage Resulting from Exploration for and Exploitation of Seabed Mineral resources. This convention regulates the civil liability of oil well operators.

Bonn 1969: Bonn agreement concerning pollution of the North Sea by oil providing for cooperation between states In order to report and dispose of oil spills in the North Sea area.

HNS: International Convention on Liability and Compensation for Damage in Connection with the Carriage of Hazardous and Noxious Substances by Sea which regulates the civil liability of shipping operators.

Basel: Basel Convention on the Control of Transboundary Movements of Hazardous Wastes and Their Disposal, prescribing regulations for the transport and disposal of hazardous wastes other than oil.

CSC: International Convention for Safe Containers, which provides standards for shipboard cargo containers.

Waigani 1995: Convention to Ban the Importation into Forum Island Countries of Hazardous and Radioactive Waste and to Control the Transboundary Movement and Management of Hazardous Waste within the South Pacific Region.

Carriage of Nuclear Material 1972: Convention Relating to Civil Liability in the Field of Maritime Carriage of Nuclear material, setting out the rules governing civil liability arising from nuclear incidents at sea.

Shipping and Navigation

SOLAS: International Convention for the Safety of Life at Sea, which regulates safety requirements on passenger and cargo ships.

SPACE: Special Trade Passenger Ships Agreement, which supplements SOLAS in the case of ships designed to carry large numbers of special trade passengers. This provides for special rules concerning construction and equipment.

PAL: Athens Convention Relating to the Carriage of Passengers and their Luggage by Sea, which applies rules covering liability in respect of injury to passengers or damage to luggage. The convention sets a maximum level of liability for shipping operators.

SFV: Torremolinos International Convention for the Safety of Fishing Vessels, which imposes regulations covering matters of construction, propulsion and equipment on fishing vessels over 24 metres in length.

STCW: International Convention on Standards of Training, Certification and Watchkeeping for Seafarers.

ILO 147: Convention Concerning Minimum Standards in Merchant Ships, which requires members ratifying it to have laws respecting safety standards, competency standards, hours of work and manning as well as respecting social security measures and conditions of work.

SAR: International Convention on Maritime Search and Rescue, which prescribes responsibility to states to carry out search and rescue operations over particular areas of ocean.

Load Lines: International Convention on Load Lines, which regulates the loading of ships engaged in international voyages in order to ensure stability.

Tonnage: IMO Convention on the Tonnage Measurement of Ships which provides for the determination and certification of gross and net tonnages to be carried out by governments.

Collision Regulations: Convention on the International Regulations for Preventing Collisions at Sea, setting out steering and sailing rules, standard sound and light signals and providing for traffic separation schemes in navigable waters.

FAL: IMO Convention on Facilitation of International Maritime Traffic, which provides for standard documents and procedures in order to facilitate and expedite international maritime traffic and prevent unnecessary delays to ships.

Registration of Ships: United Nations Convention on Conditions for the Registration of Ships, which sets out requirements for a connection between vessels and the registering (or flag) state.

Statute of Ports: Geneva Convention on the International Regime of Maritime Ports, which provides for access to ports by vessels of contracting states on a non-discriminatory basis. The statute does not apply to fishing vessels.

Port State Jurisdiction MOUs: These non-binding memoranda of understanding (Paris, Tokyo, Latin America, Caribbean, Mediterranean, Indian Ocean) apply on a regional basis. The MOUs provide a system to enable states to monitor and enforce internationally recognized safety and construction standards in respect of vessels in their ports.

IMO Guidelines: IMO guidelines and codes regulating ship routing (ship routing code), the carriage of various cargoes and materials (International Maritime Dangerous Goods Code (IMDG), Guidelines for the Packing of Cargo Transport Units (CTU), Code for the Safe Carriage of Irradiated Nuclear Fuels, Plutonium and High Level Radioactive Waste in Flask Aboard Ship (INF), International Grain, Carriage of Timber on Deck, Code of Practice for the Safe Loading and Unloading of Bulk Carriers (BLU), and cargo codes), and standards for the prevention of marine pollution (the NOx technical, bulk liquids, ballast water, survey guidelines, oil spills, shipboard oil pollution, and sewage codes).

Maritime Zones

Geneva Conventions: Largely overtaken by UNCLOS, the Geneva Conventions on the Territorial Sea and the Contiguous Zone, the Continental Shelf, and the High Seas set out basic principles in respect of coastal state jurisdiction over maritime zones.

---

to how they are met by individual parties, and universality of involvement and cooperation among key groups of stakeholders – developed and developing countries on the one hand, and government and industry on the other. The Montreal Protocol shows how a well-balanced system can get traction and momentum; however, it may be that ultimately it will not succeed without at least a degree of compliance enforcement. Therein lies the rub.

Furthermore, the challenges facing us, particularly in climate change and oceans, are likely to be far greater than any posed by the need to eliminate ozone-depleting substances. It will need all the skill of lawyers, diplomats, politicians and non-governmental stakeholders to develop rules-based systems with the right balance and sequencing to ensure that countries are not deterred from joining in collective action, and are prepared to apply progressively tighter constraints in what are – for the most part – matters of individual sovereign prerogative.

Above all, it will require political will. In this regard, I would like to conclude by underlining the challenge of overfishing on the high seas. This is an area where there are applicable laws, but the question is: do governments have the will to enforce them? If governments are not prepared to stand up to industry pressure in this area and take their obligations under the Convention of the Law of the Sea seriously, then there is a strong risk that the peaceful order for oceans so painstakingly negotiated in that convention will unravel, opening up the prospect of threats to international peace and security. The convention will not work unless there is a commitment to making it work; order will not prevail in the face of behaviour that devastates the bases of human life.

NOTE

1   Secretariat of the Convention on Biological Diversity (forthcoming) *Handbook of the Convention on Biological Diversity*, London: Earthscan Publications Ltd

2

Implementing Agenda 21:
A United Nations Perspective

Nitin Desai

INTRODUCTION

The United Nations Conference on Environment and Development
(UNCED, also known as the Earth Summit) was a landmark event. It
launched an unprecedented global partnership for economic and
social development and environmental protection, founded on
consensus and commitment at the highest political level. It adopted
the Rio Declaration, the Forest Principles and Agenda 21, an ambitious
and comprehensive programme of action including many innovative
initiatives and imaginative visions for sustainable development. It saw
the opening for signature of the first international conventions on
climate change and biological diversity.

UNCED raised high expectations for sustainable development.
Although the challenges facing the international community were
numerous and daunting, the Earth Summit showed a clear commitment by governments and civil society to join forces to reverse the
trends of environmental degradation, to use natural resources with a
view to long-term development, and to grapple with the maladies of
hunger and poverty. The task then was to harness that political will
and turn it into action and results.

Five years later, at Earth Summit +5, world leaders noted that
progress had been made in a number of areas, that commitment
remained strong in many countries, and that sustainable development

programmes had been established in many local communities. But they were deeply concerned that the overall trends in environment and development were worse than in 1992. They concluded that the implementation of Agenda 21 was more urgent than ever.

Why have many major goals of sustainable development eluded us? Why has there been improvement in some areas but not in others? What needs to be done to accelerate progress, to promote economic and social development, and to reverse environmental degradation? This chapter seeks to examine these questions from a United Nations perspective and to share some ideas on possible answers and remedies.

UNFAVOURABLE DEVELOPMENTS IN THE INTERNATIONAL ENVIRONMENT

In 1992 when delegates gathered at Rio, along with thousands of NGO representatives, the world was witnessing a promising transition to a post-Cold War era. The spectre of nuclear war had faded, and a spirit of cooperation and partnership based on mutual interest was prevalent. At Rio, developed countries accepted the principle of common but differentiated responsibilities and recognized the need to provide increased financial and technical assistance to developing countries. Developing countries took responsibility for implementation in their countries, with support from the international community.

Subsequently, however, the momentum for action gave way to concern over economic and social instability in many developed and developing countries and increasing global competition. In many developing countries, the implementation of Agenda 21 slowed as governments coped with financial crises, debt burdens, social conflicts, and other problems. Some countries experienced political instability and violent conflict, bringing development efforts to a standstill. It soon became clear that the transition to a more open, prosperous, secure and democratic world would be an arduous process, punctuated by crises and conflicts. While a number of developing countries achieved high growth for the better part of the 1990s, many fell behind. The situation of the least-developed countries was particularly worrisome. The financial crises that embroiled East Asian economies in 1997, and went on to disrupt other developing economies and economies in transition, further undermined prospects for sustainable development.

The difficulties faced by developing countries have been compounded by the failure of most developed countries to provide the financial and technical assistance needed by developing countries for the implementation of Agenda 21. The result has been a widening gap between the rich and poor. While annual per capita income in developed countries jumped from about US$18,000 in 1980 to over US$25,000 in 1998, an increase of almost US$7500 or over 40 per cent, per capita income in developing countries registered an average increase of less than US$300 or 28 per cent, rising from about US$1000 in 1980 to US$1300 in 1998. Per capita income of the least-developed countries actually fell from US$282 in 1980 to US$258 in 1998, and that of sub-Saharan African countries declined from US$438 to US$353.[1]

UNEVEN PROGRESS AND WORSENING TRENDS

Lack of resources in developing countries – financial, human and technical – has been the critical missing factor in the implementation of Agenda 21. Nowhere is this more evident than in freshwater and sanitation. Access to safe drinking water and sanitation in developing countries is sorely inadequate, and investment in infrastructure has not been forthcoming. The adverse effects on human health and human resource development have been well documented, but progress in combating them has been slow. Scarcity of freshwater has become a major constraint to socioeconomic development in many developing countries, and the number of such countries will certainly increase in the coming decades.

Lack of resources for development has contributed to worsening trends in other areas. In tropical developing countries, deforestation and forest degradation remain serious problems, in part due to commercial logging and clearing for pastures and commercial agriculture, but also because poverty is forcing people to exploit forest resources in unsustainable ways. The increasing loss of habitats as a result of deforestation is threatening biodiversity.

Another obstacle to sustainability is the energy and material-intensive production and consumption patterns of the industrialized countries. Agenda 21 recognized such unsustainable production and consumption patterns as the main cause of the continued deterioration of the global environment and advocated a three-pronged approach to the problem. The approach, reaffirmed at Earth Summit +5, requires all countries to strive to promote sustainable consumption patterns, with developed countries taking the lead, and developing countries guaranteeing the provision of basic needs while avoiding unsustainable patterns.

Since Rio, some progress has been made in changing consumption and production patterns in a number of areas. Encouraging headway has been made in some countries in fostering cleaner production and in improving efficiency in energy and material use. Green products have been developed and eco-labelling schemes set up to enable consumers to make informed choices. A number of these schemes have been in operation for several years and have yielded important insights and lessons on how to foster sustainable consumption patterns. Advances in science and technology have enabled industry to improve productivity and efficiency in resource use, with resource use per unit of output falling in manufacturing, transportation and other sectors. Recycling rates, notably for metals and paper products, have been on the rise. In developed regions, forest cover and major protected areas have expanded.

Notwithstanding these efforts, overall consumption of resources has continued to increase. World consumption of minerals, fossil fuels and forest products have all registered increases. Waste and pollutants, notably solid waste, toxic waste, acid rain and greenhouse gases, are continuing to increase, with harmful effects on ecosystems. Emissions of some pollutants in industrialized countries have declined in recent years, due to technological innovations or cleaner fuels, but such success stories are hard to replicate in developing countries where the appropriate technology is not yet available or is prohibitively costly.

NATIONAL POLICIES AND ACTIONS

What factors have contributed to this uneven record and the overall worsening trends? What role have national policies and actions played in the implementation of Agenda 21?

As recognized at UNCED, and reaffirmed at Earth Summit +5, sustainable development embraces sustained economic growth based on equity, enhancement of the social well-being of all groups, and protection of the environment. Achieving sustainable development requires integrated policies and actions in all those interdependent and mutually reinforcing areas.

In the implementation of Agenda 21, governments have proceeded along several tracks, but some common elements have been identified among the policy measures used. At the national level, governments generally have taken steps to establish high-level mechanisms for policy-making and coordination. In many countries, such a body is headed by the head of government or a senior minister. In some instances, the policy-making body works alongside a technical advisory body. Many governments have upgraded environmental protection agencies and strengthened institutional capacity.

However, recent studies, including those by National Sustainable Development Councils, demonstrate that the effectiveness of these mechanisms often depends on the priority the government accords to the implementation of Agenda 21. By itself, the establishment of a high-level policy-making or coordination body does not guarantee successful integration of policy measures.

Many governments have also taken steps to update and strengthen legislation and regulatory frameworks. New laws have been enacted to comply with international commitments; new regulations have been promulgated to ensure implementation; and increasingly, local authorities have moved beyond national standards and adopted and implemented local Agenda 21 programmes.

An encouraging trend has been the formulation of national sustainable development strategies, mapping out overall direction, sectoral plans and targets. In implementing those strategies, countries are employing a broad range of tools, including environmental impact assessments and environmental management systems. Many governments are using economic instruments, including reduction of environmentally harmful subsidies and internalization of environmental costs, to change production and consumption to more sustainable patterns. Some countries are undertaking tax reforms to shift the incidence of taxation from labour to natural resource consumption.

Broader participation by major groups, through NGOs and local initiatives, represents another significant development since UNCED. Participation by all stakeholders in the implementation of Agenda 21 is essential to attaining the goals and objectives of sustainable development. Major groups, including young people, women, indigenous people, and the scientific community bring energy, wisdom, vision and specialized knowledge to sustainable development efforts. Business and industry, as both producer and consumer of goods and services, affects economic and social development, resource consumption and the environment in a direct way. These groups have made important contributions to more sustainable practices, and they should be encouraged to take an active role on pressing issues such as climate change and changing unsustainable production and consumption patterns.

Combined, these efforts at national and local levels should have led to significant achievements in sustainable development. Why have recent reviews and assessments concluded otherwise? In considering these questions, we need to realize that governments are faced with extremely difficult challenges in their efforts to reverse environmental degradation and achieve sustainable development. Most developing countries have to contend with an unfavourable international environment and a lack of human, technical and financial resources. In terms of policy design and execution for sustainable development, governments are still struggling to achieve coherence and synergy in their policy initiatives and measures. Policy-makers are still learning how to effectively integrate policy measures within a unified strategy in pursuit of the multiple objectives of sustainable development. In short, we need to recognize that despite a growing awareness of the inter-linkages of sustainable development, we are still, to a large extent, approaching problems in a piece-meal fashion. We are still searching for a model or a paradigm that can effectively guide our efforts to design and execute policy measures in an integrated manner.

ACTION AT THE INTERNATIONAL LEVEL

Since Rio, significant strides have been made at the international level, notably in multilateral agreements. These include the conventions on climate change, biodiversity and desertification, together with their protocols, the Programme of Action for Small Island Developing States (SIDS), and the Global Programme of Action for the Protection of the Marine Environment from Land-Based Activities. Together with other existing international instruments, these provide an overarching policy framework for resolving the most pressing sustainable development issues. They are also testimony to the global nature of such issues and the need to address them through international action. Full implementation of the commitments embodied in those agreements remains an arduous task. In some cases, further strengthening of the provisions and greater efforts to meet the targets continue to be a top priority.

Deliberations and actions by various intergovernmental forums have provided essential guidance and strong impetus to international and national efforts to implement Agenda 21. The CSD, in particular, has played a pioneering role in promoting dialogue among stakeholders and in fostering partnerships for sustainable development. Efforts by the commission to involve major groups in its activities have not only expanded the impact of the commission's work beyond the confines of intergovernmental debates but have also given the commission the benefit of the views and expertise of NGOs.

Since its establishment, the CSD has reviewed the implementation of all chapters of Agenda 21, as well as the SIDS Programme of Action. Since Earth Summit +5, the commission has focused on some critical sectoral and cross-sectoral themes as well as the overriding issues of poverty and changing consumption and production patterns. It has catalysed new action and has become the principal body of the UN for promoting and monitoring national implementation of Agenda 21. In the course of its work since Rio, the commission has developed and refined its methods of work in light of its enormously complex tasks. The innovations, such as the ministerial segment and the multi-stakeholder dialogues, have enhanced the efficiency and effectiveness of its work.

Under the aegis of the CSD, the Intergovernmental Panel on Forests (IPF) and the Intergovernmental Forum on Forests (IFF) have elaborated proposals for action to be implemented at the national level. The IPF and IFF have conducted their work in an open, transparent and participatory manner. To further coordinate global action on forests, the international community could establish the UN Forum on Forests to promote and facilitate implementation of the proposals for action emanating from five years of intergovernmental deliberation on the issue.

ACTIVITIES OF THE UN SYSTEM

For many organizations of the UN system, UNCED brought about a substantial reorientation of their programmes and methods of work. Effective implementation of Agenda 21 as well as the need to provide expert multidisciplinary support for the CSD and other intergovernmental bodies have posed a serious challenge to the agencies and programmes of the UN system. Never before have UN organizations in the social and economic fields been required to work collectively for such a broad common agenda. We believe that the UN system is meeting this challenge effectively through the contributions of the United Nations Environment Programme (UNEP), the Food and Agriculture Organization (FAO), the United Nations Industrial Development Organization, the UN Conference on Trade and Development (UNCTAD), the World Bank, and other specialized agencies. The specialized agencies, programmes and financial institutions have made structural, programme and budget changes in support of the implementation of Agenda 21.

The Inter-Agency Committee on Sustainable Development has worked effectively to coordinate the initiatives of UN agencies and to marshal their expertise through a system of task managers for each area of Agenda 21. It has proved to be a cost-effective mechanism by drawing on system-wide resources.

The work of UN organizations is closely tied to that of the intergovernmental machinery. With intergovernmental bodies moving towards a more interactive relationship, especially in the follow-up to the major international conferences on sustainable development, social development, population and women, UN organizations need to further strengthen their coordination at the programme level, including with regional commissions and country offices and field projects.

POSITIVE LESSONS FROM EXPERIENCE

In the 1990s, the international community focused its attention on economic and social development and environmental protection through a series of major international conferences. Experience in implementing the outcomes of those conferences has demonstrated that sustainable development requires an enabling international environment, supportive national policy frameworks, and effective policy implementation. Strengthening each of those areas is essential to real progress in implementing Agenda 21.

As a result of globalization, the world economy has become increasingly integrated, and international markets are playing a critical role in determining the success or failure of developing countries in their development efforts. The growing gap between rich and poor countries points to the continued need for an enabling international economic environment, including access to investment capital and modern technologies, debt relief and access to international markets. If the goals of sustainable development are to be achieved in all countries, developed countries must increase their support to developing countries in those areas.

At the national level, a supportive policy framework providing direction and coordination to all sectors is indispensable to the success of national and local efforts, given the cross-cutting nature of sustainable development. It has long been recognized that cross-sectoral sustainable development strategies are important mechanisms for integrating priorities in economic and social development and environmental protection. At Earth Summit +5, member states agreed that by the year 2002, all countries should have formulated national sustainable development strategies. In the years ahead, efforts should be focused on the effective implementation of these national strategies. Increased international cooperation, exchange of experience and critical assessment of progress achieved will be essential to that process. Local Agenda 21 programmes and initiatives by major groups should play a major role in national implementation efforts.

A national policy framework supportive of sustainable development should consist of an integrated package of policy instruments, including laws and regulations, economic instruments, measures to internalize environment costs in market prices, environmental impact analyses, education and training, research and development, and information dissemination. The design and implementation of these policies and programmes should be a transparent and participatory process, involving not only governments but also the various stakeholders of civil society.

To ensure success in implementing national policies, institutional capacity must be strengthened, particularly in developing countries. A high-level coordinating mechanism within the government should be established and empowered to coordinate government activities, including at local levels. Environmental protection agencies and environmental research institutes should be established and strengthened to ensure monitoring and enforcement of national standards in support of sustainable development. National Sustainable Development Councils, whether sponsored by governments or formed by civil society, have played an important role in many countries in advancing the goals of sustainable development.

Attaining the goals of sustainable development requires specific measures in different economic and social sectors. Since 1992, Agenda 21 has provided a comprehensive, detailed programme of action for many sectors and issues. Since Earth Summit +5, the CSD has addressed a few key sectors and issues each year, allowing an exchange of views on effective measures and possibilities for international coordination of measures. The issues addressed include water resources and technology transfer in 1998, consumption and production patterns, tourism and oceans in 1999, and finance, trade and agriculture in 2000. Energy and transport will be a focus in 2001.

Business and industry, together with labour organizations and consumers, are playing a more active role in sustainable development. Progressive enterprises are improving the design and production of goods and services, reducing waste and often reducing costs and becoming more competitive in the process. Public policy frameworks should be designed to promote and reward such efforts by business and industry to go beyond basic compliance with laws and regulations. Government procurement can also be used to build markets for goods and services that support sustainable development.

Consumers in many countries, including some developing countries, are demonstrating a willingness to pay somewhat higher prices for goods and services that contribute to sustainable development. Industry, government and consumer organizations are promoting such products through consumer education and environmental and social impact assessments, taking into account the full product life cycle from design to final disposal. Eco-labelling and fair-trade schemes, combined with efforts to facilitate access by producers in developing countries to these developed country markets, can support sustainable development in all countries through informed consumer behaviour.

International trade and investment can be an important force for sustainable development, providing developing countries with the capital and technology they need. Improved access for developing countries to developed country markets, combined with international cooperation for improving productivity and cleaner production, is needed to support sustainable development, particularly in the context of declining development assistance.

However, trade and private investment are too concentrated and selective to provide an adequate basis for sustainable development in developing countries, particularly in Africa and the least-developed countries. Increased financial and technical assistance is required if the objectives of Agenda 21 are to be met.

Promoting public and private investment to improve water supply and sanitation is an urgent component of sustainable development, with a pricing system that both encourages efficient use of water and ensures access to clean water to all.

Renewable energy sources and energy conservation are a current focus of attention, and substantial progress is being made. Renewable energy sources are often proving to be the most economical way to meet the energy needs of the two billion people in rural areas of developing countries who are currently without access to modern energy sources. Cleaner fuels and new types of engines for motor vehicles with greatly reduced emission levels are being introduced both for public vehicle fleets and private automobiles, allowing reductions in urban air pollution. Rapid technological development in these areas is steadily reducing the cost of cleaner energy and transportation systems.

EARTH SUMMIT 2002 AND BEYOND

In 2002, the UN will undertake the ten-year review of the implementation of Agenda 21, assessing progress to date, drawing conclusions from the experience of all countries, and drawing up a work programme for the future. This review will be a participatory process, including analysis of trends, national assessments, regional reviews, inputs from civil society, and intergovernmental deliberations. In addition to reviewing implementation of Agenda 21, the process will identify new issues that have emerged since 1992, such as globalization, consider how they should be integrated within the international work programme, and identify priorities for the future work programme on sustainable development.

The ten-year review promises to be a participatory event with a high political profile. It offers a critical opportunity to revitalize national commitments and international cooperation for sustainable development and to renew the global commitment to implement the full programme of Agenda 21 through global partnership.

NOTE

1   E/1999/50/Rev.1 *The World Economic and Social Survey*, 1999

3

Who is Aware of Agenda 21?
Missing Conditions: Three Major Barriers

Victoria Elias

Introduction

Almost ten years have passed since heads of states and governments adopted Agenda 21 at the first Earth Summit in Rio. The last decade of the 20th century was a remarkable period of human history. What has been done to achieve the goals of Agenda 21 at different levels – from local to international – and what are the roadblocks on the way to a sustainable future for the planet?

Being a member of the NGO community and working for the last 11 years on issues of environmental protection and sustainable development in such an unstable region as the Newly Independent States (NIS) of the former Soviet Union, I would like to highlight some urgent problems relating to implementing the principles of sustainability.

There are three major barriers which slow down the move towards a sustainable society:

1   Lack of peace and security.
2   Lack of resources.
3   Lack of public involvement and access to information.

LACK OF SECURITY ON THE PLANET

The first main limiting factor is the lack of peace and security on the planet. Moreover, talking about security, we should take into account not only political but also social and environmental security issues.

Different countries and nations come together at international level to solve economic and environmental problems, discuss and launch transboundary projects and to sign protocols and conventions. At the same time, they are very much separated from regional political climates, regional groups and society's marginalized players. On the one hand, this separation process has historical and economic roots. On the other, it refers to problems of a multipolar world and global security.

National conflicts, regional fragmentation and ethnic problems can result in civil wars. These conflicts drive populations in many regions away from sustainability in the long term. This situation is seen in the Balkans, Middle East, Asia, Africa, Northern Caucasus and many other 'hot spots' around the world. Moreover, during last decade world balance has been much changed. After the collapse of the Soviet Union and the whole communist block, a number of NIS have been created in Europe and Asia. They all have transitional economies and enormous economic difficulties causing unemployment, social problems, thousands of refugees, new health epidemics and environmental degradation. Sometimes economic decline 'helps' these countries to limit hazardous substance emissions into the environment. However, even this 'positive' effect is counteracted by the of destruction of waste treatment and recycling facilities and the use of old unsustainable technologies.

Processes of democratization in transitional states resulted in the establishment of new public institutions, and a growth in the number of NGOs. Worldwide, NGOs are at the front line of those working for sustainability, but there are still many barriers. Nonetheless, NGOs often play the role of educators and promoters of sustainable development ideas in developing countries to a much greater extent than elsewhere. Attention in these countries is very much focused on solving urgent domestic problems and fighting for the survival of families. Politicians also concentrate their attention and attempts on conflict resolution, economic difficulties, budget deficits and other priority survival issues. In general, the NGO community (which is usually comprised of academics from transitional countries) becomes the main initiator of sustainable development initiatives and programmes.

SUFFERING WITHOUT RESOURCES

Sustainability initiatives, knowledge of principles and process expertise is not enough to ensure the successful implementation of such programmes at any level. Here we meet the second 'barrier' hampering movement ahead. This concerns a lack of resources. In the majority of countries, issues of environment and development are very much underestimated at the state level. Usually the ministries dealing with environmental protection are responsible for domestic sustainable development plans and strategies. Outside of highly developed countries these are not the most powerful, well-financed governmental bodies. They often face extreme difficulties due to the lack of human and financial resources made available to them. This presents a good opportunity for cooperation with NGOs and other stakeholders.

However, in many cases special assistance to such countries is needed at all levels. This assistance should be monitored by multistakeholder groups to ensure that it is effectively used, that funds are correctly allocated and that foreign experts have relevant knowledge for a given country. In practice, it often happens that 90 to 95 per cent of funds are spent on the salaries of foreign experts. There should be more opportunities to use national expertise involving different stakeholder groups. For example, being a diverse group of people with different backgrounds and often having relevant knowledge, NGOs can provide experience of many sectors and on a range of issues. Other stakeholders can also effectively contribute to the process in a similar way.

The whole issue of effective use of both domestic resources and foreign assistance should be addressed at Earth Summit 2002. This would help to look at the missed opportunities from the implementation of Agenda 21.

PUBLIC INVOLVEMENT AND ACCESS TO INFORMATION: DOES IT REALLY EXIST?

Agenda 21 highlights the urgent necessity for public involvement and participation in decision-making processes. This is one of the key principles for a successful transition to sustainable development. In fact, the most active and responsible members of society are its diverse community of NGOs which are often home to very dedicated people who are concerned about the urgency and necessity to solve outstanding environment and development problems.

An example of the positive role NGOs can play is taken from regions with strong ethnic difficulties, such as the Balkans or Northern Caucasus, where communication between some nationalities or religious groups is nearly impossible. In these circumstances, NGOs can break down barriers and work together with all groups. This is well illustrated by a trans-Balkans NGO coalition, which includes NGOs from all former Yugoslavian countries with the support of ANPED (the Northern Alliance for Sustainability). All political contradictions give way to the common goal – the path to sustainable development. The Eco-Urban Workshop (a Belgrade NGO) has reported for a long time in its publications that effective cooperation and dialogue between Serbians and Albanians from Kosovo was possible at NGO level where political difficulties were forgotten in favour of shared agendas. There are many other examples of cooperation among NGOs in other regions as well.

Multistakeholder cooperation in the framework of environment and development programmes can produce very fruitful results. There are many success stories in this area in different countries. However, public participation can be effective only in cases where there is informed participation.

In this respect, I would like firstly to question the general delivery of Agenda 21 ideas. Obviously, the main message of Earth Summit 1992 – the necessity to establish a new global partnership, where economic, environmental and social factors are taken into account by different stakeholders while developing plans, strategies and actions – was delivered to decision-makers at international and national levels. High-level officials who participated in the 1992 Earth Summit signed Agenda 21 on behalf of their countries. What has since been done? There are a number of success stories from developed countries (for example, in northern Europe and the UK) where Agenda 21 principles are implemented at national and local levels and Local Agenda 21 programmes are being developed.

However, even now, eight years after Rio, the idea of sustainable development and the principles of Agenda 21 are still not widely known by the public in all parts of the world. There are informed individuals in the NGO community and in other sectors, but in general there is still a great lack of knowledge and awareness on this issue. It is rare to find people who are not directly connected to development programmes or environmental protection and who know about Agenda 21. The idea of sustainability is not discussed in the mass media, nor included within the curricula of schools and universities. The world is still at the very early stage of awareness in this area. If people on the streets of Moscow, for example, were asked whether they know about sustainable development and Agenda 21, I am sure that not many of them would be able to give a positive answer. Moreover, during a visit to Moldova and Romania in September 1999 with the international multistakeholder group of specialists working on environment and development, I met a number of farmers following sustainability principles while developing organic agriculture; however, they had never heard about Rio or its principles of sustainable agriculture. Such information has never been delivered at this level.

In general, low access to information and low awareness of sustainability issues is the next important barrier which creates a serious roadblock for implementing Agenda 21. Furthermore, awareness is low not only among the general public, but sometimes even among officials. We have to admit, for example, that at state level, in countries in transition, there are a number of officials who take little consideration of Agenda 21 and the principles of sustainable development. At the same time, a lack of information and knowledge is visible already at the next stage – in local and sub-regional government. The experience of my organization – Centre for Environment and Sustainable Development 'ECO-Accord', an NGO from Russia – shows that awareness by both the public and government officials of sustainable development in the NIS is extremely low. We have disseminated documents on these issues and established special information services on environment and development and have received favourable feedback from all sectors.

Often NGO news releases and publications are the only up-to-date sources of information on international events and initiatives, even for ministerial officials in the NIS. As the pan-European Eco-NGO Coalition's NIS Focal Point for the Fourth Ministerial Conference on Environment for Europe (held in Denmark in 1998), we published a range of material as the official preparation for the conference. This included news from the negotiations, the history of the process and other related material from our newsletters and environmental newspapers in the NIS. According to the letters received from several NIS ministries of environment, many universities and NGOs, our material was the only source of systematic information on the subject. Taking into account that access to the Internet is still a problem in many regions, information hunger is often only really satisfied by such NGO initiative. Of course, funding is an urgent problem for NGOs. However, NGOs have human resources and almost unlimited enthusiasm to fulfil their task. This process is helped when it is initiated in cooperation with decision-makers and other stakeholders. It is very important that NGOs receive support for their information and awareness initiatives from different funds and governmental agencies and are able to work for all stakeholders without barriers. This possibility should be maintained at all levels: local, national and regional.

LANGUAGE ALSO CREATES BARRIERS

The problem of access to up-to-date information is even more urgent in non-English speaking countries. Official translation is usually late.

Sometimes it is not absolutely precise or includes other meanings. The level of English language skills is quite low for both officials and the public. In transitional and developing countries, there are usually no funds for translation at national level. As a result, some important documents are not sufficiently discussed and may end up unsigned by some countries. This was, for instance, the case with transport issues at the Third Ministerial Conference on Environment and Health (held in London in 1999), when the Russian Federation officially declared that the Russian translation of the document was too late and, as a result, there was insufficient time to work with it at national level.

Of course, this is just one particular example; but working in an NGO, my colleagues and I often face this difficulty. Cooperation with other stakeholders can sometimes help to solve the problem of translation. On the other hand, initiatives of this kind come from non-state actors. Unfortunately, until now they continue to have many problems in obtaining up-to-date information at the international level and even from the UN. This relates primarily to non-English (UN) languages. Even access to the UN Optical Disk Service (ODS) where one can find UN texts in Arabic or Russian is restricted to NGOs. The UN's websites provide only a small number of translated documents and usually not the more recent ones. Those regions where English is not a common language are effectively cut off from accessing recent publications and documents. In cases such as these, the goodwill of NGOs is not that effective. Such NGO input can only help in cases where officials have full access to all required information, which in itself is doubtful without the human, financial and technical resources and language skills available. The issue of availability and access to information in different languages and for all major groups should be addressed and discussed at Earth Summit 2002 by all delegates who represent stakeholders.

INTERNATIONAL DEBATE: WHAT CAN NGO PARTICIPATION BRING?

This access is, of course, not absolutely restricted. NGOs are welcome to participate in international debates on sustainable development. They can participate in different processes such as the CSD, negotiations on global and regional conventions, important high-level conferences and many others. Decisions and experience obtained there are very helpful at national and local levels.

Reporting in 1997 in New York on the progress made five years after Rio, many countries have shown that they have already developed and adopted their sustainable development strategies, established national councils for sustainable development with multistakeholder representation and implemented Local Agenda 21 programmes in many regions. The CSD became the forum for international discussions and decision-making in this area. Participating in CSD sessions from the very beginning, major groups' representatives, for the first time in history, have obtained the possibility to really take part in UN debate with high-level officials and to address human development and environmental protection issues. However, this participation was quite limited with only ECOSOC NGOs and some business and trade union representatives taking part in CSD sessions. They were able to return home with information about decisions and agreements made in the UN forum. Some NGOs and union representatives disseminated this data at other levels. Nonetheless, there was no real possibility for major groups to bring their experience and knowledge directly within the CSD negotiations. The exception was side events, which were scheduled to take place during lunch or in the evenings.

Established in 1998, multistakeholder dialogue sessions in the framework of the CSD agenda allowed both governments and other stakeholders to effectively exchange their visions and to discuss ideas for implementing sustainability principles in different sectors and areas. It is very important that through these dialogues local experience is brought to the UN level. This helps to create a positive link between real practice and international decision-making. One can obviously say that this kind of 'bottom-up' flow of information is helpful and that it would be useful to develop similar mechanisms in other UN and regional commissions and agencies. It is also important to establish the relevant forums for multistakeholder dialogues at national levels. This would work towards increased information availability, exchange of knowledge and experience, and finally for more effective implementation of development programmes.

It has already been mentioned above that one of the key elements for successful Agenda 21 implementation is active public participation in the decision-making processes. When looking at agreements and official documents over the last ten years, it is possible to see that progress has been made at both international and national levels to create better conditions for public participation. However, in practice the situation is still far from ideal. Even when analysing NGO participation in the most open UN process – the CSD – one can identify a number of problems. Yes, NGOs are represented at country delegations, but mostly only from developed countries. This is due not only to a lack of funds at the national level to have NGO representatives on government delegations – though, of course this may be taken as the main obstacle! Unfortunately, however, responsible officers at national levels who prepare delegation lists often have no clear picture of how to go about inviting major groups to select their representatives.

This is quite a typical situation for many transitional and developing countries. Is it a fault of governmental officials? Surely yes, but to a much greater extent this is a fault of national NGOs. Having been the first NGO representative in the Russian delegation to CSD in 1998, I was very welcome to fully participate in the process. The initiative for this cooperation came from NGOs. Both parties have benefited from this cooperation, and will hopefully work further together; but it has taken six years since Rio for the first attempt to be made. There are still a number of countries who miss this possibility.

This level of NGO participation relates specifically to CSD. At the national level, the situation is much less advanced. Of course, in some highly developed countries (for example, The Netherlands) the public is found to participate actively in environmental and development decision-making. However, looking at the current situation in the NIS states, we see that very often this participation is made just on paper. Why? Besides bureaucratic tendencies and lack of responsibility, public participation truly is a disturbing and expensive exercise for authorities. In situations where environmental problems are high on the list of urgent state priorities, there is not enough knowledge, expertise and funds to involve the public. This problem requires quick solutions in a very short space of time.

On the other hand, without relevant knowledge and experience for both sides, public involvement would only create more problems. How can we avoid this? Some authorities prefer to avoid public involvement in general. Others limit the circle of invited representatives. However, the preferred method is to raise public awareness on environment and development issues and to provide full access to information on these issues at national and international level, as was indicated in Principle 10 of the Rio Declaration and in many further documents.

The Way Forward

Most of the states in the UN-ECE region signed the Aarhus Convention 1998, which regulates public participation, access to information and access to justice on environmental matters. This document opens a new era of multistakeholder cooperation and information availability in Europe. It should become a good example for the international community for further development of global regulations in this area. An agreement to develop and sign a global framework convention on access to information would be the best solution and a victory for Earth Summit 2002. Such a convention would help to create the necessary conditions for the way forward on implementing Agenda 21.

When discussing further actions for implementing Agenda 21, Earth Summit 2002 delegates should place emphasis on promoting further cooperation with non-state actors as well as on establishing a new international mechanism or a body. This body should be made to respect sectoral, regional and gender differences. This would help to monitor free, equal and up-to-date information access and exchange on environment and development matters. One can respond to this by emphasizing that there are already many different organizations world-wide who provide information through the Internet and by other means. However, multistakeholder councils on access to information would help to coordinate these activities and to summarize options. Such councils could work closely with the UN-ECE Aarhus Convention Secretariat and at the same time promote the globalization of the convention. It is crucial that such councils are established at Earth Summit 2002 with the commitments of governments to donate core money for their existence.

Of course the three barriers described are not the only limitations and roadblocks to implementing Agenda 21. However, decisions taken at Earth Summit 2002 and their implementation at global, national and local levels would help to solve many of these problems along the way.

4

Agenda 21 and the Role of Local Government

Jeb Brugman

INTRODUCTION

The rapid response of the local government community, via the Local Agenda 21 (LA21) process, to the inauguration of Agenda 21 has provided ample real-world experiences from which to identify barriers to sustainable development. Indeed, with more than 2000 local communities in countries engaged in LA21 action planning, any rigorous assessment of Agenda 21's progress must factor the progress of related initiatives in cities and towns.

What requires little assessment is the fact that few cities and towns stand today as models of sustainability. Many have made significant and even bold progress in specific areas, such as reductions of air pollutants, waste diversion, improved governance, or increased sanitation services. However, these 'best practices' are not a sufficient basis on which to claim success, particularly in the face of continued negative global trends.

This lack of global progress cannot be attributed simply (and as is customary among the 'major groups') to the policies and actions of national governments and their international institutions. If cities and their local governments can claim a central role in the global sustainable development agenda, then they must also assume direct responsibility for the agenda's inadequate progress.

Clearly, many policies of national and sub-national government have been hindering local-level initiatives. These policies were the focus of the International Council for Local Environmental Initiatives' (ICLEI's) special report to CSD-7, entitled *Barriers to the Implementation of Local Agenda 21*. ICLEI also has issued a more detailed report on the sustainable management of urban land resources to the 9th Session of the CSD, which reflects the special function of urban land use in sustainable urban development. These reports focus on barriers arising from the lack of policy coordination between levels of government. This chapter will focus on barriers that are internal to local government and local communities, based on experiences drawn from ICLEI's LA21 field work since 1993.

Reflecting the ethic of responsibility and constructive self-criticism cited above, I will draw from examples in my own area of residence – greater Toronto in Canada – to illustrate my points.

THE CONTEXT FOR LOCAL ACTION: DECENTRALIZATION AND LOCAL AGENDA 21 IMPLEMENTATION

As a strategy aimed at reforming the process of development, the fate of Agenda 21 is directly linked to the priorities and reforms within the states which have endorsed it. Since 1992, governments worldwide have been undergoing profound reorganization, largely in response to the process of globalization. A primary response has been decentralization and the devolution of basic responsibilities to local government, a process that has been underway in more than 70 nations.

In some instances, decentralization has reflected a weakening of the state and its role in the economy. In these cases, local governments have been confronted with increased pressures from senior levels of government, as well as from local stakeholders, to perform basic societal functions previously managed at the national or sub-national levels. Revenue transfers have not generally accompanied these pressures. Local governments have been left, therefore, to make hard decisions about whether to increase local taxes (thereby potentially hindering global competitiveness) or to eliminate basic public services (thereby often reducing their economic, social and/or environmental sustainability).

In some instances, as in South Africa, decentralization has reflected a strategy to strengthen the state, and to adapt it to global economic realities, by building a nation's economic future on a foundation of healthy urban 'economic engines' managed by empowered 'city-states'.

Under either scenario, during the 1990s a large number of nations have been seeking effective mechanisms to facilitate decentralization.

Whether initiated by a local mayor or through a national ministry, the LA21 process has proven to be an effective supportive mechanism to this process, because it:

* effectively engages stakeholders;
* facilitates the review and formulation of new policies; and
* can factor sustainability issues within corporate and economic development strategies.

ICLEI's continuous review of LA21 activities around the world confirms that these processes have supported decentralization (or the general strengthening of local government); have effectively engaged many (but not all) stakeholders; and have facilitated reformulation of many (but not all) policies. However, an assessment of the true impacts of these processes must address the following two key questions.

HAVE LOCAL AGENDA 21 PROCESSES EFFECTIVELY INFLUENCED THE ECONOMIC DEVELOPMENT STRATEGIES AND POLICIES OF MUNICIPAL CORPORATIONS?

A municipal corporation is in many respects a microcosm of a nation, a transnational corporation, or a Bretton Woods institution. Each institution must ultimately respond to its specific stakeholders, and must choose the mechanisms for stakeholder engagement. Each must define its policies and development strategies according to specific governance procedures. And each must constantly transform its day-to-day operational practices in response to evolving policy without undermining its ability to deliver its most basic services.

Many municipal corporations have used LA21 planning to redefine their corporate missions and strategic plans. Hundreds of local governments have incorporated sustainability principles and specific commitments to sustainable development within their formal planning documents. Such commitments are often reflected in economic development strategies, but application of these commitments in day-to-day economic decision-making can be surprisingly inconsistent.

An interesting example is the case of Hamilton-Wentworth, Canada, which, with ICLEI's support, has served as a 'best practice' model for LA21 throughout the 1990s. Yet the Hamilton-Wentworth case highlights the tension between old and new ways of doing business that can be found in most active LA21 communities.

The regional municipality of Hamilton-Wentworth (Ontario), Canada, started its sustainable community initiative (LA21) process in the late 1980s, thus responding to the 1987 WCED report before its conclusions found expression in Agenda 21. At that time, the region was still recovering from a steady decline in its primary industry: steel manufacturing. This decline left the municipality to address high unemployment, a declining population and tax base, and considerable environmental problems. The concept of sustainable development seemed a perfect starting point for mapping the region's future.

With strong support from the regional chairman and CEO, key municipal departments joined forces with the main, local social and environmental stakeholders – as well as with those willing business representatives – to prepare a regional sustainable development strategy. Council authority over this process was granted to the council's planning and economic development committee to ensure integration of economic issues as well as political support. However, during the initial years of consultation and assessment, the community's major business organizations pursued a separate strategic planning process for economic development and rejected the notion of sustainability as a foundation principle for that strategy. In due time, this gap was bridged – a task often left unaccomplished in many LA21 communities – and a unified, regional 'Vision 2020' action plan was prepared.

The regional municipality proceeded to integrate the Vision 2020 mandates within its policies and operations. For example, an interdepartmental working group of high-level professionals was established in 1993 to review all departmental decision-making procedures, budgets and policies relative to Vision 2020.

During the period of 1993–1994, the Province of Ontario instituted dramatic reductions in traditional provincial financial transfers to municipalities. At the same time, the province transferred a variety of new fiscal responsibilities for public housing, transit and social welfare. In the course of one year, many Ontario municipalities had to reduce their operating budgets by 20 per cent. To its credit, the CEO of Hamilton-Wentworth used Vision 2020 plan criteria, in part, to determine where to cut its municipal budget.

However, during the same period, the regional council approved the construction of a major roadway through an important, environmentally sensitive area, in spite of vocal and organized public opposition. The project (which was ultimately subsidized by the provincial government) was a blatant contradiction of Vision 2020 objectives. Shortly thereafter, the council eliminated new bicycle lanes in response to complaints from private motorists. These actions were condemned by local environmental organizations as demonstrations of the region's lack of commitment to Vision 2020.

These kinds of stories can be found in most LA21 communities. They are indicative of the difficulties that municipalities and their stakeholders face in fully integrating sustainability criteria within their development and investment decisions. During the 1990s many municipal actors have been satisfied to apply sustainability concepts at the strategic level, as part of a stakeholder consultation or 'visioning' exercise. However, following the high-profile public processes, they often fail to ensure rigorous follow-up and changes in practice, particularly by those council committees and line departments that oversee development activities. The implementation of LA21 action plans is often started where it is easiest – by creating new environmental programmes or social initiatives.

Such practice is inadequate, but is to be expected. All communities operate within the parameters of longstanding power relationships and unwritten understandings between economic interests and elites. Many development proposals that have been decided in the 1990s have been building political momentum for decades. Although it should be easy to turn small ships, communities are complex systems in their own right, compelled by the momentum of earlier priorities and choices. They also are not trained to see inherent synergies between economic, social and environmental agendas. In the meantime, they continue to apply traditional formulations of these agendas, through which they see the inherent conflicts between economic development and sustainability. In this way, many critical choices have been made in the 1990s on the basis of these old visions.

HAVE LOCAL AGENDA 21 PROCESSES TRANSFORMED DAY-TO-DAY OPERATIONAL PRACTICES IN RESPONSE TO EVOLVING POLICIES?

Perhaps more insidious are the micro-level decisions, often left to an individual staff person, that hinder innovation and the establishment of a new development momentum. The reasons for contradictory behaviours, as exemplified in the case of Hamilton-Wentworth, often can be found in the day-to-day operational practices of local governments and, in particular, the specific council committees or line departments that are assigned with development promotion and control.

The council committees have control over the laws (such as by-laws or ordinances) that define what is and is not an acceptable development. These local laws determine the densities, infrastructure requirements, and required amenities (for example, stores, schools) of new neighbourhoods. Generally, these laws reflect antiquated concepts about an ideal development pattern and the required technologies for housing (for example, flush toilets, storm water connections to sewerage systems). The templates of these laws – often based on the ideals of Los Angeles or Long Island, New York, in the 1960s – have been transferred, often with the support of international development assistance, from continent to continent.

Local councils often have distinct committees to make case-by-case decisions about development proposals that vary from these laws. In these discussions, the opinions of individual municipal staff can have great influence. These detailed discussions – rather, negotiations – can focus on things as mundane as the width of sidewalks or the orientation of windows. These mundane decisions determined how much land, materials and infrastructure is required for a new neighbourhood. Therefore, at this detailed level the economics of what can and cannot be developed are actually defined.

Of course, in many nations formal municipal planning and development control systems still lack the capacity to rigorously apply local development laws; in this case, actual development approvals are granted via informal agreements. Alternatively, developments may proceed without approvals at all. The 1999 Bribe Payers' Survey of Transparency International identified the construction (development or building) industry to be most active in the use of bribes.

The greater Toronto area is a centre for the North American 'new urbanism' movement – an effort to transform laws requiring sprawling, inefficient, automobile-centred suburban development into frameworks for higher-density communities that are transit- and pedestrian-friendly. These efforts focus on two fronts: more sustainable designs for new housing developments in suburbia, and the 'infill' of existing urbanized areas to increase their residential densities.

Sprawling suburban subdivisions, North American municipalities have long argued, are approved – often on prime agricultural land – because this is the only form of housing that local residents wish to buy. However, Toronto has the fortune of a few large housing developers who have been willing to take the risk of applying new urbanist concepts.

In 1997 I visited a subdivision in a suburban Toronto-area community that was applying new urbanist concepts in a project with more than 100 new homes. The project featured wider sidewalks and narrower roadways than in the abutting developments. A church and village stores were integrated within the new neighbourhood to reduce automobile trips. A natural area and parks were designed within the development site. The developer explained that he had wished to include a number of other new urbanist features within the project, in particular the use of less land for paved roads and alleyways. The local municipal engineers rejected these efforts after persistent efforts by the developer to address municipal concerns. When asked what was the major barrier to more new urbanist construction, he cited not the market but the local municipality. The municipality, he reported, was just not willing to accept much innovation, and the time required to overcome the resistance of individual municipal professionals undermined the economic viability of such projects.

A similar story can be told of efforts to innovate within Toronto's existing, older neighbourhoods.

The city of Toronto's 1991 CityPlan (its official development plan) gives strong support to the intensification of existing city neighbourhoods through 'infill' development, particularly in areas serviced by public transit. Supportive of such an effort, in 1991, the Canadian Housing and Mortgage Corporation, an agency of Canadian government, launched a nationwide competition for the design of a state-of-the-art, healthy and environment-friendly family home. A Toronto design was selected.

The design employed 15 state-of-the-art technologies to create a three-storey, two-family home that is completely self-sufficient. The so-called 'healthy house' produces its own electricity from solar panels, provides its own water supply from rainwater collectors, and fully treats its waste water using a system of biological filters and ultraviolet light. The home is constructed of low chemical materials, employs a sophisticated, energy-saving ventilation system, as well as high efficiency appliances, lights and windows. Furthermore, the house is built on an 'infill' lot on an unserviced city alleyway, so that no new, undeveloped land is used for its construction. As the house requires no energy, water or sewage utility services and is located on existing transportation infrastructure, operating costs for the house are eliminated or severely reduced for both the municipality and the homeowner.

This being said, the developer had to spend four years to obtain the necessary approvals and variances from both provincial and municipal agencies. Existing building regulations prescribe, on the basis of old technologies, what a builder can do and what kinds of systems a builder can install. Many of the systems and materials used in the 'healthy house' are not prescribed in the provincial building code. As a result, extensive time was spent determining which provincial agency had responsibility to grant special approvals for each individual system. The building materials used in construction of the 'healthy house' required individual review by the Ontario Building Code Commission. As provincial legislation has only eight categories for sewage management and none cover on-site sewage treatment, the biofiltration system – which allows all waste water to be recycled for bathing and washing – required approvals from the municipal board of health and the Ontario Ministry of Environment. The construction of a house that would not receive electricity services from Ontario Hydro (the provincial energy utility) also required review.

The house was finally completed and offered for sale in 1996, and continues to serve as a 'best practice' – as well as an example of the barriers to best practice. Naturally, the elapse of time increased the expense of the project and local market conditions changed, reducing the economic replicability of the design. (The process did not result in changes to legislation that would reduce barriers for similar projects in the future.) But the project offered clear financial benefits to the municipality. The replication cost of building and installing the 'healthy house's' water and waste water system in future houses would be approximately US$7000, in comparison to the US$105,000 cost associated with connecting a traditional house, at the same infill location, to municipal water and sewer services.

Although the 'healthy house' model provides opportunities to reduce municipal operating costs, the slow and detailed process of changing traditional legislation to support new technologies prevents most municipalities from approving of even one such housing project. LA21 processes generally encourage these kinds of sustainable practices. But implementation will only begin to occur following quite intensive reviews and reforms of numerous detailed laws and procedures.

In addition to legal reform, the professional groups that staff municipal planning and engineering departments will need to change their standards of practice. This will require both mid-career training for established professionals as well as revised curriculums for university degree programmes.

CONCLUSIONS

Of course, the other barriers to sustainable local action remain: perverse and hidden subsidies; insufficient municipal finance and institutional capacity; restricted jurisdictions in some areas and confused and overlapping jurisdiction in others. The roots of these problems are often traced, justifiably, to national and sub-national policies. Increasingly, they are being addressed in the context of decentralization processes. Nonetheless, by taking these external barriers too seriously, local governments have traditionally also created their own self-imposed barriers. For example, municipal solicitors often provide the most conservative possible interpretation of municipal legal powers, even when many aspects of the law are open to interpretation (in the courts or similar mechanisms) and could be developed to support innovation.

The good news is that thousands of local governments have been stridently shedding their self-imposed notions of weakness, and are actively engaged in the business of innovation for sustainable development. This is why we can today report about the many detailed barriers –boring, mundane local details that require our diligent attention – more barriers than can be touched upon in this chapter. Local governments and their LA21 processes are pressing up against the barriers, and are facing the resulting conflicts and difficult choices with far greater commitment, capacity and openness than in 1992.

Sometimes we need to climb a mountain just to see how far the road is that we must travel. The worst that can be said of the progress of local governments in implementing Agenda 21 is that many mountains have been climbed.

5

Workroom versus Boardroom Approaches to Sustainable Development: Reversing the Downward Spiral

Winston Gereluk and Lucien Royer

INTRODUCTION

In *The Way Forward*,[1] prepared for the UN General Assembly Special Session in 1997, we traced the history of the movement for sustainable development back to the earliest stages of history, when workers began the struggle against the worst forms of unsustainable production. The first trade unions paved the way for increased participation in the workplace, and what has subsequently developed into an extensive field of occupational health and safety. We examined political, economic and institutional factors that affected our efforts and impeded the implementation of Chapter 29 in Agenda 21.

This chapter develops a critical analysis of the lack of progress in implementing Agenda 21, especially with respect to changes in the workplace. In particular, it focuses on the mindset among CSD stakeholders that refuses to attribute a central role to workplaces, workers and trade unions in the search for sustainable forms of production and consumption. The current downward spiral in the state of the world's ecology is bound to continue unless nations and major stakeholders agree that the joint engagement of workers and employers is necessary to bring about the level of changes that are required.

Trade unions have been active at the CSD since its inception, represented by the International Confederation of Free Trade Unions (ICFTU), which brings together 124 million members, represented by union affiliates in 143 countries and territories.[2] In 1998, it was joined by the Trade Union Advisory Committee to the OECD (TUAC), with its 55 affiliates and 70 million members in OECD countries. Since then, a growing number of International Trade Union Secretariats have become involved in CSD special reviews or special dialogue sessions, signalling the importance accorded to sustainable development by the trade union movement.[3]

In 1998 trade unions began to participate as a major group in dialogue sessions, as part of the New Programme of Work recommended by the United Nations General Assembly at its Special Session in June 1997 (UNGASS).[4] In 1999, they were able to build significantly on the core positions advanced by trade unions at the previous five general sessions, as they took part in discussions on unsustainable tourism as well as Oceans and Seas.[5,6] By Earth Summit 2002, trade unions will have coordinated the input of workers into two further dialogue sessions: agriculture and transport.

PAYING THE PRICE FOR UNFULFILLED PROMISES

Earth Summit 1992 marked a high point in worldwide awareness of the deteriorating state of our global environment. It was an event full of promise that inspired millions of individuals and major groups around the world to make environmental change a priority. Trade unions were one such major group. Chapter 29 of Agenda 21 signalled a commitment by governments to recognize a special role for workers and trade unions in the implementation of change at the workplace.

THE FUTURE OF OUR PLANET IS AT STAKE

Since Earth Summit 1992, however, concern about the future continues to grow. Member states have not lived up to commitments made in Rio and funding for Agenda 21 by developed nations *has actually decreased*. There is yet no clear 'agenda' for concrete implementation of change. Although climate-related changes are a major concern in almost any area – such as water, energy, agriculture, land-use or forest-related issues – the natural environment is losing ground, and losing ground very rapidly.[7] Reports, received almost daily, foretell an increasingly bleak future, and examples of progress seem to pale in comparison.[8]

WORKERS' STAKE IN SUSTAINABLE WORKPLACES IS HIGH

Over 1.1 million workers die each year (almost 3300 per day) from unsustainable forms of production according to national statistics: nearly double the number of people who die from war, and triple the number who die from HIV or AIDS.[9] Approximately 335,000 of these are attributable to known occupational accidents, of which 12,000 claim the lives of children. Around 325,000 deaths are due to occupational diseases, most from exposure to hazardous substances, with asbestos the largest single killer claiming 100,000 lives per year. Over 630,000 workers die per year because of health-related effects of work, and over 160 million new cases of injury or work-related diseases are reported each year. Doubling or tripling these 'official' figures would likely provide a more accurate figure.

It is against this backdrop of delayed environmental and workplace improvements that the world must now make drastic adjustments not previously contemplated.

ROADBLOCKS ENCOUNTERED BY WORKERS AND THE TRADE UNION MOVEMENT

Workers' stake in the environment goes back in history as production has always entailed risks to the health and safety of those engaged in production, be they slaves, serfs, independent producers or waged employees. In fact, the particularly unsustainable forms of production characterized by the industrial revolution are responsible for some of the earliest work towards developing sustainable, healthy workplaces and communities.[10]

Early in the Agenda 21 process, trade unions saw the importance of becoming involved in the CSD process and in other bodies where sustainable development would become a focus, such as the OECD, the International Labour Organization (ILO/ACTRAV), as well as the WHO.[11,12,13]

Nevertheless, our desire to be involved and a unique capacity to contribute have not been sufficient in themselves. For all our efforts, and the positive wording of adopted texts, the acceptance of workers and trade unions as 'full partners' in plans for concrete workplace changes continues to remain limited. A new action plan is needed, one that seeks, as never before, the support of the greatest majority of stakeholders, including workers. To develop such a plan it is important to understand what the roadblocks have been for workers and trade unions.

ROADBLOCK 1: THE RIO AGENDA REQUIRED 'QUANTUM LEAPS' – A NEW WAY OF MAKING AND IMPLEMENTING DECISIONS AFFECTING PRODUCTION AND CONSUMPTION

Rio proposed changes in patterns of production and consumption that were radical in nature – nothing less fundamental than a wholesale change in the way we live, work and make decisions. Furthermore, these patterns are deeply ingrained in our way of life and our economic and political decision-making structures; they are, in turn, supported by the most powerful structural and organizational elements on the planet (eg economic systems, trade and investment patterns, and the international banking system).[14]

Furthermore, Agenda 21 occurred just when some of the world's poorest nations were beginning to experience industrial growth. They understandably resisted suggestions that they should reject the patterns of development which have brought relative comfort to industrialized countries. In general, the demands and implications of Agenda 21 appeared to ask for too much from developing countries too soon, and with little effort to build capacity. This was clearly visible in climate change negotiations where developing countries refused to join as signatories. The inability of developing countries to fully implement Agenda 21 will not change soon, given the continued reluctance of industrialized countries to engage in the redistribution necessary to meet the costs.

These negative factors must be considered in the context of lost or delayed opportunities for change, referred to earlier. Taken together, they reinforce prospects of a downward spiral for some time. The future faced by those at Rio cannot be compared to the one that awaits Earth Summit 2002. Actions avoided since Rio are not simply delayed in a linear fashion; rather, social and environmental costs of damage and future mitigation increase exponentially. The future climate for decision-making is also bound to change. The calls for public participation at Earth Summit 2002 will most likely be threatened by a growing temptation among nations to set aside their commitments for consultation and planning in order to deal with the daily realities of local crises, disasters or ecological emergencies.

A precautionary approach cannot fully account for unknown factors that will require drastic and unprecedented actions in response to future conditions – the 'quantum leaps'. Given the current state of the world, it is now time to plan for changes that are qualitatively different from changes that might have been sufficient had they been taken yesterday or today.

The concept of quantum leaps first emerged at a Friends of the Earth workshop held in Switzerland, 1995.[15] Participants agreed that, even with known changes to current consumption and production patterns needed to fulfil Agenda 21, quantum leaps in changes would have to be considered. The concept refers not so much to size, as to the nature of required changes: it demands qualitative as well as quantitative shifts from traditional strategies, tools and time lines. It also implies changes to decision-making; fundamental change is needed not only to the way we produce and consume, but also to the way we make and implement decisions affecting change.

Instead of quantum leaps, the recommendations emerging from the CSD, other intergovernmental bodies and governments since 1992 have, essentially, exhibited a 'business-as-usual' approach, all the while seeking ways to improve it here and there or to make it slightly more efficient from an environmental standpoint. In our view, schedules for change put forward by government and business are either insufficient, or will not be implemented quickly enough to counter environmental events. Change has not been adequate in response to the growing number of warnings about our environment; we are now awakening to the realization that moderate changes to production that might have sufficed at one time are no longer adequate.

ROADBLOCK 2: A FAILURE TO RECOGNIZE THE WORKPLACE AS A FOCAL POINT OF CHANGE

Nowhere is the failure to embrace a fundamentally different way of making and implementing decisions more evident than in the reluctance of CSD members to recognize the workplace as a focal point of production and consumption. For trade unions the argument has always been clear: workplaces must be a prime focus of attention because they are at the hub of the world's production, and are also major consumers of the world's products and 'environmental capital'.

Even more importantly, workplaces serve as major determinants of patterns of consumption. Firstly, because most of the world's people work for a living, the workplace occupies a central place in their lives. Secondly, workplaces shape the character of their host communities. It is therefore unfortunate that most of the places and processes of work around the world are 'unsustainable' – and even more regrettable that this has yet to be identified as a major problem by most CSD stakeholders.

In this respect, Agenda 21 never 'got off the ground'. There has been virtually no recognition of the role workplaces play in production and consumption, and certainly no recognition that they should be a focal point for change. Instead, frequent references to business and production in CSD circles have served to marginalize the notion of workplaces.[16] As well, individuals who work in the world's workplaces have yet to be officially recognized as agents of change; the public participation espoused by CSD apparently stops at the plant gate.

At times, it was agreed that it would be foolhardy to attempt changes in workplaces without the participation of workers; and the CSD even occasionally accepted that, without unions, worker participation is unlikely. Such conclusions are only now beginning to emerge at the CSD. The ICFTU and TUAC represent workers in about 2.5 million workplaces throughout the world, but the capacity of these workers to engage in creative action has yet to be called upon. This must change. Clearly, responding to such a call will not be an easy task and will require the full support of all stakeholders. However, as we shall see later, the first task before us is to agree that this is important. The second task is, then, to begin taking progressive steps in that direction.

Instead, country delegates and stakeholders have tended to focus on 'successes' that are technical in nature, and do not involve shifts in the relations of production. Technological innovations by themselves cannot solve the problems of the unsustainable workplace, since even the most massive, integrated technological changes do not imply either negative or positive impacts. Their effect depends upon the way they are conceived and applied; more to the point, they reflect the purposes of the people who bring them into the workplace and dictate their use. The historical fact is that the vast majority of affected people, especially workers, are typically left out of the decision-making process. Their agendas and interests are completely ignored.

Decisions that emanate from the corporate boardroom, without the participation of workers and trade unions – or any other stakeholders for that matter – will do little to reverse the downward spiral. Most 'cleaner production' approaches or 'eco-efficiency' measures of the last decade, for example, focus on investments, productivity, consultants, and enlist workers only for narrowly prescribed tasks. They fail to involve the workers who represent the greatest potential for change, or the trade unions who have proven their instrumentality in coordinating efforts across sectors and national boundaries by educating and planning change with employer organizations, governments and communities.

The raison d'être of unions is to challenge the one-sided exercise of power that has traditionally existed in the workplace, and to replace it with a new regime in which the parties to the employment contract are more evenly matched, and begin to share some control and governance of the workplace. Collective bargaining is an institution developed to accomplish this, and we believe it holds some of the keys to help solve some of the real problems of unsustainable development and production. It is only when workers feel secure and are not subject to arbitrary dismissal and discrimination that they will have the power to participate in effecting positive changes. This requires union recognition and collective bargaining.

ROADBLOCK 3: THE PERSISTENCE OF TAYLORISM

Trade union delegations have repeatedly offered to work with social partners at the CSD and in other venues to make the sustainable workplace a reality. However, this has implications for industrial relations as it is currently practised throughout the world. Surprisingly, the sustainable development aspects of current industrial relations policy, as it affects production, have never been the subject of a discussion at the CSD. One would have the feeling that there is an unspoken agreement to remain silent about it. This is no longer acceptable.

The underlying problem in most of today's workplaces, we believe, is a 'problem of work': the place workers occupy in the work process. This problem is contained in the concept of Taylorism, which not only prescribes a certain relationship of workers to their work, but also dictates that they will have little say about terms and conditions under which they work.[17] It dictates that conception (thinking, decision-making) belongs to management, and that workers simply execute predetermined tasks (appropriately 'idiot-proofed'). At its extreme, Taylorism denies that workers may think for themselves, or take any responsibility for the product, the process or the community in which they work.

Taylorism fragments and damages workers, through their domestic and community life, since it invariably affects how they conduct themselves as consumers. This was clearly illustrated in the 1999 CSD dialogue sessions, where it was noted that the way workers become 'tourists' on vacations, holidays or other defined 'time off work' periods suffers from the separation of life at work from life away from work.

In too many cases, where crude Taylorism is superseded, it is replaced by another form of management that retains its essential premises. Modern human relations strategies, for example, often serve to *deepen* unitarist control of the workplace and process – an observation that is missed by very few of the workers involved.

Using collective agreements, unions have consistently promoted qualitative changes that involve workers in decision-making and provide access to information and redress when unacceptable practices continue.[18] In short, workers must become part of the dynamic of change, as whole persons, not as cyphers with muscle and labour time. Their spirit and capacity to care and be creative must be harnessed as an integral part of any strategy. It is crucial that Earth Summit 2002 explore this area fully.

Unions and collective agreements are instrumental as the means through which workers can gather, organize and articulate their interests and concerns as a party to the employment contract. The conventional wisdom that equates a 'collaborative' approach with unitarist forms of management, and an 'adversarial' approach with trade unions, is damaging and simply untrue. An adversarial relationship is implicit in the employment contract itself, in the sense that employers have some important different interests, and efforts to suppress the contract by imposing unitarist relations have produced some of the most disruptive forms of adversarial expression in the workplace, along with unsustainable forms of production. The most damaging is the 'passive resistance' that results in lost productivity and missed opportunities for improvement. A more constructive approach builds cooperation around the real expression of the voice and interests of both parties. The CSD must open up discussions on the positive role that collective agreements can play in implementing sustainable development.

Collective bargaining has already produced environmental agreements that are models for voluntary initiatives and agreements (VIAs) or self-regulated mechanisms (SRMs).[19] SRMs targeted at sustainable development have increased to the extent that CSD-6 initiated a full-scale review by trade unions, NGOs and businesses.[20] They include a wide range of codes of conduct, environment management systems, partnership agreements and framework agreements.

Trade unions will support SRMs only if they complement and strengthen government regulation, not replace it. Furthermore, they must form part of an integrated regulatory reform process and be coordinated with other intergovernmental bodies to strengthen regulatory compliance and improve standards.[21] The interests of developing countries should be integrated within any programme for promoting VIAs. Finally, it would be necessary to ensure that SRMs never undermine minimum standards based on agreed sets of indicators for environmental, economic and social factors of sustainable development. The ILO's labour standards for association and employment equity, for example, would form part of the body of social indicators.

Literally, thousands of codes of conduct or VIAs currently exist. Many contain commitments to the community or work environments for planning and development of management practices, cooperation with other sectors and public awareness. Most lack credibility and are seen as little more than PR exercises. The most certain claim to credibility would be the involvement of workers themselves, right from the initial stages of goal-setting to disclosure of information about activities at the workplace level.

ROADBLOCK 4: FAILURE TO USE THE WORKPLACE AS A VEHICLE OF EDUCATION TO MAKE 'CONSUMERS' INTO 'ENVIRONMENTAL CITIZENS'

Even where workers are recognized as vital to any strategy for sustainable production, their role as consumers is too often misunderstand. We believe that this is key to understanding current patterns of consumption and unsustainable consumer behaviour. Too many recommendations to change consumer behaviour have focused on individual choice or attitude. Consumption patterns, however, derive from social and economic factors, including industrial relations in the workplace, and it is in this light that we must begin to tackle the most negative forms of a 'consumerist' approach to the world, its people and its resources, including advertising and other market processes that portray unsustainable behaviour as desirable.

Transformation to sustainable consumer behaviour demands a 'quantum leap' in changes to lifestyles, one that will occur only when people are sufficiently aware of the effect their consumption has on the community and natural environment. It requires a willingness to forego a certain degree of comfort, if necessary, to minimize use of the world's resources, to opt for alternative products and services and, in general, an enthusiasm to actively protect the natural and built environment

This level of change can be promoted by workplace and work-related education. When provided with appropriate challenges and opportunities, workers have the ability to absorb vast amounts of knowledge and skill on the job. When empowered with knowledge and institutional support, they have become a 'market force' for change. Trade unions are in a position to facilitate this change by engaging their members as both producers and consumers. This process was described in the clearest terms at CSD-7, where it was agreed that changes to unsustainable tourist behaviour depended upon merging workers' work time with their leisure time.

Involving workers in changes to production is the most direct way of influencing their habits as consumers. Workers who are involved in changes at the point of production become aware of environmental and social issues, a shift that brings new attitudes towards personal consumption. Questions about the workplace are soon applied to domestic affairs – consumption patterns in homes, in transport, in communities. For this reason, we have proposed strategies to make workplaces centres of learning, to shape new attitudes for the good of the workplace parties and the community.

Once again, this requires an end to Taylorist relations, which engages workers only in the strict execution of assigned tasks and presumes that 'personal life' begins only when the worker is off work. The challenge is to engage the worker as a whole person: with hearts and minds as well as labour power. Trade unions have shown that education and communication can empower workers to take full responsibility for themselves, their fellow workers, and community. Such 'best practices' must be transferred to other and small- or medium-sized operations, however, as they account for the bulk of the world's workplaces, including the extension of industrial relations to those workplaces.

ROADBLOCK 5: INCREASED CONCENTRATION OF DECISION-MAKING AND CONTROL MILITATES AGAINST LOCAL PLANNING OR ACTION

Since Rio, the labour movement has promoted meaningful involvement of stakeholders in decision-making. Many roadblocks can be overcome if development is planned and implemented with citizens, employers and workers in host communities that have most to gain from sustainable development. These communities must also be key beneficiaries of any development that takes place. This is especially true of aboriginal communities, where a respect for traditional values, knowledge and ways is a prerequisite to sustainable development.

Stakeholder involvement demands workers' right to organize. Death, injury and illness are the human cost of unsafe workplaces, and inadequate provision for worker participation is a key ingredient in most of these. A keen determination to deny workers a voice is evident, however, in the extent employers and states go to deny workers freedom of association and expression. Violations of trade union rights are symptoms of unsustainable forms of production; in 1998 alone, 123 trade unionists were murdered, 1650 attacked or injured, 3660 arrested, and 21,427 sacked for trade union activities.[22] Countries where trade union rights are least respected are those in which workplace casualties are highest.

The democratization of the workplace goes hand-in-hand with our vision of the 'environmental citizen', able to make sound decisions and act instinctively to protect the Earth. Other major groups have endorsed this vision – particularly at CSD-7, where all groups agreed that sustainable tourism required worker and citizen participation, including the sharing of information and decision-making.

Unfortunately, such agreement flies in the face of reality outside the UN. The CSD and other bodies may favour broad-based stakeholder involvement, but in the years since Rio 'quantum leaps' have taken place in the opposite direction, towards concentration of control.

Today, a small number of corporations and international organizations wield a degree of control over both consumption and production that would have been inconceivable a decade ago. This must be identified as a major obstacle to the realization of Agenda 21.

Concentrated ownership and control of the means of production suggests that decision-making is often far removed from the locus of production and the affected communities. Moreover, this type of decision-making affects patterns of consumption, as an increasingly small and concentrated group of decision-makers determines what will be available, etc. Globalization of control has also changed the process of work, contributing to patterns of worker behaviour that have negative implications for consumption.

Workers have demonstrated their ability to lead the process of public participation, especially where learning and self-improvement are encouraged, as in cities and regions with Local Agenda 21 action plans. Participation cannot take place in a political vacuum, however; minimum conditions must guarantee local elections, free press, free speech and due process. Wherever these are lacking, union workers have played a key role in advancing political reform.

Finally, globalization has advanced a culture of development shaped by the world's bankers and the investment community, which has affected the capacity of nations and communities to plan for social and economic transition. This 'bankers model' too often promotes a form of development that is synonymous with the expansion of production and consumption, and views sustainable development from the point of view of 'marginal cost', concerned with protecting market competition and eliminating so-called labour market rigidities (which can be taken to include workers' demands for just and equal remuneration). Unhappily, social and environmental aspects of development are still not equal, as Agenda 21 proposed; economic demands are still dominant.

This model, or mindset, has been particularly damaging where it has produced a reaction to change in communities and among trade union members, which can be summarized as jobs versus the environment. This debate has placed well-meaning individuals and organizations against changes that could promote Agenda 21 goals, and must be overcome before any meaningful progress can be made.

An answer lies in 'just transition' programmes, yet to be addressed by the CSD. Put simply, because jobs will be lost in the process of change, employment security, or livelihood security, must be a key element of national and regional programmes of change. Workers will be involved – they have no choice – but their involvement will be positive only if governments and employers establish credible and effective 'social transition', which includes employment transition for workers' programmes.

Without such programmes, it is unrealistic to expect support from most of the world's workers; quantum leaps will simply not occur, however, without the involvement of these workers, even though all industries will be affected, and most of them will face fundamental changes to their work. History has supplied too much clear evidence that they, their families and communities will bear the major burden of any change. Clearly the time has come to address 'just transition' programmes and their institution must be integrated with the recognition that employment and employment creation are a cornerstone of sustainable development.

The OECD has identified economic instruments that can be used by member countries to fund such programmes, such as charges, taxes, marketable permits, deposit refunds and subsidies. We see a role for each, but any negative impacts on employment and other social factors must be well understood, and social costs minimized. In addition, such measures must form part of an overall sustainable development strategy that includes green jobs. Subsidies that promote unsustainable practices must be eliminated, and all revenues directed to promote sustainable development, including compensation for regressive effects on income distribution and social factors.

The Way Ahead

Work with the CSD has given trade unions an opportunity to reach a measure of agreement with other major groups. As we prepare for Earth Summit 2002, we believe that broad-based support could be built for the following objectives in the search for sustainable development:

- A multistakeholder process that involves all legitimate stakeholders to ensure that development policies, programmes and projects are developed in accordance with their needs, priorities and unique attributes, as well as the natural and cultural 'carrying capacity' of host communities and countries.
- A recognition of the pivotal role of the workplace as the centre of much of the world's production and consumption patterns, a main source of environmental problems, and therefore a logical focus for change. This includes the unique position of workers to contribute to change in the workplace. Core labour standards must be respected, including employment equality and the prohibition of child and forced labour.
- An industrial relations focus which recognizes collective bargaining as a way of producing needed change, and in which the tools and programmes for workplace health and safety are applied to

environment and community issues. Support from such bodies as UNEP, governments, NGOs and academic institutions is vital.

- Effective management tools and decision-making, which includes stock-taking and target-setting, supported by reliable workplace auditing, reporting and evaluating, undertaken jointly by workers, employers and trade unions. These tools are to be aimed, initially, at meeting low-cost and reachable targets related to water uses, energy and resource uses, waste and toxic substance management, as well as health and safety.[23]

- SRMs, VIAs that clearly supplement regulations or standards within an integrated regulatory reform process, recognize the interests of developing countries, and abide by minimum social, environmental and economic standards of sustainable development and do not undermine the role of government and public services, especially in policy development, standard-setting and enforcement.

- A special focus on employment creation, 'just transition' measures, and poverty alleviation in all local, regional and national programmes to promote sustainable development. Workers must see that a continued livelihood and an orderly conversion have been secured through reliable transition programmes.

- A commitment to joint action and partnerships that recognizes that the workplace is a part of the community and is promoted through all stages of production and consumption. Workers and their trade unions, community representatives and other stakeholders must be involved from the outset, setting common targets, training and education, design and implementation and, finally, in assessment, evaluation, and reporting.

- Involvement as a means of changing attitudes, understandings, and capacities of people, institutions and nations – the only way to bring about 'quantum leaps' in production and consumption patterns. Involvement in changes to production increases awareness, changes attitudes and provides a link between production and personal consumption patterns; in short, this develops the type of 'environmental citizens' who will work in a community to change consumption patterns.

Challenging the CSD

Promises made at Rio were not kept because they implied a fundamental change to the way we live, work and make decisions, beginning at the workplace and extending into international circles. Although this chapter focuses on roadblocks to progress, it also points to an important and exciting role for the CSD in the new millennium. The

CSD has already taken the first steps by bringing together representatives of business, trade unions, NGOs, local authorities and other major groups who were able to move quickly beyond their differences to search for points of agreement. All this happened at the lofty, removed level of the UN; but nonetheless, it proved that it could be done and, in this respect, clearly distinguished itself from other international agencies which have yet to move towards any comparable form of major group input.

Earth Summit 2002 and the CSD must now move to a higher level. With concern about the environment growing dramatically, and awareness that environmental degradation is more than 'scare mongering', member states must be pressed to honour the agreements they signed in the heady weeks at Rio by instituting the broad-based type of stakeholder involvement envisioned in Agenda 21. They might begin by including worker representatives on all national delegations to the CSD and other agencies devoted to sustainable development. In other words, it is time for them to demonstrate more than a paper commitment to Chapter 29 of Agenda 21. It is in the power of the CSD to promote this change among its members.

NOTES

1   Gereluk, W and Royer, L (1997) 'Trade Union Action: A Paradigm for Sustainable Development', in F Dodds (ed) *The Way Forward: Beyond Agenda 21*, London: Earthscan Publications Ltd

2   *Sustainability Through Trade Union Action at the Workplace* (20 case studies from around the world), published for CSD 'Day of The Workplace', April 1996; and *The Challenge of Collective Engagement – Trade Union Dialogue Session*, 5th Session of the CSD, 1997, Brussels: ICFTU

3   International Federation of Building and Woodworkers (IFBWW), International Federation of Chemical, Energy, Mine and General Workers' Unions (ICEM), International Textile, Garment and Leather Workers' Federation (ITGLWF), International Union of Food, Agricultural, Hotel, Restaurant, Catering, Tobacco and Allied Workers' Associations (IUF), and International Transport Federation (ITF) and Public Services International (PSI)

4   *Commitments For Sustainable Development – Trade Unions at the CSD*, 'Special Business and Industry Segment', 20 April–1 May 1998, Brussels: ICFTU

5   *Workers in the Web of Tourism*, CSD, Paris: ICFTU, TUAC and IUF, April 1999

6   *Troubled Waters (Fishing, Pollution and FOCs)*, CSD, London: ICFTU, TUAC, ITF and Greenpeace International, 1999

7   *Action Against Climate Change: The Kyoto Protocol and Beyond*, prepared for the OECD Economic Policy Committee, Paris, 5–12 October 1999

8   United Nations Environment Programme (1999) *Global Environmental Outlook 2000*, London: Earthscan Publications Ltd

9   Takala, J (1999) 'Global Estimates of Fatal Occupational Accidents', *Epidemiology*, vol 10, no 5, Philadelphia, September

10 Gereluk, W and L Royer, op cit, p1

11 *OECD Work on Sustainable Development: A Discussion Paper on Work to be Undertaken over the Period 1998–2001*, Public Affairs Division, July 1998

12 ILO (1996) *Using ILO Standards to Promote Environmentally Sustainable Development – Discussion Booklets*, Workers' Education and Environment Project, ILO

13 WHO (1999) *WHO Declaration*, Third Ministerial Conference on Environment and Health, London, 16–18 June

14 Policy changes and reviews brought in by the president of the World Bank Group, John Wolfensohn, and his new environment director, Robert Watson, provide some basis for hope

15 Friends of the Earth (1995) *Towards a Sustainable Europe*, London: Friends of the Earth

16 The words 'work' (as related to production), 'worker(s)' or 'workplace(s)' have not yet made their appearance into any of the CSD's adopted text since 1992

17 Refers to the 'scientific management' introduced by American engineer F W Taylor in the early 20th century, who was credited with advocating a strict segregation in the work process between tasks involving 'conception' and those involving 'execution', with workers being restricted to the latter

18 Collective agreements are legal contracts between employers (or employer associations) and trade unions which act as bargaining agents for units of workers. Provisions govern terms and condition of employment, as well as the settlement of disputes internally between parties. Increasingly, they contain green clauses whereby the parties agree to joint actions to protect the environment, as well as the health and safety of workers. There are over three million such agreements currently in existence

19 Collective bargaining is the process whereby a trade union and employer reach a collective agreement, and occurs when the workers' union has been recognized through legal certification or otherwise. Freedom of association, along with employment standards (including prohibition of child labour), constitutes a core of rights and freedoms that have proven fundamental to workers' participation as a means of ensuring workplace implementation of Agenda 21

20 UN Economic and Social Council (1992) *Voluntary Initiatives and Agreements*, report of the Secretary-General, (E/cn17/1999/12) April, New York: United Nations

21 OECD (1999) *The State of Regulatory Compliance: Issues, Trends and Challenges*, Paris: OECD – Public Management Service, PUMA/REG(99) 3 June

22 ICFTU (1999) *Annual Survey of Trade Union Rights*, Brussels, International Confederation of Free Trade Unions

23 A special project initiated in central and eastern Europe by the ICFTU
    and TUAC may serve as a model, and all stakeholders are challenged to
    promote similar joint worker–employer initiatives. This special project
    involves only 70,000 members. However, 130 million workers are affili-
    ated to our trade union centres, and with sufficient support and
    agreement among key stakeholders, many more can be encouraged to
    engage in simple actions, creating a snowball effect that points to the
    type of quantum leaps that are required

6

Women and Sustainable Development: From 2000 to 2002

Minu Hemmati

'Women are not the feel-good factors of international policy.'

Kofi Annan, 1999

INTRODUCTION

Earth Summit 2002 offers a unique opportunity to 're-engender' the debate on sustainable development – to ensure that women's concerns, needs and contributions are an integral part of reviewing the implementation of Agenda 21 (United Nations, 1992) and the Programme for Further Implementation (1997), as well as an integral part of forward-looking analysis and decisions for the future. The women's movement will have to stand up to this challenge. Governments, UN bodies and other stakeholders can play a significant role in making this happen. This chapter aims to outline some suggestions on how stakeholders can contribute to re-engendering the debate.

'Human development, if not engendered, is endangered'(UNDP, 1995, p1). Sustainable development requires the full and equal participation of women at all levels. None of the three aspects of the goal of sustainable development can be achieved without solving the prevailing problem of gender inequality and inequity.

Environmental protection requires a solid understanding of women's rights and roles in environmental planning and management; acknowledgement and incorporation of women's knowledge in environmental matters; and an understanding of gender-specific impacts of environmental degradation.

Economic well-being is a goal which requires gender-sensitive strategies. At least 70 per cent of the world's estimated 1.3 billion people who live in absolute poverty are women. Segmentation of labour markets – horizontally and vertically – has improved only little. The economic well-being of a society cannot be proclaimed if one group is massively underprivileged compared to the other. An economy cannot be called healthy without the contributions and skills of all members of society.

Gender equity is a fundamental part of *social equity*. Sexism, racism, discrimination on the grounds of ethnic group membership, faith, political opinion or sexual orientation are all indicators of social inequity. No society can survive sustainably and allow its members to live in dignity if there is prejudice and discrimination on the grounds of any kind of social group membership.

It is clear that gender equity is an essential building block of the three pillars of sustainable development. It is not necessary to justify women's full and equal participation. Women's rights are human rights. Also, it is clearly inappropriate and inefficient to try to address problems, identify the appropriate strategies, and implement the solutions if half of the people concerned are not involved.

This has been argued at length and the international community has laid down in numerous agreements how gender inequity needs to be overcome. For example, Agenda 21 urges governments 'to consider developing and issuing by the year 2000 a strategy of changes necessary to eliminate constitutional, legal, administrative, cultural, behavioural, social and economic obstacles to women's full participation in sustainable development and in public life' (Agenda 21, Chapter 24: 'Global Action for Women Towards Sustainable and Equitable Development', Objectives, para 2c).

This chapter will not discuss the historical, cultural, economic, social and religious reasons why women, in most countries and over long stretches of recorded history, have been oppressed, and have been deprived of power in decision-making, of access to and control of resources and of the right to fulfil their roles towards achieving peace, justice and sustainable development. Women's studies and social and economic sciences have produced sound theoretical approaches, vast empirical evidence and fruitful discussions which help us to understand traditional gender roles, discrimination of women and obstacles to overcoming this. The increased understanding has found its way into international policy-making, largely due to intensive efforts from the women's movement and contributions of expertise as well as political pressure. This is documented not only in Chapter 24 of Agenda 21 but also throughout the entire document in specific chapters on women and gender issues, in other global plans of action, and most strongly in the Beijing Platform for Action – the outcome of the Fourth World Conference on Women in 1995. Gender mainstreaming has been established as an essential component of planning and decision-making processes in all areas of sustainable development.[1]

The goals set out in international agreements, and many of the strategies outlined in national laws and institutional mechanisms for the advancement of women, are well deliberated and seem attainable. However, these goals, conclusions and recommendations are not a reality. Agreed strategies are either not being followed through or are less successful than hoped. It seems that we have agreed the goals, and that we have set many good strategies – but change is slow and we suffer many setbacks every year. The little improvement – as compared to goals and necessities – points us to further obstacles which might not have been sufficiently understood or clearly stated. Some of them shall be addressed in this chapter. The main emphasis, however, will be placed on some suggestions regarding the way forward.

Not all of the obstacles and suggestions discussed are specific to women or gender issues. This is due to the fact that, on the one hand, women are not only the largest but also a very specific major group in their cultural diversity and their commonality of a long history of oppression. Women's rights are human rights and their right to participation does not need to be grounded on anything else but that: a fundamental human right. Also, women's roles in sustainable development are not limited to contributions in specific areas of expertise, but their knowledge needs to be brought into all decision-making processes.

On the other hand, women as a major group share certain characteristics with other major groups: many of them have a history of exclusion and oppression. Many of them are able to make specific contributions due to their traditional roles, knowledge and expertise. Many of them are sceptical and hesitate to become involved in existing power structures and institutional systems which have been set up in the past primarily without them. Many of them are wrongly being perceived as a homogenous group rather than the multitude of sub-groups of diverse characteristics, concerns and interests.

> *'As long as women are prevented from attaining their highest possibilities, so long will men be unable to achieve the greatness which might be theirs.'*
> 'Abdu'l-Baha

A LOT HAS BEEN ACHIEVED...

There have been considerable efforts to achieve full and equal participation for women and to make women's rights and roles a reality.

Research on obstacles and reviews of experiences such as good practice analyses have been carried out by many institutions and organizations, including UN agencies, governments, women's NGOs and research institutions. These efforts have produced evidence of a remarkable range of activities, achievements and challenges in increasing women's involvement and improving the lives of women. They have also identified ways forward which stakeholders are striving to implement at various levels. In many cases, women's NGOs and grass-roots women's groups have been at the forefront of activities towards change and implementing the international agreements in the area of women and sustainable development (see Hemmati et al., 2000).

It is not possible to give a full account of achievements here. However, as an example, there have been efforts which focused on including women in environmental decision-making that were conducted by NGOs, community associations or governments. More than 60 countries affected by drought and desertification in Asia, Africa, Latin America and the Caribbean have established participatory national action programmes. These groups have launched awareness-raising campaigns focusing on women's participation, resulting in positive responses from the women towards whom the campaigns were aimed. As a result, there have been efforts in many countries to ensure that women are members of environmental decision-making bodies. In some cases, Local Agenda 21 processes have begun to look seriously at increasing the participation of women. Gender-sensitivity training and guidelines have been developed in many institutions. These are but a few examples of many activities which stakeholders have been involved in over the last decade and more. Women's NGOs have certainly played the key role in these efforts and have achieved much with very little resources (see, for example, Mawle, 1997; SocialWatch, 1999; WEDO, 1997, 1998; WomenWatch Online Working Group, 1999).

> '*In the beginning of any innovative development there is a small group, an active minority — who in the end answers the needs of the majority.*'
>
> Serge Moscovici

...BUT IT IS BY NO MEANS ENOUGH

Women hold 11.7 per cent of the seats in the world's parliaments. The percentage of female cabinet ministers worldwide has risen from 3.4

in 1987 to 6.8 per cent in 1996. In all, 28 women have been elected heads of state or government in the last century. Of the world's nearly one billion illiterate adults, two-thirds are women. Two-thirds of the 130 million children worldwide who are not in school are girls. The majority of women earn an average of about three-quarters of the pay of males for the same work, outside of the agricultural sector, in both developed and developing countries. In most countries, women work approximately twice the unpaid time that men do. Approximately 585,000 women die every year, over 1600 every day, from causes related to pregnancy and childbirth. Each year an estimated two million girls suffer the practice of female genital mutilation (see Johnson, 1999). Reviews being carried out at the moment for the UN General Assembly (GA) special sessions to review implementation of the Beijing Platform for Action and the outcome of the World Summit for Social Development show that progress has been slower than hoped and that obstacles prevail. The review processes will be discussed later in this chapter.

Despite the efforts – consulting about the problems, negotiating the international action plans and agendas, and efforts towards implementation – the situation of women remains absolutely unacceptable and we are continuing to follow the path of unsustainable development. Many reasons have been put forward to explain the lack of achievements.

Firstly, there is a lack of political will in many governments and decision-making bodies. Closely related to insufficient political will is the lack of resources, which poses another major obstacle. This has been named time and again by all stakeholders as the barrier that holds back implementation and suffocates creative and practical projects at all levels. Lack of political will and resources are essentially ethical issues. For example, the life expectancy of citizens in least-developed countries is about half as long as that of citizens in developed countries. Being born in the developed world is nothing but luck. However, what a privilege it is to live long, be able to develop oneself, see children and grandchildren grow up and enjoy contributing to the well-being of all. How can one not strive to change this – unless driven by selfish greed for power and wealth? We should not accept simple explanations that problems are too complex and practical barriers are insurmountable. As stated above, complexity has been, and can be, analysed and many agreed strategies are based on solid knowledge and understanding. It is not true that we do not know what needs to be done.

Although the level of understanding documented in many international agreements is relatively high, there are still considerable gaps of awareness, information and knowledge among delegates and decision-makers. This has often been mirrored in the language used in CSD decisions – the famous half-sentences, such as 'and particularly women' or 'with a particular emphasis on vulnerable groups such as women, youth and the elderly', etc. Many of these half-sentences are meaningless and are put in place to fulfil an obligation rather than to reflect competent analysis and creative problem-solving.

> *'Never doubt that a small group of thoughtful committed citizens can change the world. Indeed it's the only thing that ever has.'*
>
> Margaret Mead

WHAT THE UNITED NATIONS AND MEMBER STATES NEED TO DO

RESOURCES

Financial resources need to increase significantly in order to implement agreements. Donors need to live up to their commitments, otherwise all agreements and the cumbersome and expensive processes to reach them will have been undertaken in vain. The agreements will also become more and more harmful as a testimony of untruthfulness and lack of reliability.

Resources need to be invested in awareness-raising and education for women and men; in relevant research; in making gender-disaggregated information available in all countries; and in community development that creates space for women and shared fora for women and men. Donors must change their criteria and effectively gender-mainstream their work, applying gender-sensitive analysis, indicators, monitoring and evaluation to all projects.

The UN, governments and other stakeholders need to invest in the participation of women at all levels: in their communication, outreach and networking, their effective preparations, and their ability to attend relevant meetings. Active participation of competent women's NGOs at international meetings is necessary to provide the expertise required to raise awareness of gender-sensitive aspects and to help make wise and practical decisions.

AWARENESS-RAISING AND CAPACITY-BUILDING

Many international agreements state that it is necessary to raise awareness on gender issues and to build capacities for effective gender mainstreaming. This needs to be done within governments and inter-governmental bodies, for all stakeholder groups as well as the general public. Gender-sensitivity training is necessary at all institutional levels, including the top decision-making level. It must be relevant to the issues, continuous and regularly updated. It must link different groups and activities and be monitored and evaluated to enable improvement and ensure effectiveness over time.

Gender issues need to be incorporated within regular curricula in schools and higher education; gender mainstreaming should be promoted to the general public. Obviously, governments have a key role to play in this regard. However, they should seek collaboration with women's NGOs when engaging in campaigns and capacity-building activities.

Furthermore, women themselves need to be informed about their rights, roles and responsibilities. Public awareness of international agreements and action plans is very low. The UN and governments have not sufficiently invested in informing citizens about their decisions and plans. Much information is spread by women's NGOs. However, a lot remains to be done to ensure that every woman and every man knows what sustainable development is about and why it requires gender mainstreaming.

RESEARCH

There is a great need to invest in relevant research and the development of gender-sensitive indicators. We must identify systematic and methodologically sound approaches to learning from experiences such as good practices, using qualitative and quantitative means of gathering information and ensuring that participants develop a real ownership of the process. Many collections of case studies and good practice examples are available. However, most of them lack a systematic meta-analysis which would allow individuals to draw general conclusions in terms of success factors and transferability.

In preparation for Earth Summit 2002, a major outreach into the academic community should be undertaken in order to draw in women's studies specialists, social scientists and economists who have a solid understanding of the problems involved and access to the latest research findings available. Many academics would be eager to contribute their outstanding expertise to the process if they only knew how. Academic communities should become aware of the responsibility placed upon them by the fact that they have been acknowledged as a major group in Agenda 21. To date, academic institutions primarily contribute upon demand as experts being brought in by governments, UN bodies and other stakeholders. They need to contribute in their own right and at their own initiative. Given the ethical and political background and motivation of many researchers in the area of women's studies, gender issues could be a pioneering example for involving academia at a significant scale.

INSTITUTIONAL MECHANISMS FOR THE ADVANCEMENT OF WOMEN

As agreed in the Beijing Platform for Action (1995), governments and intergovernmental bodies need to install efficient institutional mechanisms for the advancement of women – gender departments, women's units, etc. We know that these have been effective to a certain extent in the past and they urgently need to be strengthened, including significant increases of their resource bases. Otherwise, they remain but lip service, will be marginalized quickly and have no effect towards gender mainstreaming and equity. Institutional mechanisms offer these opportunities if installed rightly, at the highest level and centre of government, with sufficient resources and clear formal links to the whole of the institutional structure (UN DAW / ECLAC, 1998). However, installing them is by no means the sole strategy: they need to be linked with major efforts towards increasing the number of women in decision-making positions at all levels and in all areas.

MULTISTAKEHOLDER PROCESSES: A NON-REVOLUTIONARY REVOLUTION

It is difficult to negotiate international agreements and to develop consensus among over 180 countries and all relevant international and regional institutions and stakeholders. However, it has proven even more difficult to put broad goals and complex agreements into practice. Implementation requires universal participation, based on transparent and democratic consultation. Everybody who is part of the problem and everybody who needs to be part of the solution has to be involved. New patterns of interaction and participation, especially among individuals and groups that have previously been excluded from decision-making, such as women, can open the door to new possibilities and novel solutions.

In the past, we have seen many a revolution which brought about radical changes in a society – some for the better, some for the worse. The principle of revolution is based on the assumption that one group – which is not (yet) in power – can govern better than the group in power, and therefore seeks to replace the existing leaders. Universal participation, 'broad public participation in decision-making' (Agenda 21, Chapter 23) is not a revolutionary approach in this sense. It is based on the assumption that no one represents an objective point of view but has to speak from a specific perspective, based on group memberships and individual characteristics.

In that sense, women do not seek a 'revolution': women do not seek to replace men. Rather, they seek to participate equally with men, thus completing the skills and knowledge available to the decision-making process. Denying women the right or opportunity to participate is not only discriminatory and oppressive but also inappropriate and ineffective. Men have not been and will not be able to solve by themselves the problems we face today. However, multistakeholder processes and equal participation of women are truly revolutionary: we have not acted this way in the past.

There is a great need for financial resources to be allocated to multistakeholder processes and to share our experiences with them. Private foundations might be interested in supporting such open-ended, sometimes initially weakly defined, processes.

TOWARDS EARTH SUMMIT 2002: PROCESS AND RESOURCES

In preparation for Earth Summit 2002, the UN needs to ensure a wide, participatory and transparent process, involving all stakeholders, to:

- review the implementation of Agenda 21 (1992) and the Programme for Further Implementation (1997);
- provide analysis of the present situation and emerging issues;
- develop projections and make decisions for the future.

Women need to be involved in all these steps towards a renewed commitment to sustainable development and there must be new recommendations on emerging issues such as globalization and HIV and AIDS. There is an urgent need to review the implementation of Agenda 21 Chapter 24 –'Global Action for Women Towards Sustainable and Equitable Development' – and other decisions and recommendations throughout Agenda 21, the subsequent CSD decisions and the outcome of Earth Summit II in 1997. The recommendation in Chapter 24.2.c, as quoted above, was benchmarked for the year 2000. However, no audit has been planned so far. A review on women and sustainable development needs to be an integral part of the preparations for Earth Summit 2002. It should begin with an overview of all relevant agreements in the area and stress cross-links between processes as much as possible. We cannot afford to duplicate efforts in several fora and run the risk of lack of resources as well as diluting efforts.

- By mid 2000, a large amount of relevant data will be available due to the review processes for Beijing +5 and for Copenhagen +5 (both UN GA special sessions are scheduled for June 2000).

- In 2000, the review process regarding the Habitat II Agenda begins, leading to a UN GA special session in 2001 (Istanbul +5).
- The follow-up process for the World Food Summit reaches a major stepping stone in September 2000 with a meeting of the FAO Committee on World Food Security.[2]
- National reporting to the CEDAW Committee, by governments as well as NGOs, provides information on progress towards eliminating all forms of discrimination against women and should be taken into account.
- Progress on the conventions, particularly the Convention to Combat Desertification (CCD), with its strong emphasis on the participation of women, should equally be brought into the process of reviewing and looking forward.[3]

CSD should call upon the UN agencies dealing with the above-mentioned processes to provide relevant material and contribute to the preparatory process for 2002.

- UNDP should consider focusing the *Human Development Report* (HDR) for 2001 on sustainable development, including a strong emphasis on gender issues and gender-disaggregated data.
- UNEP should, in its *Global Environment Outlook* (GEO) report for 2002, include a section on women and the environment, reporting gender-differentiated impacts of environmental degradation, as well as consider gender aspects of each environmental sector covered in the report.
- The World Bank, in its *World Development Report* (WDR) for 2002, which will be covering the theme of sustainability, should also include a distinct section on women and sustainable development, as well as cover all other sections without omitting the necessary gender perspective.

All three reports – HDR, GEO and WDR – should be developed with a strong participatory component and include gender specialists in the preparatory research teams.

Such a process needs political support and substantial resources to be able to pay more than lip service to gender mainstreaming. In the spirit of Agenda 21, stakeholders should have the opportunity to develop their own views as well as to engage in discussions among themselves at national, regional and international levels. As with other stakeholder groups, it is particularly important to ensure participation of representatives from developing countries. Women's participation needs to be regionally balanced to make sense.

The CSD should:

- Ask UN Division on Sustainable Development (DSD) to issue a questionnaire to governments on implementing Agenda 21 and its emerging issues; this should contain a detailed section on women and sustainable development issues.
- Urge governments and donor agencies to support national, regional and international networks of women's NGOs to produce their own 'alternative reports' (learning from the strategies NGOs have employed in preparation for Beijing +5).
- Take stakeholders' alternative reports into account when producing secretary general's reports on implementation and emerging issues.
- Urge governments to engage in multistakeholder processes to review implementation of Agenda 21 and to look forward.
- Ensure participation of women's NGOs at regional and global PrepComms and other preparatory meetings towards Earth Summit 2002 (providing funds and urging donor support).
- Ensure participation of women's NGOs in ongoing and future multistakeholder processes developed on the basis of CSD decisions (providing funds and urging donor support).
- Provide electronic discussion fora on emerging issues well in advance of Earth Summit 2002; this needs to be done with a particular emphasis on the participation of developing countries (for example, by using UNDP country offices and UNEP regional offices) and with a transparent policy on how to use the information.

Formal links between participatory structures and governance structures are very important for the preparatory process. Women's NGOs should have a clear idea how their involvement will be supported and how their contributions will be used.

- CSD should discuss modalities of involvement and its transparency; an important political question is how much weight major groups' input will be given.
- UN DSD should develop suggestions regarding strategies towards fruitful collaboration of unlikely partners in multistakeholder processes. The suggestions should be discussed at CSD to set up appropriate structures and rules and to agree recommendations to all stakeholders.

> *'It is important that groups who work towards change help society to realize what it is capable of.'*
> Felix Guattari

What Women's NGOs Need to Do

The year 2002 offers a unique and extremely important opportunity to re-engender the debate on sustainable development and its implementation. It is my sincere hope that the women's movement will stand up to this challenge.

The CSD NGO Women's Caucus needs to deliver according to two basic strategies. Firstly, we need to claim women's rights and pressure governments to put into practice what is agreed upon – in other words, enabling effective preparations and participation by women's NGOs. Secondly, we need to deliver substantive contributions on specific issues, spelling out what precisely are the gender-sensitive issues being discussed and suggesting policies and strategies based on solid information and up-to-date research. The first strategy can take the shape of powerful 'wake-up calls' in statements and submissions to the CSD and PrepComms. The second strategy should involve the participation of women directly affected by particular problems, as well as bringing research to the table. Women's NGOs have in the past used both strategies. We have employed the common political strategy: a dual approach of working 'outside the system' and criticizing it, and working 'within the system' and using it for our goals. On our side, the dual strategy requires a certain amount of tolerance towards ambiguity, respect for each other's strategic preferences and a pragmatic approach to our involvement with the UN system.

The Women's Caucus is operating within the framework of the CSD NGO Steering Committee. For the process towards Earth Summit 2002, we need to carry out a number of initiatives. To ensure a successful process we must:

- Outreach to networks of women's NGOs around the world, working to ensure participation of developing country NGOs and to include grassroots women's groups.
- Outreach into women's networks around other UN processes: given the list of relevant processes and material above, we can see which networks we have to tap into to involve the women's NGOs who work in these areas. These NGOs must be involved in the preparations for Earth Summit 2002. Not many women's NGOs are involved in several processes; instead, we have experienced considerable drop-offs and compartmentalization;
- Be as inclusive and transparent as possible in order to build trust and ensure effective collaboration.
- Mutually support each other's work and strengthen solidarity through collaboration and teaming up on issues among participants from around the world.

- Provide information about the CSD process and Earth Summit 2002 for newcomers; develop mentoring relationships between experienced people and those eager to learn.
- Actively take part in existing and future multistakeholder processes connected to the CSD process and in preparation for Earth Summit 2002.
- Build strong links with other NGO caucuses to ensure gender mainstreaming of their work and strengthen the network of the CSD NGO Steering Committee.
- Build bridges with other stakeholder groups, particularly women's associations within them, such as business and professional women's associations, women's trade union groups, women's initiatives in local authority associations, researchers on women's studies.
- Build bridges with UN agencies dealing with women's issues and gender programmes and with women's units in UN agencies concerned with environment, development and economic issues.
- Build bridges with agencies likely to produce a significant share of the data available when preparing for Earth Summit 2002, such as UNDP (HDR office), UNEP (GEO group), World Bank (WDR office).
- Actively participate at all upcoming meetings and work to ensure that funding is available for women's NGOs from developing countries.

Regarding substantive contributions, we need to:

- Identify our priorities for Earth Summit 2002 through open, transparent and inclusive consultation among the widest range of women's NGOs possible.
- Identify the gender-sensitive areas under the priority issues stated in the NGO non-paper on 2002; other areas will be identified by CSD and PrepComms.
- Develop Women's Caucus background material and position papers, drawing on the widest range of contributions possible; documents should preferably be coauthored by several people, ensuring regional balance of contributions.
- Disseminate information about our priorities and gender-sensitive areas to all stakeholders in order to ensure that reviews and forward-looking discussions are being carried out to cover these areas.
- Disseminate developed material to NGOs, UN, governments and other stakeholders well in advance of upcoming meetings to ensure a gender-mainstreaming effect on their work.

'Even a superficial look at history reveals that no social advance rolls in on the wheels of inevitability; it comes through the tireless efforts and persistent work of dedicated individuals. Without this hard work, time itself becomes an ally of the primitive forces of irrational emotionalism and social stagnation.'

Martin Luther King, Jr, 1962

What We All Need to Do

Learning how to consult

Sustainable development is a process, ideally, of consultation with all stakeholders as partners; these stakeholders:[4]

- together define the problems;
- design possible solutions;
- collaborate to implement solutions;
- monitor and evaluate the outcome;
- and through this process develop a more appropriate understanding and more sustainable solutions to new challenges.

For example, do we know how to develop a water supply system that alleviates the workload of women and girls – and at the same time does not challenge the status of women in the community as having been the ones responsible for supplying this important resource for their families? Do we know how to bring together all stakeholders in tourism development – how local communities, women's groups, indigenous peoples, international corporations, local authorities, national tourism boards, trade unions, and government departments of environment, development, health and education, etc should get together and discuss a potential tourism development long before land is sold and airports, hotels or roads are built? Do governments or UN bodies know how to make transparent the way that stakeholders' inputs feed into their decision-making pocesses?

I am not sure we do. We need to experiment and to share our experiences, successes and failures alike. The CSD has been an example forum of experimenting with consultation processes since 1998, namely through its multistakeholder dialogues which inform the negotiations and have sparked off follow-on processes and joint projects of several stakeholder groups.

Many consultation processes will need to be culturally specific and dependent upon the problem area and the stakeholders involved. However, there are some practical rules to be taken into consideration:[5]

- Information should be gathered from the widest possible range of sources in order to seek a diversity of points of view.
- During discussions, participants must make every effort to be as frank and candid as possible, while maintaining a courteous interest in the views of others. Confrontation, blank ultimatums and prejudicial statements are to be avoided. An atmosphere that cultivates openness, objectivity and humility can be viewed as prerequisite for successful consultation.
- When an idea is put forth, it becomes at once the property of the group. This sounds simple but it is perhaps the most profound principle. All ideas cease to be the property of any individual, subgroup or constituency. This principle encourages those ideas that spring forth from a sincere desire to serve, as opposed to ideas that emanate from a desire for personal aggrandizement or constituency building.
- Groups strive for unanimity, but a majority vote can be taken to bring about a conclusion and make the decision. Once the decision is made, it is incumbent on the entire group to act on it with unity – regardless of how many supported the measure. This way, it will be evident if a measure is feasible or not.
- All participants need to be open to change when embarking on a consultation process as outlined above. When listening to others carefully, when striving for unanimity, when giving our ideas to the group, we are likely to change because we have learned.

THE CHALLENGE OF DIVERSITY

Multistakeholder processes aim to improve decision-making. They benefit from a diversity of views and a wealth of information which would otherwise not be available to the process. Multistakeholder processes also help to ensure commitment from participants which will support implementation. Any multistakeholder process poses the challenge of dealing with diversity. This is not only the cognitive or logistical challenge of the sheer number of views to be dealt with. It is equally the challenge of respecting people and groups who differ from ourselves and whose views can be diametrically opposed to our own.

Rarely in history have human beings been very successful at dealing with diversity: usually, differences are perceived as 'better' or 'worse', not as 'different but of equal value'. Agenda 21 and its urge for broad public participation and the resulting strategy of multistakeholder processes, however, demand from us to learn exactly that: 'us' and 'them' need to become 'we, as different members of one process'. Our various points of view are equally important elements of a consultative problem-solving approach.

Probably more than any other major group, women constitute a very heterogeneous group. It is important that all stakeholders are aware that women come from very diverse backgrounds. In the CSD NGO Women's Caucus, we have experienced our diversity as we have in other fora. Members come from all parts of the world; there are academics, practitioners, newcomers, experienced experts, grassroots women's groups, etc. We are not a decision-making body and therefore do not necessarily need to come to a consensus. Instead, we try to put forward the diversity of our views; however, this is and should be based on discussions which help to clarify and develop views and recommendations.

The challenge of diversity is to respect and celebrate each other's specific characteristics and at the same time look out for commonalities. As social psychiatry and sociological research have demonstrated, minorities are much more effective if they act in unison and are consistent over time (see, for example, Moscovici, 1980). As women, we need to balance the need to act as effectively as possible with the need to represent the diversity of views and recommendations. In many cases, this will mean putting forward recommendations which are specific to certain political, cultural or geographic regions.

Overcoming stereotypes and habits: Obstacles inside ourselves

It is amazing how we can live with our current unsustainable behaviour – which continues even in the knowledge that this will lead to further suffering, destruction and death. There are some powerful forces behind the continuation of unsustainable development, not the least the appalling greed for extreme power and obscene wealth which people and organizations continue to exhibit. Yet there are also more psychological, but equally powerful, sources behind the lack of change – in particular, two remarkable fundamental characteristics of the individual human being.

Firstly, there is our amazing capacity of imagination. We are able to live in our own 'realities'; we are able to ignore facts and sometimes live in more of a fantasy than the 'real' world. When it comes to facing uncomfortable realities, we are able to shut them out and continue with what seems comfortable and secure. If we don't want to face it, we can avoid it. But – using the same abilities – we can turn away from obstacles and use our imagination to develop visions; we can develop solutions where problems seem insurmountable.

Secondly, human beings have enormous capacities to learn and develop behaviour patterns which can quickly become strong habits. This is an important tool – for example, we learn to ride a bike and this complex activity can very quickly become a rather automated process, quickening our reactions and leaving us free to draw our attention to other things, such as enjoying the surroundings. But our strength of habit is a problem when it comes to changing our behaviour – habits tend to strongly resist change. However, once we decide to change and feel a strong urge to do so, we can change very quickly, again through learning and developing new habits.

To move forward, we need to make use of our imagination and we need to learn to embrace change – in other words, we can fall in love with the future we envisage and accept change as the path towards this future.

> *'You know, for every dollar a man makes*
> *a woman makes 63 cents.*
> *Fifty years ago, that was 62 cents.*
> *So, with that kind of luck, it'll be the year 3848*
> *before we make a buck.'*
>   Laurie Anderson, *Beautiful Red Dress*, 1998

I am aware that it is not strategically wise to point out that changes take time – especially in a text meant to urge readers to develop rapidly. However, we should be aware of the true size of the changes required of all of us. Let us not lose faith in our ability to change. We will live in dignity by proving that we can indeed learn and grow. We will prove our humanity and our love for life itself.

REFERENCES

Annan, K (1999) Speech at an advance ceremony celebrating International Women's Day, UN Headquarters, 4 March

CSD NGO Women's Caucus at http://www.csdngo.org/csdngo – click on 'Women' under 'Major Groups' (gender-sensitive areas under upcoming issues; position papers; summary of recommendations to CSD-8; etc)

Hemmati, M and CSD NGO Women's Caucus (2000) *Women and Sustainable Development 2000 – 2002*, Recommendations in Agenda 21 and Related Documents and Suggestions for a Review on Implementation, available at http://www.csdngo.org/csdngo – click on 'Women' under 'Major Groups'

Instituto de Tercer Mundo (1999) *SocialWatch*, no 3, Montevideo, Uruguay, SocialWatch

Johnson, K (1999) UN Statistics on Women. Via the Know-How-Conference electronic list server (knowhowconf@nic.surfnet.nl), 4 July

Mawle, A (1997) 'Women, Environment and the United Nations', in: F Dodds (ed) *The Way Forward: Beyond Agenda 21*, London: Earthscan Publications Ltd, pp146–157

Moscovici, S (1980) 'Toward a theory of conversion behaviour', in L
    Berkowitz (ed) *Advances in Experimental Social Psychology*, vol 13,
    New York, Academic Press, pp209–239
National Spiritual Assembly of the Baha'is of the United States (1994) *Unity
    and Consultation: Foundations of Sustainable Development*. Available
    at http://www.bcca.org/~glittle/docs/unity.html
Sustainable Cities Programme (UNEP/UNCHS – Habitat) (1998) International
    Workshop on Gender Responsive Environmental Planning and
    Management, Preliminary Report, Nairobi, SCP
United Nations (1992) *Report of the United Nations Conference on
    Environment and Development: Agenda 21*, Rio de Janeiro, 3–14 June
United Nations (1995) *Report of the Fourth World Conference on Women:
    Action for Equality, Development and Peace*, Beijing, 4–15 September
United Nations (1995) *Report of the World Summit for Social Development*,
    Copenhagen, 6–12 March
United Nations (1996) *Report of the World Summit on Human Settlements,
    Habitat II*, Istanbul, 4–13 June
United Nations Development Programme (UNDP) (1995) *Human
    Development Report 1995: Gender and Human Development*, New York
    and Oxford: Oxford University Press
United Nations Food and Agriculture Organization (1996) *Report of the
    World Food Summit: World Food Summit Plan of Action*, Rome
United Nations Division for the Advancement of Women (UN DAW)/UN
    Economic Commission for Latin America and the Caribbean (ECLAC)
    (1998) 'National Machineries for Gender Equity', Expert Group Meeting
    Report, Santiago, Chile, 31 August–4 September
Walker-Leigh, V (1999). *Action Proposals for the CSD Women's Caucus:
    Linking Sustainable Agriculture, Global Food Security and
    Women's/Gender Issues*, New York: Women's Caucus
Women's Environment and Development Organization (WEDO) (1997)
    *Lighting the Path to Progress: Women's Initiatives and an Assessment of
    Progress since the 1992 United Nations Conference on Environment and
    Development (UNCED)*, New York: WEDO
Women's Environment and Development Organization (WEDO) (1998)
    *Mapping Progress. Assessing Implementation of the Beijing Platform
    1998*, New York, WEDO
WomenWatch (1999) Online Working Group on Women and the
    Environment, September / October 1999, archived at
    http://wwww.un.org/womenwatch

NOTES

1   'Mainstreaming a gender perspective is the process of assessing the
    implications for women and men of any planned action, including
    legislation, policies or programmes, in any area and at all levels. It is a
    strategy for making women's as well as men's concerns and experiences
    an integral dimension of the design, implementation, monitoring and
    evaluation of the policies and programmes in all political, economic and

societal spheres so that women and men benefit equally, and inequality is not perpetuated. The ultimate goal is to achieve gender equality.' (E.1997.L.10.para.4. Adopted by ECOSOC, 17 July 1997)

2   The FAO Committee on World Food Security (WFS) (18–21 September 2000, Rome) will review WFS follow-up reports and action proposals from regional conferences (1999–2000) on WFS commitments 1, 2, 5, 7 and decide on further action. Subsequent reviews will take place biannually, leading up to the mid-term review of 2006 (see Walker-Leigh, 1999)

3   United Nations Convention to Combat Desertification in Countries Experiencing Serious Drought and/or Desertification, Particularly in Africa, 1996

4   In many cases, partners in consultation will need to address power gaps. Ideally, unlikely partners such as international corporations and local women's groups will engage in an explicit exchange about this problem and involve a mediating body to facilitate consultation whenever necessary

5   This is based on the principles of consultation outlined in the writings of the Baha'i Faith as well as on latest findings in social a organizational psychology research

Part II

A New Charter

7

A People's Earth Charter

Maximo Kalaw

INTRODUCTION

For over a decade diverse groups throughout the world have endeavored to create an Earth Charter. Hundreds of groups and thousands of individuals have been involved in the process. Representatives from government and non-governmental organizations worked to secure adoption of an Earth Charter during the Rio Earth Summit in 1992. However, the time was not right. A new Earth Charter initiative was launched by the Earth Council and Green Cross International in 1994.

An Earth Charter Commission was formed in 1997 to oversee the project and the drafting of the charter. The secretariat for the commission is at the Earth Council in Costa Rica. In March 1997, at the conclusion of the Earth Summit II in Rio de Janeiro, the Earth Charter Commission issued the *Benchmark Draft Earth Charter*. The commission also called for ongoing international consultations on the text of the document.

Between 1997 and 1999 over 40 national Earth Charter committees were formed, and numerous Earth Charter conferences were held. Comments and recommendations from all regions of the world were forwarded to the Earth Council and the drafting committee. Guided by these contributions to the consultation process, the text of the charter has been extensively revised. In April 1999, the Earth Charter Commission issued *Benchmark Draft II*. The consultation process continued throughout 1999 in order to provide individuals and groups

with a further opportunity to make contributions to the drafting
process. As a result of the worldwide consultation process, the Earth
Charter Commission issued a final version of the Earth Charter after
their meeting on 12–14 March 2000 at the UNESCO headquarters in
Paris. The Earth Charter Commission plans to review responses to the
document in two or four years and consider possible amendments.

OBJECTIVES OF THE INTERNATIONAL EARTH
CHARTER CAMPAIGN

The objectives of the Earth Charter campaign include the following:

*   Promote a worldwide dialogue on shared values and global ethics.
*   Draft an Earth Charter that sets forth a succinct and inspiring vision
    of fundamental ethical principles for sustainable development.
*   Circulate the Earth Charter throughout the world as a people's
    treaty, promoting awareness, commitment and implementation of
    Earth Charter values.
*   Seek endorsement of the Earth Charter by the United Nations
    General Assembly by the year 2002.

A DECLARATION OF INTERDEPENDENCE AND PRINCIPLES
FOR SUSTAINABLE DEVELOPMENT

As indicated by the preamble, the Earth Charter is a declaration of
interdependence and responsibility and an urgent call to build a global
partnership for sustainable development.

The principles of the Earth Charter are closely interrelated.
Together they provide a conception of sustainable development and
set forth fundamental guidelines for achieving it. These principles are
drawn from international law, science, philosophy, religion, recent UN
summit meetings and the international Earth Charter conversation on
global ethics.

The goal of sustainable development is full human development
and ecological protection. The Earth Charter recognizes that humanity's environmental, economic, social, cultural, ethical and spiritual
problems and aspirations are interconnected. It affirms the need for
holistic thinking and collaborative, integrated problem-solving.
Sustainable development requires such an approach. It is about
freedom, justice, participation and peace as well as environmental
protection and economic well-being.

THE DESIGN OF THE EARTH CHARTER

Some groups would prefer a short Earth Charter that is a prayer or poem or a declaration with only five to ten principles. Others strongly favour a more substantial document that is more like an intergovernmental declaration.

In an effort to address these different concerns, the drafting committee has created a layered document with a preamble, 16 main principles, various supporting principles and a conclusion. The principles are divided into four parts.

The supporting principles offer clarification and elaboration of the ideas in the main principles. The supporting principles provide an overview of the many issues that have been raised by various groups in the course of the international consultation process. Those who favour a very short Earth Charter would like to see the supporting principles significantly reduced in number or eliminated. Others feel passionately that the supporting principles are an essential part of the charter because they make explicit the practical meaning of the main principles with reference to critical issues. The supporting principles are especially important to groups that feel marginalized and excluded from decision-making processes.

A further thorough analysis of the structure of the charter and of the place and function of the supporting principles is underway. A commentary on the principles is being prepared.

THREE WAYS TO PRESENT THE EARTH CHARTER VISION

1   Use the four general principles only as a short version.
2   Use the two-page abbreviated version with the full preamble, the 16 main principles only and a conclusion.
3   Use the full document with the preamble, the main principles together with the supporting principles and the conclusion.

THE EARTH CHARTER WEBSITE

Explore the Earth Charter website for more information: www.earthcharter.org.

BOX 7.1 THE EARTH CHARTER

Preamble

We stand at a critical moment in Earth's history, a time when humanity must choose its future. As the world becomes increasingly interdependent and fragile, the future at once holds great peril and great promise. To move forward we must recognize that in the midst of a magnificent diversity of cultures and life forms we are one human family and one Earth community with a common destiny. We must join together to bring forth a sustainable global society founded on respect for nature, universal human rights, economic justice and a culture of peace. Towards this end, it is imperative that we, the peoples of Earth, declare our responsibility to one another, to the greater community of life and to future generations.

Earth, our home

Humanity is part of a vast evolving universe. Earth, our home, is alive with a unique community of life. The forces of nature make existence a demanding and uncertain adventure, but Earth has provided the conditions essential to life's evolution. The resilience of the community of life and the well-being of humanity depend upon preserving a healthy biosphere with all its ecological systems, a rich variety of plants and animals, fertile soils, pure waters and clean air. The global environment with its finite resources is a common concern of all peoples. The protection of Earth's vitality, diversity and beauty is a sacred trust.

The global situation

The dominant patterns of production and consumption are causing environmental devastation, the depletion of resources and a massive extinction of species. Communities are being undermined. The benefits of development are not shared equitably and the gap between rich and poor is widening. Injustice, poverty, ignorance and violent conflict are widespread and the cause of great suffering. An unprecedented rise in human population has overburdened ecological and social systems. The foundations of global security are threatened. These trends are perilous – but not inevitable.

The challenges ahead

The choice is ours: form a global partnership to care for Earth and one another or risk the destruction of ourselves and the diversity of life. Fundamental changes are needed in our values, institutions and ways of living. We must realize that when basic needs have been met, human development is primarily about being more, not having more. We have the knowledge and technology to provide for all and to reduce our impacts on the environment. The emergence of a global civil society is creating new opportunities to build a democratic and humane world. Our environmental, economic, political, social and spiritual challenges are interconnected, and together we can forge inclusive solutions.

Universal responsibility

To realize these aspirations, we must decide to live with a sense of universal responsibility, identifying ourselves with the whole Earth community as well as our local communities. We are at once citizens of different nations and of one world in which the local and global are linked. Everyone shares responsibility for the present and future well-being of the human family and the larger living world. The spirit of human solidarity and kinship with all life is strengthened when we live with reverence for the mystery of being, gratitude for the gift of life and humility regarding the human place in nature.

We urgently need a shared vision of basic values to provide an ethical foundation for the emerging world community. Therefore, together in hope we affirm the following interdependent principles for a sustainable way of life as a common standard by which the conduct of all individuals, organizations, businesses, governments and transnational institutions is to be guided and assessed.

Principles

I Respect and care for the community of life
1 Respect Earth and life in all its diversity.
   a Recognize that all beings are interdependent and every form of life has value regardless of its worth to human beings.
   b Affirm faith in the inherent dignity of all human beings and in the intellectual, artistic, ethical and spiritual potential of humanity.
2 Care for the community of life with understanding, compassion and love.
   a Accept that with the right to own, manage and use natural resources comes the duty to prevent environmental harm and to protect the rights of people.
   b Affirm that with increased freedom, knowledge and power comes increased responsibility to promote the common good.
3 Build democratic societies that are just, participatory, sustainable and peaceful.
   a Ensure that communities at all levels guarantee human rights and fundamental freedoms and provide everyone an opportunity to realize his or her full potential.
   b Promote social and economic justice, enabling all to achieve a secure and meaningful livelihood that is ecologically responsible.
4 Secure Earth's bounty and beauty for present and future generations.
   a Recognize that the freedom of action of each generation is qualified by the needs of future generations.
   b Transmit to future generations values, traditions and institutions that support the long-term flourishing of Earth's human and ecological communities.

II Ecological integrity
In order to fulfil the four broad commitments listed above, it is necessary to do the following:

5 Protect and restore the integrity of Earth's ecological systems, with special concern for biological diversity and the natural processes that sustain life.

a   Adopt at all levels sustainable development plans and regulations that make environmental conservation and rehabilitation integral to all development initiatives.

b   Establish and safeguard viable nature and biosphere reserves, including wild lands and marine areas, to protect Earth's life support systems, maintain biodiversity and preserve our natural heritage.

c   Promote the recovery of endangered species and ecosystems.

d   Control and eradicate non-native or genetically modified organisms harmful to native species and the environment, and prevent introduction of such harmful organisms.

e   Manage the use of renewable resources such as water, soil, forest products and marine life in ways that do not exceed rates of regeneration and that protect the health of ecosystems.

f   Manage the extraction and use of non-renewable resources such as minerals and fossil fuels in ways that minimize depletion and cause no serious environmental damage.

6   Prevent harm as the best method of environmental protection and, when knowledge is limited, apply a precautionary approach.

a   Take action to avoid the possibility of serious or irreversible environmental harm even when scientific knowledge is incomplete or inconclusive.

b   Place the burden of proof on those who argue that a proposed activity will not cause significant harm, and make the responsible parties liable for environmental harm.

c   Ensure that decision-making addresses the cumulative, long-term, indirect, long-distance and global consequences of human activities.

d   Prevent pollution of any part of the environment and allow no build-up of radioactive, toxic or other hazardous substances.

e   Avoid military activities damaging to the environment.

7   Adopt patterns of production, consumption and reproduction that safeguard Earth's regenerative capacities, human rights and community well-being.

a   Reduce, reuse and recycle the materials used in production and consumption systems and ensure that residual waste can be assimilated by ecological systems.

b   Act with restraint and efficiency when using energy and rely increasingly on renewable energy sources such as solar power and wind.

c   Promote the development, adoption and equitable transfer of environmentally sound technologies.

d   Internalize the full environmental and social costs of goods and services in the selling price, and enable consumers to identify products that meet the highest social and environmental standards.

e   Ensure universal access to health care that fosters reproductive health and responsible reproduction.

f   Adopt lifestyles that emphasize the quality of life and material sufficiency in a finite world.

8 Advance the study of ecological sustainability and promote the open exchange and wide application of the knowledge acquired.

   a Support international scientific and technical cooperation on sustainability, with special attention to the needs of developing nations.

   b Recognize and preserve the traditional knowledge and spiritual wisdom in all cultures that contribute to environmental protection and human well-being.

   c Ensure that information of vital importance to human health and environmental protection, including genetic information, remains available in the public domain.

III Social and economic justice

9 Eradicate poverty as an ethical, social and environmental imperative.

   a Guarantee the right to potable water, clean air, food security, uncontaminated soil, shelter and safe sanitation, allocating the national and international resources required.

   b Empower every human being with the education and resources to secure a sustainable livelihood and provide social security and safety nets for those who are unable to support themselves.

   c Recognize the ignored, protect the vulnerable, serve those who suffer and enable them to develop their capacities and to pursue their aspirations.

10 Ensure that economic activities and institutions at all levels promote human development in an equitable and sustainable manner.

   a Promote the equitable distribution of wealth within nations and among nations.

   b Enhance the intellectual, financial, technical and social resources of developing nations, and relieve them of onerous international debt.

   c Ensure that all trade supports sustainable resource use, environmental protection and progressive labour standards.

   d Require multinational corporations and international financial organizations to act transparently in the public good, and hold them accountable for the consequences of their activities.

11 Affirm gender equality and equity as prerequisites to sustainable development and ensure universal access to education, health care and economic opportunity.

   a Secure the human rights of women and girls and end all violence against them.

   b Promote the active participation of women in all aspects of economic, political, civil, social and cultural life as full and equal partners, decision-makers, leaders and beneficiaries.

   c Strengthen families and ensure the safety and loving nurture of all family members.

12 Uphold the right of all, without discrimination, to a natural and social environment supportive of human dignity, bodily health and spiritual well-being, with special attention to the rights of indigenous peoples and minorities.

a   Eliminate discrimination in all its forms, such as that based on race, colour, sex, sexual orientation, religion, language and national, ethnic or social origin.

b   Affirm the right of indigenous peoples to their spirituality, knowledge, lands and resources and to their related practice of sustainable livelihoods.

c   Honour and support the young people of our communities, enabling them to fulfil their essential role in creating sustainable societies.

d   Protect and restore outstanding places of cultural and spiritual significance.

IV Democracy, non-violence and peace

13   Strengthen democratic institutions at all levels, and provide transparency and accountability in governance, inclusive participation in decision-making and access to justice.

    a   Uphold the right of everyone to receive clear and timely information on environmental matters and all development plans and activities which are likely to affect them or in which they have an interest.

    b   Support local, regional and global civil society, and promote the meaningful participation of all interested individuals and organizations in decision-making.

    c   Protect the rights to freedom of opinion, expression, peaceful assembly, association and dissent.

    d   Institute effective and efficient access to administrative and independent judicial procedures, including remedies and redress for environmental harm and the threat of such harm.

    e   Eliminate corruption in all public and private institutions.

    f   Strengthen local communities, enabling them to care for their environments, and assign environmental responsibilities to the levels of government where they can be carried out most effectively.

14   Integrate into formal education and life-long learning the knowledge, values and skills needed for a sustainable way of life.

    a   Provide all, especially children and youth, with educational opportunities that empower them to contribute actively to sustainable development.

    b   Promote the contribution of the arts and humanities as well as the sciences in sustainability education.

    c   Enhance the role of the mass media in raising awareness of ecological and social challenges.

    d   Recognize the importance of moral and spiritual education for sustainable living.

15   Treat all living beings with respect and consideration.

    a   Prevent cruelty to animals kept in human societies and protect them from suffering.

    b   Protect wild animals from methods of hunting, trapping and fishing that cause extreme, prolonged or avoidable suffering.

    c   Avoid or eliminate to the full extent possible the taking or destruction of non-targeted species.

16 Promote a culture of tolerance, non-violence, and peace.
  a   Encourage and support mutual understanding, solidarity and cooperation among all peoples and within and among nations.
  b   Implement comprehensive strategies to prevent violent conflict and use collaborative problem-solving to manage and resolve environmental conflicts and other disputes.
  c   Demilitarize national security systems to the level of a non-provocative defence posture, and convert military resources to peaceful purposes, including ecological restoration.
  d   Eliminate nuclear, biological and toxic weapons and other weapons of mass destruction.
  e   Ensure that the use of orbital and outer space supports environmental protection and peace.
  f   Recognize that peace is the wholeness created by right relationships with oneself, other persons, other cultures, other life, Earth and the larger whole of which all are a part.

The Way Forward

As never before in history, common destiny beckons us to seek a new beginning. Such renewal is the promise of these Earth Charter principles. To fulfil this promise, we must commit ourselves to adopt and promote the values and objectives of the charter.

This requires a change of mind and heart. It requires a new sense of global interdependence and universal responsibility. We must imaginatively develop and apply the vision of a sustainable way of life locally, nationally, regionally and globally. Our cultural diversity is a precious heritage and different cultures will find their own distinctive ways to realize the vision. We must deepen and expand the global dialogue that generated the Earth Charter, for we have much to learn from the ongoing collaborative search for truth and wisdom.

Life often involves tensions between important values. This can mean difficult choices. However, we must find ways to harmonize diversity with unity, the exercise of freedom with the common good, short-term objectives with long-term goals. Every individual, family, organization and community has a vital role to play. The arts, sciences, religions, educational institutions, media, businesses, non-governmental organizations and governments are all called to offer creative leadership. The partnership of government, civil society and business is essential for effective governance.

In order to build a sustainable global community, the nations of the world must renew their commitment to the UN, fulfil their obligations under existing international agreements, and support the implementation of Earth Charter principles with an international legally binding instrument on environment and development.

Let ours be a time remembered for the awakening of a new reverence for life, the firm resolve to achieve sustainability, the quickening of the struggle for justice and peace, and the joyful celebration of life.

Part III

Overriding Concerns

8

International Forest Initiatives

Stephen Bass[1]

TRENDS FACING FORESTS AND STAKEHOLDERS

In attempting to comprehend the mixed bag of international forest initiatives, each with their own economies and politics, it is sometimes hard to keep sight of the actual issues they are trying to address. Thus, we might summarize the main physical forest problems as:

- Declining quantity of natural forest assets. This is felt most strongly by stakeholders with strong economic and livelihood dependence on forests.
- Declining quality of forest environmental processes. Local stakeholders bear the costs, but so also does the international community in losing environmental services such as carbon storage and bioquality.

International initiatives have not always been built on a good understanding of the underlying causes of forest problems. These are complex, and interacting policy, institutional and market-related failures include the following:

- Not all forest values are fully recognized in real-world agendas and decision-making (especially environmental and livelihood-level values). There are particular clashes between global and local values – with weak efforts to reconcile them at national level.

- Policy, markets and stock markets signal that forest-asset stripping for timber or land 'pays'; yet sustainable forest management (SFM) is unprofitable. Short-termism in electoral politics, valuing companies, etc, mean that those with ready access to political processes and resources are able to get the lion's share of forest assets.
- Institutions perpetuate inequalities in benefit/cost-sharing from forests, with few mechanisms for stakeholders to make their claims to forests, and to negotiate with other stakeholders.
- Capacity to practise SFM is weak – or is not fully recognized – for example, the capacity of local traditional stakeholders.

PLAYERS IN INTERNATIONAL FOREST INITIATIVES

The first point is that the different international players have varying expectations and interests in what can be achieved.

Governments view forest issues differently on the international scene, depending upon their forest assets and state of development. For example, some may be major timber exporters and wish to protect their markets. Others may have few forests, importing practically all their needs for forest goods and services, and thus wish to see other countries' forests managed accordingly. Others again may view forests as 'frontiers' or land banks and wish to exercise sovereign rights to 'develop' forests – or to gain access to finance, technology and trade. Each may have other foreign policy agendas which may compromise their forests agenda. Thus intergovernmental forest initiatives are not the product of a uniform vision.

Multinational corporations often have more economic power than governments. They want forests to be viewed as economic assets in international agreements, and not solely as environmental assets. Many of them want access to cheap forest assets, and therefore prefer weak or chaotic policies. Others want long-term investment and prefer stable policies for SFM – if they face the right incentives.

Environmental and social NGOs increasingly have more international political power than do some governments. They aim for social and environmental services from forests, and tend to want binding commitments, targets and monitoring of international agreements.

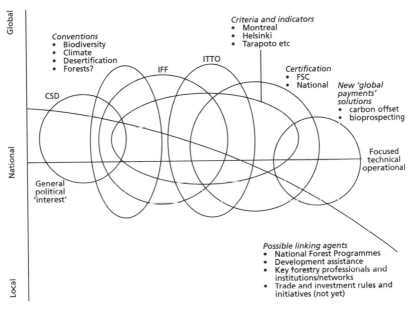

Source: after Thomson, 1996

Figure 8.1 *Global initiatives in forest policy*

How International Initiatives Are Doing in Tackling Forest Problems: An Overview

There is a wide range of international initiatives, ranging from the political to the technical, and with varying degrees of interaction at national and local levels (see Figure 8.1).

Intergovernmental Initiatives

Intergovernmental initiatives tend to be bounded by similar constraints – they do not infringe on the sovereignty of participating nations, and may merely promote lowest common denominator rules and standards. There are varying degrees of participation in them, but they are increasingly becoming open to NGO and private sector inputs.

- *Intergovernmental institutions:* FAO, UNDP, ITTO and UNEP all have increasing concerns for forests. They are beginning to cooperate better through the UN Interagency Task Force on Forests, but there is no obvious lead body in all matters concerning forestry. Issues of institutional survival restrict their degrees of freedom.

- *Intergovernmental forestry processes:* following the 1992 Earth Summit (at which rather bland Forest Principles and a deforestation chapter in Agenda 21 were agreed), two processes have proceeded in attempts to further forest agreements. The Intergovernmental Panel on Forests (IPF) addressed many issues, producing some excellent syntheses of knowledge in the process, but could agree on little more than a paralysingly comprehensive menu of approximately 130 'proposals for action' and the need to continue through an Intergovernmental Forum on Forests. The latter is in some ways a backward step: it has traversed old ground and produced little of new value, thus signalling that practical action is difficult.
- *Multilateral environmental agreements (MEAs):* touch on various aspects of forestry (CBD, FCCC, CITES). Their existence for certain forest services, as well as ITTO for tropical timber trade, has caused many to doubt the need for an international forest convention. With the prospect of international payment transfers for biodiversity conservation and carbon offsets now somewhat closer, following a period of voluntary markets, MEAs may become increasingly important for the future shape of forests.
- *Development assistance initiatives:* have been tied closely to intergovernmental agreements. The Tropical Forest Action Plan process – covering dozens of countries from 1985 onwards – was a well-meaning but essentially 'top-down' technocratic process of expert-developed plans which could rarely be fully implemented, since they did not match entirely with local needs, resources or capacities. The post-IPF donor agenda is in support of more bottom-up national forest programmes (NFPs). These may have more potential, as they are supposed to be driven by stakeholders in each country. But the irony is that they are not being started in many countries and may be awaiting the usual international 'push' complete with 'instructions' on how to undertake them.
- *Regional and country-group governmental agreements:* are often more focused because of shared geographical concerns – for example, the Central American forest convention and conference of ministers – or because of a shared concern to move forward on particular themes of mutual interest. Both the varied strands of international debate, and the practical searching for 'SFM' at national and forest level, led inevitably to demands for greater clarity of definitions and goals. With a political and professional climate in the mid 1990s that was more accommodating of local differences, this led to a major phase of defining criteria and indicators (C&I) for good forestry – Montreal (a North–South country group), Helsinki (Europe), Tarapoto (Amazon) or dry-zone Africa processes. These C&I processes have the advantage of

drawing attention to the dimensions of good forestry, but allowing local interpretation to differ – as indeed it should, with so many differences in forest endowments and their properties.

NGO AND CIVIL SOCIETY INITIATIVES

NGO and civil society initiatives have become among the most powerful of influences in the last decade, with campaigns directly influencing the international positions of many countries. There has been a gradual improvement in facilities and rules circumscribing NGOs' abilities to affect intergovernmental outcomes. These have progressed from demonstrations outside UN halls, to open-mike sessions within the halls, to actually taking part in the drafting of policy text. ITTO provided a valuable training ground for NGOs in this respect. The CSD generally, and the IPF and IFF in particular, have helped the gradual progression from intergovernmental antipathy of NGOs, to partial partnership. However, while intergovernmental processes have opened up debate, NGOs remain sceptical as to just how far they can.

NGOs' practical influence is especially strong when they link up with powerful financial and political players. One such is the WWF/World Bank Alliance, which promotes targets of 200 million hectares of extra protected forest area, and 200 million hectares of certified forest by 2005. Others are with market players (the various national buyers groups of traders and retailers which will buy only certified forest products).

- Forest certification is one of the more significant influences in recent years. Certification is a tool to verify that forest management meets defined standards, thus providing access to markets which differentiate in favour of 'environmentally sound' forest products. It is built on C&I with varying degrees of local multi-stakeholder input (a source of credibility). There is now an almost exponential growth in certified area. The Forest Stewardship Council (FSC), which has been promoted by WWF, has certified nearly 20 million hectares worldwide (mostly larger companies with economies of scale and ready access to markets). Regional or national certification schemes are recent or in development in about 25 countries, some in connection with FSC. With such a rapid development and proliferation of schemes, there is an urgent need to clarify the following. What is meant by 'certified forests' (the standards vary and need some form of mutual recognition)? What is certification actually achieving in terms of improving management of individual forests (it tends to recognize

already good forests at present, and there are too many information, cost and technical barriers for small producers to be
certified)? What is certification's influence on the policy process
(already significant – it has forged agreement on what good
forestry is, how to assess it in the field, who should be responsible, how to improve transparency, and it has legitimized previously
marginal stakeholders)?

- The World Commission on Forests and Sustainable Development
  (WCFSD) is an interesting example of a new type of global multistakeholder initiative, started by a committee of 'wise people'
  through the UN Interaction Council (ex-heads of state) in an
  attempt to look for and promote both local needs and best
  practice, and thereby counteract some of the failings of the (parallel) IPF process. It made admirable attempts to reach the
  grassroots through its regional (continental) hearings, but these
  could only scratch the surface and the commission was
  constrained by lack of resources. It's report *Our Forests – our
  Future* makes interesting reading. Although it was supposed to
  'hand over the baton' to institutions and initiatives that its findings
  showed to be promising, it is also promoting a global forest trust,
  with a component forest management council (to bring different
  standards together), ForestWatch (to publicize good or bad
  practice), a forest ombudsman (to arbitrate) and a forest award. It
  is equally open to governmental, NGO and private sector support
  in its ambitions.

PRIVATE-SECTOR ASSOCIATIONS AND INITIATIVES

There has been extraordinarily weak international coherence among
private-sector forestry actors who still do not have a global forum.
Spurred on, however, by the 'policy inflation' of other international
forestry initiatives, a few groups have come to some prominence – but
are still looking for the best way to influence the governmental and
NGO actors.

- *World Business Council for Sustainable Development (WBCSD)*
  has a forestry working group which is attempting to encourage
  industry leaders to make commitments to SFM and therefore to
  improve the image of both the forest industry and wood products.
  It supported IIED's major study of the global 'sustainable paper
  cycle' and is promoting the concept of eco-efficiency.
- *International Forest Industries Round Table (IFIR)* meets
  annually. It is currently promoting the mutual recognition of certification schemes.

- *International Chamber of Commerce* works with both the WBCSD and IFIR, and would like to see ISO environmental management system standards used more routinely in forestry.

So, which Initiatives Seem to be Working?

- For dealing with specific global forest services: some of the MEAs are the result of much preparation and include (under-utilized) implementation provisions. They need information about good forestry and need to be better recognized in key trade, although there is current disagreement on this in WTO.
- For developing a *lingua franca* about SFM, but allowing for local differences: the C&I processes encompass broad SFM needs, but allow for local interpretation. Through certification they are being tested with rigour. However, they need application to the key areas of trade, investment and MEAs.
- For improving transparency and incentives: the process of certification can provide real incentives for SFM if linked to stable markets. The process of developing national standards helps to review and build on local policy, livelihood and land-use realities. But its mechanics need to be suited also to non-market situations and to small players in order to solve real problems – and not only to service the needs of a few 'green' markets.
- For reconciling and responding to pressures of globalization and localization: country-led NFPs could be a major vehicle; however, they need to be built on local-level knowledge and institutions as well as the internationally agreed elements such as the IPF proposals for action.
- For integration of local and international needs: focused regional agreements offer the right political and operational environment, but need to ensure that they are strongly purpose-led, and do not become hijacked by other agendas.

Problems with International Policy Initiatives

At their best, international policy initiatives accommodate local perspectives, convene multiple stakeholders, and allow local interpretation and subsidiarity in their implementation. They catalyse local initiative, build capacity and offer common language and political momentum behind shared challenges and truly global needs.

At their worst, international initiatives are dominated by certain players: they impose precepts which reflect the demands of a few countries only (or possibly none at all), remove national incentives and freedom to use forests for development and welfare, and destroy local institutions and other sources of resilience which had sustained forests and livelihoods.

Caught somewhere between the best and worst, most international initiatives have spent too much time and energy engaging with what we might call 'common national problems' – which might be better addressed by national or local initiatives – and have made little progress with truly global problems. Thus, there are four general problems with most of these international initiatives.

Firstly, there is a genuine confusion over what is a truly global forest issue, and when it is relevant. We suggest that the security of global forest services (such as carbon sequestration or important biodiversity), or global causes of problems (such as trade or debt), are properly international issues and should be dealt with as such. Sovereignty – or the need for compensation – gets in the way of everything else.

Secondly, the initiatives still focus mostly on forests and are not engaged with the big 'extra-sectoral' policies – environment, peoples' rights, technology, trade and finance. Many people behind international forest initiatives are uncertain about how to handle the two big phenomena facing forestry today: globalization of markets, information flows and communication, and localization – increasing trends towards democracy, seeking to improve local peoples' rights to forests for multiple local benefits, or other decentralization from governmental downsizing. This means that many of them simply do not tackle the underlying causes – they have effect only at the margins of the forest problem. This is involves theoretical master plans or just fiddling while Rome burns.

Thirdly, none of the established international initiatives are truly multistakeholder. Those that do bring many stakeholders together – notably certification and fair trade – are attracting interest but are still weak on government involvement. With many of the underlying causes relating to weak communications and coordination, it would seem an obvious need to work towards an international multistakeholder forum.

Finally, intergovernmental initiatives have taken us a long way, but are no longer sufficient to help progress and are out of touch with on-ground realities. There are too many 'lowest common denominators', justifications for inaction, inequitable coalitions and divisions, obfuscations or diversions from real problems and unrealistic 'dreams'. The 'talk shops' continue to be populated by the usual suspects. We are now at a phase when we need more strategic actions. Civil society initiatives such as WCFSD and certification, in contrast, appear to push progress forward – even if they are not ideally constituted to begin with. They focus on strategic issues and suggest innovative actions.

WHERE NEXT FOR INTERNATIONAL INITIATIVES?

We should build on the proven and promising international tools to date – the C&I, the NFPs, certification, the specific MEAs, and purposeful regional agreements. In doing so, progressive stakeholders have begun discussing some of the following possibilities:

- Agreement on a simple set of C&I which provides an accepted international *lingua franca* for SFM. This should become integral to MEA protocols, payment schemes and certification programmes for global forest services; to trade policies for standards equivalency/mutual recognition and legitimacy of technical barriers to trade; and to investment, so that finance authorities can lend and judge environmental and social performance.
- The extension of certification/verification to global environmental services (there are already carbon offset certification schemes, and moves towards certifying protected forest areas to deal with the 'paper parks' problem), and to other real forest issues (perhaps domestic markets in countries facing severe forest problems).
- A review of the potential and performance of existing intergovernmental instruments and institutions. There is much scope for applying the climate change and biodiversity conventions, and some other existing environmental agreements, to certain aspects of forestry. This would have to be preceded by a performance gap analysis of existing initiatives. The same applies to the intergovernmental agencies.
- Better integration of the international initiatives on NFPs and national strategies for sustainable development. This should improve the way that cross-sectoral links to forests are addressed. This demands recognition of 'what works' at national and local level, which will often mean building on 'second best', as opposed to promoting unachievable perfect master plans.
- Involvement of important, but thus far marginalized, actors in international processes, and notably representatives of local forest-dependent groups and the private sector. At present, the 'higher up' the local-to-global hierarchy, the more depauperate the means of representation and participation;
- Finding better means of representation and involvement of the private sector. Real efforts are needed to form private-sector bodies for constructive engagement with other groups, to explore their impediments to SFM, to improve their own commitment to SFM, and to help all groups work out practical ways forward using the resources available to the private sector.
- We might consider ways of moving towards an effective international multistakeholder forest forum that integrates the above. In

this, and indeed all other international forest initiatives, we can learn from the most effective national policy initiatives, which are based on:

a   institutions for experimentation and learning, with performance reviews and mechanisms for accountability;
b   parity between government, civil society and business;
c   getting more marginalized forest-dependent groups to the table;
d   better coordination between policy instruments.

Finally, and as stressed at the beginning of this chapter, for international processes to stand any chance of success it is essential to improve participatory national policy processes and capacities. These are the main links between the forces of globalization and localization, where 'win–wins' can be identified and trade-offs made where necessary.

NOTES

1   The principal source for this chapter is J Mayers and S Bass (1999) *Policy that Works for Forests and People*, London: IIED

9

A Sustainable Transport Convention for the New Europe

Deike Peters

'A *human right, a human pleasure, an economic resource and a servant of economic activity: transport is many things to all people.*'
European Commission, Directorate General Transport
(1994, p1)

'We speak of sustainable transport
not because we fear
that we might one day pass the limits of nature
but because we know that we have already done so.'
Kågeson (1994, p1)

INTRODUCTION

The advent of the European Union (EU) and the break-up of the Soviet Union in the 1990s have brought profound new challenges to all levels of policy-making across the European continent. At the same time, late 20th-century transport innovations have caused dramatic increases in the accessibility and mobility of goods and people, resulting in what Anthony Giddens (1990) has termed 'time-space compression' in an increasingly uneven European geography. Transport innovations arguably provided the original, spatial foundation for European integration long before the political idea of the European Union was born. Starting with the advent of the railway in the latter half of the 1800s, boosted by the proliferation of motor vehicles, and further accelerated by the rise of high-speed rail and commercial air transport in the last decades, Europe has now 'shrunk' to a continent that can be crossed in a matter of a few hours.

Meanwhile, with as many as 12 eastern and southern European countries now involved in accession talks with the European Union, the political integration of the continent is continuing at a faster pace and more dramatic scope than ever before. The central European front runners for accession are already struggling to bring their national laws and regulations in accordance with EU policy, prompting sweeping changes in their commercial, social and environmental sectors. Clearly, the time has come for European political leaders to convene together and articulate a clear and powerful common vision of sustainable mobility for the new millennium.

The overreliance on this century's most notable transport innovation, the private motor vehicle, continues to lie at the heart of the environmental challenge both in Europe and the rest of the world, diminishing the 'livability' of our cities and towns and threatening the environmental sustainability of the entire planet. This chapter reviews past and present transport sector policies in Europe in light of this global threat, highlighting the dramatic environmental and social costs of motorization and sprawl. Unfortunately, the encouraging new sustainability rhetoric of recent official EU and UN policies continues to clash with a reality of ever-increasing mobility and (road-biased) investments into large-scale transport infrastructures. There is thus an urgent need for a reinvigorated effort towards a pan-European agreement on sustainable transport. The steps (and hurdles) towards the realization of such a vision are outlined below.

THE PROBLEM: THE ENVIRONMENTAL AND SOCIAL COSTS OF TRANSPORT

The transport sector is responsible for over a quarter of the world's primary energy use, and for about 54 per cent of all world oil consumption. Despite rapid motorization in developing countries, industrialized countries will remain responsible for the majority of this energy use for another 25 years or so. While they host the majority of the world's population, developing countries currently only account for 14 per cent of the world's car fleet. By 2020, this figure will only rise to about 33 per cent (Banister, 1998). Transport is a major contributor to the greenhouse effect, accounting for about a quarter of all

CO_2 emissions from fossil-fuel use. As the European Commission (1998a, p5) recently warned:

> *'In 1995, CO_2 emissions from transport represented 26 per cent of total EU CO_2 emissions. On unchanged trends, a significant further increase in the order of 40 per cent is expected by 2010, outstripping growth in all other sectors. It is clear that, if left unchecked, growth in transport CO_2 emissions would make it extremely difficult to achieve the CO_2 emission reduction target agreed at Kyoto (an economy-wide reduction of 8 per cent from 1990 levels by 2008–2012).'*

The only ways to reduce transport sector CO_2 emissions are to travel less, to use less fuel and/or substitute it with renewable forms of energy.

Transport's share of a variety of other major pollutants is even greater. Transport accounts for about 80–90 per cent of carbon monoxide (negatively affecting morbidity and fertility rates), 80 per cent of benzene (a major carenogenic), 60 per cent of nitrogen oxides (responsible for acid rain and resulting forest degradation, and, together with volatile organic compounds, photochemical smog), 50 per cent of hydrocarbons (toxic trace substances), 50 per cent of lead (seriously affecting children's mental development) and about 27 per cent of particulates (linked to a variety of inflammatory and cardiovascular diseases). In major city centres, road traffic alone can account for as much as 90–95 per cent of carbon monoxide and lead (where leaded fuel is not phased out), and up to 70 per cent of nitrogen oxides and hydrocarbons (World Bank, 1996, p50). Transport's overall share of sulphur dioxide, a major cause of respiratory illnesses, is about 5 per cent, but this share can rise fourfold and more in locations where a majority of the vehicle fleet runs on diesel fuel. Very small particulates, an increasing focus of concern, are also mainly found in diesel fuel. By extrapolating results from US cities, scientists have estimated that up to 10,000 people die prematurely from these particulate emissions in the UK alone (Banister, 1998, p5).

The negative impacts of transport on natural ecosystems are equally profound. Besides rapidly depleting the world's natural energy sources, transport sector needs destroy vast amounts of fertile land and threaten natural wildlife habitats. Other important environmental impacts such as noise, vibration, severance effects and aesthetic impacts are typically less recognized externalities of transport, partly because they are harder to quantify. However, there is little doubt that continued exposure to constant vibration and high noise levels (over 55 to 65 A decibels) results in sleep disruptions, anxiety, depression and stress, in turn negatively affecting people's economic performance. Other quality of life effects such as the loss of community caused by a new bypass or highway and children's inability to play on busy urban streets may not carry a direct monetary value, but certainly illustrate transport's additional ill effects on human settlements.

While European cities are typically denser than their US counterparts, where the transportation system often occupies over 30 per cent of the developed land, automobiles still have come to dominate urban landscapes. As a recent EU Commission working paper on transport and the environment notes (CEC, 1998b, p2):

> *'...[s]patial and city planning has, over the past decades, accommodated the increasing role of road transport and in many cases even facilitated it. Urban sprawl, the decline of city centres and industrial relocations to places with good access to motorways resulted in many cases. This, in turn, not only fuelled further demand for road transport, but also undermined the competitive positions of other modes.'*

Two of the most easily quantifiable societal costs of car-dependent transport systems are accidents and congestion. Traffic congestion is responsible for increases in pollution, including noise pollution, and further rises in fuel consumption. Approximately half a million people die each year in road accidents and another 750,000 are seriously injured (World Bank, 1996, p50). The yearly death toll in EU and European Free Trade Association (EFTA) countries is around 55,000 (Kågson 1994, p4).[1]

Despite the availability of sophisticated public transport systems in most urban areas, private automobile travel remains the dominant mode of travel for most Europeans. In western Europe motorization rates are at an alarming 450 per 1000 people, and car ownership levels in the central European transition countries have been skyrocketing over the last 10 to 15 years, now averaging 250 cars per 1000 people, reaching as many as 400 per 1000 people in urban areas such as Warsaw. Rising car ownership directly translates into lower occupancy rates and diminished mode shares for more environmentally friendly modes such as bicycles and public transport, all of which in turn increase the overall energy consumption in the sector. Trip lengths have also consistently increased as a result of travel patterns becoming more car-dependent. It should be noted that the greater fuel efficiency of the modern western European vehicle fleet has recently become outweighed by added energy use due to the fact that vehicles are much heavier and more powerful now and have much added hi-tech equipment (especially air conditioning).

The provision of adequate access and mobility thus emerge as a key challenge in the building of sustainable societies. The efficient functioning of transport systems obviously remains an essential prerequisite to successful economic development. Yet accessibility and mobility gains are often reaped at the expense of severe damage to human health and global biodiversity, with problems accelerating for future generations. This clearly violates the sustainability principle. It is therefore the pressing task of national governments and international cooperative institutions to provide successful measures, regulations, taxes and other incentives to better internalize the environmental and social costs of the transport sector.

THE LEGACY: A SHORT HISTORY OF EU TRANSPORT POLICIES AND PLANS

In the 1958 Treaty of Rome establishing the original six-member European Economic Community (EEC), transport, agriculture and external commerce were identified as the only sectors for which common policies were to be developed immediately, making transport truly 'one of the foundations of the Community' (Whitelegg, 1989, p6). Yet while substantial agreements were soon reached on agricultural and trade issues, for over three decades minimal progress was made in developing a Common Transport Policy (CTP) (Whitelegg, 1989; Erdmenger, 1983). Without any solid basis for intervention, EU transport CO_2 emissions increased by 37 per cent between 1985 and 1996 alone, while GDP only increased by 26 per cent. Transport emission growth thus outstripped economic growth. Official EU sources estimate that as much as 20 per cent of this growth was due to a modal shift to less energy-efficient modes of transport (CEC, 1998a, p6) – largely shifts from non-motorized transport, public transit and rail to private vehicles and trucks.

EU ambitions in the transport sector dramatically changed with the 1992 European Union Maastricht Treaty. In this new basic treaty, the European Union member states officially proclaimed their goals of harmonious, balanced development; sustainable growth; economic and social cohesion; and improved quality of life and solidarity between member states (Article 2). Concretely, Article 130r of the Maastricht agreement obliges the European Community to integrate environmental protection with other community policies, including transport.

Also in 1992, the *White Paper on Transport* was finally passed as the European Union's official transport policy document. Its full title is *The Future Development of the Common Transport Policy – a Global Approach to the Construction of a Community Framework for*

Sustainable Mobility. However, the crucial term sustainable mobility is never once concretely defined in the document. Paragraph 123 vaguely defines it as 'efficient, safe transport under the best possible environmental and social conditions'. The paper falls short of a true call for sustainable transport development in numerous ways. Bowers (1992) provides a very useful section-by-section explication of the White Paper, noting, for example, that:

> '...*there is no commitment to reducing transport volume, merely a need to "address the demand", and indeed there is no mention at all of reducing transport demand in the action programme... [The White Paper] does not mention the syndrome that new roads can generate new journeys, nor does it mention the syndrome that road space freed up by anti-congestion can fill up again very quickly if there are no accompanying car use disincentives. The bicycle finally gets a mention in paragraph 176, but walking is never mentioned as a means of transport.*'

But the White Paper dedicates numerous paragraphs to the establishment and development of the so-called Trans-European Networks (TENs). Since their first official mention in the Maastricht Treaty, the creation, upgrading, expansion and optimization of these plans for large-scale pan-European road, rail and water transport infrastructures has emerged as one of the now most hotly debated issues within the challenge of creating an ever expanding 'sustainable Europe'.[2] The commission's 1992 White Paper already treated the TENs as an accepted plan, stating that '[a] reasonable estimate of the volume of investment required during the period 1990 to 2010 to guarantee adequate funding of the total transport system is of the order 1000 to 15,000 billion ECU, or 1 to 1.5 per cent of GDP, and probably towards the higher end' (CEC, 1992, §143).[3]

At the 1994 European Council at Essen, the EU then expanded its own domestic mandate by declaring the preparation of priority transport links to and within the central and eastern European (CEE) countries applying for EU membership – a major task related to future enlargement. This led to the development of the so-called Crete Corridors. These are in essence CEE extensions of the EU TEN corridors. More recently, the so-called Transport Infrastructure Needs Assessment (TINA) programme led and funded by the EU Phare Unit developed an additional, supposedly complementary map of secondary links likely to receive priority EU and international funding support. Transport infrastructure investments are thus firmly established on the European political agenda as a key topic to be addressed as the continent moves towards 'ever closer union' in the 21st century.

Unfortunately, the environmental and economic effects of increased investments in large-scale transportation infrastructures are much more complicated and problematic than official EU rhetoric asserts. Powerful pro-growth interests in Europe equate network expansion with economic prosperity to justify enormous investments that will have important distributional and environmental consequences. Official EU policy claims that the large-scale TEN links hold the key to successful European integration and sustainable growth (European Commission, 1995, 'Conclusion'):

> *'Only the European Union can make the integrated transport network a reality in time to avoid the environmental and mobility crisis which faces us... An integrated trans-European transport network will bring economic and social benefits to all of Europe. It will play an important part in easing the long-term job crisis, it will be good for the environment, and it will improve the quality of people's lives.'*

This is not only an overly simplistic but, in fact, a misleading rendering of the situation. For one, it clearly overstates transport infrastructure's direct influence on economic growth. Even mainstream neoclassical transport economists such as Button et al (1995, p192) conclude that: 'Perhaps the most objective position is to say that the role of adequate transport and other infrastructure is now seen by many as being a necessary but not sufficient condition for economic development.' The academic debate over the importance of infrastructure as a stimulant to economic development remains inconclusive (see, for example, Aschauer 1989; Biehl, 1986; Vickerman, 1991; Böhme et al, 1998; p14ff). However, a variety of recent studies, including several done by the British Standing Advisory Council on Trunk Road Assessment (SACTRA), suggest that previous arguments regarding road investment's positive stimulus on regional growth and employment were vastly exaggerated, and that the social and environmental costs of excessive road building are enormous and often unevenly distributed between core and periphery regions (SACTRA, 1999; T&E, 1995a; Whitelegg, 1993; Bina and Briggs, 1996; Hey et al, 1995; BirdLife, 1999).[4]

It therefore seems clear that simply completing an expensive network of new highway and high-speed rail links will not in itself provide a sustainable solution to Europe's transport needs. To the contrary, it may prove detrimental to long-term sustainability. Given the magnitude of the planned investments, closer scrutiny of the institutional and political decision-making process directing and informing

European and regional-level transport policies and plans is necessary. Past experience suggests that powerful pro-growth interests may seriously jeopardize the successful implementation of Agenda 21 goals in the European transport.[5] A renewed and strengthened pan-European political consensus thus needs to be forged around sustainability issues.

THE PRESENT: A NEW CONSENSUS ON SUSTAINABLE TRANSPORT

RECENT EU INITIATIVES AIMED AT PROMOTING SUSTAINABLE TRANSPORT

Several recent EU initiatives point in a more positive direction. In particular, the issue of the internalization of the social and environmental costs of transport, often summarized under the heading 'Getting the Prices Right' (T&E, 1995b), has slowly but surely entered official policy documents. Most importantly, it was partly taken up by the EU *White Paper on Fair Payment for Infrastructure Use* (EU, 1997). However, the 1995 European Community's *Green Paper on Fair and Efficient Pricing* showed that taxes and charges in the sector are still not consistent across modes and do not adequately reflect external costs. The cost of not internalizing these costs is enormous. According to two EU working papers (CEC, 1998b, p17):

> 'At the Community level, the policy of internalizing all external costs of transport would reduce CO_2 emissions on average by 11.5 per cent. In addition to CO_2 reductions, the net benefit to European citizens from reduced time spent suffering congestion, and from decreased accidents, noise and other emissions, would range between 28–78 billion ECU per year.'

Meanwhile, a variety of important community initiatives are underway. The European Community's 5th Environmental Action Programme – 'Towards Sustainability' – set ambitious targets for environmental standards and also made transport one of five special target sectors. The EU's Auto-Oil Programme identified a series of measures aimed at the reduction of road transport emissions, ranging from cost-effective vehicle emission and fuel-quality standards and improved vehicle maintenance to local policy measures. If carried out in full, set air-quality targets, with the important exception of ozone, could be achieved by 2010. This does not mean that select localities would not continue to exceed WHO standards, however.

In 1995 an EU communication outlined the potential of short sea shipping as an environmentally friendly mode (European Commission, 1995). The EU also published a *White Paper on Revitalizing the Community Railways* (CEC,1996a), followed by a *Communication on Trans-European Rail Freeways* aimed an unlocking the potential of railways (CEC, 1997a). Another CEC communication developed an action programme for creating an integrated intermodal freight transport system (CEC, 1997b). A *Green Paper on the Citizens' Network* examined the potential of public transport as a means of reducing urban congestion (CEC, 1996b). The development of a Car-Free Cities Network has also found increasing support from the community in recent years. Also, after years of NGO calls for strategic environmental assessments (SEAs) to be done on the TENs, the commission is finally developing a methodology for this.[6]

Last, but not least, EU policies are slowly beginning to take Agenda 21 recommendations more seriously by stressing the importance of local measures and of integrating land-use and transport planning. The EC's *Communication on Transport and CO_2* refers to an official Austrian study that calculated the possible combined reduction of CO_2 emissions through cycle promotion, speed controls, higher car-parking charges, car and trucking restrictions in cities and information campaigns at 14 per cent. For land-use measures, the EC (1998b, p20) refers to an Institute of Spatial Planning University of Dortmund (IRPUD) study to suggest that emissions per capita per day can be reduced to about one third by 2010 using the following bundle of measures:

- increased prices for car use and financial incentives to use more efficient cars;
- increased inner-city parking charges;
- faster public transport (25 per cent) and reducing car speeds by 40 per cent;
- land-use management in the periphery in order to reverse the trend of urban sprawl.

Improved logistics, strategies to reduce CO_2 emissions from passenger cars; revitalization of railways; promotion of non-motorized modes, public transport, short sea shipping, and intermodal transport; the stepwise introduction of fair and efficient pricing in all modes of transport; strategic environmental analysis of TEN-T transport infrastructure investments; and the promotion of a series of complementary land-use measures and charges to be implemented by national, regional and local authorities thus emerge as key policy approaches for promoting sustainable transport and for actively reducing greenhouse gas emissions (also see CEC, 1998b).

PAN-EUROPEAN DECLARATIONS IN SUPPORT OF SUSTAINABLE TRANSPORT DEVELOPMENT

Although impressive in their rhetoric, by themselves the above described EU-wide white papers and communications are not sufficient for ensuring active policy change throughout Europe. Their translation into national legislation will provide many individual challenges and only a few of the central European transition countries will manage to become EU members within the next decade. Although the accession process will ensure a general convergence of legal and administrative systems in the region, large policy gaps between EU and non-EU countries will remain for some time. The formulation of a pan-European sustainable transport consensus must thus also build on two other important initiatives that are pan-European in scope; these are listed below.

THE VIENNA DECLARATION ON TRANSPORT AND THE ENVIRONMENT

The 1997 UN-ECE Regional Conference on Transport and the Environment resulted in the Vienna Declaration on Transport and the Environment.[7] The declaration recalls the importance of the sustainable transportation principles developed at the 1996 OECD conference in Vancouver, urges remaining states to ratify the Convention on Long-Range Transboundary Air Pollution and the related protocols, and draws attention to increasing pollution from air and maritime transport. The declaration also encourages phasing out leaded fuels and considers providing ECE member countries in transition with appropriate assistance in restructuring the vehicle and oil-refining industries. It refers to the 1991 Espoo Convention on Environmental Impact Assessment in a Transboundary Context in encouraging more effective environmental impact assessment of transport infrastructure projects in transboundary contexts and calls for further development of SEA methodologies. Even several more radical measures receive active mention – for example, the establishment of national environmental and health targets in the transport sector within national strategies, dedicated cycle networks and road pricing.

The annex to the declaration contained a detailed programme of joint action (POJA) in the fields of transport and environment, listing possible measures and solutions at the international and national level. The 1998 and 1999 progress reports from the resulting UN-ECE joint meetings on transport and environment show mixed results at the international level.[8] Impressive strides have been made in areas such as improved environmental assessment, but for ambitious goals such as 'develop[ing] and tighten[ing] environmental standards for off-road and rail vehicles and ships', 'regulations to avoid new registration in other ECE countries of vehicles already withdrawn' or developing 'reference criteria for appropriate charging of infrastructure costs and external costs', the last report shows that 'no new relevant activities [are] underway or foreseen at the international level.'

Overall, however, the POJA activities are wide ranging and many of the individual actions are indeed effectively designed to advance sustainable transport goals in Europe. The Geneva-based programme is therefore the logical home of any joint efforts towards a pan-European transport convention.

THE 1999 WHO CONFERENCE ON TRANSPORT, ENVIRONMENT AND HEALTH

The June 1999 WHO Conference on Transport, Environment and Health resulted in an ambitious charter that was signed by European health, environment and transport ministers, together with the relevant WHO representatives. Building directly on the Vienna Declaration and other relevant documents, the charter highlights the specific and wide-ranging impacts of transport activities and infrastructures on human health. A first annex, supported by several sophisticated background papers, provides up-to-date scientific evidence on key issues (for example, the quantifiable positive effects of cycling and walking and the enormous social costs of motorized transport from accidents, noise and pollution). In a very commendable effort, a second annex then provides a detailed overview of existing relevant international actions, differentiating between legally binding documents (for example, the Convention on Transboundary Air Pollution) and non-binding efforts and declarations.[9] The spirit and approach in the charter clearly aims at effectively integrating existing efforts within future action plans, so it is hardly surprising that it was this document where the concrete idea of a European transport convention first received weighty support in the form of an official mention in an international charter (see quote below).

FROM VISION TO ACTION: TOWARDS A EUROPEAN TRANSPORT CONVENTION

The new emerging consensus that current road-based transport systems are unsustainable needs to be more urgently translated into an international action programme for improved transport sustainability. Taken together, the 1997 UN-ECE Vienna Declaration on Transport and the Environment, the 1999 WHO Charter on Transport, Environment and Health and the transport-related EU policy statements reviewed above already present a clear outline for a European Convention on Sustainable Transport. This chapter therefore emphatically underscores the concluding statement of the 1999 WHO Charter on Transport, Environment and Health in which the respective ministers and representatives of the European member states of WHO call on WHO, the UN-ECE and international organizations to:

> *'...provide an overview of relevant existing agreements and legal instruments, with a view to improving and harmonizing their implementation and further developing them as needed. A report on this overview should be submitted at the latest by spring 2000, recommending which further steps are needed. That report should cover the possibility of new non-legally binding actions and* the feasibility, necessity and content of a new legally binding instrument (eg a convention on transport, environment and health), *focusing on bringing added value to, and avoiding overlaps with, existing agreements* [emphasis added].'

Such an instrument with a legally binding character is necessary in addition to existing non-binding agreements in order to ensure improved articulation and, most importantly, implementation of concrete goals that could be achieved by individual governments in the short, medium and long term. By making the passing of such a convention their core contribution to the preparatory process to Earth Summit 2002, European countries would then be able to impress the world by leaving Earth Summit 2002 with a concrete result, not just a vague plan for future measures.

REFERENCES

Banister, D and Berechmann, J (eds) (1993) *Transport in a Unified Europe – Policies and Challenges*, Amsterdam: North Holland, Studies in Regional Science and Economics

Bina, O, Briggs, B and Bunting, G (1995) *The Impact of Trans-European Networks on Nature Conservation: A Pilot Project*, Bedfordshire: The Royal Society for the Protection of Birds and Cambridge: World Conservation Monitoring Centre

Bowers, C (1992) *The EC White Paper on Transport – a guide for the environmental campaigner*, T&E Paper 92/8, Brussels: European Federation for Transport and Environment (T&E)

Button, K (1993) *Transport, the Environment and Economic Policy*, Aldershot: Edward Elgar Publishing

Commission of the European Communities (1998a) *On Transport and CO2 – Developing a Community Approach*, Communication from the Commission to the Council, the European Parliament, the Economic and Social Committee and the Committee of the Regions, Brussels: Commission of the European Communities

Commission of the European Communities (1998b) *Transport and the Environment*, Brussels: EU Directorate General for Transport, Working Paper (1979) 'The Common Transport Policy: a case of lost direction', *Transportation Science*, vol 13, no 4, pp343–357

ECMT (1993) *Report of the 95th Round Table on Transport Economics; Transport Infrastructure and Systems for a New Europe*, Paris: ECMT

European Commission (1995) *The Trans-European Transport Network: Transforming a Patchwork into a Network*, Luxembourg: Office for Official Publications of the European Communities

European Commission, Directorate General Transport (1994) *The Trans-European Transport Network*, Luxembourg: Office for Official Publications of the European Communities

Giddens, A (1990) *The Consequences of Modernity*, Stanford, CA: Stanford University Press

Hey, C, Pfeiffer, T and Topan, A (1996) *The Economic Impact of Motorways in the Peripheral Regions of the EU – A Literature Survey for the Royal Society for the Protection of Birds and BirdLife International*, Freiburg: EURES, Institute for Regional Studies in Europe

IRPUD (1994) *New Time–Space Maps of Europe*, IRPUD Working Paper No 132, Dortmund: Institut für Raumplanung Universität Dortmund

Kågson, P (1994) *The Concept of Sustainable Transport*, T&E Paper 94/3, Brussels: European Federation for Transport and Environment (T&E)

Kirlazidis, T (1994) *European Transport: Problems and Policies*, Aldershot: Avebury

Nijkamp, P, Vleugel, J, Maggi, R and Masser, I (1994) *Missing Transport Networks in Europe*, Aldershot: Avebury

Ross, J (1998) *Linking Europe: Transport Policies and Politics in the European Union*, London: Preager

Standing Advisory Committee on Trunk Road Assessment (SACTRA) (1998) *Transport Investment, Transport Intensity and Economic Growth*, London: UK Government Publications and http://www.detr.gov.uk/heta/sactra98

Spiekermann, K and Wegener, M (1998) 'Socio-Economic and Spatial Impacts of Trans-European Networks: The SASI Project', Paper presented at the Eighth World Conference on Transport Research, Antwerpen, 12–17 July 1998

'Trans-European Networks and Unequal Accessibility in Europe', *European Journal of Regional Development (EUREG)*, vol 4/96, pp35–42

Vickerman, R (ed) (1991) *Infrastructure and Regional Development*, London: Pion

Whitelegg, J (1989) *Transport Policy in the EEC*, London: Routledge

Whitelegg, J (1993) *Roads, Jobs and the Economy*, London: Greenpeace

NOTES

1   By comparison, just over 1000 people were killed in rail accidents in 1990, and more than 2000 injured

2   It is also interesting to note that by calling for the formation and completion of the TENs, the Maastricht Treaty first established the European Union as a de facto supra-national infrastructure planning institution. At the time, however, the actual status of the TENs was illegal and remains ambivalent to date. The hi-level Christopherson Working Group, suggesting the key list of priority projects of pan-European importance, did not include any environmental NGOs and even ignored the EU parliament. An article by Ann Doherty and Olivier Hoedeman in *New Statesman and Society* (10 March 1995, p29) quotes a September 1994 European parliament working document as stating that 'the failure to involve the European Parliament in the Christophersen Group's work, or to inform it about this work, must be condemned in the strongest possible terms'

3   The completion of the ambitious plans requires about 220 billion ECU in investments until the year 2000 alone (Spiekermann and Wegener, 1998). Since 1992, the European Investment Bank, the 'house bank' of the EU, alone has allocated 42 billion ECU towards infrastructure projects related to European integration

4   Core-periphery arguments are often closely related to arguments regarding the uneven effects of EU regional policy. The central contention is that the central European core has in fact always benefited more from investments than peripheral regions, and some scholars specifically contend that new transport corridors have detrimental effects on weaker, peripheral regions. Fifteen years ago, Pinder (1983, p84) already talked of 'the growing view that transportation improvements do not guarantee more equitable centre-periphery balance [in the EU]. Polarization, rather than trickling down, may be accentuated by the reduction of regional isolation'

5   Although Agenda 21 does not contain a specific chapter on transport, the document nevertheless contains clear recommendations for transport planners and policy-makers. According to Agenda 21, all government should:

- Integrate land-use and transportation planning to encourage development patterns that reduce transport demand [number of trips and distance] (para 7.53).
- Adopt urban transport programmes favouring high-occupancy public transport in communities, as appropriate (para 7.53).
- Encourage non-motorized modes of transport by providing safe cycle-ways and foot-ways in urban and suburban communities, as appropriate (para 7.53).
- Develop or enhance, as appropriate, mechanisms to integrate the transport planning strategies and urban and regional settlement patterns, with a view to reducing additional needs for transport (para 9.12)

A renewed and strengthened pan-European political consensus thus needs to be forged around sustainability issues

6   Unlike project-specific environmental impact assessments (EIAs), which cannot influence unsustainable mode choices or route selections any more, SEAs aim at providing timely environmental assessments of policies, plans or larger corridors, thus preceding project selection

7   It is important to note that this document reaffirms both the Rio declaration and recent European initiatives, but also cautiously warns that 'the different geographic and economic circumstances of [UN-ECE] member states may necessitate differentiated approaches and flexibility of choice within that framework [of sustainable development] ' and therefore recognizes 'the special circumstances and priority needs of ECE member countries in transition' (paras g and n)

8   All relevant POJA documents, including the final versions of the Vienna Declaration and the joint programme of action, as well as the progress reports, are available online on the UN-ECE website (www.unece.org). Links to key EU, ECMT/OECD and WHO documents are also provided

9   All of these documents are, of course, available online on the WHO website

10

Poverty and the Environment

Cletus A Avoka

INTRODUCTION

As preparations for Earth Summit 2002 gather pace, the urgent need to prioritize poverty has become increasingly apparent. Events such as the Ghanaian Meeting of Environment Ministers that I chaired in September 1999 have clearly identified poverty elimination as one of the lead issues for the Sustainable Development Agenda for the start of the millennium. Earth Summit 2002 – ten years after Rio – provides a timely opportunity for the global community to make serious commitments towards bettering the basic standards of living of many of the world's inhabitants.

Poverty has been defined in diverse ways by various authors. The concept of poverty, according to O Alhimir (1979), implies the incapacity of a person to become part of the socioeconomic environment in a way that continually allows for the satisfaction of basic necessities of life.

According to UNEP, the two basic causes of the environmental crises are poverty and misuse of wealth: the poor majority is forced to destroy, in the short term, the very resources they will need for their long-term subsistence, while the rich minority makes demands on resources that are unsustainable in the long term, thus transferring the costs to the poor. It must be emphasized, therefore, that the poor are not, of course, the only or the major cause of pressures on the environment. Environmental degradation from logging and other commercial activities in and around forests, for example, are likely to be appropriated by the rich minority.

Alleviation of poverty has been a major goal of past and present governments of Ghana since independence in 1957. However, since 1990 sustainable reduction in poverty has taken over poverty alleviation. Governments have also realized that in addressing poverty issues, there are attendant gains with respect to the better management of the country's natural resources. Thus, some poverty alleviation programmes have had indirectly associated with them the concept of reducing the impact of the population on the environment and natural resources.

WHY ARE POVERTY AND ENVIRONMENT OVERRIDING CONCERNS?

Human development connotes improvement in the quality of life and well-being of individuals. The basic goals, therefore, target inter-alia poverty reduction, sustainable livelihood and well-being for the wider population, particularly for vulnerable groups. These social goals are best attained through development activities that aim at improving human resources, health, sanitation and human settlement, and seek to promote food security, household water security and nutrition. Furthermore, such development goals target the provision of access to safe and potable water and clean air while generating and supporting employment that raises incomes and distributes equitably the benefits of such developments.

One of the major factors that significantly militates against the achievement of such noble goals of human development is environmental degradation; this potentially aggravates poverty through the adverse impacts of eroding and undermining the achievements of human development goals that improve the quality of life.

The available information on the poverty profile of Ghana (*Ghana Living Standard Survey*, 1987–1988) indicates that about 36 per cent of the population live below the poverty line, which is defined as two-thirds of the national average income. The majority of this poor live in the rural or peri-urban areas of the country. The livelihood of the rural population and the urban poor, who represent a greater percentage of vulnerable groups, is almost entirely dependent upon the environmental resource base for meeting the socioeconomic needs of the country, particularly from mining, forestry and logging and agriculture.

Paradoxically, the socioeconomic development activities of the rural population tend to degrade environmental resources, and threaten the life support systems necessary to meet the needs and aspirations of the general population, thus aggravating poverty.

Degradation of the environment is a global phenomenon, but its impact is more strongly felt among the poorer segments of the rural population since the degradation of their natural resource base is significantly worsening their poverty. Rural poverty and the degradation of the environment are mutually reinforcing. When people's survival is at stake, they are forced to increasingly farm on marginal soils, to reduce fallow periods, to cut vital forests, to overstock fragile range lands and to overfish rivers, lakes and coastal waters (Jazairy, 1992).

To understand the complex relations between poverty, land degradation, high birth rates and diminishing food security, it is important to appreciate the following. Poor smallholders who till land in the most ecologically fragile regions need to maintain high fertility levels. This satisfies the labour demand for maintaining household subsistence on lands with diminishing returns. Clearly, this is a result of unsustainable farming practices as well as a lack of capital to invest in labour-saving or productivity-increasing technologies. The net result is increasing populations to provide for the needs of families and communities.

The increasing population in turn increases pressure on the use of a nation's natural resources. There is an increased demand for fuel-wood, which leads to forest degradation with its attendant problems. In addition, high population growth puts pressure on the land by reducing fallow periods under the shifting cultivation system, hence decreasing soil fertility and depressing crop yields. The decrease in fallow reduces the availability of pastures and leads to overgrazing, which has a direct consequence on soil erosion.

In urban areas, the rapid increase in population and the inadequate development of urban infrastructure has also led to pollution and degradation of the urban environment. This in turn leads to pollution-related health hazards, especially those arising from air and water pollution.

ECONOMIC ACTIVITIES

Pressure on the environment is resulting in declining crop yields and overgrazing. Fuel-wood needs are met by attacking the forests – cutting down trees for firewood and charcoal. Other traditional practices are sand and gravel mining, small-scale mining of precious metals, popularly named 'Gallamsay' (literally 'get them for sale'), bushfires, inappropriate farming practices and agro-chemical application. The resultant key environmental problems of priority concern in Ghana, which have been identified at the local level, include air and water pollution, deforestation and land degradation, loss of biological diversity and drought.

Other significant impacts include both the degradation of soils through erosion and the loss of structure and fertility, and degradation of vegetation through deforestation and overuse. The two problems are interrelated and represent the most serious environmental problems facing the country in terms of their economic impact and the area and number of people they affect.

One major environmental problem relates to water abstraction from streams, rivers, most reservoirs and underground water. Generally, water has been treated as a free good over the years. Water use had, therefore, been virtually unregulated so there was little, if any, effort to conserve this resource. With the establishment of the Water Resources Commission in 1998, arrangements have been put in place to promote conservation of water. The full economic costs of water have not been brought into play because of the social importance associated with the commodity. The emphasis, however, has been on promoting the sustainable management of the country's water resources. Despite these arrangements, the poor tend to pay more for the water they use compared to the rich in the society.

Deforestation and reduction in vegetative cover, coupled with cultivation and mining close to river and stream banks, have significant impacts on run off and stream flow with marked seasonal extremes. Such streams and rivers can become totally dried up during the dry season.

Large-scale surface mining began in Ghana around 1986. Since then there have been significant numbers of surface mines established in the country. The environmental impacts of these mines are very serious in comparison to underground mining. Recent occurrences at some mining centres in the country have shown that communities in mining areas are becoming increasingly concerned about the impacts of surface mining. The key environmental problems include:

- Dust and noise pollution.
- Pollution of water bodies.
- Insufficient potable water from boreholes for resettlement communities, especially during dry weather periods.

URBAN POOR

Most individuals of the rural–urban migration resettle along the coastal zone of the country, resulting in many of these areas becoming very densely populated. About 60 per cent of Ghana's large-scale industrial establishments are located in the Accra-Tema areas. There is only a limited capacity to cope with the human and industrial wastes generated in these areas. Improper disposal of these wastes constitutes a threat to the fragile coastal ecosystems. Most of these settlements are made up of the urban poor.

These factors, combined with uncontrolled discharge of domestic and industrial waste, impact on water quality and supply, and pose significant threats to human health in these areas. Water-borne and water-related diseases such as typhoid, diarrhoea, dysentery, cholera, malaria, guinea worm, schistosomiasis and onchocerciasis are quite predominant in these areas.

Exploitation of coastal area resources also impacts on the coastal zone, most obviously through the demand for fuel-wood for artesian fish-smoking enterprises; this has led to extensive felling of trees in and beyond the coastal zone. Urban fuel-wood demand has also encouraged the urban poor to engage in tree felling in the coastal zone.

GENDER

In many parts of sub-Saharan Africa, women represent approximately 60 per cent of the labour force in some sectors, grow about 80 per cent of the food, and yet earn 10 per cent of the income and own about 1 per cent of the assets. Extreme poverty is highest among women. This economic pressure on women forces them to be the major degraders of the environment.

As the primary food producers in the developing world, women have a stake in the preservation of the environment and in environmental sustainable development. However, because of their lack of access to agricultural resources, women farmers who try to eke out an existence on marginal lands often have no choice but to contribute to their further degradation. Lack of access to credit limits the ability to purchase less environmentally damaging technologies. This sets up a cycle of declining productivity and increasing environmental degradation.

STATUS OF FOREST RESOURCES AND RECENT DEVELOPMENTS IN FOREST CONDITIONS: THE GLOBAL TREND

The area of the world's forests, including natural forest plantations, was estimated to be 3454 million hectares in 1995, or about one fourth of the land area of the earth. About 55 per cent of the world's forests are located in developing countries, where poverty is a major problem. Only about 3 per cent of the world's forests are forest plantations. The remaining 97 per cent are natural or semi-natural forests.

Data published in the *State of the World's Forests, 1997* (FAO, 1997) provides a picture of the trends in forest cover over a 15-year interval (1980–1995) and makes a comparison between the 1980–1990 and 1990–1995 periods. Between 1980 and 1995, the extent of the world's forests (including both natural forests and forest plantations) decreased by some 180 million hectares. There was a net increase of 20 million hectares in developed countries but a net loss of 200 million hectares in developing nations, primarily due to poverty.

Between 1990 and 1995, there was an estimated net loss of 56.3 million hectares of forest worldwide. This represented a decrease of 65.1 million hectares in developing countries and an increase of 8.8 million hectares in developed countries. The estimate of forest cover change in natural forests of developing countries (which is where most deforestation is taking place) was an annual loss of 13.7 million hectares between 1990 and 1995, compared with 15.5 million hectares per year over the decade 1980–1990.

The major cause of the change in trend in forest cover in the tropics appears to be the expansion of subsistence agriculture in Africa and Asia and large economic development programmes involving resettlement and deforestation. Other significant causes are insect pests and disease, fire, overharvesting of industrial wood and fuelwood, poor harvesting practices, overgrazing and air pollution.

Globally, 1997 and 1998 were the worst years for worldwide fires in recent times.

SOLUTIONS TO POVERTY-RELATED ENVIRONMENTAL PROBLEMS

Environmental degradation can be minimized in areas of widespread poverty if accurate assessment of micro- and macro-level causes for degradation are made. Moreover, appropriate institutional measures must be taken to assist poor communities to enhance their resilience in the face of economic and environmental shocks and risks. This might include the provision of soft credits, particularly during extended periods of macro-economic change, or serious natural disasters and hazards, as well as the regular supply of cheap fuel and clean drinking water.

Other measures include the following:

- Drastic reduction in the distribution of permits to obtain land in forest areas, to both farmers and loggers.
- Reduction in the number of logging companies.
- Creation of incentives for logging companies to replant and protect their forest concessions by increasing the period of concession, with contracts requiring minimum replanting and conservation.
- Introduction of export duties and stumpage fees on timber production; this should discourage excessive cutting and exports and, while not eliminating them, set the levies so as to permit environmentally sustainable cutting.

- Expansion of national parks and development of tourist infra-structure in these parks.
- Development of industrial plantations as alternative sources of fuel-wood and lumber.
- Employment opportunities for the poor: the presence of jobless and underemployed people has a negative effect on the environment; these people represent the potentially productive group whose activities can easily degrade the environment within a very short period of time.
- Improving the conditions of women, which would undoubtedly release the pressure they exert on the environment.

This could be done in the following ways:

- Provide opportunities for women to improve their economic position through increasing their assets.
- Increase the productivity of their assets (for example, access to credit, agricultural extension services).
- Ensure more equitable treatment on the wage-earning segments of the labour market.
- Introduce more environmentally friendly income-generating activities which do not put substantial pressures on the environment.

WHICH ACTIONS ARE BEING TAKEN TO ADDRESS THE PROBLEM OF POVERTY?

Ghana's Vision 2020 provides the long-term (1996–2020) develop-ment framework and policy thrust of the country. This has the overriding objective of satisfying human needs and realizing the poten-tial of all members of the Ghanaian society. The long-term human development objectives are to improve the quality of life by expanding the opportunities and developing the capacity of all Ghanaians, and to provide for the special needs of the vulnerable by implementing poverty-targeted programmes and projects.

To address the problem, a National Poverty Reduction Programme (NPRP) has been put in place as a major government programme to reduce poverty in Ghana. The objectives of the programme are to:

- improve management;
- develop skills;
- make poverty-reducing techniques more available; and
- improve the position of women, the handicapped and girl-child education.

In the medium term, the goal of the programme is to make significant progress towards reduction of poverty through:

- enhancement of human capital (skills and managerial development); and
- increased opportunities for sustained income generation.

Actions have been put in place in the following areas between 1997–2000:

- Economic growth, employment and access to productive assets.
- Access to basic social services and safety nets.
- Food security and nutrition.
- Population management.
- Governance and decentralization.
- Addressing the needs of women.
- Institutional and coordination arrangement.
- Poverty indicators and monitoring.

In addition, other actions have been taken to address poverty, including:

- Institutional mechanisms for coordination of poverty-reduction programmes.
- Establishment of continuous poverty monitoring systems.
- Formulation of a new agriculture strategy.
- Formulation and harmonization of sectoral and district poverty-reduction programmes.
- Decentralization and participatory decision-making.
- Better policies for gender and environment to help poverty reduction.
- Relative poverty-reduction initiative.

A specific poverty-reduction programme, which is linked to the environment, is the Government of Ghana/International Fund for Agricultural Development Rural Enterprises Project. The programme focuses on the transitional zone of the country: the geographic zone between the northern savannah and the southern forest zones of the country. Through this project, efforts are being made to introduce good business practices and appropriate technologies to rural communities. Through these efforts, the income-generating capacities of rural populations have been improved. In addition, the introduction of alternative business opportunities has led to the acquisition of new skills. This has moved much of the rural populace away from its overdependence on the natural resource base to other income-generating activities. Employing appropriate technologies has also helped in the more efficient use of resources.

WHO BEARS THE ENVIRONMENTAL COSTS?

It is the poorer groups in society who generally bear most of the ill-health and other costs of environmental problems. They are the least able to afford good-quality housing in neighbourhoods with piped water, and adequate provision for sanitation, garbage collection, paved roads and drains.

The scale of the differentials between richer and poorer groups in their access to natural resources (from adequate supplies of freshwater, to safe land sites for their housing and open spaces suitable for children's play) is a revealing indicator of the level of equality within society. So too are the differentials in the scale and type of household waste generation from different income groups. Poorer households often separate glass, metals and paper from their wastes since these can be sold. Their vegetable wastes may go to feeding livestock; waste may also go to making composts where people have access to land on which food can grow.

In many communities, there is a strong correlation between indoor air quality and income because poorer groups use more polluting fuels and more inefficient stoves or open fires, which leads to worse indoor air quality. The fact that poorer groups also live in much more cramped and overcrowded conditions is obviously a clear indication that the transmission of infectious diseases among this group cannot be over-emphasized.

Many studies of the differentials in health status or infant mortality rates between city districts show conditions in poorer areas being much worse than in more wealthy areas (Bradley et al, 1991). Infant mortality rates are often four or more times higher in poorer areas than in richer areas. Large differentials between rich and poor are also common with regard to many environmentally related diseases, for instance, tuberculosis and typhoid.

THE FUTURE

Though it is appreciated that both the rich and the poor undertake activities which have adverse environmental impacts, in developing countries it is the poor whose activities need to be addressed as part of the process of promoting sustainable development. This should be addressed not through stand-alone projects: it is important that the total concept of sustainable development is used in all development projects. This will ensure that the economic status of the population is considered as programmes are put in place to ensure good environmental stewardship.

The rural enterprises project concept may be seen as the type of approach which developing countries will have to use in their efforts at addressing poverty. Purely environmental projects should be seen as only addressing one aspect of the poverty-environment cycle. Where the poor have been economically empowered to appreciate the value of the environment in which they live, they will ensure that the resources on which their livelihoods depend are adequately protected for the good of the whole society.

11

Financial Resources for the Transition to Sustainable Development

Barbara J Bramble

INTRODUCTION

This chapter asks the question: where will the financial resources come from to promote the transition to sustainable development, which is needed in both rich and poor nations? Rich nations need to restructure perverse subsidies, incentives and other aspects of their economies, using the 'polluter pays' principle and similar concepts, so as to maintain quality of life while reducing the ecological damage caused by consumption. Developing countries need financial assistance because they have to achieve many of the same efficiency gains as industrialized nations, while reducing poverty, providing education, clean water and health care to their citizens, improving regulatory and judicial systems and developing alternatives to economic dependence on exports of primary commodities. This is a tall order and not one that many countries can implement on their own.

However, instead of meeting these needs, which were articulated clearly during the Rio Earth Summit in 1992, most industrialized nations have reduced their commitment to international financial assistance. This chapter looks at the failed promise of the financial bargain made at Rio, the profound changes in the economic landscape since then, and the prospects for a new agreement that could move this now stagnant debate off dead centre.

THE WIDER CONTEXT: THE FERMENT OF THE 1990s

For much of the world, the decade of the 1990s brought major change, not least in the realm of economics and finance. With the end of the Cold War, and the dismantling of centrally planned and heavily statist economies, the certainties of life for millions of people broke down, ushering in a period of increased freedom paid for with insecurity, social disarray and what some have called 'predatory capitalism'. In the fast-growing newly industrializing countries, primarily in South-East Asia and Latin America, after years of economic growth the bubble burst, first in Mexico in 1995 and then in the frightening and contagious financial meltdown of 1997–1998, plunging back into poverty many millions of people who had only recently struggled out. Simultaneously, in Northern industrialized countries, the imperative to accommodate new competition from low wage producers has pitted factions in favour of streamlining social services and regulations, ending welfare, and downsizing corporate payrolls against those believing in the long-cherished role of the state in smoothing the rough edges of commerce.

During this decade, the pace of globalization accelerated, taking most people and nations by surprise. Electronic communications mushroomed, including networking among millions of individuals and non-governmental organizations (NGOs). All nations, but developing countries in particular, felt the international pressure accompanying the formation of new trade agreements to reduce tariff barriers and regulation of international investing. These forces, along with the rise of instant currency speculation, have encouraged the cross-border movement of people, money and jobs, which has weakened national barriers and national authority. The free exchange of capital, information and new ideas brings with it not only easy tax evasion, but also the increased vulnerability of almost all nations to outside pressure, reducing their ability to maintain domestic policies and values.

The decade has brought improvements in many measures of human welfare, including increased life expectancy; in 1997 almost 50 developing countries enjoyed an average life expectancy at birth of more than 70 years. UNDP reports that school enrolment and adult literacy each rose significantly and the share of the world population with access to safe water supplies nearly doubled, from 40 per cent to 72 per cent. But this progress was spotty, with some countries making little headway, and many of the former Eastern bloc countries reversed former progress, notably in life span. Today, poverty levels continue to stagnate, with nearly 1.3 billion people still living on less than US$1 a day. Both within and among nations, the averages mask a troubling increase in the gap between rich and poor. In the last decade, the share in global income of the richest fifth of the world's people reached 74 times that of the poorest fifth, up from 30 times in 1960, with the assets of the richest 200 individuals exceeding the combined income of 41 per cent of the world's people.[1]

The debt crisis of the 1980s continues to plague scores of developing countries because the partial solutions promoted in the 1989 Brady Plan, and the subsequent Trinidad, Naples and highly indebted poorer countries (HIPC) initiatives, never produced settlement of a significant proportion of the outstanding debt.[2] The majority of low-income countries still face year after year of debt overhang, which crowds out public expenditures for 'new'-looking priorities such as sustainable development. Many have a persistent net outflow in their balance of payments to the industrialized creditor nations and international funders. At the same time, many observers blame the structural adjustment requirements, including stringent budget caps and deflationary measures, along with rapid trade and capital liberalization, imposed over the last 15 years as part of debt workout deals for promoting anti-sustainable economic trends, such as reductions in government expenditures for social needs, increases in unemployment and consequent overreliance on exploiting fragile natural resources.[3]

The growing prominence of the Jubilee 2000 campaign for debt relief, and the recent announcement of the International Monetary Fund to emphasize poverty reduction in debt workout plans, perhaps finally will lead to real progress on debt relief.[4] But meanwhile, scores of countries have opened their economies prematurely without the necessary domestic regulatory, tax and legal structures in place, and before the crucial investments in human development, social services and infrastructure.[5]

The result is boom and bust investment, volatile capital flows and untold riches for some while ruin suddenly faces many more, as in the South-East Asian financial crisis of the late 1990s. In some societies, new computers are the birthday present of choice for children, and most families have several cellular phones and automobiles. In others, including almost a billion people who cannot meet their basic consumption requirements for food and shelter, the hope for a brighter future seems to be receding.

We as a world society seem to be replaying the free-for-all of the late 19th-century phase of industrialization. The winners, understandably, see this as the inevitable price of progress but the losers are frightened and angry.[6] During this decade, a reasonable consensus on what must be done to promote sustainable development was outlined in several landmark UN conferences, but the pace of economic change and the resultant uncertainty and fear have jeopardized that consensus.

RIO: THE FAILED COMMITMENT

In the preparations for the UN Conference on Environment and Development (UNCED) otherwise known as the Earth Summit (1992), the gulf between the positions of the G77, representing the developing nations, and that of most of the industrial countries was stark. Many Southern governments were expecting the negotiations to result in an increase in official development assistance (ODA) specifically to finance sustainable development. The UNCED secretariat was asked to prepare preliminary rough estimates of the costs to the developing countries of the transition to sustainability. It estimated that US$625 billion per year in total was required to implement Agenda 21 and, of that total, there was a requirement for US$125 billion to be transferred from developed to developing countries. In 1992 external aid then averaged less than US$60 billion per year, depending on the method of calculation – thus the implication was clear that more than a doubling of financial assistance would be required.[7,8] The required transfer, perhaps by coincidence, worked out to approximately 0.7 per cent of the GNP of industrialized countries – the target that most of them had agreed to in 1970 following the report of the Pearson Commission.[9]

During the negotiations in 1992 the G77 leadership frequently and ardently pressed their case for continuing the existing aid pipelines and priorities, with the new demands of Agenda 21 being financed from 'new and additional resources'. The industrialized countries were of mixed views, with several European nations accepting the need for substantial new and additional resources, and the US in the lead of those who felt that 'sustainable development' should be funded by shifting existing aid flows to more sustainable uses. Most European negotiators made considerable efforts to sound accommodating to the G77, whether or not they agreed with the US position, while the latter refused to make any new commitment to meet a development assistance target.[10] NGOs also have sought funding mechanisms that would make financial resources preferentially available to those official and non-governmental actors who were undertaking projects embodying the characteristics of sustainability and were democratically organized and managed. National environmental funds have since come into being in over a score of countries in response to this call. In the shadow of this dispute over financial assistance, Agenda 21 was negotiated as the broad outline of mutual national commitments and understandings for action and policy change to achieve sustainable development.[11]

In the end, a sort of subterfuge was adopted, embodied in principles 6, 7 and 9 of the Rio Declaration, and section 13 and 14 of Chapter 33 of Agenda 21. This language allowed all parties to read into the agreement what they wanted to see.[12] With this history of the negotiations, it was almost inevitable that expectations among the participants for future aid allocations from donor countries would be sharply divergent.

FINANCIAL FLOWS SINCE THE RIO EARTH SUMMIT

OFFICIAL DEVELOPMENT ASSISTANCE

With the end of the Cold War, the tacit public support in many Northern countries for aid as a form of anti-communist bribery has evaporated. And there seems inadequate interest in enhancing the development prospects of the world's poor, as a moral imperative. Thus the G77 nations feel that a promise for financial help was made and broken; leading spokesmen for nations of the South have warned against 'backtracking' and 'lack of political will'. At the same time, there are many new claimants to assistance. In 1992 the countries of eastern Europe and the former Soviet Union were not significant borrowers or donees, nor was South Africa, and since they were going through their historic changes during the preparatory process for Rio, many of them felt left out of the Earth Summit altogether. Furthermore, increased priorities for assistance to the Middle East can be envisioned with the peace process continuing.[13] These additional requests on a shrinking pie have contributed to the feeling that the industrialized countries are not serious about sustainable development. But the industrialized countries feel there were commitments made by all participants to adopt certain policy changes to promote sustainability, and to improve the use of existing financial resources, which are not being kept. As a result, there is a pervasive sense of betrayal among all parties.

BILATERAL

Looking back, it is ironic that 1992, the year of the UNCED negotiations, saw the high-water mark of development assistance, measured in constant dollars. Since then overall aid levels receded, and by 1997, when the UN General Assembly held a Special Session (UNGASS) to review the progress on implementation of the Rio accords, only four countries – Denmark, Sweden, Norway and The Netherlands – had met their 0.7 per cent of GNP target.[14] Bilateral development assistance from most OECD countries fell steadily, and was not fully compensated for by the additional US$4 billion from the Global Environment Facility (GEF) and increases in assistance from the EU.

For some countries, such as France and Germany, the declines continued in 1998. In France, where the government has committed itself to 'a high level of public aid', the percentage fell throughout the decade, from 0.63 per cent of GNP in 1992 to 0.41 per cent in 1998. Germany, where it had been hoped the new government would increase levels, aid remains below 0.3 per cent where it fell from the 1992 level of 0.39 per cent.[15]

Collectively, the OECD countries reduced their ODA to 0.22 per cent of GNP in 1997, falling from 0.33 in 1992.[16] But the 1997 UNGASS meeting may have been a turning point for some countries which are now reversing their decline in ODA: the UK pledges to reach 0.3 per cent by 2001 and then to increase again (up from 0.27 per cent in 1998); Ireland committed to reach 0.45 per cent by 2002 (up from 0.31 per cent in 1998); Norway committed to reach 1 per cent by 2001 (0.91 per cent in 1998); Portugal committed to reach 0.7 per cent by 2006 and is soon to reach 0.36 per cent (0.24 per cent in 1998); The Netherlands and Sweden have committed to continue giving approximately 0.8 per cent; and Denmark 1 per cent.[17] And most significantly, the US, which has averaged approximately 0.1 per cent of GNP for the last four years, raised its contribution by over 10 per cent in 1998.[18] Although it is too soon to know if this indeed portends a new trend, the OECD Development Assistance Committee reports a halt in the years of decline. In their 1999 report, they calculate a rise in combined ODA of almost 10 per cent in real terms, even though some of the largest volume donors have not yet reversed their negative trends.[19]

Aside from the debate over the amount, the effectiveness of aid remains controversial. The Development Assistance Committee of the OECD is still striving, after years of exhortations, to convince donor nations to improve the coordination among their multiple agencies that compete for the attention of hard-pressed local counterparts; it has also encouraged donors to end the 'ties' that even today often obligate recipients to use the funds to purchase products and services from the 'donor', instead of devoting them to locally determined priorities.[20] Moreover, there is very little information about whether, or how much of, development assistance is devoted to purposes that further Agenda 21. Statistics are not collected in many of the necessary categories, and a significant portion of technical cooperation is excluded from key compilations.[21]

MULTILATERAL

Disbursements from the multilateral development banks have held their own, but the future is clouded by US reluctance to negotiate its continuing share in these institutions. Moreover, much of this funding has been made available in the form of quick disbursing structural-adjustment loans, often in order to facilitate external debt repayments by the poorer countries (many of the loans were essentially accounting moves, which made a quick 'round trip' or never even left the financial centres in the North). The public financial institutions assisted payback of bad loans to many of the private banks, with the result that the World Bank, the IMF and the other international agencies now hold most of the outstanding debt of the highly indebted countries.[22]

PRIVATE AND COMMERCIAL FINANCIAL FLOWS

Since the Rio Summit, what has grown, instead of the expected ODA, has been direct foreign investment, commercial bank lending and bond lending. Over the last ten years, net flows from private and commercial sources of funding increased from approximately US$44 billion to over US$227 billion in 1998. This includes direct corporate investment from OECD countries, which grew from US$24.5 billion in 1990 to US$155 billion in 1998; commercial bank lending, which rose from US$16.3 billion in 1992 to US$60.1 billion in 1997, before falling back to US$25.1 billion, due to the financial crisis in South-East Asia; and bond lending, which rose from US$11.1 billion in 1992 to US$53.5 billion in 1996, then tumbling to US$30.2 billion in 1998, again because of the South-East Asian crisis.[23]

The increase in private-sector flows over this decade has been marked by surges and slow downs, as investors followed a herd instinct. Both the influx and the exodus of capital were sudden and extreme in many countries, and this volatility caused problems in both directions. The large inflows were concentrated in short-term debt, affecting exchange rates, reducing international competitiveness and inviting overextended lending.[24] The reversal of flows then wreaked havoc, not only with private-sector credit, but also with government revenues, development plans and social expenditures, as millions were thrown out of work.

Small and medium enterprises, which generate the majority of wage employment, are at a particular disadvantage in this economic climate. Although the Mexican and Asian financial crises are considered 'over' for the investors, evidence is mounting that the social costs for individuals and communities lasts for many years.[25]

Moreover, this growth in capital flows was unevenly distributed among the developing and transitional countries. More than 80 per cent of the direct corporate investments were made in less than 20 countries and almost none of them were made in the countries of sub-Saharan Africa.[26]

Looking specifically at the group of low-income countries, there has been an increase in total private flows from US$5 billion in 1992 to US$15.2 billion in 1998, though it only represents around 5 per cent of the flows of capital to emerging markets as a whole.[27]

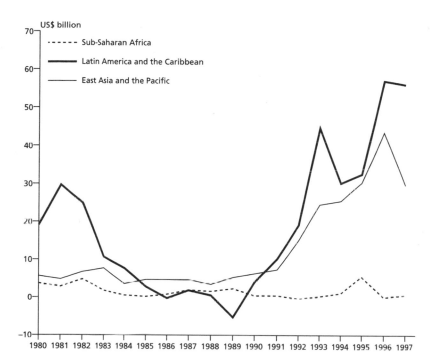

Source: UNDP (1999) Human Development Report, Figure 1.7, p41

Figure 11.1 *Volatility of Portfolio Flows in Selected Markets*

Crucially for the progress on sustainable development, there is no way to know whether any of this investment was made to promote the objectives of Agenda 21. This points to an obvious research agenda that could be pursued in preparation for the next major debates on finance in 2001 and 2002.

Unfortunately, much too late, quiet voices are emerging to say 'I told you so' that the scale and timing of this surge of investment, whether for privatization or new plants, and especially its volatility, have had perverse effects on the development prospects of many of the poorer nations.[28] It seems clear in hindsight that the majority of countries failed to take advantage of the investment to improve the lives of their citizens, and instead suffer gross increases in corruption and a widening gap between rich and poor, while their natural resource base is degraded, because of the very same factors that put them into the category of 'developing countries' to begin with. It is a commonplace for business leaders today to observe that respect for the rule of law, competent courts and the enforcement of contracts, transparency in procurement, as well as availability of basic infrastructure, are essential to attract foreign investment. In the former Eastern

Table 11.1 *Net private capital flows to low-income countries (US$ billions)*

	1990	1991	1992	1993	1994	1995	1996	1997	1998
Total private flows	3.5	4.9	5	11.2	13.1	11.3	14.6	17	15.2
International capital markets	2.4	1.8	1.8	6.3	7.6	4	5.3	6.4	4.7
Debt	2.3	1.8	1.4	4.2	0.5	1. 3	-0.4	4	4.3
Banks	2.2	0.4	1.6	3.7	0.4	1	-0.6	1.7	4.7
Bonds	0.1	1.4	-0.3	0.6	0.1	0. 3	0.2	2.3	-0.4
Portfolio equity flows	0.1	0	0.4	2.1	7.1	2. 7	5.7	2.4	0.4
Foreign direct investment	1.1	3.1	3..2	4.8	5.5	7. 3	9.3	10.6	10.6

Source: World Bank (1999) *Global Development Finance 1999*, Table 2.11, p37

bloc at least, it seems that it was a mistake to aggressively pursue privatization until these elements were in place. But these factors, essential for investors, are only part of the story. When these are missing, it is equally likely that the local economy and workers suffer from the failures on the other side of the institutional coin. Citizens need a government that monitors the safety of working conditions and enforces anti-pollution laws; that affords labour the right to organize and demand a living wage; that collects taxes from all, on a progressive scale; and that ensures basic health care, education, clean water and sanitation are provided to all citizens, so that the economic activity benefits the society as a whole. Under the best of circumstances, this institution-building agenda would be a work of many years. In the throes of the wildly fluctuating modern 'global casino' economy, it seems all but impossible for many nations.[29]

NGO FINANCE GOALS FOR THE UN SPECIAL SESSION (UNGASS) IN 1997

In order to advance beyond stalemate, and in preparation for the five-year review of progress since the 1992 UNCED, which many called Earth Summit II, a group of NGOs began to explore the many reasons behind the failure to fulfil the financial commitments made in Rio. In 1996 and 1997, NGOs sponsored a series of dialogues in which representatives of Northern and Southern governments and social groups participated; these dialogues revealed the sense of frustration and betrayal described earlier in this paper.[30] Out of these dialogues, NGOs distilled a proposal that the CSD establish an Intergovernmental Panel on Financing for Sustainable Development that would explore a specific list of issues and report back to the CSD in 2000. This was one plank of the major finance issues that environment and development NGOs prioritized in their position paper Towards Earth Summit II.[31] The NGO proposal outlined several purposes of the panel including the following:

• Identify those costs of the transition to sustainable development that are best financed by external assistance and how best to focus scarce development assistance funds.
• Analyse and formulate recommendations on options for new sources of funds and new mechanisms for delivering finance for sustainable development, such as micro-credit and national environmental foundations.
• Review the implications for sustainable development of corporate international investment, currency speculation, privatization, structural adjustment and debt.

The concept for the panel was modelled on the Intergovernmental Panel on Forests, and its intent was to support the Southern countries' call for increased development assistance, while pushing for sustainability reforms and public accountability in both national and international financial institutions. The NGOs saw the panel as a way out of the stale 'ping-pong' game of diplomatic accusations, in which the Northern failure to provide increased aid was pitted against the Southern failure to undertake sufficient 'structural reforms', eliminate subsidies or collect more taxes. This finger-pointing argument had been bouncing back and forth for years between industrialized and developing countries without result. It was hoped the panel would be able to separate out the useful issues for resolution – such as to highlight the dangers, as well as the benefits, of foreign direct investment (FDI) and portfolio capital; and to facilitate a practical discussion of the techniques of domestic resource mobilization through such mechanisms as green taxes and user fees. Above all, the hope was for a serious and systematic review of potential new financial mechanisms and sources of funds for development assistance.

Not surprisingly, the panel proposal failed to be approved, essentially because of the enormous frustration felt by developing countries over the unfulfilled promise of 'new and additional financial resources' from 1992.[32] The demise of the panel proposal, part of the overall failure of the Special Session to make progress on financing for sustainable development, was a major factor contributing to the general disappointment in the whole UNGASS event.[33] However, the next year, the UN General Assembly decided to hold a high-level event on financing for development, scheduled for 2001, and some elements of the 1997 NGO concept remain alive in the agenda for this event.[34]

GOALS AND RECOMMENDATIONS FOR 2001 AND 2002

Major groups, including NGOs and businesses, as well as governments and international bodies, have the opportunity to prepare for two upcoming UN events which will highlight the issues presented in this chapter. In 2001, as noted above, the UN General Assembly will hold a high-level discussion on financing for development; and in 2002 the CSD will undertake a comprehensive review of progress since the Rio Earth Summit.[35] The latter will open up the question of the need for financing to assist developing countries in implementing Agenda 21 (including the whole sustainable development agenda) and will highlight the conspicuous failure of the industrialized nations so far to provide it. If a substantive accord on finance is to result from these events, progress must be made, starting in 2000, to clarify the steps needed to achieve Agenda 21.

The UN's Ad-hoc Open-ended Working Group on Financing for Development has identified five broad topics for these discussions:

1   domestic financial resources;
2   international resources: trade, FDI and other capital flows;
3   international financial cooperation for development, including ODA and debt relief;
4   enhancing coherence and consistency of the international monetary, financial and trading systems in support of development and avoidance of international financial crises and excessive financial volatility, and enhancing effective participation and integration of developing countries and countries in transition within the global economic system, including capacity-building;
5   special needs of Africa, least-developed countries (LDCs), small-island developing states (SIDS), land-locked developing countries and other developing countries with special difficulties in attracting financing for development.

These categories seem reasonable, and in fact may represent a genuine compromise. The Group of 77 has been reluctant over the years to discuss international resources, and the role of trade, FDI and other capital flows, in the context of financing sustainable development.

Similarly, the industrialized countries, led by the US, have been unwilling to admit to the downside of their open trading and investment ideology, and the special needs of disadvantaged countries, so that items 4 and 5 on the list have been off limits. Thus, this agenda by itself may be an advance in the discourse. The major missing element is the recognition that there is no guarantee that any of these flows will move countries in the right direction – that is, towards sustainable development.

While even optimists know it will be difficult to achieve agreement on significant new financial mechanisms, or pledges of large amounts of new and additional financial resources by 2002, it should nevertheless be possible to make progress on several fronts under the five items just listed as the agenda for the upcoming financing for development event.

INTERNATIONAL DEVELOPMENT COOPERATION: ODA AND DEBT RELIEF ESPECIALLY FOR DISADVANTAGED COUNTRIES

This will be the topic of greatest interest to developing countries. The high-level event of 2001 and the Earth Summit 2002 should concentrate attention on three aspects of this issue:

1 Delineate more clearly the specific role of the ODA, perhaps including a selection of two or three sectors as the highest priority for implementing concerted international action plans.
2 Complete the unfinished business of debt relief for the poorest countries.
3 Make progress on ways to raise additional dedicated sources of new and additional resources.

THE ROLE OF ODA

Progress on reversing the falling ODA contributions is more likely if the specific uses for the funds are clearly spelled out. There seems to be an emerging consensus that capacity-building is an essential role for ODA, especially for the government and civil society institutions necessary for nations to take part in the global economy.[36] But, of course, there are many other critical needs as well.

In the preparations for the 2001 and 2002 events, there is an opportunity for the recipient nations to clarify what kinds of capacity-building and other work they need, and which agencies and programmes are best suited to contribute to the effort. Some of the general categories are fairly obvious:

- building institutions to oversee delivery of health, education, fresh-water, sanitation, micro-credit and other services, especially for the poor;
- strengthening financial, taxation, health, safety and environmental regulatory systems, including monitoring, enforcement and other legal infrastructure;
- enhancement of mechanisms for channelling private-sector economic activity (including FDI) into areas of national priority;
- natural resources management expertise in such areas as forestry, agriculture and fisheries.

However, much more substantive information is needed to clarify this debate and to formulate recommendation for the 2001 and 2002 events.

RECOMMENDATION

The Ad-hoc Open-ended Working Group for the 2001 event and the CSD should commission substantive research on what kinds of programmes have actually delivered results that the recipients value; they should also prepare case studies of both successes and problems. In addition, there is a need to examine the results of recent efforts to improve coordination among donor programmes. The CSD should ensure that the preparations for Earth Summit 2002 incorporate and build upon this work for the ten-year review of Rio.

A more concrete step forward is proposed in a recent analysis of the ODA stalemate by Professor Morris Miller of the University of Ottawa. He advocates selection of two priority sectors, which would have a dramatic impact on the quality of life of billions of people, for implementation of major new international action plans.[37] These would be on the scale of the immunization initiatives of the World Health Organization (WHO) and the agriculture research and extension programmes of the Consultative Group on International Agricultural Research (CGIAR). Professor Miller recommends considering the following two sectors as appropriate for this scale of effort:

- communications technology – to make available equipment, related software and connections for modern communications technology adapted for poor communities; and
- energy technology – to develop low-cost modern energy technolo-gies that utilize local sources of energy in biomass, solar, wind, shallow gas deposits, and micro-hydro.[38]

The upcoming development finance negotiations in 2001 and 2002 could be focused on a very few high-priority sectors such as these, with the specific goal of enlisting the international community in a coordinated effort to adapt new technologies for widespread delivery and low-cost operation. In this way the often abstract topic of financial resources would be concentrated on developing an action plan with specific concrete components and associated costs, such as: establishing an international research and development capability and delivery mechanisms for the technologies; analysis of how to utilize existing agencies; estimates of costs and their allocation among international donors and recipients; the potential for international agreement on a 'bit' tax to help pay for the communications action plan (see 'New Sources of Financial Resources' overleaf); and the possible participation of private foundations, which were instrumental in the establishment of the CGIAR.

RECOMMENDATION

In the preparatory process for 2001 and 2002, governments should agree on two or three high-priority sectors, and conduct research on what kinds and amounts of ODA or FDI are being spent on these sectors now. The Ad-hoc Open-ended Working Group for the 2001 event should commission a review of the status of research and development in those sectors; flesh out a detailed action plan for a coordinated international-scale effort; and identify the scale of financial resources needed. By the end of 2002 the member governments of the CSD should adopt the international action plan and commit the financial resources to implement it.

RECOMMENDATION

The recent modest increase in ODA, reversing the downward trend of the 1990s, should be maintained, and commitments should be made by all OECD countries to future increases, in particular Japan, France, Germany and the US. NGOs in the US need to be more forthright about how little their government devotes to foreign assistance, since the US general public is not aware of the low level.

DEBT RELIEF

The Jubilee Campaign for debt forgiveness in the year 2000 has been partially successful, with the recent announcement of the new IMF poverty-oriented debt-relief facility and the G8 leaders' commitment last summer to enhanced bilateral debt forgiveness. But critics characterize the efforts as minimal actual debt reduction, requiring years to qualify, and with too much unrealistic structural reform as the prerequisite. NGOs will continue to call for faster, deeper and more realistic terms, and the 2001 and 2002 events will focus even more public attention and pressure on the failure to wipe the slate clean for at least the poorest nations.

RECOMMENDATION

Creditor nations and international financial institutions should arrange complete debt relief for the 52 poorest countries before or during the 2001–2002 negotiations.

NEW SOURCES OF FINANCIAL RESOURCES

Over the last ten years a number of innovative proposals have emerged to raise funds among the industrialized nations and wealthy publics to support increased assistance to countries that implement their own sustainable development action plans. At the last count, there were at least 30 different kinds of fees and taxes mentioned as possible candidates. Most of the proposals break down along the following lines:

- Dedicate a share of national fees or taxes on pollution or other activities related to sustainability (such as a carbon tax) to assist developing nations to solve a similar problem (eg the transition to renewable sources of energy).
- Use revenues from an international fee or charge which is established for an unrelated purpose. The most well-known and feasible example of this category would be a 'Tobin'-type fee, which is intended primarily to reduce dangerous volatility in the currency markets.[39]
- Through an international agreement, impose a fee for the exploitation of resources over which no nation currently has sovereignty (the global commons) – for example, deep-sea minerals, airspace used by civil aviation, or satellite parking rights.[40]

At the 1997 UN Special Session, the main 'new financial resource' that was discussed was an example of the first category above: the introduction of an air-fuel tax.[41] More recently, one of most intriguing new ideas for raising financial resources has been that of the 'bit' tax on internet communications, which has been brought to prominence by the UNDP's 1999 Human Development Report. This proposal is based on the realization that the Internet, the worldwide computer link-up, is 'the fastest-growing tool of communication ever', with the number of users expected to grow from 150 million today to more than 700 million in 2001, but with access extremely limited outside of the industrialized countries.[42] One way to help close the gap between the rich and poor in their access to the world of communications, and to finance the technology initiative mentioned above, is to charge a miniscule fee, amounting to only one US cent for 100 emails, but potentially raising significant revenue.[43]

RECOMMENDATION

The participating governments and major groups should analyse and negotiate the first steps towards the adoption of dedicated air-fuel and bit charges during the 2001 and 2002 processes.

DOMESTIC FINANCIAL RESOURCES

This will be the topic of most interest to many industrialized countries. Although this chapter and much of the debate over financing for sustainable development has primarily considered external financial flows, both public and private, it has always been true that even in the poorest countries the bulk of resources for development has always been derived from domestic economies. In fact, in recent years the combined total of ODA and FDI only provided about 15 per cent of the investment capital in developing countries.[44] Therefore, in this context, the phrase 'financing for sustainable development' can mean something very different than either ODA or FDI – instead, it might be seen to cover the whole subject of how an economic system (international as well as domestic) can be modified to give the right cost and price signals to enterprises, individuals and governments in order to promote sustainable behaviour.[45] Some of the methods of redesigning incentives which are already being developed, and which may become even more effective when they are undertaken more generally among many nations, include the following:

- charging fees and/or reducing subsidies for economic activity that cause ecological and social damage, both to pay for repairing the damage and to discourage the activity;
- charging fees to enterprises sufficient to cover the costs to society of reasonable regulatory systems, including research, monitoring and licensing as appropriate, and enforcing rules to protect humans and the environment;
- reducing fees and in some cases providing 'green subsidies' to activities that enhance human and environmental health, education and other aspects of sustainability.

If these incentives and cost signals all pull in a sustainable direction, nations can harness the engine of domestic private-sector activity to help pay for the necessary conversion to sustainability.[46] Many treatises have been written on the efficiencies that these changes would initiate, and that far from being disadvantageous they may enhance a nation's competitive edge. In addition, much study has been devoted to methods of ensuring that the process of making such changes would not harm disadvantaged groups, within or among nations.[47]

But this is the subject for another chapter. Suffice it to say that most countries are reluctant to be in the vanguard of the experiment, and even the richest nations are just learning some of the steps.[48] These changes in subsidies, taxes and fees cannot be effective without several basic domestic institutional prerequisites, such as competent and respected legal, regulatory, taxation and judicial systems; research, monitoring and enforcement bodies; and an active and engaged civil society to push for reform. Some of the newly industrializing nations may be ready to move in this direction as they analyse recent demonstrations of the benefits of fee-based approaches. But many among the poorer nations first have to build the requisite institutions, and that is a long, slow process which itself may require substantial external technical cooperation and assistance.

Even though not all countries are in a position to implement these techniques yet, the topic of generating domestic financial resources for sustainable development through environmental taxes, fees and incentive reforms fits well into the discussion of financing for sustainable development. Those countries that are ready to try out these techniques will benefit from learning of the successes and failures of some of the early experiments.

RECOMMENDATION

In the preparations for the 2001 and 2002 finance discussions, substantive research should be conducted on experience with the techniques discussed above, and case studies should be compiled to analyse the necessary conditions for success in order to provide meaningful information to national governments and civil society organizations.

INTERNATIONAL CAPITAL FLOWS: PROMOTING COHERENCE AND CONSISTENCY OF ECONOMIC SYSTEMS, INCLUDING EFFECTIVE PARTICIPATION OF DEVELOPING COUNTRIES

Among the topics on the agenda for the 2001 high-level event listed on page 144, item 4 sets out a number of issues related to the flaws that currently beset the international economic system, including periodic financial crises, dangerous volatility and excess export capacity, as exhibited in the recent South-East Asian 'meltdown'. This topic should be of interest to all countries, although the US and some other industrialized nations may pretend it is unnecessary. The presence of this set of issues on the agenda for 2001 raises the challenge of whether it is possible to regulate the international economic system to support society's aspirations of sustainable development, and to foster the participation of the developing nations and economies in transition.[49]

Perhaps it is time for the US and other industrialized nations to recognize how inappropriate is the tone of ideology, or theology if you will, that has characterized their belief in open trade and investment regimes to solve all ills. Missionary zeal is not useful to advance rational economic debate. If the upcoming finance discussions can result in a collective taking of a deep breath, and a calm assessment of the state of global monetary, trade and investment regimes, much progress can be made. The task before national governments is to assess and implement rules to harness the world economy for sustainable development (including social equity and environmental health), since 'capitalism, for all its wondrous creativity and wealth, has not yet found a way to clothe the poor and feed the hungry unless they can pay for it...the market cannot deliver certain values to people and must be governed by them.'[50]

This chapter will not attempt to summarize the accumulating evidence that governments have abdicated their essential role in the recent bout of accelerated globalization. But it appears that far from 'free' trade and investment capital flows, society needs a moderating force of concerted regulatory action by governments, with input from civil society groups, to balance the boundless and ruthless energies of capitalism. Suffice it to say that the entire 20th century has been a history of painful learning among some nations about how to tame the worst elements of industrialization, to reduce inequality and to ensure that society as a whole benefits from the results of private enterprise, not just a lucky few. If that effort is thrown away, as seemed likely in the latter decade of the past century, the rifts caused by fear and resentment, on the part of those that are marginalized, may one day engulf the world again as occurred in the 1930s and 1940s.

There is no short cut to development, and neither trade nor investment on their own will foster human institutions of competence and fairness, or ensure education and health care for those in need. Developing countries and economies in transition must build human and social capital, and this will take time. This is not a quick fix that can be undertaken on demand in order to attract and retain foreign investment capital.[51] On the other hand, volatile, unregulated 'boom-and-bust' global financial flows can make it almost impossible for countries to build the institutions they need, and to nurture steady improvement in living standards. There is no point in discussing how to raise or spend modest aid resources that are dwarfed by almost instantaneous currency fluctuations and drastic changes in commodity prices. Thus, any discussion of financing for development has to include an agreement among governments to return to their responsibility to ensure financial stability, not leaving it to the poorest people and nations to bear the brunt of 'the global casino'.

A useful starting place for the financing for development debate may be to admit that the forced opening of economies was probably too rapid for some countries, and may have gone too far for all – at least in the absence of well-functioning global regulatory institutions. In particular, there is no need to rush forward into new rounds of trade and investment negotiations until the parties have ensured that the developing countries are reaping the expected benefits from past agreements. Moreover, many developing countries were not able to fully participate in the previous rounds of negotiations, both because of the complexity of the subject matter and the restricted logistical arrangements of the negotiations. And the exclusion of civil society from the negotiation process must also be remedied before further talks are undertaken. Furthermore, there is no humane option for governments but to slow down the dizzying pace of further 'liberalization', until they regain control of the system, in order to ensure that reasonable rules are in place to protect against the excess of exuberance that comes with capitalism.[52] The utility of a 'Tobin' toll to discourage short-term, round-trip currency gambling is but one example of the innovations that are available for this purpose.[53]

RECOMMENDATION

The participants in the 2001 and 2002 finance discussions should begin a serious assessment of the options for reducing volatility and financial crises, beginning with some variant of the 'Tobin' toll. No further rounds of investment or trade liberalization talks should proceed until the expected benefits for developing countries of previous rounds are fully implemented, and more equitable participation in the negotiations is assured.

NOTES

1   UNDP (2000) 'Human Development Index' *Human Development Report 1999*, Oxford: Oxford University Press, Tables 4, 6, 7, 8, 10, 16; pp22, 36, 38

2   Morris Miller (1999) 'Beyond Aid: Cooperative Approaches to Achieve Effective International Programs for Poverty Alleviation', Paper for 49th Pugwash Conference: Confronting the Challenges of the 21st Century, Rustenberg, South Africa, September 1999, n11. Professor Jeffrey Sachs observed in a 12–13 June op-ed piece in *The International Herald Tribune* that 'the financial bankruptcy of the poorest countries has been evident for at least 15 years, but the IMF, the World Bank and the rich countries have delayed real solutions to this chronic problem'

3   Mohsin Khan (1990) 'The Macro-economic Effects of Fund Supported Adjustment Programs', IMF Staff Papers, vol 37, no 2, p222, cited in Michel Chossudovsky (1998) *The Globalization of Poverty: Impacts of*

IMF and World Bank Reforms, London: Zed Books, p69; Morris Miller (1995) 'Debt and the Environment: Converging Global Crises', New York: UN Publications; even *The Economist* admitted that 'structural adjustment has neither restored growth nor eased poverty' in 'Nothing to Lose but Your Chains', 1 May 1993

4   At the June 1999 meeting of the G8 heads of state, the key industrialized countries launched the Cologne Debt Initiative and committed themselves to additional debt relief for the poorest countries of up to US$100 million (G8 Final Communiqué). But many observers doubt this is more than another public relations effort. See Miller (1999) op cit Note 2, p8

5   UNDP (2000) op cit Note 1, see Figure 4.1, p85; Joseph Stiglitz (1999) (former chief economist of the World Bank) 'Who Will Guard the Guardians?' *Challenge*, November–December 1999, p61

6   See William Greider (1997) *One World, Ready or Not, the Manic Logic of Global Capitalism*, New York: Simon & Schuster for a full discussion of the risks inherent in failure to rein in the excesses of 'free-running' capitalism. Even George Soros warns of serious deficiencies of the global capitalist system which must be corrected including, 'the uneven distribution of benefits, the instability of the financial system ... and the question of values and social cohesion': 'Toward a Global Open Society', *The Atlantic Monthly*, January 1998, p22

7   Development Cooperation – 1995 Report (1999) 'Total Net Resource Flows to Developing Countries', Paris: OECD, Table 1

8   In providing its estimate of financing needs for Agenda 21, the UNCED secretariat assigned approximate costs to the long list of major sector- and resource-based environment and development problems under discussion for the UN conference. See A Markandya (1994) 'Financing Sustainable Development Agenda 21,' Harvard. Harvard Institute for International Development, Harvard University. This was a different approach from that taken at the Cairo International Conference on Population and Development, where costs were assigned to a specific agreed-upon action plan with limited objectives

9   Lester Pearson et al (1969) *Partners in Development*, Report of the Commission on International Development, New York: Praeger

10   During and after this debate among the governments, a number of NGOs took a different tack. After several years of following the lending practices of multilateral development banks (MDBs) and some bilateral agencies, they knew that simply making additional financial resources available was not necessarily a solution. In fact, they had found that much MDB financing had serious adverse impacts on both poor people and the environment. They had been pushing for MDB reforms to emphasize the basic elements of sustainable development, even before the term was well understood:
  •   social equity and public participation in decision-making;
  •   broad-based economic improvement, with an emphasis on reducing poverty; and
  •   environmental health, for both people and ecosystems.
Throughout the UNCED negotiations and the later CSD sessions, the

NGOs pressed for public participation and transparency, and monitoring of all development assistance, with accountability to the supposed beneficiaries. They also recognized that debt relief, reduction of Northern trade barriers against products from the South, and innovative funding sources would prove more important than aid flows. See, for example, 'Informal NGO Paper on Financial Resources and Mechanisms' presented to the 1st Session of the CSD, 16 June 1993

11 Many of these agreed commitments were only briefly sketched in Agenda 21; they needed further articulation and specific action plans to bring them to implementation. Details on a number of the key subject areas were filled in during the simultaneous negotiations on the conventions on biological diversity, climate change and desertification, and in the subsequent UN conferences of the 1990s on population and development (Cairo, 1994), social development (Copenhagen, 1995), women and development (Beijing, 1995), and human settlements (Istanbul, 1996). These agreements in total comprise the 'sustainable development agenda'

12 See, for example, section 33.13, where nations agreed that 'developed countries reaffirm their commitments to reach the accepted United Nations target of 0.7 per cent of GNP for ODA and, to the extent that they have not yet achieved that target, agree to augment their aid programmes in order to reach that target as soon as possible'. The point to remember here is that the US had never made any commitment to reach that target, so they had no commitment to reaffirm. Beyond that they only agreed to try to reach that target as soon as possible, which is no more than business as usual. European countries, many of whom had made the commitment to reach the 0.7 per cent target over the years, faced a more difficult ethical dilemma

13 Nineteen nations reached agreement in 1996 to establish a new Middle East and North Africa Development Bank

14 OECD Development Assistance Committee (1999) *Development Cooperation – 1998 Report*, Paris: OECD

15 Ibid

16 Ibid

17 Reality of Aid Management Group (1999) 'World Aid at a Glance', in J Randel, A German and D Ewing (eds) *The Reality of Aid 2000*, London: Earthscan Publications Ltd, pp3–6

18 Ibid

19 *Development Cooperation – 1998 Report* (2000) Paris: OECD

20 Ibid

21 'Official Development Assistance Data', Review of the DAC Statistics, Reporting on the Purpose of Aid, OECD Development Assistance Committee Working Party on Statistical Problems, Paris: OECD, 1996

22 In the process of debt restructuring negotiations, the multilateral creditors required the imposition of a series of macro-economic 'reforms' aimed at creating new markets for the industrialized nations, whose capital-based voting shares dominate the bank and the fund. These included the precipitous opening up of fragile economies to foreign trade and to volatile foreign investment, before the establishment of the

necessary regulatory and social institutions; in addition, adjustment pressure, especially from the IMF in the 1980s, often resulted in the reduction of the very education, health, environmental and other social investments that are needed to prepare for participation in the global economy. See Giovanni Andrea Cornia, Richard Jolly and Frances Stewart (1987) *Adjustment with a Human Face, Protecting the Vulnerable and Promoting Growth*, volume I, Oxford: Clarendon Press. These measures have had perverse effects on the future prospects of many developing countries, and their citizens are too poor to serve the hoped-for role as buyers of Northern products. Greider (1997) op cit Note 6, p49. In its new emphasis on poverty reduction as an explicit goal of debt reduction, the IMF seems to have finally heeded 15 years of outcry by civil groups, UN agencies and even the World Bank against its earlier approach

23   World Bank (2000) *Global Development Finance, 1999*, Washington, DC: The World Bank, Table 1

24   UNCTAD (1998) *Trade and Development Report 1998*, New York and Geneva: UNCTAD

25   UNDP (2000) op cit Note 1, p40

26   Those countries include Argentina, Brazil, Chile, Mexico, Venezuela, China, Hong Kong, India, Indonesia, Korea, Malaysia, Singapore, Taiwan, Thailand, Hungary, Poland and Russia. *World Development Indicators*, 1999, Washington, DC: The World Bank, CD-ROM; and UNDP (2000) op cit Note 1, p 27

27   Humberto Campodonico (1999) 'The Context of International Development Cooperation', in J Randel, A German and D Ewing (eds) *The Reality of Aid 2000*, London: Earthscan Publications Ltd, p9

28   Stiglitz (999) op cit Note 5; Greider (1997) op cit Note 6; UNDP (2000) op cit Note 1

29   However, developing nations face not only their own vast gulf of development needs but also a global economic milieu of wildly shifting interest and exchange rates, inexorably deteriorating prices for primary commodities and continued protectionist barriers in the industrialized countries against many of their key exports. Their task is equivalent to running up the down escalator, and not many can be successful. See Miller (1999) op cit Note 2, p18

30   See 'Financing Sustainable Development into the 21st Century', summary of a series of NGO-government panel discussions at the UN CSD, sponsored by UNED-UK and National Wildlife Federation of the US, under the auspices of the CSD NGO Steering Committee (1996–1997, in manuscript)

31   Among other matters, NGOs called for:
   • an overall increase in funding for ODA, and the creation of new revenue sources such as an international aviation fuel charge, along with redesign of aid and private finance to support sustainability;
   • specific recognition of countries' rights to regulate investment, and obligation to reform taxation, eliminate perverse subsidies and focus budgets, all aimed at the goals of sustainability;
   • establishment of a stronger global regulatory framework for international capital flows, particularly speculative financial transactions, to

curb cross-border tax evasion and to ensure that corporations, including transnationals, comply with national codes, and international law; see 'Towards Earth Summit II', NGO Steering Committee for CSD, New York, March 1997

32   The proposal for the panel was supported by the US and Norway and eventually by the European Commission after a campaign in European capitals by NGOs. There was some support among key G77 countries, including at times Brazil and Malaysia. Ambassador Amorim of Brazil, who co-chaired the first Preparatory Committee meeting (PrepCom) for UNGASS, called for all countries to seriously consider the proposal put forward by the NGOs. However, Tanzania, whose ambassador was chairing the G77 at the time, was a key opponent. The ambassador instead renewed the old call for simply increasing aid levels to meet the 0.7 per cent Rio commitment, saying that all that is lacking is 'political will that starts with the grassroots people of the North and works up to the politicians and political agencies...A panel on finance will not provide political will, only more bureaucracy', *Earth Summit II – Outcomes and Analysis*, 1998, London: Earthscan Publications Ltd, p55. Tanzania, with the eventual support of China and India, was able to defeat the establishment of the panel during the UN Special Session, and again later that year at the UN Economic and Social Council

33   Undersecretary-General Nitin Desai later summed up the conference: 'The Special Session did not result in any major breakthroughs. It did not fully meet the expectations of developing countries which had hoped for new commitments and initiatives from developed countries, particularly regarding the provision of new and additional financial resources', *Earth Summit II – Outcomes and Analysis, 1998*, London: Earthscan Publications Ltd, 'Foreword', px

34   See General Assembly Resolution 179, A/RES/52/179, 14 January 1998. The UN General Assembly further agreed that: 'The high level intergovernmental event for the year 2001 will address national, intergovernmental and systemic issues relating to financing for development in a holistic manner in the context of globalization and interdependence...Within this context, the event should address the mobilization of financial resources for the full implementation of the outcomes of major conferences and summits organized during the 1990s by the United Nations and of the agenda for development and in particular for poverty eradication.'

35   This review is starting to be dubbed 'Earth Summit 2002'

36   Even the US has recognized that it must contribute to this capacity-building effort – at least in the narrow context of assistance for institution-building efforts related to attracting and keeping foreign investment. It is increasingly apparent that the resistance to its 'open economy' agenda has been growing because so many countries are not in a position to benefit from the process of liberalization

37   Miller (1999) op cit Note 2, p17. Professor Miller was an executive director for Canada on the board of the World Bank in the 1980s

38   Another critical sector that could be added to this list is freshwater supply, which over the next decades will see a growing conflict among

human uses and between human use and maintaining ecological balance

39   Professor James Tobin recognized over 20 years ago that it would be necessary to slow down the furious pace of speculation on currency exchange rates after they were freed from the gold standard in the early 1970s. He proposed that governments impose a tiny exit-and-entry fee to be charged at the major foreign exchange centres, which would not discourage productive investment but would throw 'sand in the wheels' of the huge daily cross-border capital flows and reduce instability in currency values. The logistics and consequences of imposing such a toll have been debated for years; a recent variant of the proposal would set up a two-tiered fee to reduce the levy on longer-term investments. Several investigators of this concept have proposed to dedicate at least part of the revenues to support the UN sustainable development agenda, particularly in developing countries. See Mahbub ul Haq, Inge Kaul and Isabelle Grundberg (eds) (1996) *The Tobin Tax: Coping with Financial Volatility*, Oxford: Oxford University Press; *Futures: The Journal of Forecasting, Planning and Policy*, Special Issue: the United Nations at Fifty – Policy and Financing Alternatives, vol 27, no 2, March 1995; David Felix (1995) 'The Tobin Tax Proposal: Background, Issues and Prospects', UNDP Policy Paper

40   All of these proposals raise a host of questions, including the following. Does the tax or fee promote sustainable development itself? Does it further distort appropriate market incentives or does it correct for market imperfections? Are its distributive effects neutral, or could it be deliberately slanted to benefit a particular group? Could it be easy and cheap to collect, and hard to evade? Who would benefit, who would lose out, who would oppose it and how could agreement be reached? Are there any legal barriers in existing treaties or new instruments needed? What might be the yield from imposing the fee and what objectives or organizations might lay claim to the revenue? See Overseas Development Institute (1996) 'New Sources of Finance for Development', Briefing Paper, London, February 1996. Among these, the biggest stumbling block at present is that any such solution would require the agreement of all the members of the UN. With the conservative US Congress challenging the nation's participation in the UN on many fronts, the prospects for agreement on an international fee or tax at this time seem slim indeed. If this remains true after the 2000 elections, then two possible options remain for the foreseeable future: another attempt to persuade the EU to go it along on the air-fuel tax, and working with the Internet companies for voluntary introduction of a bit charge

41   In the 1997 UNGASS, many Northern NGOs campaigned for a global tax on aviation fuel, proposing that the revenue be dedicated to ODA for sustainable development. When it became clear that it would not gain support from either the US or Japan, or even some key developing countries, European NGOs lobbied for the EU to go it alone and introduce the tax within their own boundaries. In the end, there was insufficient time to create the political momentum to deliver this at UNGASS, but it remains a priority goal of many European NGOs

42   The 'network society is creating parallel communications systems: one for those with income, education and – literally – connections ... the other for those without connections, blocked by high barriers of time, cost and uncertainty and dependent on outdated information ... threatening greater marginalization of those left out and left behind', UNDP *Human Development Report 1999*, pp58, 63

43   In Belgium, such a tax would have yielded US$10 billion on the volume of email traffic in 1998, and globally the tax would have yielded US$70 billion in 1996 – more than total of ODA that year. Ibid, p6

44   Miller (1999) op cit Note 2, p6

45   It is well to remember that all countries must change their economic policies to achieve sustainability; this is not a task that should fall disproportionately on developing countries. In fact, to curb excessive use and abuse of natural resources in their processes of production and consumption, and the waste inherent in their economies which were designed before the understanding of sustainability emerged, it is the industrialized countries who have the greatest responsibility to reshape economic incentives to promote behaviour change and who may have the harder time making the necessary shift

46   In fact, with proper encouragement, including the implementation of the 'pollutor pays' principle, the great majority of funds needed for investment in clean industrial technologies; energy, water and sanitation services; housing and improved mass transit; and sustainable agriculture, soil conservation and wetlands rehabilitation can come from private landowners and investors. This can be accomplished either through requirements imposed by regulation, such as pollution emission limits, through targeted financial incentives, such as favourable interest rates, tax credits, speedy permit procedures, or tradable permit systems, or through a mixture of these approaches

47   Robert Costanza, John H Cumberland, Herman E Daly, Robert Goodland and Richard B Norgaard (1997) *An Introduction to Ecological Economics*, Boca Raton, FL: CRC Press – St Lucie Press; Glenn Jenkins, Ranit Lamech (1994) *Green Taxes and Incentive Policies: An International Perspective*, San Francisco: ICS Press; Theodore Panayotou (1993) *Green Markets: The Economics of Sustainable Development*, San Francisco: ICS Press; Robert Repetto, Roger C Dower, Robin Jenkins, Jacqueline Geoghegan (1992) *Green Fees:How a Tax Shift Can Work for the Environment and the Economy*, Washington, DC: World Resources Institute; David Malin Roodman (1997) *Getting the Signal Right: Tax Reform to Protect the Environment and the Economy*, Worldwatch Paper 134, Washington, DC: Worldwatch Institute; Ernst U Weizsacker, Jochen Jesinghaus (1992) *Ecological Tax Reform: A Policy Proposal for Sustainable Development*, London and New Jersey: Zed Books

48   The problem in implementation, in both North and South, is to surmount the short-term political 'hump', when interest groups object to changes in the current order. Financial resources may be needed to cushion the distributional costs which vulnerable groups face during the conversion. For all countries, there are significant start-up costs in the form of changes in regulatory and enforcement systems, and providing adequate information and credit to overcome initial investor reluctance

49 As William Greider logically points out: 'The standard claim of the global financiers – that governments are impotent to regulate their behaviour – is always quickly put aside when a large crisis like Mexico's collapse develops. Then the national governments are expected to step in and provide the funds and regulatory supervision to clean up the mess...Global capital that needs the protection of the nation-state needs to learn to live by its rules and obligations.' Greider (1997) op cit Note 6, p318

50 Ibid, pp468–469

51 There is unlikely to be any reasonably attainable level of financial transparency or 'good behaviour' sufficient to inspire investor confidence that most developing nations can aspire to, given that the UK was successfully forced by currency speculation to devalue the pound sterling in 1992

52 The minimum objective would be to ensure that there is an economic climate conducive to the sustainable development of the poorer nations. It may be required to go even farther in order 'to bias the global economic/financial system to make its operations especially congenial for the developing countries'. This would be equivalent to a 'structural adjustment for the global economy' and would require support by the donor community for measures to lower real interest rates, dampen the volatility of interest and exchange rates, open up the industrialized countries to the exports important to the developing nations, and tap new sources of funds for sustained ODA. See Miller (1999) op cit Note 2, pp2–3, 18–26

53 See Note 39

12

Trade, Investment and Sustainable Development

Andrew Simms

'[There was] a planet in another galaxy, where the little green people ... could get food only if they could sell goods or services to somebody else. The planet ran out of customers, and nobody could think of anything to do about that. All the little green people starved to death.'
Kurt Vonnegut, Timequake

'The predicted gains to developing countries from the Uruguay round have proved to be exaggerated...Income and welfare gaps between and within countries have widened further... the world economy is deeply divided and unstable... Asymmetries and biases in the global system against the poor and underprivileged persist unchecked.'
UNCTAD, Trade and Development Report 1999

INTRODUCTION

Once, it was assumed that the way to tackle poverty was with charity. But, as aid from rich to poor countries has dwindled, many people have turned to the private sector in the hope that it will help deliver sustainable development and contribute to meeting international poverty reduction targets. However, huge expectations have been created without proper assessment of the problems. Poor countries especially face difficult terms for international trade and problematic relations with multinational enterprises. Investment, though eagerly sought, can create harmful volatility. At the same time, there is upheaval among the major, big business players in the global economy. Public opinion is forcing such corporations to address why there is a lack of trust surrounding their activities. This chapter looks at some of the structural problems that get in the way of poor countries benefiting from trade and investment. It should be read in accompaniment with Chapter 13, which looks at the agenda businesses are grappling with to improve their environmental and social responsibility and, as a result, to build public confidence in what they do.

Not As I Do... Hypocrisy and the Global Economy: A Tale of Trade and Investment

Trade liberalization: a shark swims up to a fish and says: 'You can take a bite out of me if I can take a bite out of you.' There is a 'dirty little secret' in the analysis of international trade according to the leading trade economist Paul Krugman. Though an advocate of free trade, he says that the costs of protectionism 'are not all that large', while the 'empirical evidence' of great benefits from liberalization 'is at best fuzzy'.[1]

The question has never been whether or not to trade, but how and to what end. Now that there are several internationally agreed development and poverty reduction targets, it is clearer than ever that economic activity should not be an end in itself but a means to an end.

The most important question, then, becomes: under what circumstances will trade and investment maximize social benefits where they are most needed, and will they preserve and enhance the environment we all depend upon? It is an enquiry that leads more into the dense undergrowth of power and politics than into the abstract world of economic theory.

The current official consensus ranging from the US Treasury Secretary to the UK's International Development Secretary is that nothing should get in the way of trade liberalization and extended WTO authority over a growing list of issues.[2] In the aftermath of the WTO's chaotic Seattle meeting *The Economist* magazine's front cover neatly expressed the latest favoured argument of ardent free-traders, showing rag-wearing hungry children beneath the caption 'The real losers from Seattle'.[3]

Yet, it is well known, if rarely acknowledged, that the big business lobby for trade liberalization is more interested in removing barriers to its control and manipulation of markets, than it is in removing barriers which will expose it to more vigorous competition.

'WTO obligations reflect little concern for development and little appreciation of the capacities the least-developed countries have', was the conclusion of the World Bank's head of trade policy. He added that: 'The context of the obligations imposed by the World Trade Organization agreements... can be characterized as the advanced countries saying to the others: do it my way.'[4] Many poor countries have seen no real liberalization in the markets most important to them: those of industrialised countries. Separately, where liberalization has occurred, its effects on poor countries have been at best hard to predict, and at worst clearly negative.[5]

So, can further liberalization deliver sustainable development and the internationally agreed poverty-reduction targets focused on the year 2015?[6]

As existing trade rules are removed and new ones written that will lever more countries into the global economy, where those countries start is likely to determine where they finish. Once a pecking order is established, only upheaval and special circumstances will tend to change it. If anything, the progressive liberalization of the last few decades has entrenched and ossified the international economic hierarchy. Since the 1960s, the income gap between the richest and poorest fifth of the world's population has grown from a ratio of 30:1 to over 70:1.[7]

Benefits from the last Uruguay round of trade talks were, and continue to be, highly unevenly distributed. Industrialized countries are expected to account for, and profit from, 70 per cent of increased trade over a ten-year period. The 48 least-developed countries, who account for only 0.4 per cent of world trade (approximately half their level 20 years ago), are expected to be worse off – in the case of sub-Saharan Africa, by up to US$1.2 billion a year.[8]

There are good and well-understood reasons why this situation came about. So why are these reasons not properly addressed by the dominant trading nations who are trying to justify accelerated trade liberalization, stressing its universal economic and social benefits?

That the least-developed countries are doing so badly is not because they cannot compete due to innate weakness. The costs of protectionism to some domestic economies may not be all that large according to Krugman, but the collective protectionism of the industrialized countries towards developing countries is devastating.

In a great irony, rich countries, whose policy-makers urge poor countries to open their domestic markets and export their way to economic development, are responsible for denying those poor countries US$700 billion per year by maintaining trade barriers to their exports in low-tech industries alone.[9] In addition, the OECD group of industrialized countries subsidized their own farming to the tune of US$353 billion in 1998. At the same time, since the end of the cold war, instead of the promised peace dividend we have seen a peace deficit. The downturn in aid since 1992 left aid giving by the OECD US$21 billion below what it should have been in 1998 if previous trends had continued. Even the OECD admit that if more donors had met the UN aid target of 0.7 per cent of GNP, 'the mass poverty and humanitarian emergencies which persist in many parts of developing world today might have been largely avoided.'[10]

'The hypocrisy is there. We all know how subsidies have helped the agriculture of these giants: yet having used them to develop their exports, they turn round and say subsidies are bad,' said Kofi Larbi, the trade lawyer responsible for preparing Ghana's position for the Seattle 1999 meeting of the WTO.[11]

Former chief economist at the World Bank, Joseph Stiglitz, declared that poor countries are being left with 'neither trade nor aid', and that 'it is not surprising that critics of liberalization... raise cries of hypocrisy'.[12]

There is a sense that, not only are rich countries pulling up the ladder, they are also mocking poor countries from their comfortable heights. According to Stiglitz, rich countries play down political problems faced by developing countries telling them to 'face up to hard choices' – but then excuse their own trade barriers and agricultural subsidies by citing 'political pressures'. And it is not only political problems that poor countries face, including high unemployment and 'weak or non-existent safety nets', but also greater economic volatility; and that 'opening to trade in fact contributes to that volatility'.[13]

Like all legal systems the WTO is biased in favour of those who can afford to play it. Developed countries have around seven people each in their trade delegations in Geneva at the organization's head offices, not including bought-in legal advice. Thirty poor members of the WTO, including 19 from Africa, have no permanent trade representative.[14]

Consequently, they cannot properly participate in negotiations and protect their countries' interests when trade rules are set. The benefit of the so-called regulatory level playing field is also flawed in its conception. Imagine the unequal outcome of, for example, the US being given permission to take retaliatory action against a small country such as Mozambique following a trade dispute, and the consequences for both countries if Mozambique took action against the US.

The lack of legal and technical capacity is increasingly important as industrialized countries push to expand the range of issues covered by the WTO to include ever more of the normal daily functions of national government, from health and education to investment. During the last round of trade talks, where poor countries lacked capacity they were 'taken to the cleaners', according to one of the authors speaking at the British launch of the 1999 World Bank *World Development Report*.

Even before the list of trade-related issues grew potentially longer, the World Bank advised its own board in a confidential briefing for its 1999 annual meetings that 'multilateral negotiations have become increasingly complicated, making effective participation difficult for many low-income countries'.

The same briefing conceded that 'rapid liberalization' of the kind seen in central and eastern Europe, for example, 'may create adverse social impacts'. It also said that rich countries failed to 'implement the spirit of their obligations' and that the last round of trade talks created 'little sense of ownership' among developing countries. Given the scale and protracted nature of civil society criticism, it candidly admitted that problems faced by poor countries in implementing the GATT agreements were all along 'underestimated'.[15]

Changing the Balance of Power

To benefit from trade and investment, poor countries have to be able to strike positive deals with the global firms who dominate these activities.

Over two-thirds of world trade is controlled by a small number of mostly Northern-based multinational enterprises, and over one third is wholly contained within the conglomerates of individual global corporations. The concentration of economic power is growing, and trade and foreign direct investment are increasingly inseparable. UNCTAD says there is no simple answer to the question 'does trade lead to FDI, or FDI lead to trade'.[16]

The problems that poor countries face when negotiating with global firms echo the difficulties they face at the WTO. Rubens Ricupero, the head of UNCTAD, observed: 'The outcome of foreign direct investment depends significantly on how well the host economy bargains with international investors', but that 'the capacity of developing host countries to negotiate with TNCs is often limited'. Ricupero also stated that 'weak bargaining... can result in an unequal distribution of benefits or abuse of market power by TNCs'.[17]

Another sobering assessment comes from a comprehensive survey of 'empirical evidence' by economist and TNC analyst Richard E Caves. He concluded that 'no trustworthy conclusion' could be reached on the basis of available information on the contribution of TNCs to the economic development of the least-developed countries.[18]

While concrete evidence of benefits is missing, several definite problems are well known. They will need to be solved before the least-developed countries can rely on rich country-based TNCs to be the agents of their integration within the global economy.

Foreign direct investment (FDI) is generally considered the most benign form of capital flow, essential to development; yet its story is complex. Investors see poor countries as higher risk and therefore demand higher returns. This makes FDI expensive for regions such as sub-Saharan Africa. One scenario raises the spectre of a new generation debt crisis emerging in the shadow of growing foreign exchange liabilities.[19]

FDI also tends to focus more on technologically intensive sectors, which creates two problems. This is an area where the poorest countries are especially weak, and where rich countries and firms, through patents, control the vast proportion of intellectual property. Although rarely seen this way, property rights are also a right of exclusion. Food biotechnology is a clear example. Developed countries and their TNCs hold 97 per cent of all patents worldwide, granting monopoly powers.[20] As a result, poor countries tend either not to attract investment at all, or they attract investment, but under terms where most of the benefits return to the investor.

FDI is overwhelmingly in the form of mergers and acquisitions. Where these take the form of a simple change of ownership, UNCTAD says they can be of 'lesser developmental value' and that take-overs can 'lead to asset stripping'.

The experience of Asia stands testimony to the way in which large inflows of investment can become large outflows, leading to 'exchange rate volatility and discouraging productive investment'. FDI can also 'crowd out' local infant economic activity. The list goes on. Where TNCs 'seek to acquire created assets embodied in competitive host country firms', this can 'lead to a restructuring of these firms not necessarily beneficial for host countries'.

The gallery of obstacles to benefits from trade and investment is long and could go on to portray problems with emerging monopolies in the food industry, which *The Financial Times* said should be ringing 'alarm bells' in national capitals.[21] It could also show global restrictive business practices and tax evasion by multinational enterprises through transfer pricing. A poor country denied legitimate tax revenue, it should be noted, cannot invest in environmental protection, health and education.

While companies argue for new global laws on trade and investment liberalization to restrict the scope for government action, they insist that only voluntary codes and standards are needed for business.

A two-tier legal system has emerged which treats international treaties on environment and development as inferior to economic agreements. Only the WTO with its dispute mechanism backed by sanctions has real teeth. Its agreements and legal procedures contradict the precautionary principle enshrined in the 1992 Rio Declaration; undermine environmental agreements ranging from the Kyoto Protocol on Climate Change to the Convention on Biodiversity; and signal the end of governments' ability to actively promote development.[22]

The general public is often more in tune with these problems than politicians. In a poll by National Opinion Poll (NOP) for the New Economics Foundation just prior to the 1999 Seattle meeting of the WTO, people thought that poor countries got a bad deal when they traded with rich countries by a ratio of over four to one. On attitudes to transnational corporations, 84 per cent thought that they needed binding global rules to get them to stick to social and environmental standards.[23]

Trade and investment are only a means to an end, not an end in themselves as the obsession with liberalization suggests. The minimum necessary action for the future is to have full social and environment accounting of trade and investment in rich and poor countries. Instead of trying to make the world safe for trade and investment, we can shape trade and investment to meet our social and environmental needs. In this light, the WTO must be subordinated to the global obligations underlying the international development targets and multilateral environmental agreements.

We must ask questions. How will everyone benefit from the frenzy of economic activity we call globalization? How can it be sustainable? How can we concentrate and keep wealth, properly defined, where it is needed in poor communities? And how can we give those communities the control over their own lives they need to guarantee their well-being?

If we ask these questions we will stop being spellbound and prostrate before globalization and its false prophet: trinket technologies such as food biotechnology. Instead, we will see the need to design regulation for the global economy which will allow real democracy, real choice and local economies to flourish.

The core justification for trade liberalization is to maximize conventional economic growth. But economists now realize that the scale of growth beyond a certain point is 'ushering in a new era of "uneconomic growth" that impoverishes rather than enriches'.[24] Even the OECD has said that 'the negative scale effects of globalization may turn out to be very large, effectively swamping any positive...effects'.[25] Subsidiarity, the principle rediscovered in the 1970s by the economist EF Schumacher that activities are least harmful when they happen at the lowest possible level, takes on new importance today. It is a principle to guide trade and investment.

The train from the meeting in Marrakech, that concluded the Uruguay round of trade talks, to the WTO in Seattle did not stop in Rio, where the world agreed environmental objectives; Kyoto where it decided to tackle climate change, or Copenhagen where the world agreed to end poverty. It is time for the trade train to head for a new destination.

There is now an historic opportunity for the UN apparatus to move us beyond the current system of unbalanced, one-legged economic government and restore legitimacy to the way the global economy is managed.

From now on, to ensure that economic activity actually benefits the majority, concrete social and environmental objectives agreed under the sponsorship of the UN must not be subordinated to the abstract economic theories that steer the WTO. Progress on the biosafety protocol has set an important precedent.

In the build up to the tenth anniversary of the Rio Summit, if bodies such as UNCTAD can overcome past problems, they can begin a wide-ranging conversation aimed to fill the vacuum of regulation needed at the international level outside of the WTO, linking trade and investment to sustainable development.

The original Earth Summit led to a growing body of multilateral environmental agreements. Now is the time to set up legitimate global economic agreements and institutions of the kind we take for granted at the national level. Their role will be to hold corporations accountable and prevent the abuse of market power. There is now an opportunity to bring forward a global competition commission and international office for fair trading for example, with powers to act. Among many other missing pieces in the economic jigsaw is an international investment agreement to balance social, environmental and corporate priorities. These are the new directions in which the globalization engine can take us.

NOTES

1   Krugman, P (1995) 'Dutch Tulips and Emerging Markets', *Foreign Affairs* vol 72, no 4, July/August
2   Summers, L (1999) 'Personal view', *The Financial Times*, 29 November 1999; Short, C (1999) *Making the trade round work for the world's poor*, Department for International Development
3   *The Economist*, 11–17 December 1999
4   Finger, J M (head of trade policy, World Bank) and Schuler, P (1999) *Implementation of Uruguay Round Commitments: The Development Challenge*, Washington, DC: The World Bank
5   Woodward, D (1996) *Globalisation and Liberalisation: effects of international economic relations on poverty*, Geneva: UNCTAD
6   These include halving the proportion of people in absolute poverty and universal primary education by 2015, and all countries to have strategies for sustainable development in place by 2005

7   UNDP (2000) *Human Development Report 1999*, New York: UNDP
8   UNCTAD briefing, 9 July 1999; UNDP (1997) *Human Development Report 1997*, Oxford: Oxford University Press
9   UNCTAD (2000) *Trade and Development Report*, Geneva: UNCTAD
10   OECD Development Assistance Committee (2000) *The DAC Journal of Development Co-operation 1999 Report*, Geneva: OECD; 'Loaded against the poor – World Trade Organization', Position Paper, November 1999, Oxford: Oxfam
11   The *Financial Times* (1999) 'Little nations prepare to speak up before the goliaths of world trade', 19 November
12   Stiglitz, J E (1999) *Two Principles for the Next Round: Or, How to Bring Developing Countries in from the Cold*, Geneva: the World Bank
13   Ibid
14   More power to the World Trade Organisation? The international trade controversy, Panos Briefing, November 1999, London: Panos; Stiglitz (1999) op cit Note 12
15   IBRD, Office of the Vice-President and Secretary (1999) World Bank Support for Developing Countries on International Trade Issues, 25 August 25 1999
16   UNCTAD (1998) *World Investment Report 1998*, Geneva: UNCTAD
17   UNCTAD (1999) *World Investment Report 1999*, Overview, Geneva: UNCTAD
18   Caves, R E (1996) *Multinational Enterprise and Economic Analysis*, second edition, Cambridge: Cambridge University Press
19   Woodward, D (1997) *The Next Crisis? Direct and Portfolio Investment in Developing Countries*, EURODAD, mimeo
20   ActionAid UK (1999) *Trade-Related Intellectual Property Rights (TRIPS) and Farmers' Rights*, London: ActionAid UK
21   The *Financial Times* (1999) 'Seeds of a monopoly', 17 September
22   The WTO Ministerial Conference in Seattle: Implications for the Environment and Sustainable Development, WWF-UK Briefing, November 1999
23   Simms, A (1999) *Behind our Backs: Public opinion, international trade and the World Trade Organisation*, London: New Economics Foundation/NOP Solutions
24   Daly, H and Cobb, J (1998) in *International Environmental Law and Policy*, quoted in CIEL (1999) *WTO High-Level Symposium on Trade and Environment*, CIEL Briefing, March, Geneva: Centre for International Environmental Law
25   OECD (1997) *Economic Globalisation and the Environment*, OECD, quoted in CIEL (1999) op cit Note 24

13

Civil Society, Business and Sustainable Development: Regulating (almost) Without the Regulation

Rob Lake

WHAT INFLUENCES BUSINESS?

It is sometimes easy to forget in a discussion of trade, investment and sustainable development that trade and investment are actually carried out by private companies, not by governments or international organizations. Goods are bought and sold, and investment decisions made, by the private sector. A large proportion of global trade and investment is now accounted for by a small number of enormous multinational companies: 359 companies account for 40 per cent of world trade, and the world's largest 100 companies have revenues that exceed the gross domestic product (GDP) of 50 per cent of the world's countries.[1] If the huge economic power of these companies and the trade and investment flows they control are to be harnessed for sustainable development, it is vital to understand what influences multinational corporations.

International and national policy and law are of course important. They provide part of the strategic framework within which all business is conducted. It is essential that international agreements in areas such as the environment and labour standards are enforced at the national level, and that new agreements are put in place to ensure that companies operate within basic standards that will promote sustainable development. But the years since Rio have demonstrated vividly the importance and effectiveness of civil society as a 'non-regulatory regulator' of business. Governments find it difficult to make standards laid down by law and international agreements stick – sometimes because of a lack of political will under the influence of business, sometimes because of lack of resources and capacity to run the necessary institutions (such as factory and pollution inspectorates). Civil society is stepping into the breach, holding business to account for its performance in relation to international standards, and demonstrating that the public has expectations of companies and their role in society that extend far beyond the relatively unambitious standards of current legislation.

In 1997 Shell, one of the biggest companies in the world, was forced by public pressure to reverse its decision – which had been supported by the UK government – to dispose of the Brent Spar oil platform in the North Sea. The company has also been forced by an alliance of local communities and international NGOs – brought together by the 'CNN world' of virtually instantaneous international communication – radically to rethink its approach to its operations in the Niger Delta.

The fair trade movement in Northern countries has been steadily building consumer support for an approach to South–North trade that tips the balance of power in favour of disadvantaged Southern producers, guaranteeing fair prices and decent working conditions and creating new livelihood opportunities. When offered a choice, more and more consumers are showing a willingness to 'shop for sustainable development'. The Ethical Trading Initiative in the UK is bringing together companies, trades unions and NGOs to develop ways of achieving International Labour Organization (ILO) core labour standards in global supply chains through companies' voluntary codes of conduct.

This non-governmental enforcement mechanism for standards agreed by governments has been made possible by public pressure on large retailers to demonstrate that the goods they sell are not manufactured in unacceptable conditions in developing countries. The chief executives of supermarkets, sportswear companies and clothing retailers do not like headlines revealing that their goods have been made by children in sweatshops, or that their suppliers' workers are paid a fraction of a living wage.

The risks to business linked to sustainable development issues of concern to civil society can no longer be ignored by companies. Indeed, the quality of a company's response to these challenges is becoming a new arena for business competition – Nike, Reebok and Adidas are now competing explicitly on their commitment to tackle issues such as child labour in their supply chains. As the chairman of

British Telecommunications, one of the world's largest telecommunications companies, says: 'There are those who believe that a concern with ethics, values or, indeed, the community at large is incompatible with the business aim of creating shareholder value; that managers should focus on making profits and steer clear of the difficult compromises and trade-offs involved in trying to balance the interests of the various constituencies. That is a misplaced belief.'[2] A senior Shell executive has said: 'What we fear most is not new legislation but consumer revolt.'[3] The remainder of this chapter explores what Earth Summit 2002 can do to strengthen civil society's ability to play this role as a 'regulator without the regulations', and to encourage steps the business world is taking to internalize the challenges civil society is laying down into key aspects of the way business and investment work.

TRANSPARENCY

Transparency and information disclosure by companies are central here. As Ann M Florini of the Carnegie Endowment for International Peace puts it: 'Transparency is always closely connected to accountability. The purpose of calls for transparency is to permit citizens, markets or governments to hold others accountable for their policies and performance. Thus, transparency can be defined as the release of information by institutions that is relevant to evaluating those institutions.'[4] Civil society is already moving a long way beyond simply calling on companies to be transparent. It is actively developing tools and standards to enable them to do it. The Global Reporting Initiative (GRI) is an international NGO alliance that aims to develop a comprehensive sustainability reporting standard for business. This will cover all three pillars of sustainable development – environmental, social and economic. Under the GRI, companies will report within a standard framework on their environmental impacts, their social performance in areas such as labour standards and contributions to local economies, and their overall economic performance.

Frameworks such as this, requiring information to be reported in standardized, comparable ways, are essential to allow comparisons of one company's performance with another. This enables civil society to encourage competition among companies in their sustainability performance. A slightly different approach to standard-setting for transparency and accountability is being taken by the UK-based Institute for Social and Ethical Accountability (ISEA). ISEA, whose members include both companies and NGOs, has recently launched the AA1000 standard for social and ethical accounting, auditing and reporting. Rather than prescribing specific areas of performance for reporting, as GRI does (for example, pollution emissions per unit of product), AA1000 is a standard for the processes an organization needs to go through to demonstrate its accountability to a wide range of stakeholders. Thus, a company can choose its operating standards – such as ILO core labour standards – and plug these into AA1000 as a means of demonstrating how it is complying with them. At Earth Summit 2002, governments should commit themselves to take every possible step to support the development of these voluntary standards and their adoption by companies.

CORPORATE GOVERNANCE

There has been much debate in sustainable development circles about the need for new forms of international governance – new institutions, reallocation of responsibilities among existing institutions, and new ways of working between governments and international organizations. However, little attention has been given to the importance of good corporate governance for sustainable development. The way companies are run and the way they conduct their relationships with their various stakeholders – shareholders, employees, customers, local communities, regulators, NGOs, etc – is vital to achieving social, environmental and economic sustainability. The issue of corporate governance has been steadily rising up the agenda in the business world for several years. High-profile corporate collapses and scandals (such as the misappropriation of pension funds and controversy over top executives' pay levels) have focused attention on the company boardroom and how it works. Then in 1998 the Asian financial crisis brought home to western investors how little they knew about some of the companies to which they were entrusting their funds. OECD governments became concerned. As a result, the OECD has now adopted a set of principles of corporate governance that are formally viewed by the G7 as an integral part of the new 'international financial architecture' – the 'rules of the road' for the international financial system.[5] The World Bank has launched a work programme to promote good corporate governance.[6]

To make the maximum contribution to sustainable development, corporate governance needs to be based on the principle that a company should maintain balanced relationships with a wide range of stakeholders. Focusing on shareholders to the exclusion of all else will not guarantee the necessary standards of environmental performance, relations with the community, compliance with social standards, etc. A company must understand and try to meet the expectations of all its stakeholders – all those that affect it, and all those it affects. A test of good corporate governance should be whether it recognizes that companies must operate within the boundaries set by international agreements on human rights, labour standards and the environment, and within other societal expectations. The operation of the company board, management systems and information disclosure by the company should all be designed with this in mind.

It is vital that the World Bank's corporate governance programme adopts this approach. Bringing together key international institutions such as the International Monetary Fund (IMF) and international securities regulators, governments, companies, and major institutional investors who control billions of dollars of international capital, the programme will be crucial in determining whether corporate governance helps or hinders sustainable development. Earth Summit 2002 should ensure that this programme has the necessary links with the key international and national sustainable development institutions. Governments should commit themselves to an approach to corporate governance at the national level that is based on the same principle.

REGULATING BUSINESS FOR TRANSPARENCY

We have briefly reviewed voluntary, market-based initiatives to increase the contribution of business to sustainable development. But signs are also emerging that the actions of civil society in urging business towards greater social responsibility are helping to bring about change in some of the core aspects of regulating business and capital markets. As noted earlier, companies are recognizing that poor social and environmental performance exposes them to business risk. Campaigns by NGOs and adverse media coverage can damage a company's reputation – which is a crucial intangible asset in today's fiercely competitive market. In certain industries it is now also accepted that 'social' or 'environmental' issues represent core operational risks for a company, not just reputational risks. An oil company that has such poor relations with local communities that local people disrupt its operations will lose money. One person's human rights issue is another's business risk.

From this perspective, the quality of a company's relationships with a wide range of stakeholders is vitally relevant to its prospects for business success. Shareholders are increasingly seeking more information from companies to enable them to understand these issues and factor them into their decisions to buy or sell shares. As a result, the UK Stock Exchange has recently made it a condition of listing – having a company's shares traded on the exchange – that companies report information on the risks to which their businesses are exposed. This specifically includes environmental and reputation risks – and we have seen that the latter will embrace a host of 'sustainable development' issues of concern to civil society. Thus, all companies seeking access to one of the world's leading capital markets face new requirements to disclose their performance on key social and environmental issues.

London is so far the only Stock Exchange to have taken this step. Reputation and risk issues are perceived differently in other markets. Yet, as investors' understanding of these issues matures, and capital moves globally, they are seeking information from companies listed on other stock exchanges, including those in developing countries. Investors in London or on Wall Street are now asking about labour conditions in companies listed in Bangkok or Kuala Lumpur. Earth Summit 2002 could make a major contribution to encouraging governments to include disclosure of information on companies' compliance with core international sustainable-development standards in local Stock Exchange listing rules.

Stock Exchange listing rules by definition apply only to publicly traded companies; the information of concern to investors is likely to be more limited than that required by civil society at large. Information disclosure requirements for all companies are set out in company law. The growing expectations of society for greater transparency by business are reflected in the debate on the review of UK company law. Serious consideration is being given to requiring all companies to report on their relations with stakeholders and on environmental matters. For the largest companies, comprehensive, audited environmental and social reports should be compulsory. At Earth Summit 2002 governments will have the opportunity to debate how the needs of sustainable development can be incorporated within company law – and a commitment to new reporting obligations on core environmental and social issues should be a key outcome of that debate.

For many years a small group of 'ethical' or 'socially responsible' investors has sought to reflect ethical, social and environmental concerns in investment decisions. The total value of funds invested in this way is now something over UK£2 billion in the UK and around ten times that in the US. Persistent worries that 'ethical' investment would underperform 'conventional' investment, meaning that a clear conscience had to be bought at the cost of reduced pensions or investment earnings, have not been borne out. By and large, ethical funds do not seem to perform worse on average than conventional funds. Strong public demand for an ethical choice in investment products has spurred mainstream finance houses to launch ethical products – pensions, individual savings accounts, etc. As the big investment houses start to ask blue-chip companies about their environmental and social policies – to decide whether they should be on their approved investment lists – senior managers are taking more notice of these issues.

Alongside this, more and more pension funds – which control around 35 per cent of the UK stock market – are raising sustainable development issues with the companies they invest in. From July 2000 UK pension trustees will be required by law to disclose what consideration they have given to social, environmental and ethical concerns. The changing understanding of business risk, noted above, means that to fulfil their core legal duty to get the best investment return for their pension scheme members, trustees will – in many cases – have to focus on issues that have historically been categorized as purely 'social' or 'environmental'. Earth Summit 2002 should review these trends and encourage governments worldwide to follow the example of requiring greater transparency in the way pension funds and other assets are invested.

The mayhem on the streets of Seattle at the opening of the WTO conference in December 1999 demonstrated vividly the public's lack of confidence and trust in business. Promoting a model of business that takes account of interests other than those of shareholders, and that defines success not just in terms of profits but in terms of contributions to sustainable development, will require a range of action. International agreements need to balance rights and opportunities for companies with responsibilities, and to open up new trading opportunities for the poorest countries. A key challenge for Earth Summit 2002 is to take an overall view. It should recognize and take steps to underpin the 'non-regulatory regulator' role of civil society – strengthening transparency requirements on companies as a cornerstone of this function. It should also press for more transparency in stock-market listing rules and more disclosure by institutional investors on sustainable development issues, allowing civil society greater scrutiny of business' real contribution to the Rio agenda which is still as vital and pressing as it was in 1992.

NOTES

1   UNDP (2000) *Human Development Report 1999*, Geneva: UNDP
2   *BT Social Report 1999*, London: British Telecommunications
3   John Vidal (1999) 'Consumer power ready to take on corporations', *The Guardian*, 27 November
4   Does the Invisible Hand Need a Transparent Glove? The Politics of Transparency. Paper prepared for the Annual World Bank Conference on Development Economics, Washington, DC, 28–30 April 1999. Available at http://www.worldbank.org/research/abcde.papers.html
5   Available at http://www.oecd.org
6   cf http://www.worldbank.org/html/fpd/privatesector/cg/index.htm

Part IV

Emerging Issues

14

Environment and Security*

Margaret Brusasco-Mackenzie

INTRODUCTION

'There can no longer be the slightest doubt that resource scarcities and ecological stresses constitute real and imminent threats to the future well-being of all people and nations. These challenges are fundamentally non-military and it is imperative that they be addressed accordingly.'[1]

The words above, composed more than a decade ago as part of the WCED's report Our Common Future (commonly known as the Brundtland Report), remain as true today as when they were written. The relationship between environment and security has become increasingly apparent; resource scarcity and ecological stress have worsened considerably since the publication of the Brundtland Report. However, knowledge of the seriousness of the situation and its relationship to the security of all mankind unfortunately still seems to be confined to a knowledgeable and active minority. Even among the environmental community, the emphasis is laid more upon stress in a

* Much of the material for this chapter was gathered and written when working for the EC Environment Directorate General, as adviser for the follow-up to the Rio Summit. The views expressed here are the responsibility of the author and in no way engage the European Commission. I should like to acknowledge the major contribution made by Ranak Pandya, trainee European Commission, March–July 1999, for which I am deeply indebted.

particular sector, such as destruction of forest or biodiversity, than upon the holistic questions of overall security.

It is imperative in areas such as trade, development and environment, that governments, NGOs and other social partners begin to use joined-up thinking to address issues of environment and security. Some excellent work has been done in the academic community and think tanks and some governments have also been working on the issue.[2] However, most of the work by governments to date has been done from the premise of security than environment. In other words, it has addressed predominantly the effects on the environment caused by security policies – such as damage by the military to the environment as a result of armed conflict, weapons testing and contaminated sites.

The purpose of this chapter is to concentrate on the environmental aspects, in other words to look at the problem from upstream rather than downstream. How can we stimulate the right kind of sustainable policies so that less stress will be placed upon the environment in future, and greater security of resources will be provided for the present and future populations of the world?

As part of the preparation for Rio, governments became aware of severe environmental degradation and the problems created by the diminishing resource base, particularly in regard to the destruction of biodiversity and the link that this can have to security, especially food security for rural and indigenous populations. Agenda 21 and the follow-up process in the UN-CSD and UNGASS have developed these themes. The terrible problem of water stress – not having sufficient clean water – which affects already one third of the world's population, was brought out strongly at UNGASS; water stress also has a major negative effect on agriculture. This, combined with the decrease in arable land by more than 25 per cent according to Food and Agriculture (FAO) statistics since 1950, can lead in turn to problems of food insecurity. Drought and desertification are taking tens of thousands of hectares of arable land out of cultivation each year and making marginal arable land increasingly more fragile.[3]

To be added into this equation of double insecurity (food and water) are the effects of global climate change (which as a minimum is resulting in more and more extreme weather events), and the disappearance of biodiversity, particularly forest cover. This leads to a downward spiral in relation to human security and natural resource degradation, which may also exacerbate one another. Added to this is the growth in population, with a 50 per cent increase to nine billion foreseen for the middle of this century. We therefore have two curves which coincide disastrously: upward population and increasing need for food and water, and downward availability. The consequences of this have already been seen in some countries in Africa, particularly Sudan, Ethiopia and Eritrea. The lack of security in relation to the basic necessities of life has already led to conflicts. It is suggested that this can eventually lead to armed conflict, because there will be competing groups struggling to occupy what fertile land is left in order to assure food supplies to feed their families and to sustain the group.

It is also suggested that economic hardship has already caused an upsurge in migration, particularly from North and West Africa to richer countries, such as the EU and also the US. There are also well-known tensions in several European countries between locals and the Northern African emigrants.[4] Sudden increases in immigration, which have already taken place after famines, have led to considerable social tensions and unrest among African countries – for example, between Zimbabwe and Mozambique. The situation concerning environment and security is already serious in many areas and could rapidly deteriorate.[5] The issue has already been taken up by the G8 environmental ministers and by the Organization of Security and Co-operation in Europe (OSCE). It is an issue which is likely to be raised, particularly relating to water and food security in the framework of the preparation for Earth Summit 2002.

WHAT DO WE MEAN BY ENVIRONMENT AND SECURITY?

The link between environment and security has only been made over the last 10 to 15 years. Traditional concepts of security have been centred on the state, with the maintenance of state sovereignty as its cornerstone related to military and armed conflict. The definition has recently been widened to include environmental degradation of resources, especially of non-renewable resources, as well as a rising scarcity of resources deemed vital to the security of individual nations. Since the end of the Cold War some governments have reflected (and in a few cases taken action) that the military should promote environmental security – for example, by releasing global monitoring data and reacting to environmental emergencies and clean-up operations for their own contaminated sites and bases.

This is a major area of concern. There are numerous sites across the face of the Earth that are littered with the fallout from war and lesser conflicts. This, of course, is particularly serious where areas have been mined, and has led to many humanitarian disasters in countries such as Mozambique. This has also resulted in large swathes of arable land being taken out of production in countries where there is a population which frequently experiences food shortages and, in some cases, famine. Other examples of highly mined areas can be found on other continents – for example, in Vietnam and in Bosnia with attendant consequences both for human well-being and the environment. In Vietnam, there is still the legacy of the chemical weapons that were used there 30 years ago and which are still poisoning soils and aquifers and having a negative effect on health. Deposits and decommissioning of weapons, especially chemical and nuclear weapons, are often responsible for environmental pollution. This is an issue which has been the subject of much research, predominantly by the academic and military communities, and would certainly be worthy of a major treatment. It is not, however, the focus of this chapter.

Since the Brundtland Report, there has been a more holistic definition of security which takes the environment as the starting point. Thus, recent concepts of environmental security are based on coordinated and international action in the search for adequate solutions to situations of stress and conflict. A rethinking of the traditional concept of security should address the relationship between the individual and the environment, as well as the state and the environment. In turn, a more proactive and preventive approach to environmental problems needs to be adopted, which looks to causes rather than simply dealing with consequences. Sustainable development has a central role in promoting the long-term good of the environment and of the individual's security.

This chapter will focus on the burden of environmental destruction as a cause, rather than the result of, political tensions and insecurity, and which can and does lead to armed conflict. What is required is an approach which recognizes new threats and looks at means other than the military to deal with them. Environmental security is not synonymous with sustainable development but it does suggest integrating environmental policy within other policies so that situations of water, food and biodiversity stress will not give rise to conflict.

Emphasizing the urgency of environmental destruction in terms of security issues will also help to move environmental concerns further up the political agenda into areas of 'high politics'. In this way, the concept of environment and security should gain wider credibility and attention, and ultimately become an issue that will generate a coordinated international and adequate response. It must always be borne in mind that conflict rarely arises because of environmental issues alone; instead, it is a result of a web of economic, social and environmental factors.

SOME EXAMPLES OF THE CONNECTION BETWEEN ENVIRONMENTAL DEGRADATION AND SECURITY

According to Professor T Homer-Dixon, (University of Toronto), environmental scarcity is caused by three main factors:

1   Environmental change.
2   Population growth.
3   Unequal social distribution of resources.[6]

Under these conditions, the likelihood of conflict is augmented, result-ing in various social problems. Social stress caused by environmental crisis can be manifested in a number of ways. Firstly, environmental problems such as soil erosion or water scarcity could lead to urban migration, overpopulation, poverty and instability. Homer-Dixon identifies two resulting phenomena: 'resource capture' – how lack of resources and population growth may encourage the powerful elite to shift resource distribution in their favour (eg Brazil, India, Pakistan – land tenure issues); and 'ecological marginalization'– how unequal access to resources coupled with population growth may lead to migration to a fragile region and thus result in chronic poverty (eg Mozambique, Ethiopia).[7]

It is clear that under circumstances of environmental stress, the potential for conflict is accentuated. Traditionally, any analysis of conflict examines issues such as ethnic, religious or cultural tensions as their cause, but 'disputes are often sharpened or even triggered by glaring social and economic inequities'.[8] Thus, the growing pressures of population growth, resource depletion and environmental degrada-tion are key factors in causing conflict. Environmental security is an issue that can affect all societies at various levels. The problems of overexploitation of water resources, soil erosion, desertification and deforestation can be seen the world over. Clearly, rural areas in the developing world are the most vulnerable, since their relative social and economic standards put them in a weaker position to deal with problems such as population growth, unequal land distribution, decline in land fertility and scarcity of water, increasing the chance of conflict. It is not only developing countries that are affected. Some of the countries of the EU and central and eastern Europe are also facing threats to environmental security that must be rapidly addressed – for example, water stress and land degradation in particular.

WATER STRESS AND SCARCITY

'Wherever population is growing, the supply of freshwater per person is declining.'[9] Nearly a billion people in 50 countries live with severe water shortages every day of their lives, and by 2025, as much as two-thirds of the world's population could be experiencing moderate to high water stress.[10] In addition, 20 per cent of the world population lack access to safe water and about 50 per cent lack access to adequate forms of sanitation.[11]

Evidence of water scarcity can be seen on every continent. The overexploitation of rivers and aquifers for pumping means less water is available and there is a gradual depletion of groundwater. In the light of global climate change, both the threat of rivers running dry and sea-level rise can lead to severe cases of environmental stress. Inequalities in the distribution of water supplies are also increasing, exacerbated by poor water management. This has serious consequences for food production and social well-being, increasing the potential for conflict, particularly in the context of population growth. It is estimated that the population grows by 87 million each year.[12] In addition, the transboundary nature of river systems means that about two billion people depend on international cooperation to ensure their water supply. With over 300 transboundary river networks across the globe, 40 per cent of the world's population live alongside shared river resources.[13]

It is clear that the role of water scarcity in shared river basins has a great potential to trigger or intensify regional instability and other security issues, particularly health problems. There is also potential for internal conflict within states over water resources, often having severe impacts on the local population. A study by the International Rivers Network found that the construction or expansion of 604 dams in 93 countries displaced (in several cases forcibly) at least 10 million people during 1948–1993.[14]

NILE RIVER BASIN

One of the clearest examples of water conflict is within the Nile River Basin. Out of the nine nations through which the Nile passes, only Egypt and Sudan have cooperated in its management, in the form of the 1959 Nile Waters Agreement. The immediate problem lies between Egypt, Sudan and Ethiopia, who have experienced different levels of development and have relied upon a local approach to water allocation rather than a basin-wide approach. The most imminent threat to water resources is Egypt's rising level of population growth, placing an added demand on water for human and livestock consumption. Furthermore, the desire for economic growth in all three countries means that a large amount of water is needed for industrial purposes. It is estimated that Egypt's total water demand in 20 years will exceed its allotted share by almost 60 per cent.[15] It is clear that water scarcity has a serious impact on security within the Nile Basin, on humans, the Nile ecosystem, as well as the nations involved. The results are self-explanatory: dehydration, disease, hunger and the potential for conflict. The last factor could pose the greatest threat to Egypt, especially if Ethiopia threatens to reduce the availability of water for nations downstream. Cooperative water management agreements are essential in regulating water supply and bringing conflicting interests together. The role of the international community may be vital to act as a catalyst for change, for example via donor funds.

MIDDLE EAST: EUPHRATES-TIGRIS BASIN

The Middle East is an effective example of severe water-related tensions. Turkey's Grand Anatolia Dam project has created an upstream–downstream conflict between Turkey on one hand, and Syria, Iran and Iraq on the other. The Kurds, in particular, are worried that their homelands will be flooded and they will be left landless. According to the UK Defence Forum, the dam has the potential to cause a war within the region as various parties quarrel over access to water.

MIDDLE EAST: JORDAN BASIN

About 40 per cent of the groundwater that Israel depends upon, and uses for extensive agricultural irrigation, originates in the Occupied Territory. This severely restricts water use by Palestinians on the West Bank and, as a result, Palestinian wells have run dry, so that many have abandoned farming and moved to the towns where there is little employment and social unrest. It is suggested that Israel's demand may outstrip supply by 40 per cent within three decades, indicating the grave pressure on water supplies and the strategic importance it plays in the peace process.[16] The Palestinians are only prepared to negotiate on the basis of an 'equitable' share of existing resources, and with the Jordan Basin facing a serious lack of rainfall in 1999, tensions regarding demand and supply are likely to escalate. The international community has a clear role in trying to prevent conflict.

THE SLOVAK–HUNGARIAN CONFLICT OVER THE GABCIKOVO–NAGYMAROS DAM SYSTEM ON THE DANUBE

The joint hydroelectric barrier system between Slovakia and Hungary on the River Danube has negatively affected relations in central Europe during the 1990s. Conflicts arose between Slovakia and Hungary in the early 1980s, and in 1992 Hungary unilaterally terminated the treaty. Meanwhile in late 1992, Slovakia diverted the river, so that the whole of the project was built within Slovak territory. Consequently, both sides charged the other with breaking the treaty and tensions escalated into a major international political and legal dispute. The case was finally submitted to the UN International Court of Justice in 1993, after pressure from the EU and a complicated ruling followed, resulting in a compromise agreement for future arrangements. Although there were many strategic factors shaping the conflict, it is interesting to note both the lack of regional conflict-mitigating institutions, and the usefulness of subsequent intervention of larger global institutions as agents for cooperation between the states.

ARAL SEA BASIN

The conflicts in the Aral Sea Basin clearly demonstrate examples of how water stress can lead to violence. Located in Central Asia, the fertile and densely populated Fergana Valley is home to many different ethnic groups, particularly Uzbeks and Tadjiks. The shared system of irrigation led to riots in 1989, with more than 200 casualties based on water distribution conflicts. This case indicates a whole range of environmental problems and their social consequences, from contaminated drinking water to loss of habitats, prompting reactions by institutions such as the World Bank and EU as well as of several local and international NGOs. The Interstate Council for the Aral Sea, comprising the former Central Asian republics, has therefore been set up as a key step towards cooperation, with a view to prevent further conflict.[17] The problems of the Aral Sea represent in a particularly dramatic way the consequences of adopting environmentally unsuitable policies, and the enormous difficulty to subsequently repair the damage done. It will involve considerable political will, and goodwill by all the populations involved, including investment by international institutions in order to address the problems and to recreate environmental security.

LAND DEGRADATION AND SOIL EROSION

Another example of how environmental decline can cause conflict is land degradation. This has serious consequences for grain production and world hunger, in many cases leading to a poor level of health and a deepening cycle of poverty. Although the 20th century has been a revolutionary one for world agriculture, 841 million people across the globe still remain hungry and undernourished. During the first half of the 21st century, heavy cropland losses are expected in many areas of the world due to degradation, soil erosion and, increasingly, climate change. From 1984 to 1998, growth in the grain harvest has fallen behind that of the population, dropping output per person from 343 kilogrammes in 1984, to 312 kilogrammes in 1998, a total decline of 9 per cent or 0.7 per cent a year.[18] This is a worrying situation for food security, as cropland is likely to be further reduced due to the pressures from population rise and the increased demand for land for urban development.[19] It is possible that up to one third of the world's arable land will be depleted within the next 20 years.[20] Even within the EU, farmland territory has dropped from 53 per cent in 1975, to 44 per cent in 1997.[21] Parallel to this, world population has more than doubled, climbing from 2.5 billion in 1950 to 5.9 billion in 1998.

In the past, the trend has been to clear more land in order to meet the demand for food. However, most high-quality agricultural land is already in production, and the environmental costs of converting remaining forest, grassland and wetland habitats into cropland are well recognized. Thus, food insecurity is a veritable threat across the world and is likely to become more severe in the future. The problem is not necessarily the supply of food; rather, it is matching global food supply with actual food needs at a local level.[22] Coupled with the pressure on water availability, the shape of world grain trade patterns is likely to alter significantly, driving world grain prices up and increasing the pressure to import food supply.

In 1995, the Food and Agriculture Organization (FAO) estimated world cereal stocks at 267 million tonnes – their lowest level for 20 years. Developing countries' cereal imports are expected to reach 160 million tonnes by 2010.[23] The prospect of increasing food imports in sub-Saharan Africa is particularly worrying. The OECD forecasts an increase in net cereal imports from 30 to 47 million tonnes by the year 2000, highlighting the grave financial reality of food scarcity in this region.[24] Brazil also faces a similar situation, with food imports at a level of 10 to 15 per cent of total imports.[25] At the same time, world food aid has sharply declined by 35 per cent, from 15.1 million tonnes in 1992–1993, to 9.8 million tonnes in 1994–1995, although the European Community has increased its commitments from 578.9 million ECU in 1993, to 646 million ECU in 1995.[26]

The threat of famine often leads to the displacement of civilians. This can become an entire region's problem, since even countries not experiencing conflicts can be drawn in, bearing the pressure of migration from their neighbours. It has been claimed that as the difficulty in feeding 90 million more people each year becomes apparent, food security may replace military security as the principal preoccupation of many governments.[27] Thus, the problem of land degradation has very serious consequences for environmental insecurity. An inability to meet rising demands for food leads to acute famine and poverty, as has been seen in Ethiopia and Sudan in the last decades, and subsequently results in declining health and increased migration.

RWANDA

A clear example of how land degradation can contribute to violent conflict is in Rwanda, where tensions between the Hutu and Tutsi ethnic groups resulted in the slaughter of one million people in 1994. This was triggered by many interlinked factors – above all, ethnic hatreds – but also by population growth, severe land shortages, land degradation, lack of non-agricultural employment and structural adjustment of the economy.[28] The problems in Rwanda were very acute; since it is a highly agricultural country, most of the disputes have centred around the distribution of pastureland and farmland. The World Bank lists Rwanda as the least urbanized country in the world and the most densely populated in Africa.[29] As a result of limited access to arable land and intense population growth between 1954 and 1993, farmers were pushed into arid and hilly regions, leading to intense cultivation and erosion. Thus, environmental pressures accentuated existing tensions within the country, contributing to large-scale violence and genocide.

THE MEDITERRANEAN

The problem of land degradation can also be seen in the countries of the EU. Around 25 million hectares are seriously threatened by soil erosion in western and central Europe.[30] Changing patterns of land use, as well as harsh climatic events, have significantly altered the dryland regions of the Mediterranean. Growth in agriculture has led to pressure on water resources and overgrazing has had deleterious effects on the land. It is suggested that soil erosion (moderate to serious) affects 50 per cent to 70 per cent of agricultural land.[31] In addition, urban and tourist developments on the coastline have displaced populations, resulting in new pressures on patterns of land management and competition for limited water supplies. It is suggested that in Spain alone, almost one million hectares of land were to be considered as desert and another seven million were identified as being as being at high risk of desertification in 1993.[32] Although fortunately there has been no violent conflict as a result of these factors, it is clear that this is an area where environmental degradation has led to social stress and migration to the coastal zones. As a result, there is increasing competition for jobs in an era of high unemployment, and frequently there are tensions between the local population and the North African migrant workers (who are also fleeing infertile lands). There is a clear need for much more sustainable policies both in relation to agriculture and the development of coastal zones, particularly for tourism, throughout the Mediterranean region.

RESOURCE SCARCITY

FISH

With one billion people relying on fish as their primary protein source, the trend towards global overfishing has taken its toll over the last 45 years. According to the FAO, 60 per cent of the world's important fish stocks are 'in urgent need of management' to rehabilitate them or keep them from being overfished.[33] Of the 15 major oceanic fisheries, 11 are in decline. The limit to fish supply has inevitably led to conflicts among countries over scarce resources, accentuated by the fact that fish are highly mobile and disregard national boundaries. Although cases of violent conflict over depleted fish stocks are rare, political tensions have been manifested in all regions of the world. The UN recorded more than 100 disputes over fish in 1997.[34] Examples include cod wars between Norwegian and Icelandic ships, disputes between Canada and Spain over turbot off Canada's eastern coast, and tensions between South Africa and Spain over fishing rights. Within the EU, the accession of Spain and Portugal in 1986 has brought new challenges as the number of EC fishermen doubled overnight, and consumption increased by a half. This has been manifested in Africa, where the displacement of fishing activity by EU fleets has led to overexploitation of local waters and to tension between the EU fishermen and local populations, as well as numerous protests by NGOs.

DECLINE OF BIODIVERSITY AND FORESTS

Another factor which can undermine the security in a region is the threat to natural habitats, necessary for the survival of species. The world's species are disappearing at an alarming rate, with 3000 endangered and 27 faced with extinction in the EU alone.[35] This is largely due to the intensification of many human activities, such as agriculture, forestry, industry, transport and tourism, exacerbated by the effects of global climate change on the extinction of plant and animal species. This has clearly been the case in the Pacific Islands, where pressure to expand the economy has resulted in erosion, flooding and loss of biodiversity and where global climate change is already making itself felt.

Such situations have negative effects on biodiversity, destroying species – many of which could provide tomorrow's foods – and thus have serious consequences on future human health and issues of security.[36]

One of the most pressing global issues is that of deforestation. As a result of population growth and the need for more urban land, the FAO estimated a net loss of 180 million hectares of forest in developing countries between 1980 and 1995.[37] Analysts at the World Resources Institute claim that overgrazing and overcollection of firewood to meet the demands of a growing population are also threatening large areas of virgin forest. In addition, we have seen the chilling consequences of forest fires set by traditional farmers and private companies (for example, in Brazil and Indonesia) to clear land for cultivation or pasture across the globe. Continued forest loss and degradation have serious implications at local, regional and global levels. As far as security is concerned, the lives of indigenous people may be threatened, as well as the destruction of habitats and biological diversity.[38] Cases range from the conflict over copper and gold

mining in the rainforests of Papua New Guinea, to large-scale deforestation in the Mount Apo region of the Philippines and in disputes
between Burma and Cambodia.[39] In many cases, conflicts arise
between the government and/or private industry and the local population, displacing communities who then have to face the consequences
of migration and poverty.[40]

Indonesia holds the second largest tract of tropical forests on the
planet, covering 92 to 109 million hectares. As an important source of
state revenue and a tactical political resource, forests can often trigger
cases of violent conflict, particularly between local communities and
state agents, as well as between elite groups over the control and use
of rents from forest exploitation. Indonesian forests are therefore
highly vulnerable to pressure from human demands: logging, mining,
conversion to agriculture and spontaneous settlements have had the
aggregate effect of stripping forestlands and stunting regrowth. It was
estimated that between 1950 and 1989, 43 million hectares were lost
to deforestation. Ultimately, this leads to natural resource scarcities,
unable to sustain population growth and multiplying the potential for
migration conflict and disorder. One of the most prolific examples of
threat to environmental security were the 1997 forest fires. At least 20
million people were affected by the smoke caused when Indonesian
forests caught fire because of burning on agricultural plantations by
private companies. This resulted in haze, severe flooding and soil
erosion. In addition, political and social tension was exacerbated,
including between the countries in the region. Malaysia, Borneo and
Singapore were also more or less seriously affected by the 'haze', with
its attendant health risks and effects on agricultural and industrial
production.

BRAZIL

Latin America is richly endowed with natural resources, including the
world's largest expanse of tropical forest, although it is plagued by
both rural and urban conflicts. More than 20 per cent of the population still face absolute poverty. The issue of land distribution is a
particularly controversial one. The richest 1 per cent of Brazilians
control nearly half of the country's land; five million rural families
have no land at all. In addition, the expansion of agricultural production has had devastating effects on the forests, which have been cleared
for cattle ranches and subsistence farms, or have been subject to heavy
logging. As a result, many of the landless Brazilians have tried to settle
on unoccupied land. During the past ten years, 1000 people have been
killed in confrontations with landowners in Brazil. The loss of
woodlands also destroys communities of indigenous peoples and
destroys their traditional livelihood in the commercialization of nuts,
fruits and medicinal plants growing in the forest.

CONCLUSION

The examples discussed here illustrate the potential of environmental degradation to affect security. The cases examined are, in fact, only a sample of what is happening in many countries, both developed and developing, all over the world. Although the environmental factor as a cause of conflict is not always measurable, many of the cases indicate that the environment often plays a role in addition to political, economic and social variables. What is most striking is that the fundamental resources needed for survival – food and water – are severely under threat in many areas of the world, with grave consequences. The results of past environmental stresses portray a bleak future: poverty, inequality, migration and tense international relations.

GLOBAL MONITORING AND ENVIRONMENTAL CONFLICT

Much of the data on environment and security to date has relied on information from specific case studies. However, in order to establish coherent policy objectives, it is necessary to build up a representative picture of environmental degradation across the globe. Systems and models that enable us to quantify and develop patterns of environmental stress are important in identifying areas that need remediation and in defining future strategies in order to prevent stress and conflict (hotspots).

GLOBAL ENVIRONMENTAL MONITORING

Although the primary aim of global environmental monitoring is not to prevent conflict, the techniques available give a scientific basis to a largely human problem. UNEP was first in the field with the GEMS-GRID monitoring system, which has performed creditably but which needs reinforcement. Substantial work has already been done in the field of global climate change and satellite imagery to track the disappearance of tropical forests. International monitoring systems need to be improved and extended to develop a more sophisticated picture of global environmental security. Information through monitoring is essential for policy formulation and, consequently, should enhance the implementation process. A commitment to monitoring programmes by the international community is specified in the conventions on biodiversity, climate change and desertification and this information, when available in more comprehensive form, would assist the identification of preventive measures and flashpoint zones. Release of non-sensitive military data (as has been done to some extent in the US) could also be very helpful in this area.

Within Europe there are several ongoing programmes for monitoring – for example, on energy, environment and sustainable development. A water project has been launched: 'application of space techniques to the integrated management of a river-basin water resources' (ASTIMWR). This aims to use Earth observation techniques to help manage water resources in a river basin shared by Spain and Portugal through examining how its customers currently use the information they receive from conventional sources.

Another European programme is the Cereal Yield Estimation System (CEREAL YES). This will provide reliable and objective estimates of cereal yield for agricultural districts, using data from high-resolution, remote sensing satellites which could be incorporated into existing forecasting programmes.[41] Such projects are vital in identifying sensitive areas so that preventive measures can be taken to avoid cases of environmental stress, especially water and food security. If these techniques are successful, they could be extrapolated to other areas of the globe, and it is suggested they could also be used by UNEP.

Predictive models are also being developed by universities such as the University of Michigan (Professor G Schultink) and by the University of Kassel (Professor J Alcamo) to try to quantify the link between environmental change and human security. In conjunction with global monitoring efforts, it is becoming increasingly important to build up stronger databases which can actually quantify and predict the scale of the environmental conflict. Such predictive academic models are invaluable in providing a global overview of the intensity of threats of environmental change to human security and in identifying future areas of environmentally related crises (hotspots). It emerges from all the models that it is necessary to identify conditions of stress at an early stage – specifically the capacity of the state to react – in order to mitigate the effects and reduce the possibility of conflict.

The potential of modelling for environmental purposes is vast and needs to be further developed. Fragile regions of the world such as the Nile Basin, the Jordan Basin, the Euphrates–Tigris Basin and parts of Africa such as Eritrea, Rwanda and Sudan, where environmental conflicts could erupt at any given moment, would greatly benefit from early warning systems and conflict prevention mechanisms. It is therefore vital to support and broaden the work of global environmental monitoring systems and predictive modelling. These techniques play a key role in identifying patterns of environmental damage, and consequently they explore methods which promote preventive rather than remedial action. This is central to tackling problems of environmental stress. If vulnerable areas can be identified, then preventative action can be taken in time. It is clear that the most challenging hurdle is perhaps selling these ideas and their results to policy-makers, rather than any lack of activity in this field.

STRATEGIES TO IMPROVE ENVIRONMENTAL SECURITY

Many policies are involved in such strategies – for instance, environmental, development, foreign policy, trade and agriculture strategies – but how to link them together coherently is a difficult question and will be at the crux of future discussions and action.

The European parliament recently produced a report and resolution on environment, security and foreign policy.[42] It suggested that the EU must bring together the trade and development aid policies with the international environment policy to deal with:

- agricultural and food production and environmental degradation;
- water shortages and transfrontier water supply;
- deforestation and restoring carbon sinks;
- unemployment, underemployment and absolute poverty;
- sustainable development and climate change;
- deforestation, desertification and population growth; and
- the link between all of the above, including global warming and the humanitarian and environmental impact of increasingly extreme weather events.

This analysis clearly applies not only to the EU but to the whole donor community. The NGO community has an important role to play in this area to stimulate analysis of the problem and to urge subsequent action upon the donors. NGOs can also use examples of their own grassroots projects in developing countries to assist the OECD development aid agencies in approaches which engage more sustainably in food security and water management policies in the developing world; these approaches are essential to create environmental security.

THE ROLE OF DIFFERENT POLICIES

INTERNATIONAL ENVIRONMENT POLICY

Much of the thrust of international environment policy since Rio has, in fact, been preventative, with a view to reducing the stress on the natural environment towards its preservation, and hence towards greater environmental security. The two major conventions signed at Rio and subsequently widely ratified – the Global Climate Change Convention and the CBD – both have prevention and indeed precaution at the heart of their philosophy. The link between the CBD, the loss of biodiversity and environmental security is quite obvious. As examples cited above have shown, the destruction of natural resources and forests have impoverished the lives and increased the sense of insecurity of countless millions across the world, particularly in Central Africa, Amazonia and Indonesia. As we have seen, the destruction of biodiversity can indeed play a part in creating the conditions of armed conflict.

The ethos of the CBD is to ensure that the world's resources should be preserved for the good of future and present generations. One of its basic premises is that there must be a fair share for both the originating country and the developer of such natural resources. It must be made clear to those who wish to have unfettered access to natural resources and to commercialize them that the basic tenets of Rio (including common but differentiated responsibility) apply and that developing countries, as the source of many of these resources, are entitled to their just share of the proceeds from any such commercialization. Some progress in this area has fortunately been made by the recent agreement on the protocol on biosafety, but much more needs to be done.

The relationship of the Global Climate Change Convention to environment and security may seem, at first, to be less evident. However, as is well known, global climate change is already occurring and could have disastrous consequences in the medium term for low-lying countries and those already suffering from aridity and desertification. Global climate change has also increased the number and intensity of extreme weather events worldwide, such as hurricanes, cyclones and flooding of river basins.[43] All of these events, apart from the human tragedies that they entail, also degrade or destroy large tracts of arable land. This arable land is often the only livelihood of the local population. Hence, global climate change contributes to the vicious cycle of environmental disaster, forced migration, tensions between local populations and incoming migrants. Therefore, it has a direct effect in terms of land degradation and an indirect effect in relation to security and conflict.

Another issue, addressed at Rio and subsequently, is the major scourge of desertification. The framework convention set up in 1995 is beginning its work, but if we are to come to grips with this major problem, a great deal must be done and far more rapidly. Hopefully the convention will allow for more coordinated efforts to combat desertification both by the donor community and the developing countries affected by it. It is also clear that besides more efficient coordination and aid, there is need for much greater volumes of aid if we are to tackle this problem and to prevent it spreading to the drylands of Africa, Asia and Latin America. If it does spread, then we will witness an even larger population of environmental migrants seeking their livelihood, probably unsuccessfully, in major conurbations or trying to immigrate to the industrialized countries.

Another major issue linked to all of the three areas above is forest policy. It seems from the Global Environment Outlook Report (GEO-

2000) that the hopes in the mid 1990s that the destruction of forests had been slowed have not been fulfilled. There has been wholesale burning of forests in recent years, both in Asia and Latin America, with consequent destruction of habitat and biodiversity. The donor community has tried to respond to this situation. Some useful reafforestation projects are continuing. Some developing countries – for example, Costa Rica – have set up good policies to preserve their forest. But again, all of this needs to be addressed by joined-up thinking. Whether this will take the form of the Forest Convention or another instrument is not clear, given the very different and often conflicting views expressed; but it is an area which must be addressed with some urgency in the framework of Earth Summit 2002. Preservation and sustainable management of forests are essential for the environmental security of the planet.

Another area, in which environmental law-makers have recently been active, is that of public participation, information and access to justice concerning environmental decision-making. The Aarhus Convention of the UN Economic Commission for Europe (UN-ECE) is truly a major achievement in this field and its establishment and signature have been brought about by intensive cooperation between governments and environmental NGOs. Once ratified and in force, it should give the populations of Europe a truly efficient tool so that they can be involved personally and collectively in the decisions on the environment which affect their lives. This visionary convention, it is suggested, can contribute greatly to environmental security by ensuring that decisions are taken openly and in a cooperative, transboundary manner. If the convention proves to be a success in practice, it is suggested that it is an example which could be used in favour of sustainability and security worldwide. Working groups could be set up in other continents, using the same principles and, in particular, with strong involvement of NGOs from the outset to arrive at their own versions of a convention on information, participation and access to justice.

Other policies which are concerned also with international environmental policy are those on fisheries, food security and water management. As stated earlier, the world's fisheries are in many cases under extreme pressure; at the same time they provide an invaluable source of food, as well as being a commodity for much of the developing world. There have already been numerous clashes over rights to fish, and here again a much more systematic and sustainable approach to fisheries is required. The EU is at long last trying to deal with the problem of overfishing within its own waters and, in the framework of the post-Lomé negotiations, will be looking at its fisheries agreements with developing countries. It is suggested that within the framework of the UN (UNCLOS, FAO), a holistic approach must be taken since fisheries are an essential part of food security and the environment.

FOOD SECURITY AND WATER MANAGEMENT

Food security is a concept which was not much spoken of, nor indeed addressed, during the Rio Conference, but it is an essential part of environmental security and must be addressed within the framework of the Earth Summit. Food security for the developing world is the basic condition for the support of life and for the protection of the environment. As is well known, the overall problem lies with the inequality of the distribution of food rather than the world's inability to produce enough food. However, there are many situations of penury and famine. This has led to constant increase in food aid over much of the 1980s and part of the 1990s. However, food aid can only be a Band-Aid; it is not a lasting solution. Therefore, many countries, developed and developing, are beginning to develop food security policies, marking a shift in values.

The new system between donor and developing countries aims to form stronger partnerships with beneficiary countries and to prevent situations of crisis by addressing the causes of food insecurity, rather than attempting to contain the effects. Programmes for food security must be integrated within overall development cooperation policy, making the best use of local resources, and in coordination with other partners including Northern and Southern NGOs. The financing should be undertaken on a multi-annual basis, be intersectoral and cover poverty reduction, farming, transport, support for the private sector and crisis prevention. The aid should be provided both in cash and in products such as seeds, tools and credit support systems.

The EU has been running food security programmes since 1996 and in 1997 200 million ECU worth of grains were provided together with 100 million ECU in currency and 120 million ECU in support schemes, tools, etc. The best of these schemes aim not only at assuring food security; they also contain an element to supply local populations with drinking water. They aim to reduce pressure on the available arable land and to increase productivity per unit of land. Some individual donors within the EU also focus on food security as one of their basic programmes. It is suggested that these programmes should be surveyed and their methods and results relayed to the preparatory process for Earth Summit 2002 so that positive results can be incorporated. If Earth Summit 2002 can contribute globally to such a basic aspect of environmental security as food security, this will mark a major step forward.

Another basic aspect of environmental security is water management. Across the world, thousands of projects have been carried out but in most cases they have not been developed with the goal of relieving environmental stress. There is a need for a new generation of water projects based on the concept of water management which ensures water security. It is well known that two-thirds of the world's population will be living in conditions of water stress in the next 50 years unless urgent action is taken. The difficult political and legal problem of shared water resources has to be tackled. Water management in future must be done on the basis of river basins and incorporate transboundary aspects.

Some work has already begun in this direction within the Southern African Development Community (SADC) region. There has recently been a meeting of all riparian states of the Nile, which is of the greatest importance. Within Europe, there is extensive experience of river basin management (for example, on the Rhine, the Elbe and the Oder). This experience, it is suggested, could be of value to other regions. While it is clear that there is need for greater cooperation among developing countries on shared water resources, there should also be greater coordination between donors on water basins in recipient countries. Perhaps it would be too early at the 2002 summit, but we should build on the CSD's work on water management. Regional water programmes must also become a reality if there is to be environmental security.

ENVIRONMENT AND PEACE

In addressing the questions of environmental security, this chapter has concentrated on the specific areas where environmental stress can lead to conflict and has highlighted strategies to prevent this. Mention should be made, however, of an important aspect of the environment. The environment, within high foreign policy, has traditionally been regarded as a 'soft' subject. It has, therefore, been considered as suitable territory for broad agreement, even where political circumstances are extremely tense; and in some cases the parties may even be in a state of war. This, for example, was the case of the Barcelona Convention for the Protection of the Mediterranean Sea. When it was negotiated in 1975, all the states bordering the Mediterranean, including the Palestine Liberation Organization and the EEC, took part in the negotiations. Several of the Arab countries concerned were officially in a state of war with Israel. Nevertheless, after two years, the negotiations were concluded successfully and the convention itself was ratified by all the states. It has been in force for more than 20 years and is one of the more effective of regional conventions; it now has seven protocols, most of which are in force. Considering the difficult environmental issues in the region, (particularly water rights), this shows that international environmental diplomacy can work and can contribute to peace-building. Even at times of great tension, environmental authorities within the warring states have continued to be in contact with one another and to work together as far as possible.

Similarly, within the UN-ECE during the long period of the Cold War, there was constant verbal confrontation between the Western and Eastern blocs. As a result, in many areas it was not possible until after 1989 to make progress within UN-ECE. However, one area which did have substantial achievements is that of the environment, where the landmark UN-ECE Convention on Long Range Transboundary Air Pollution (1979) was negotiated and came into force, having been ratified by all the countries concerned. It also now has a series of protocols and a second generation of protocols to its credit. The contact between the environmental organizations across the iron curtain also contributed to détente, and ultimately to the 'velvet' and other revolutions in central and eastern Europe. Here again we see a positive and reinforcing role of environmental diplomacy in providing a terrain for entente even between conflicting parties. Clearly, there is sufficient joined-up thinking, even in dangerous situations, for governments to realize that in relation to the environment, we are all truly in it together and together we sink or swim.

TRADE

Trade policy, it is suggested, could also be used for environmental security. Green trade policies can lead to sustainable development in our trading partners, particularly in developing countries, whereas 'business as usual' trade policies are all too likely to lead to the rush to the bottom. This means that developing countries overexploit their natural resource base, exporting commodities and/or unsuitable cash crops which deplete or pollute their environment and lead to problems of food insecurity. It is essential that the new World Trade Organization (WTO) negotiations are conducted within the framework of sustainable development. There must be an acknowledgement that trade, environment and development are a continuum and that this new round must take the interests of developing countries into account if globalization is to be channelled positively.

It would seem from recent declarations at the Davos World Economic Forum that the protestors at Seattle have made their point. Negotiators from OECD countries must also recognize that 'business as usual' in the form of unfettered trade liberalization is not acceptable, and that the new round must include special assistance for developing countries, as well as further environmental security. Specific strategies must be developed to these ends.

The EC in its generalized system of preferences (GSP), its special tariffs for sustainable timber and core labour standards has already tried to improve the trading situation of less developed countries (LDCs). The timber concession, however, has not had the desired effect and it is necessary to examine this area carefully. The original idea of encouraging trade in sustainably managed timber is an excellent one from the point of view of environment and security (also of human security in the case of the Amazonian forest), but it has not been constructed in such a way that LDCs can easily utilize this scheme. The new suggestions for the Millenium Round related to capacity-building and technical assistance for removing constraints for LDCs would seem to be more useful strategies and tools to ensure a greater share of trade for developing countries, thereby assisting them towards greater prosperity and therefore greater security.

CONCLUSIONS

Policies are needed for remediation and prevention. Strategies for development, in particular for tackling poverty, must take into account the need for environmental security and be sustainable. Development policies must be oriented towards creating food security, not falling back on simply providing food aid in times of famine, and towards ecosystem river-basin water management. Trade policy can also offer useful tools in order to achieve greater equity in the world trading system, and the new round should be used for this purpose. International environmental policy must reinforce the element of precaution as well as security.

The connection between environment and security no longer needs to be spelled out. The decline of our environment will lead to war, local and regional, in the medium term and in some cases in the near future (for example, about water rights) unless preventative action is urgently taken. Those of us in the environmental community must marshal our facts and arguments so that we can convince the high-level policy-makers, foreign ministries and, indeed, defence ministries as well as the military establishment. While the Cold War is over, many bitter, disastrous, local and regional wars continue. Frequently, these local wars are due to poor people fighting over land to feed their families. Unless the world adopts sustainable policies in relation to food and water security, these conflicts will only get worse and immigration will also inevitably increase.

We have the tools: international environment policy, development aid policy, agriculture, fisheries and forestry policy. The donor community must think much more holistically. It must incorporate environment and security within all its foreign policies; and not only are more funds needed, they need to be spent more effectively and in a coordinated way. Developing countries have the responsibility not to destroy their own environment, and therefore not to destroy the security of their own peoples. We must all work together in order to adopt the correct sustainable strategies to ensure environment and security. Earth Summit 2002 and its preparation gives us the opportunity to discuss these issues, and to draw all the threads together, with the aim of working towards a sustainable and secure world for future generations.

NOTES

1   UN Group of Governmental Experts on the Relationship Between Disarmament and Development, taken from World Commission on Environment and Development (1987) *Our Common Future*, Oxford: Oxford University Press, p300
2   For example, Woodrow Wilson Centre, US; Ecologic, Germany; Worldwatch Institute and World Resources Institute, US
3   UNEP (1999) *Global Environment Outlook Report*, London: Earthscan Publications Ltd
4   Ibid
5   Ibid
6   Homer-Dixon, T (1994) 'Environmental Scarcities and Violent Conflict: Evidence from Cases', *International Security*, vol 19, no 1, summer, p8
7   Ibid, p13
8   Renner, M (1997) *Fighting for Survival*, London: Earthscan Publications Ltd, p25
9   Brown, L R, Gardner, G and Halweil, B (2000) *Beyond Malthus: Nineteen Dimensions of the Population Challenge*, London: Earthscan Publications Ltd, p37
10   *Strategic Approaches to Freshwater Management*, Report of the Secretary-General (Feb/March 1988), UN Department of Economic and Social Affairs/CSD
11   *Preparations of Guidelines in the Water Resources Sector*, DG VIII, October 1997
12   UNFPA
13   UNEP (1999) *Everybody Lives Downstream*, World Day for Water, UNEP, March
14   Renner (1997) op cit Note 8, p65
15   Chou, S et al (1997) *Water Scarcity in River Basins as a Security Problem*, WW Spring, p100
16   Hammond, A (1998) *Which World? Scenarios for the 21st Century*, London: Earthscan Publications Ltd, p112
17   Postel, S (1995) *World Watch*, vol 8, no 3, May/June 1995, Washington, DC: Worldwatch Institute, p14
18   Brown et al (2000) op cit Note 9, p33
19   Brown, L et al (1999) *State of the World 1999: A Worldwatch Institute Report on Progress Towards a Sustainable Society*, London: Earthscan Publications Ltd, p120
20   Radford, T 'Will the World Starve Itself to Death', *The Guardian*, 3 June, p13

21 Eurostat (1998) *Statistics In Focus – Agriculture*, Eurostat, p2
22 *World Resources 1998–99: A Guide to the Global Environment*,
    Washington, DC: World Resources Institute, p154
23 *EC Food Security and Food Aid Programme: In Support of Development,
    Activity Report 1995–96*, European Commission, Luxembourg: Office for
    Official Publications of the European Communities
24 Ibid
25 Courrier de la Planete, *Food for Development* (January–February 1998)
    European Commission, DG VIII, p20
26 *EC Food Security and Food Aid Programme: In Support of Development,
    Activity Report 1995–96*, European Commission, Luxembourg: Office for
    Official Publications of the European Communities
27 Brown et al (1999) op cit Note 19, p129
28 Renner, M (1997) *World Watch*, vol 10, no 1, January/February,
    Washington, DC: Worldwatch Institute, p18
29 Renner (1997) op cit Note 8, p118
30 *Conservation Agriculture in Europe: Environmental, Economic and EU
    Policy Perspectives (1999)* European Conservation Agricultural
    Federation, p9
31 Ibid, p7
32 *European Commission Addressing Desertification: a Review of EC
    Policies, Programmes, Financial Instruments and Projects (May 1997)*
    Luxembourg: Office for Official Publications of the European
    Communities
33 WRI (1998) *World Resources 1998–99: A Guide to the Global
    Environment*, Washington, DC: World Resources Insitute, p195
34 Brown et al (2000) op cit Note 9, p51
35 *Natura 2000: Managing Our Heritage*, European Commission DG XI
    Publication
36 Rudneva, I (1999) *Black Sea Ecosystem and Environmental Stress*,
    Institute of the Biology of the Southern Seas National Ukrainian
    Academy of Sciences
37 WRI (1998) op cit Note 33, p185
38 Kennedy, R D et al (1998) *Environmental Quality and Regional
    Conflict, Report to the Carnegie Commission on Preventing Deadly
    Conflict*, Carnegie Corporation of New York, p8
39 Talbott, K and Brown, M (1998) *Forest Plunder in South East Asia: An
    Environmental Security Nexus in Burma and Cambodia*, Woodrow
    Wilson Environmental Change and Security Report, issue 4, spring 1998,
    p54
40 Baechler, G (1998) *Why Environmental Transformation Causes
    Violence: a Synthesis*, Woodrow Wilson Environmental Change and
    Security Report, spring
41 'Space Techniques for Environmental Monitoring Research',
    Environment and Climate Programme, Provisional Catalogue of
    Contracts 1995–98, European Commission DG XII
42 'European Parliament Resolution on the Environment, Security and
    Foreign Policy', *OJC* 128/94, dated 7 May 1999
43 IPPC (1997) *Intergovernmental Panel on Climate Change Report*

15

Cities and the Culture of Sustainability

Herbert Girardet

INTRODUCTION

At the beginning of the new millennium humanity is involved in an unprecedented experiment: we are turning ourselves into an urban species. Large cities, not villages and towns, are becoming our main habitat. The cities of the 21st century is where human destiny will be played out, and where the future of the biosphere will be determined. There will be no sustainable world without sustainable cities. How can we make a world of cities viable in the long term – environmentally, socially as well as economically?

The size of modern cities, in terms of numbers as well physical scale, is unprecedented: in 1800 in the UK there was only one city with a million people – London. At that time the largest 100 cities in the world had 20 million inhabitants, with each city usually extending to just a few thousand hectares. In 1990 the world's 100 largest cities accommodated 540 million people and 220 million people lived in the 20 largest cities – mega-cities of over 10 million people, some extending to hundreds of thousands of hectares. In addition, there were 35 cities of over 5 million and hundreds of over 1 million people.

Urban growth is changing the face of the Earth and the condition of humanity. In the 20th century, global urban populations have expanded from 15 to 50 per cent of the total, which itself has gone up from 1.5 to nearly 6.0 billion. By 2020, two-thirds of humanity will live in cities, with much of the rest depending upon urban markets for their economic survival. Urban agglomerations and their resource uses are becoming the dominant feature of the human presence on Earth, profoundly changing humanity's relationship to its host planet and its ecosystems. What are the measures needed to limit the physical impact of cities on the global environment?

In a world dominated by cities, the international community is beginning to address the issue of urban sustainability. The process began in Rio in 1992 with Agenda 21 and continued at the 1996 UN City Summit in Istanbul. The 100-page Habitat Agenda, signed in Istanbul by 180 nations, states: 'Human settlements shall be planned, developed and improved in a manner that takes full account of sustainable development principles and all their components, as set out in Agenda 21... We need to respect the carrying capacity of ecosystems and preservation of opportunities for future generations... Science and technology have a crucial role in shaping sustainable human settlements and sustaining the ecosystems they depend upon.'

Many of today's cities function very differently from those we have inherited from history. Low transport costs based on the ubiquitous use of fossil fuels have rendered distances irrelevant, plugging cities into an increasingly global hinterland. The process is often facilitated by substantial government subsidies on transport infrastructure. The actual location of settlements is becoming less and less important as global trade treaties come to determine the fate of national and local economies.

Today we don't really live in a civilization but in a mobilization – of natural resources, people and products. Cities are the nodes from which mobility emanates, along roads, railway lines, aircraft routes and telephone lines. Cities also sprawl ever outwards along urban motorways and railway lines to their suburbs and shopping malls, while their centres are often devoid of life outside business hours. They are both the origin and the destination of this mobilization, which has come to define human existence.

Yet, it is unlikely that the planet can accommodate an urbanized humanity which routinely draws resources from ever more distant hinterlands, or routinely uses the biosphere, the oceans and the atmosphere as a sink for its wastes. Can cities transform themselves into self-regulating, sustainable systems – not only in their internal functioning, but also in their relationships to the outside world? An answer to this question may be critical to the future well-being of the planet, as well as of humanity.

CITIES AND SUSTAINABLE DEVELOPMENT

Large-scale urbanization is an essentially unsustainable process. It greatly increases per capita use of fossil fuels, metals, timber, meat and manufactured products, with major external environmental implications. Unlike most traditional cultural systems, modern urban systems crucially depend upon a vast system of external supply lines to rural areas and manufacturing centres, facilitated by global transport and communications infrastructures.

City people often have very limited understanding of their use of resources. Energy is a case in point. When city dwellers think heat and light, they usually don't think firewood; instead, they think of electric or gas appliances – yet they are hardly aware of the power station, refinery or gas field that supplies them. And they hardly reflect the impacts of our energy use on the environment because they are rarely experienced directly, except when they inhale exhaust fumes on a busy street.

Demand for energy defines modern cities more than any other factor. Most urban activities depend upon fossil fuels – to warm, cool or illuminate us, to commute or to supply us with goods and services. Without the routine use of fossil fuels, mega-cities of ten million people and more would not have occurred. As far as I am aware, there has never been a city of more than one million people not running on coal, oil or gas. But there is a price to pay: not only is air pollution a continuing menace in cities, but most of the increase of carbon dioxide in the atmosphere is attributable to combustion in or on behalf of the world's cities. Yet, most city people find it hard to make the connection with something that is not happening here but 'out there'.

Urban food supplies are another case in point. The direct experience of growing food is largely absent in most cities; most people harvest at the supermarket and expect food to be served up packaged and branded for enhanced recognition. As city people they are hardly aware of the impacts of food consumption on the fertility of farmland supplying them, often from some distant place.

Urban standards of living have come to be the norm in the countryside as well. As we put plastic-wrapped meat or fruit in a supermarket trolley, we are blissfully unaware that humanity now uses nearly half the world's primary production from photosynthesis and that most of this is utilized by urban people. Our knowledge system fails to inform us that the human species is changing the very way in which the 'the web of life' on Earth itself functions: from the geographically scattered interaction of a myriad of living species, to which local cultures are intimately connected, into an assembly of concentrated urban centres into which one species, humanity, funnels resources from all over the world. Cities today take up only 2 per cent of the world's land surface, yet they use over 75 per cent of the world's resources.

Arising from the work of William Rees and Mathis Wackernagel, I have examined the ecological footprint of London – the land surfaces required to feed it, to supply it with wood products and to reabsorb its

CO_2 output. In total, these extend to 125 times London's own territory of 627,500 hectares, or nearly 80 million hectares. With only 12 per cent of Britain's population, London requires the equivalent of Britain's entire productive land. In reality, these land surfaces, of course, stretch to far-flung places such as the wheat prairies of Kansas, the soya bean fields of Mato Grosso, the forests of Canada, Scandinavia and Amazonia, or the tea gardens of Assam or Mount Kenya. But this global dependence of Londoners has never been a big issue. Food is there to be enjoyed – the environmental impact of food supplies, including the energy used to produce and supply them, is rarely discussed.

The same applies to the metabolism of cities. Like other organisms, they have a definable metabolism. That of traditional towns and cities was characterized by interactions between dense concentrations of people and their local hinterland, with transport and production systems centred on muscle power. Beyond their perimeters, traditional settlements were usually surrounded by concentric rings of market gardens, forests, orchards, farm and grazing land for use by townspeople. Today urban farming is still alive and well in cities in many countries. In some Chinese cities, for instance, people still practice returning night soil to local farmland to assure sustained yields of crops. With their unique systems of governance, Chinese cities administer adjacent areas of farmland and aim to be self-sufficient in food. Is this model of urban–rural linkages relevant to cities elsewhere in the world?

The metabolism of many traditional cities was circular, whereas that of most 'modern' cities is linear. Resources are funnelled through the urban system without much concern about their origin and about the destination of wastes; inputs and outputs are treated as largely unrelated. Contemporary urban sewage systems are a case in point. They have the function of separating people from their wastes. Sewage, treated or not treated, is discharged into rivers and coastal waters downstream from population centres, and its inherent fertility is lost to the world's farmland. Today coastal waters everywhere are polluted both by sewage and toxic effluents, as well as the run-off of fertilizers applied to farmland feeding cities. This open loop is utterly unsustainable.

The linear metabolic system of most cities is profoundly different from nature's own metabolism, which could be likened to a large circle: every output by an organism is also an input which renews and sustains the whole living environment. Urban planners and educators should make a point of studying the ecology of natural systems. On a predominantly urban planet, cities need to adopt circular metabolic systems to ensure their own sustainability and the long-term viability of the environments on which they depend. Urban outputs will need to be regarded as potential inputs into urban production systems, with routine recycling of paper, metals, plastic and glass, and composting of organic materials for reuse on local farmland.

The local effects of urban resource use also need to be better understood. Cities accumulate materials within them. The 1.6 million inhabitants of Vienna every day increase the city's actual weight by some 25,000 kilogrammes. Much of this is relatively inert materials, such as concrete and tarmac. Other substances, such as heavy metals, have toxic effects as they leach into the local environment. Nitrates, phosphates, or chlorinated hydrocarbons accumulate in local water courses and soils, with as yet uncertain consequences for future inhabitants.

These issues need to be addressed by national and urban policy in order to establish new ways in which to engineer and plumb our cities. They also need to be addressed at a subtler level. The value systems to which city people adhere must ascertain that this is not taken for granted indefinitely. Our separation from natural systems and our lack of direct experience of the natural world is a dangerous reality as it reduces our understanding of our impacts and of the ways in which we might lessen them.

Can cities maintain their living standards while curbing their local and global environmental impacts? To answer this question it helps to draw up balance sheets comparing urban resource flows. It is apparent that similar-sized cities are supplying the needs of their people with a greatly varying throughput of resources. Many cities could massively reduce their throughput of resources, maintaining a good standard of living while creating much-needed local jobs in the process. Cities in the North often have a much less impressive track record than those in the South, though poverty is a significant driving force for the high levels of waste recycling in the South.

FROM URBAN SPRAWL TO CONVIVIAL CITIES

Motorized transport makes it possible for cities to expand to hundreds of thousands of hectares, developing along railway lines and along new highways. It also assures supplies of food, forest products, manufactured goods, water, oil and gas to cities from ever greater distances. Today, air transport, which starts and ends at airports in the vicinity of cities, further contributes to our transport and travel options.

Motor cars and public transport systems also make it feasible to zone cities into distinct residential districts, industrial zones, business centres, cultural areas and shopping malls, ensuring the continued need of transport systems and increasingly replacing short-distance travel on foot and by bike. By tearing apart previously spatially integrated functions of urban life, dependence on motorized travel is assured, building travel distances into people's daily lives that are difficult to undo.

One thing is clear: in many cities sprawl can be contained only by vigorously applied planning legislation. London's outward growth, for instance, was curtailed by policies drawn up by Patrick Abercrombie after 1945. A clearly defined green belt, which cannot be built on, stopped London's expansion and helped protect the rural hinterland. Similar policies are now in place in many cities in Europe, though less so in the US. Portland, Oregon, where a successful green belt has curtailed the city's outward growth, is a notable exception.

It is clear that in formulating concepts for sustainable urban development we need to address the space that cities take up. It is important to limit the size of building plots, thus reducing the distances that people have to travel and encouraging efficient transport technologies and the integration of transport systems. The compact city offers a model that is of great significance for sustainable urban development, and that also applies to the potential of urban fringe agriculture.

Wherever a city sprawls, it does so on the farmland that made the growth of the city possible in the first place. By expanding on agricultural land, the long-term viability of cities is often undermined because they are in danger of becoming permanently dependent on land elsewhere, and often a long way away, in order to feed their inhabitants. In highlighting the importance of urban agriculture for urban sustainability, it is therefore crucial to develop and enact policies for preventing or countering urban sprawl.

TOWARDS SUSTAINABLE URBAN DEVELOPMENT

How can city people improve their understanding of the impacts of their life styles? Can large modern cities adopt more local, more frugal, more self-regulating production and disposal systems? How can the growth of cities be kept under control?

An answer to these questions may be critical to the future well-being of the biosphere, as well as of humanity itself. Maintaining stable linkages between cities and their hinterland – local or global – is a new task for most city politicians, administrators, business people and people at large, requiring new approaches to urban management. Many of the world's major environmental problems will only be solved by city people conceptualizing new ways of running their cities. Some cities have already made circularity and resource efficiency a top priority. In Europe, many cities are installing waste recycling and composting equipment. In many parts of the developing world, too, city administrations have made it their business to encourage the reuse of wastes.

Given that the physiology of modern cities is currently characterized by the routine use of fossil fuels, a major issue is whether people will see the potential of new, clean and efficient energy technologies for powering their cities, such as combined heat-and-power systems, heat pumps, fuel cells and photovoltaic modules. In the coming decades enormous reductions in fossil-fuel use can be achieved by incorporating photovoltaic modules in urban buildings.

URBAN FARMING TODAY

To make cities more sustainable a whole new range of initiatives is required. Urban agriculture is a case in point. If well developed, it could make a significant contribution to feeding cities and providing people with livelihoods.

Urban food growing is certainly common in the late 20th century and not just in poorer countries. A recent UNDP book called *Urban Agriculture* proves the point:

> '*The 1980 US census found that urban metropolitan areas produced 30 per cent of the dollar value of US agricultural production. By 1990, this figure had increased to 40 per cent. Singapore is fully self-reliant in meat and produces 25 per cent of its vegetable needs. Bamako, Mali, is self-sufficient in vegetables and produces half or more of the chickens it consumes. Dar-es-Salaam, one of the world's fastest-growing large cities, now has 67 per cent of families engaged in farming compared with 18 per cent in 1967. 65 per cent of Moscow families are involved in food production compared with 20 per cent in 1970. There are 80,000 community gardeners on municipal land in Berlin with a waiting list of 16,000.*'

In the Western world, few provisions have been made since World War II in providing space for urban food production. The economic boom of the last 40 years has led to the assumption that city people will buy food, not grow it themselves. But at a time when work sharing is widely seen as essential for assuring a dignified existence for large numbers of people, additional opportunities for people to create livelihoods for themselves are essential. Urban food growing is certainly one of the options.

In cities that have experienced industrial decline, provision of derelict land for food growing is certainly a planning policy option. In US cities, such as Detroit and New York, thousands of hectares of land have been given over for food growing to unemployed workers. In the UK, city farm projects have been established on areas of derelict land in some 20 cities. In Germany, land in former coal-mining areas in cities such as Essen is being set aside for urban agriculture projects.

There has been concern about the suitability of contaminated urban land for food growing, and it has been suggested that it is prudent to grow crops more than ten metres away from busy roads, particularly in countries where lead fuel is still in use. Generally, land polluted by heavy metals, such as cadmium and lead, requires special precautions. However, research in the US and the UK has shown that these problems can be tackled in a number of ways. Firstly, maintaining a high pH with additions of plenty of lime helps to immobilize heavy metals in the soil. Secondly, it is useful to add plenty of compost to the soil. People who grow food in cities tend to prefer the 'deep bed method', even building vegetable beds in wooden or brick frames on top of the soil surface.

The Chinese are famous for their highly intensive urban cropping systems, and to this day many of their large cities are largely self-sufficient in food from adjacent land areas administered by them. Beijing, now a city of over ten million people, still administers its own adjacent farmland extending to an area the size of Belgium. In Shanghai today only 30 per cent of the territory administered by the city authorities is actually built on; 70 per cent of the land, mainly in the urban perimeter, is used for crop growing, making the city region self-reliant in vegetables and producing much of the rice, pork, chicken, duck and carp. Is this model of urban–rural linkages relevant to cities elsewhere in the world?

For thousands of years the Chinese used to have a system of meticulously recycling and composting human and animal wastes, thus maintaining the fertility of their farmland by the most appropriate means. Whereas this system has been weakened, the Chinese are reluctant about abandoning it altogether. Instead, they are exploring ways of upgrading sewage recycling technology.

Urban farmers have always utilized the great variety of fertile materials they found in cities. The best-known examples are the vegetable growers in Paris who, until the end of World War I, were famous for the abundance of their crops. They used to heap up to 30 centimetres of horse manure on top of their vegetable beds every year, and used many different methods to control soil and air temperature. They were able to grow between three and six crops of fruit and vegetables a year, making a good living on no more than three-quarters of a hectare. In Paris a century ago 100,000 tonnes of high-value, out-of-season crops were grown on 1400 hectares, around one sixth of the surface area of the city, using about one million tonnes of horse manure. The crops were so abundant that they were even exported as far away as London. But the introduction of motor-powered transport ended the supply of horse manure to the marais.

In addition, more and more crops were brought in by train from the south of France.

IMPLEMENTING SUSTAINABLE URBAN DEVELOPMENT

Urban agriculture is only one aspect of a more sustainable urban lifestyle. City people need to formulate new cultural priorities and this should centre on formulating value systems for urban living, giving cities the chance to realize their full potential as centres of creativity, education and communication. Cities are nothing if not centres of knowledge, and today this also means knowledge of the world and our impact upon it. Reducing urban impacts is as much an issue of the better uses of technology as of education and of information dissemination.

As I have suggested, currently cities are not centres of civilization but mobilizers of people and goods. We need to revive the vision of cities as places of conviviality and, above all else, of sedentary living. This means reviving more local lifestyles within cities themselves, focusing on the concept of the urban village within the city where community living can be a reality. A calmer, serener vision of cities is needed to help them fulfil their true potential as places not just of the body but of the spirit. The greatest energy of cities should be directed towards creating masterpieces of human creativity.

The future of cities crucially depends upon the utilization of the rich knowledge of their people, and that includes environmental knowledge. Urban communications systems have a particularly important role to play in helping city people to understand their impacts and to bring about the necessary changes in the way we run our cities. In the future, cities need to develop communication strategies that help people to confront the global impacts of their economic power and consumer habits. City people need new communication channels to help them improve their decision-making, particularly regarding the impacts of their life styles. Here we can learn a great deal from the cultural feedback methodologies practised by traditional cultures, which use regular community meetings to reflect their impacts on the local environment. New communication systems can enable city people to monitor and ameliorate their impact on the biosphere.

Today new communication technologies should also be utilized to enhance the way cities function by improving communications within them, leading to better decision-making. Urban Intranets, now in place in a growing number of cities, should improve the communication flow between various sectors of urban society. If such changes occur, using the best of modern communication systems, we may yet learn to run our cities in more sustainable ways, improving their metabolism and reducing their ecological footprints. Large cities are not going to go away for the time being, but the way they work certainly need not be as damaging and wasteful as it is at the present time.

Cities for a new millennium could be energy and resource efficient, people friendly and culturally rich, with active democracies ensuring the best uses of human energies. Prudent investment in infrastructure could enhance employment, improving public health and living conditions.

Eco-friendly urban development could well become the greatest challenge of the 21st century, not only for human self-interest, but also to create a sustainable relationship between cities and the biosphere. Ultimately, that cannot be done without changing the value systems underpinning our cities. In the end, it is only a profound change of attitudes – a spiritual and ethical change – that can ensure that cities become truly sustainable.

16

Tourism and the Commission on Sustainable Development

Frans de Man

INTRODUCTION

In many countries tourism is regarded as an important business sector to enhance economic growth. Worldwide it certainly is: in 1998, 625 million tourists spent US$445 billion in the world economy. The amount of tourists is expected to increase to 673 million in 2000, and up to 1.6 billion in 2020. In 1999, according to predictions of the World Travel and Tourism Council (WTTC), tourism will account for 11 per cent of the world's gross domestic product (GDP) and for 200 million jobs – 8 per cent of world employment. In 2010 tourists will spend US$2 trillion creating a total of 255 million jobs.

Tourism was not on the agenda as a separate topic at the Earth Summit in 1992, but it has experienced such growth that (as an official UN Department of Public Information announcement states):

> *'Tourism is now one of the world's largest industries and one of the fastest growing economic sectors. Prior to 1997, the issue of sustainable tourism had been discussed by the Commission on Sustainable Development only in the context of the small island developing states. However, during the 19th special session of the General Assembly to review the first five years' implementation of Agenda 21, the General*

Assembly considered that there is a need to consider further the importance of tourism in the context of Agenda 21. Tourism, like other sectors, uses resources, generates wastes and creates environmental, cultural and social costs and benefits in the process. Consequently, the General Assembly placed sustainable tourism on the agenda of the commission at its seventh session in 1999.'

A Normal Economic Sector

Although often seen as a clean, friendly and romantic industry, tourism – as an economic sector – doesn't differ from other sectors. It represents an economic activity like any other. As in any transnational industry, it involves international forces and large economic powers that work according to the laws of the world economy, which also apply, for example, to agriculture. Like everywhere in the service sector, contact exists between the service provider and the client. This is comparable to banks, insurance, and the consultancy sector. For the working people of the developing world, it means jobs with advantages and disadvantages, with opportunities and threats for personal and collective development and with the problems of unequal relationships and suppression. Even the fact that the local people themselves don't consume the services they produce is not unique for the tourism sector.

Pros and Cons of Tourism

In one way, tourism does distinguish itself from other economic activities: it is a very complex sector. The end product reflects an enormous variety of holidays: from several nights on a basic campsite for a backpacker to a completely organized luxurious holiday for a senior citizen; from simple hikes for the low-budget traveller, to a trip on a leased yacht with staff for the upper market.

To make the situation yet more complex, tourism consists of several components that are being delivered by different producers, varying from big transnational corporations in the hotel sector to the souvenir vendors in the informal sector. This leads to a large number of actors and parties involved in a wide variety of views, who often disagree on whether and how tourism provides opportunities for real development.

Promoters would say tourism raises a lot of foreign currency that wouldn't enter the country otherwise; but their opponents confront them with the fact that this foreign currency leaks out of the country

through imports and payments of interest on loans, necessary for
tourism development. The jobs in tourism are not well paid, unevenly
divided and are seasonally bound; but the rhetorical reply is: what
would be the alternative? Proponents say that in the areas where
tourism is being developed, social and cultural values revive and
modernization is supported. Opponents point to the fact that modernization is not equal to improvement. They argue that crime and
prostitution increase and that vulnerable groups are being affected,
especially where it poses a threat to the position of women and
children because of bad working conditions and the sex lust of certain
tourists. Tourism is said to be bad for the environment because of the
strain tourists put on vulnerable natural resources, through the
overuse of these scarce resources, such as water and wood, through
the creation of huge piles of waste, and last but not least through the
huge pollution created by air traffic. Not true, is the reply; tourism is a
clean industry compared to mining, for example. It raises money for
nature conservation through ecotourism and air planes will be clean
in a few years.

DIFFERENT INTEREST GROUPS

Although many actors disagree on the opportunities and threats
tourism offers, all of them are directly or indirectly linked to each other
in what is called the tourism chain. This chain covers all the actors and
phases through which tourism passes, from the actual customer – the
tourist – to the person who finally delivers the touristic service – the
local. Let us take a look at the different actors who pass by if we go
along the tourism chain. We will start at one end, with the group that
constitutes the largest variety of interests: the local people in the destination regions. They are involved in a number of, sometimes
conflicting, roles. They are partly a passive part of the touristic
product: take a look at the local people, enjoy their hospitality, admire
their ferocity, etc, all without being asked. But a lot of them are also
involved in a more active way: as employees or entrepreneurs, directly
in the case of hotels and restaurants; indirectly as farmers, fishermen
or bakers; and through services such as laundries and banks.

   With the entrepreneurs at local level, we arrive in the part of the
tourism chain that deals with economics. This consists of a large group
of tourism entrepreneurs who actually bring and assist tourists in
getting from one place to the other: the tourism industry. It starts at
the level of the destination with the so-called incoming (receiving)
tour operators and goes through the national and international transportation companies, to the outgoing (sending) tour operators in the
tourist-sending countries. These companies quite often are all

combined in large transnational corporations (TNCs) and have solid links to other industries such as international hotel chains, airlines, banks and insurance companies.

Another interest group obviously are the governments, at the local as well as national and international levels. They have stakes in tourism in several ways and through several instruments, such as laws, taxes, planning and participation procedures, including immigration facilities, international declarations, health and hazard regulations, environmental, labour and tourism policies.

NGOs have been involved in tourism from the beginning of the century. There were the labour unions, on the one hand (which would save pennies from their members' salaries to offer them affordable holidays in union resorts), and elitist environmental movements on the other (conserving mountains by reserving them for the noblesse). In the last few years, the number of NGOs getting involved in tourism has grown dramatically, mainly due to the growth of the tourism sector, its environmental, economic and social effects and the number of people affected by it.

Last but not least there is the tourist, represented in great variety as mentioned above. Although national tourism is a common phenomenon in many parts of Asia and Latin America, the international tourist generally has one feature in common: he or she is from a rich part of the world. Tourism embeds the right to holidays in the struggle of the unions for days of rest from work, often confusing the right to holiday with the right to travel to anywhere they wish.

COMPLEXITIES IN TALKING ABOUT TOURISM

All these stakeholders obviously have their own opinions on tourism, highlighting pros and cons depending upon the interests they represent. But over the last two years a strange thing happened. Although it is obvious that tourism consists of a complexity of interests, in the late 1990s, it seemed that the stakeholders were merging into an agreement on the necessity and the contents of sustainable tourism. Although there is, of course, a remote possibility that all these interests agree on the necessity, there is far less likelihood that they all agree on what sustainable tourism should look like. At the CSD in 1999, it appeared more likely that this agreement is due to a lack of clarity between and among interest groups, resulting from differing perspectives when entering the discussion on sustainable tourism. Before dealing with the position of NGOs, let us therefore take some time to deal with and clarify some of the different perspectives. To start with one clarification, in this chapter we specifically address international tourism.

INCOMING VERSUS OUTGOING TOURISM

Talking about tourists and tourism, there are two different areas of concern regarding touristic activities and policy-making. The area of incoming tourism is about the infrastructure and capacity to receive tourists in your own region. The area of outgoing tourism is about organizing the facilities for your nationals to spend their holiday abroad. Although some of the facilities and actors might coincide, each involves different interests and activities. Confusion arises when actors with interests in outgoing tourism get involved in, and decide on, issues which are mainly in the realm of incoming tourism, and vice versa.

Related to this are the concepts of tourist-sending and tourist-receiving countries. Although many Western rich countries are both, many other countries in the world, especially developing world countries are only tourist receiving. It is obvious, therefore, that the way one perceives tourism is influenced by one's origin. These concepts are not only important for one's perspective of, and judgement on, tourism, but they also are relevant in policy areas such as national tourism and recreation. In some countries international tourism can lead to enhancement of the tourism and recreation facilities for nationals; in others they might compete.

EMPOWERMENT VERSUS TRICKLE DOWN

On a more conceptual level, the development of theories in tourism is mainly dominated by a belief in trickle-down concepts: if it rains on the wealthy it will trickle down and drip on the poor. Tourism has hardly ever been an area of interest for critics of these economic trickle-down theories. Scientists involved in theories of structural underdevelopment did not deal with tourism as a serious economic sector. The development of theories and the actual world of tourism development itself have both been dominated by organizations that believe in trickle-down economics and structural adjustment. Discussion on sustainable tourism on a global level took as its starting point a firm belief that an invisible hand, if assisted by codes of ethics and voluntary charters, would assure the trickling down of the benefits of tourism to local people. NGOs involved in development critique did not get involved in tourism easily and if they did, they very often denounced it.

Only recently, things have started to change and the studies and pleas to approach and develop tourism from an empowerment perspective are growing. This is mainly due to the fact that many of the target groups of these NGOs (the world's poor) were confronted with the growth of tourism. They would start to invest in small-scale tourism projects and ask NGOs for assistance, or they would invite NGOs to negotiate with the tourism industry to take a common stand against the threats of tourism, as was done in the case of the fight against child sex tourism.

From the perspective of empowerment, and acknowledging the fact that different interests might pose insurmountable conflicts, development critics would raise questions about the incompatibility of the long-term aims of sustainable tourism and the short-term interests of local people, striving to get control of their environment or just wanting to survive. In this debate, not only trickle-down assumptions are questioned, but also the presupposed harmony between ecological and social development. Where trickle-down thinking has picked up the issue of sustainable tourism, it mainly tapped into the discussion on ecotourism, accepting the value and importance of ecological resources because of their importance for the tourism product. The social contents of the concept of sustainability were seen as secondary, assuming they would follow automatically from development of ecological resources through sustainable tourism. These implicit assumptions were criticized by pointing at the conflicts that exist between the conservation of nature and the needs of local people to survive. An often mentioned example is the case of the Masai in Tanzania, who were evicted from their living grounds in order to change them into national parks for ecotourists. Now both the Masai and the park are struggling to survive: the Masai because they cannot graze their cows, the park because an essential element, the Masai and their cows, were taken away from the ecosystem.

But even within the ecological sphere of sustainable tourism there are differing and even conflicting interests, as the discussion on air traffic makes clear. What if you want to earn the money to conserve a national park through ecotourism, but in doing so are contributing to the greenhouse effect through all the air transport needed to get people from the rich part of the world to the parks?

ROMANTIC VERSUS REALISTIC

Most of the theories on sustainable tourism, leading to easy compromises, suffer from a romanticized view of what tourism is all about. They reflect only one side the dualistic approach that many Westerners have towards the developing world. When they hear of Indonesia, they think of human rights violations and the atrocities of East Timor; mention Bali and they fall into a dream about unspoiled beaches and beautiful cultural dances. Talk about Kenya, and they think of student riots and political oppression; but when you mention Masai Mara, a view of endless plains with elephants, lions and giraffes appears in their mind's eye. Talk about Guatemala, secret police killings and torture in prisons come to mind; mention Tical and a beautiful jungle opens up to a miraculously beautiful temple complex. In tourism discussions based on these trickle-down theories, only the romantic side of these equations passes the review. Many of the misunderstandings in discussions on tourism stem from this deeper conflict of perspectives.

From here, most theories on the benefits of tourism take a step further into romance, arguing that international tourism contributes to world peace. The contacts between cultures and people from different cultures is supposed to benefit the understanding of those people. While this might be hard to prove – looking at the growth of tourism and the situation of war and peace in the present world – it certainly takes us to a more dangerous aspect of the romanticized image of the development process and of tourism. The development of tourism, ideally, should never lead to changes in the culture of the destination area – the touristic version of the noble savage. Not that the dynamics of the culture of a destination area are taken as the starting point, but culture is seen as static thing. By coincidence, this static interpretation of culture is also an important ingredient of tourism and its brochures. Tourism is more interested in the static culture of my country, The Netherlands (tulips, mills, cheese, wooden shoes), than in its dynamic culture (high pressure at work, disappearing and reappearing landscape, commercializing of the media, soccer, single-parent families, mass discharges, American movies, IT, McDonald's, etc). In this reasoning, the perspective of the tourist/adventurer/traveller who is afraid that another unspoiled paradise (discovered by, and destined for, him or her) will be destroyed plays an important role.

TERMINOLOGY

Building on these underlying and confusing perspectives, a terminology developed, contributing to a touristic Babylon with terms such as ecotourism, alternative tourism and (unfortunately) sustainable tourism. These marketing myths were developed mainly to help conscientious tourists who suffer from the feelings of guilt regarding air pollution, disturbing local people and spending more money in one week than locals will earn in a year. They don't refer to the actual quality of the respective tourism product. For instance, they don't mention how ecologically responsible a holiday is, or how alternative it is to other touristic products when seen through the eyes of the local population, and they say more about the sustainability for the tourism industry than for the tourism destination. Furthermore, the same masters of terminology speak about host populations, which was considered offensive by some developing world critics because it implies that these 'host populations' cordially invited tourists to come: 'We were confronted with them without being consulted!'

Recently, the proponents of tourism gladly adopted the new mystifying hype on 'globalization'. Tourism is seen as both a cause and a consequence of it. But where economic globalization might be beneficial for some forms of tourism, the industry should view the resulting cultural globalization as a threat to tourism in general. Also relevant for sustainable tourism is the fact that globalization, while offering more choices to tourists and outgoing tour operators, means more competition for people in holiday destinations. The beaches and nature parks of Ecuador will have to compete with those of Tanzania and of Thailand, and, ultimately, low prices and willingness to compromise will decide how tourism develops on a global level. As in any sector, globalization in tourism benefits the powerful in the development process.

PERSPECTIVE OF THE NGOS

Until 1999 NGOs had not taken a collective firm position in the discussion on sustainable tourism. Although individual NGOs had participated in global events on sustainable tourism, from which statements came out stressing their NGO involvement, there were only a few moments when NGOs tried to speak with one voice. Globally, they hardly gathered among themselves. Regionally, there were NGO meetings, but they suffered from the same flaw: interests gathered on a regional basis did not reflect the global spectrum of interests. At the few global meetings of NGOs involved in tourism, the gaps between them became apparent. The problem is that most NGOs stand for the interests of particular groups or causes involved in the tourism chain. The differences of interest within the tourism chain can (and did) lead to differences between NGOs involved in tourism.

In the late 1990s, however, with the unstoppable growth of tourism affecting NGO target groups, offering threats and opportunities, many NGOs felt uneasy that they could not create a counterforce to bridle the power of tourism developers. The preparations for the CSD-99 came as a relief. NGOs involved in tourism all over the world were approached by the CSD NGO Steering Committee and asked to comment and adapt the texts that would serve as a start to create a common stand for NGOs. This was done with respect to the existing differences between NGOs from the South and those from the North. During the two weeks of the CSD, many of these differences were overcome, in the light of the importance of taking a stand together against global developments in tourism which threaten the position of people. To organize this, the CSD NGO Tourism Caucus was set up. In the process of negotiations and lobbying, leading to the final tourism document of the CSD-99, this caucus – with some 25 members – was quite successful in including its points of view. The most disappointing setback was that the document contains no direct mention of the fight against child sex tourism, one of the most important (and successful) common causes for NGOs. After the CSD-99, the caucus decided to continue its activities. To describe the tasks it took upon itself, it issued a mission statement. What follows now is an impression of it.

THE NGO TOURISM CAUCUS

The NGO Tourism Caucus of the CSD NGO Steering Committee focuses on the participation of local people and communities in the process of tourism development, referring back to Agenda 21 and the concept of sustainable development. In this process it has expressed the collective experiences of Southern and Northern NGOs on the impacts of tourism. It would like to have a wider representation so that the industry-led tourism development perspective is balanced by people's concerns and priorities, which are:

- the right to determine one's own future;
- land, water and resource rights;
- individual and community rights;
- preservation of customs and cultures;
- protection of biodiversity;
- preservation of traditional wisdom;
- the just demands of those who work in the tourism industry.

Consequently the NGO Tourism Caucus will take up the empowerment of local communities and indigenous peoples (with special attention to the workers in tourism) through a more representative and democratic exchange of information and ideas. Leading to informed participation, this should help individuals and communities to participate directly and meaningfully at all levels of decision-making. This requires broad and authentic information, education and awareness-raising.

To deal with the unsustainable aspects of tourism we have to deal with some very crucial issues, such as the mechanisms creating a world of rich and poor; the unequal use of resources on a global level; the tensions (monocultural) tourism creates in 'backward' regions; patterns of (over) consumption; unequal and unsustainable leisure and recreation patterns; the position of workers in post-industrial society; qualitative versus quantitative measuring of tourism benefits.

From all the documents that have been produced, the Tourism Caucus distilled categories which can be seen as highlighting the issues relevant for tourism in the coming years.

- Tourism development should be a multistakeholder process, involving all the major groups from the CSD process, such as women, youth, labour unions, NGOs and local authorities.
- The role of local people should be stressed in the years to come. Through informed participation, tourism should contribute to community development, with special attention being paid to the rights of indigenous peoples. Tourism should be geared to fit local economies and to benefit, not destroy, them. Only after that has been secured, links to – and the prevention of leaks from – economies should be promoted. Local entrepreneurs and local workers should get fair chances in tourism.
- Entrepreneurship, in general, should become more responsible, while fair (and ethical) tourism should become the standard, not only focusing on the ecological consequences of tourism but, first and foremost, on social, economic and cultural consequences. Voluntary initiatives, codes of conduct and stewardship can only complement fair trading practices.
- Tourists have a right and an obligation to be educated and informed on the local situation in order to prevent conflicts with, and disturbance for, local people.
- Complex as the sector is, one cannot separate tourism development from other developments; discussions on sustainable tourism have to take place in other sectors as well. Global developments in finance and economy will influence tourism development more than any voluntary initiative or code of conduct ever will.

International financial institutions and agreements will determine the limits to sustainable tourism development. Therefore, it is of the highest importance to discuss and lobby for sustainable tourism within these institutions. For the same reason, sustainable tourism should be an integral part of all discussions on biodiversity.

THE MULTISTAKEHOLDER UN WORKING GROUP ON SUSTAINABLE TOURISM

A first step in addressing the tourism issue in a way that could offer sustainable solutions was the establishment of a UN working group on sustainable tourism, which met for the first time on 20 January 2000 in the Costa Rican city of Heredia. This working group, which was called for by NGOs in the CSD process, comprises a number of different stakeholders in tourism, among them members of the UN nations family such as the World Tourism Organization and UNEP, as well as representatives of the industry and of NGOs. It has taken upon itself to address issues relevant to sustainable tourism in a common agenda, with results to be presented at Earth Summit 2002. These issues cover many of the elements that are considered crucial by the NGOs. The NGOs of the Tourism Caucus of the CSD NGO Steering Committee will therefore participate in this working group to ensure that the concerns and priorities of local communities are taken up in the agenda for 2002.

17

Sustainable Tourism: A Southern Perspective

Nina Rao

INTRODUCTION

Tourism is big business today. There is no country in the world that is not in the global network of tourism activity. As numbers grow, there is pressure to keep the growth rate up. Every other industry has a cyclic downturn, but not tourism. To be able to understand the influence of tourism at the turn of the century, we have to distance ourselves from the blurb that surrounds tourism. We have to try to get at the basic elements that drive the process of global tourism.

In our cultures, we have been participants in the process of the pilgrimage; we have been travellers, merchants, adventurers, but only very recently have we become tourists. Our tourism was always related to learning, business, family occasions and ritual. We did not travel merely for pleasure. Kings and emperors travelled for sport and for recreation, but common people travelled when it was necessary and when it was an obligation. How did we learn to become tourists?

Tourism was bequeathed to us by colonialism, which reproduced in the colonies the same form of tourism as was practised at home. We developed scenic and recreational centres where the colonial administrators moved to get away from the heat and dust. In their wake followed the well-to-do and the babus (clerks) without whom the administration could not function. The focus of tourism was now on eating, drinking, play and relaxation. The activities were the same all over the colonized world. Only the scenery changed. The holiday-come-tourism pattern was encouraged by institutional seasonality. The summer holiday was now a sacred moment in the tourism enterprise.

In the post-colonial world, there was no consciousness of tourism, no definition, no data, no marketing strategy and no tourism plan! However, the right to holiday (and subsidy) was recognized and government employees were given a leave-travel concession to make their way to all corners of the country in order to promote national integration. The state intervened to create a tourism consciousness, bringing ethnic groups and communities together in the new national enterprise: development and modernization. The need of the hour was to follow in the footsteps of the advanced industrialized countries, for whom foreign exchange was necessary, and we began to look to the rest of the world to see what we could export. Tourism, the invisible export, was a handy instrument as the UN announced its development decade in the 1960s.

TOURISM ACTIVITY AND SERVICES

As we began to set targets under the guidance of the World Tourism Organization (WTO), every developing world country began to compete with others for the same tourists and promoted similar products. The chase for numbers continues today; for some there is success and for others the correlations do not come right. The question that we all ask is: what is sustainable? Is it numbers? Is it development? Is it foreign exchange? Is it jobs and income for the poor, the displaced and the people on the margins? Is it to feature among the top ten destinations or the top ten earners from tourism? If the latter two, then no developing world country features in the list. China has just recently made, but it is outside the market economy system. Do we count this as a success story because of the numbers or because its economic system is different?

As we look at the forecasts of the WTO and the World Travel and Tourism Council (WTTC) we can observe that tourism activity and benefits are concentrated in the North (western Europe and North America). But the new destinations are coming up in the South. As the push towards tourism continues, we can also see that the old division between tourism receiving and generating countries is a false distinction. Many countries in the South are sending out more tourists than they are receiving. However, these tourists do not consume as much since they have to buy dollars at an unrealistic rate of exchange. Most countries have a much more significant domestic tourism activity, but the focus is on international tourism, since the domestic tourist does not use the same facilities and their activities are not based on international consumption patterns. Domestic tourism is being tolerated for political reasons, but the key to tourism as trade lies in international tourism. It is for this reason that the WTO has circulated a paper on tourism services and the Global Agreement on Tariffs and Trade (GATT) long before the World Trade Organization has completed the discussion on this agenda.

Liberalization of tourism services is the need of the multinational corporations (MNCs), who are seeking new destinations for profit and to ensure that numbers keep growing in demand for their services, which are based on unsustainable levels of consumption. They pay lip service to the concept of sustainability by recycling water and saving electricity, but their footprints are larger than their contribution to the well-being of the planet.

INTERNATIONAL TRADE VERSUS SUSTAINABILITY

The decade of the 1990s has been significant for us. As unequal trade and debt have ground our survival strategies into dust and broken our traditional support systems, and as structural adjustments have destroyed our safety nets, we have been thrust into the marketplace of international developmental agendas. Beginning with the Earth Summit, the Beijing Women's Conference, the new world trade order and social clauses on labour, we now have an international sustainable development order that has put the tourism issue on the agenda. As some NGOs have stated, we are now in the process of selling indulgences for developed countries to continue pillaging the resources of the world as they create a consumer class for marketing their products and life styles; meanwhile, the rest of the Earth's population sinks below the consumption line into invisibility.

How do we look at sustainability? For us the issue is not one of protecting forests and other landscapes in which tourists can view wildlife as they consume wood, water, energy, food and air. It is not to keep the pristine beauty of the mountains so that tourists can trek in a peaceful and clean environment. It is not a series of resorts strung along the coastline while fishermen and women move further down the coast. It is not farms which cater for country holidays on land and which produced food for people. The slogan for sustainable development is food, shelter and clothing for all. Has tourism helped us to realize this dream? It must be said that at the end of the century, the dispossessed will determine what is sustainable, if anything is left for them at all.

The process of sustainable development as debated at the CSD has adopted a multistakeholder methodology to give a semblance of participation in the democratic decision-making process. However, the categories identified are determined more for administrative convenience in order to draw larger numbers into the market rather than to realize their dream of minimum standards of living. Government and industry in democracy represent the same interests. Local governments carry this unholy combination to grassroots levels. People's representation through NGOs does not necessarily mean that the weakest or poorest are being represented or consulted. The programmes and models are based on self-help groups to encourage individualism and market orientation rather than to resolve the unsustainable access to resources and their consumption. Tourism development is following the same patterns.

How can we break through this web of neo-liberal subterfuge? We believe that tourism is a human right. We believe that regardless of affluence or ethnicity, we all have the same right to rest, recreation, leisure and tourism. We believe that we also have the right to culturally determine what form and type of tourism we would like to practise. The multiculturalism that Northern NGOs promote tends to gloss over not only the aspects of racism and the stereotypes that result from it, but also the fact that other cultural practices which are location specific might be more sustainable than practices which are currently determined by intergovernmental agencies, client governments and the tourism industry controlled by MNCs.

Tourism has endangered not only the Earth but also the atmosphere, as transport networks have expanded to encircle the globe. If we accept this, then we have to ensure that the distance travelled for tourism becomes less, not more. Demand for energy and water for comfort and recreation have added to the water crisis around the world. As towns and villages suffer blackouts and women walk miles to carry safe water for essential needs, can we sustain the demand for air conditioning, heating, laundry and swimming pools? As people live under the open sky, can we demand more luxurious high-rise islands? Can we demand tourism infrastructure at the expense of schools and health care in the remote mountains?

ECOTOURISM

Ecotourism has been seen as a sustainable activity, but it appears to be a new business opportunity. There are many case studies to show how ecotourism has led to displacement of people, destruction of social and cultural patterns and in some areas degeneration of the ecosystem. In India, the World Bank is funding projects to remove local inhabitants so that administrators control forests for the use of industry and commerce. Tourism is one such activity that is being pushed in forested landscapes, which have been the home of tribes and communities for generations. Their traditional relationships and knowledge systems have been replaced with pseudo-scientific development. The displaced people have been alienated from their homes and their resources so that tourists can come and learn to live with nature. We believe that ecotourism should encourage people to learn about nature but not at the cost of those who can teach them the real worth of the ecosystem and its living principles.

For us, sustainability means reducing consumption. It means respecting that what is local is often wiser than what is global. It does not mean increasing the gap between the rich 20 per cent and the poor 20 per cent. The resources needed and the waste generated by modern tourism are certainly not sustainable. This depletes nature faster than the processes under which natural and nature-based resources can regenerate. Sustainability in tourism must keep within the regeneration capacity of a destination in terms of its ecology, its economy, its culture and its social norms.

ECOLOGICAL FOOTPRINTS

In this context, we might look at the ecological footprint (EFP) concept to determine sustainability. EFP is a planning tool. It is a simple yet comprehensive tool which helps us to visualize the impact of tourism. EFP accounts for the flow of energy and matter to and from any defined economy and converts this into land and water area required to support such a flow. Therefore, we cannot only assess the sustainability of current tourism activity at current levels, but must also use it as a campaigning tool to build awareness of the crisis, as well as to help in decision-making. This tool is not to make us aware of how bad tourism is, but to help us secure a form and volume of tourism that depends on nature and its 'free' gifts. In this way our dependence on these gifts will sustain human existence and access to tourism now and in the future as well.

The first thing we understand by using this tool is that our planet is finite and the human enterprise cannot be expanded indefinitely. But who should stop: North or South? The failure to reason this out would hurt the poor first, the rich a little later; and as we watch other species become extinct, we may face the same fate. In the production–consumption–pollution cycle, human society has become a dominant system in every ecosystem. In tourism we would like to redress this imbalance. To make tourism sustainable we have to manage ourselves first.

The average North American footprint measures 4–5 hectares and is a measure of the consumption of Americans. The world average of land available is 1.5 hectares per person. North Americans are consuming three to four times their fair share. The per capita consumption of residents in rich countries has exceeded supply of resources by a factor of three. This has happened at the cost of someone else. Thus, the ecosystems that support 70 per cent of the world's tourists lie far away from where they live. These systems support populations and activities which are being crushed under the heavy footprints of tourism. Can we say that taxes and the polluter-pays principle will ensure that we get our fair share of tourism? Can we get our fair share of the resources of nature for our children?

The population of these destinations is being trampled under these over-sized footprints. To see the true impact of tourism, the EFP analysis would represent not only a scientific analysis of the flow of resources and their consumption, but would also demand political judgement to determine the sustainability of modern tourism.

CODES OF ETHICS

When we look at sex tourism and paedophilia and other forms of exploitation, the remedies suggested are difficult to implement. It is just the tip of the iceberg that is visible to activists. Every legislative regime forces these crimes underground. Governments, industry and NGOs are all required to play a role in identifying those most at risk, and then use tourism itself to invest in removing the causes of these perverted forms of 'enjoyment'. EFP will make visible the consumption of children and women to which any civilized society would object. Just as the world has taken note of the state of the planet through various awareness-raising tools, we who work in the area of wanting sustainable tourism have to develop tools that will make tourists, governments and industry sit up and take note of what is going on.

Many sociologists have explained the negative behaviour and practice of tourists (and the industry that manipulates them to consume products and to consume more) as the crossing of the threshold of liminality. Normative behaviour is locked behind the front door as a tourist leaves on holiday. At the destination, industry stereotypes (standardized activities and services) and tourist prejudices ensure that the tourist uses money power and societal advantage as justification for behaviour that would be unacceptable at home. Servers at the destination also view tourists as a stereotype and behave accordingly with them. Tourism encounters encourage this perception and push the limits of human tolerance. Codes of ethics, therefore, have to target specific areas and hold industry responsible for the way in which the traveller has given way to the pejorative term: the tourist.

18

The Titanic Transnationals: Corporate Accountability and Responsibility

Jagjit Kaur Plahe[1] and Pieter van der Gaag[2]

INTRODUCTION

Transnational corporations (TNCs) control two-thirds of global trade and investments. The total foreign assets of the top 100 TNCs amounted to US\$18 trillion in 1998, according to the 1999 World Investment Report.[3] Trade these days is not confined to goods, but also includes services and intellectual property rights (IPRs). Investment is no longer confined to the physical establishment of a plant or an office, but also includes portfolio investments. There is no doubt that the transnational nature of giant corporations in the past ten years has led to huge cuts in costs of production of goods and services, and has increased global output dramatically. There are, however, still major concerns regarding corporate accountability and responsibility among governments, civil society groups, trade unions and communities worldwide. Human rights and environmental protection are at the forefront of these concerns.

The list of the top 100 non-financial TNCs is dominated by a few western European countries, the US and Japan. Only two are based in developing countries: South Korea and Venezuela. The power of Northern-based TNCs is growing every day with rapid mergers, acquisitions, alliances and joint ventures between giant corporations. The economic reach of these corporations goes all the way down the production chain from the patents and trademarks at the top, to the smallest suppliers situated on the edges of developing country cities at the bottom.[4] A mere glance at these figures portrays a very real picture of where power lies globally. There is a clear dominance of the North over the South in terms of the production of goods and services. The sheer size of some of these corporations, and the financial capital that they generate and control, wields them immense power to protect their own interests. While TNCs dominate global markets, there is no world government or competent world authority that is capable of regulating TNCs. Instead, the world is witnessing the rapid increase in voluntary codes of conduct which corporations use to address human rights and sustainable development concerns.

These concerns have brought the issue of corporate accountability and responsibility at the forefront of advocacy work on the principles of equity and social justice and environmental protection worldwide. These issues directly relate to the implementation of Agenda 21, such as meeting, in an equitable manner, developmental and environmental needs of present and future generations (Rio principle 3); addressing the interests and needs of all countries (Rio principle 6); eliminating and reducing unsustainable patterns of production and consumption (Rio principle 8); access to information (Rio principle 10); and cooperation to further international law regarding liability and compensation for adverse effects of environmental damage (Rio principle 13).

International treaties that relate to trade have a very strong, legally binding, sanction-based enforcement mechanism. On the other hand, global treaties and agreements that are negotiated to protect human rights and the environment have a much weaker enforcement mechanism. When states want to create market conditions which are favourable to TNCs, legally binding treaties such as the ones negotiated at the World Trade Organization (WTO) or the failed Multilateral Agreement on Investment (MAI) of the OECD are introduced. When it comes to setting standards of corporate behaviour, enforcing human rights or protecting the environment, non-binding measures, or measures with weaker enforcement procedures, seem to be preferred. These non-binding measures include thousands of corporate codes of conduct, but also agreements between governments, other stakeholders and corporations.

To address this dualism in international policy making, the NGO Taskforce on Business and Industry (ToBI) was founded. Its purpose was to move the UN towards addressing the issues related to corporate accountability and responsibility.

Today, while there is a lot of information being generated on voluntary codes, there is still not much information available on the role of voluntary codes of conduct in sustainable development. Although individual case studies do exist, they have not been collated to give an overall global picture on this role. Given the increasing power and impact of TNCs on sustainable development, it is very important to review voluntary codes of conduct within a framework that reflects the relationship between such codes and sustainable development.

This chapter puts forward the argument that an international effort under the auspices of the CDS needs to be made to ensure corporate accountability and responsibility, in line with the aforementioned Rio principles. It is also argued that sustainable development needs a balanced approach in international policy-making, where powerful trade and possible investment treaties must be balanced with equally strong social and environmental treaties.

EQUITABLE DEVELOPMENT AND TRANSNATIONAL CORPORATIONS

A TNC is a manufacturing or service company which operates in several countries. Traditionally, it consists of companies in different countries which are linked to the extent that they share knowledge, resources and work interdependently. What separates the relationship between entities within a TNC and entities that do not form a TNC is the fact that there is a level of responsibility for the operations of the entities, and not a mere trading relationship. Usually this responsibility emerges from one entity registered in one country.

The reason that corporations internationalize their production is to make higher profits. By expanding their operations in countries where certain factors of production are cheaper, such as labour, corporations experience economies of scale and hence lower costs of production.[5] Corporations then become more competitive and are therefore able to gain greater clout in markets worldwide. Large corporations have the financial and capital might to invest in separate countries, maximizing their ability to gain profit from different situations (legal, economic, etc) from different countries. This is why bilateral and multilateral treaties, which seek to open up markets in previously closed countries, greatly favour TNCs.

In the past decade, with the rapid liberalization of most of the economies of the world, 'the sales and the assets of TNCs have grown faster than the world gross domestic product, faster than total global exports, and faster than gross fixed capital formation'. The estimated value of the total global sales of TNCs in 1995 alone by some 280,000 foreign affiliates of 44,000 parent corporations has been estimated at US$7 trillion.[6] In 1997 this volume increased to US$9.7 trillion by 53,000 TNCs and their 450,000 affiliates.[7]

Foreign direct investment (FDI) has, as these figures show, increased dramatically.[8] There is no doubt that FDI outweighs exports as the 'dominant mode of servicing foreign markets'.[9] However, according to the 1997 World Investment Report, this is not the case in developing countries where 'exports continue to be the principal mode of delivering goods and services to foreign markets'.[10] Although in 1997 the numbers had increased slightly in favour of the developing countries, the dominance of developed countries in FDI is still obvious.[11] The developing world is far from homogenous and trends in these countries therefore cannot be generalized. Today, there is a very small outflow of FDI from developing countries; major foreign investors are from Asia and a few from Latin America. Africa has a negligible outflow of FDI (mainly from South Africa and Nigeria). The countries in transition in central and eastern Europe and the newly independent states of the former Soviet Union show similar trends. Large TNCs are purchasing many of the existing plants. Yet inflow of investments does not equal the giant capital flight (outflow) witnessed in the newly independent states in particular.[12]

While there is little outflow of FDI from developing countries, the inflows of foreign investment are large and increasing, especially in Asia, central and eastern European, and, to a lesser extent, Latin America. For this reason, developing countries are now referred to as 'emerging markets' and unfortunately not as 'emerging producers'. The sales of four of the biggest TNCs exceed the gross domestic product of the whole of Africa.[13] This goes to show that African corporations at present are very small in terms of size and capital when compared to corporations from the North. Developing country corporations today are not major global players and therefore they do not have the same kind of power to lobby for their interests as the titanic corporations from the North have.

The outcome of the UN Conference on Environment and Development (UNCED) in Rio de Janeiro in 1992 was an effort by the world's leaders to address the problems related to environmental damage in order to ensure the sustainability of the planet. It was recognized at Rio that corporations have a major role to play in achieving sustainable development. Although there are examples that clearly demonstrate that the corporate sector has contributed to achieving this goal, these are very few, and a lot still needs to be done to ensure that development truly is sustainable. More disturbingly, corporations are in some cases the major forces behind averting measures that would ensure an equitable distribution of welfare, environmental protection and the achievement of government-controlled measures in favour of sustainability. The push for an MAI-like framework within the WTO and the push for the Africa Growth and Opportunity Bill are examples of this. This reality suggests that, in order to achieve the Rio principles, the UN system needs to focus on evaluating corporate behaviour and devising measures that are acceptable to all parties interested in, and concerned with, achieving this.

THE DUAL APPROACH IN INTERNATIONAL POLICY-MAKING

It is quite evident that it is extremely difficult to get strong, legally binding, international legislation for human rights and environmental issues. There is also plenty of evidence that it is easier for countries to negotiate and agree on strong, binding international legislation that ensures market access and protection of corporate interests. This leads to the conclusion that we seem to be entering a dual international policy-making system, where – on the one hand – economic benefits for a few strong actors are secured and – on the other hand – the rights of the majority are not.[14] The WTO is well known for its far-reaching influence in policy-making. The WTO system belongs to the first side of this dual system: namely, the side securing economic benefits for the stronger few. Regretfully, there is no equal player with the same power for securing the rights for the weaker actors in society.

The WTO has three major agreements: the General Agreement on Tariffs and Trade (GATT), the Trade-Related Aspects of Intellectual Property Rights Agreement (TRIPS) and the General Agreement on Trade in Services (GATS). Each of these agreements is about providing market access to investors. The irony is that while the WTO's ideology is based on the neo-liberal laissez-faire model, the TRIPS treaty goes against this ideology since IPRs are all about protection. IPRs actually distort the market if one is to follow the theory of competition. This clearly demonstrates the fact that, when liberalization is in the interests of the powerful players at the WTO, treaties that liberalize markets are drawn up. However, when corporate interests actually require protection, then protection treaties are negotiated, signed and enforced, and the free trade ideology in the latter case is gladly relinquished.

Rapid liberalization of countries through structural-adjustment conditions, as well as through WTO commitments, does not really guarantee efficiency through competition; in fact, such conditions and commitments can actually lead to anti-competitive behaviour. The Consumer Unity and Trust Centre of India has identified several ways in which TNCs can actually distort the global market through anti-competitive practices.[15] These include cross-border mergers and acquisitions which can create new monopolies to replace previously competitive firms; strategic business alliances where competing corporations begin to cooperate through joint marketing or other means; and import and international cartels, both of which comprise premediated action by corporations to divide up the market. This behaviour is a far cry from what liberalization is all about.

Multilateral trade agreements and regional treaties such as the Lomé Convention help to fortify the powerful positions of TNCs.[16] These agreements unfortunately do not incorporate either multilateral environmental agreements, such as the Convention on Biodiversity, or any human-rights treaties such as the Covenant on Economic, Social and Cultural Rights. This is a major shortcoming of the WTO since it enforces corporate freedoms, but not the rights of people and the environment that they live in. The WTO does have a Committee on Trade and Environment (CTE); however, there is really no serious consensus on what kind of trade-related environmental measures need to be enforced.

The WTO insists that it is a trade body and not an environmental or human rights one. Yet, trade liberalization greatly affects the extent to which poor people have access to basic needs, such as health and education. Besides, human rights and environmental agreements have a very weak enforcement system when compared to the WTO's system. Ideally, each WTO agreement should complement previously multilaterally agreed-upon human-rights and environmental agreements which are legally binding.

At present, there is no international regulation of TNCs. Anti-trust laws and competition policy only feature nationally, and while parent companies might be controlled in their home countries they can easily circumvent competition policy in host countries, especially if these host countries are developing countries with weak competition policy or none at all. TNCs might even pressure host countries to offer them protection against cheap imports, for example. To curb this behaviour, the UN attempted to set up a centre for TNCs; however, this turned out to be a failure due to strong political reasons. The only remaining governmental instrument – the OECD guidelines for multinational enterprises – have recently been reviewed. However, strong rules pushing OECD-based TNCs towards more sustainable behaviour were not established in this instrument either.

VOLUNTARY INSTRUMENTS

While treaties to uphold corporate rights are being drawn up at an international level, there are no similar treaties to ensure corporate accountability and responsibility. Instead, there are many voluntary codes of conduct which are being developed for this purpose. The past few years have seen an incredible increase in the use of voluntary instruments to address all kinds of issues. A recent survey counted more than 250,000 of these instruments to be in place.

There are several types of voluntary instruments, and the OECD, for example, categorizes them as the following:[17]

- public voluntary programmes where the government sets up a policy programme, and then invites companies to voluntarily join in;
- negotiated agreements between an industry or industry sector and a public authority;
- private agreements between different actors, such as between NGOs and business;
- unilateral commitments set by industry without any outside involvement.

Those working towards a strong international regime for sustainable development are finding that strong and binding measures find little support and preference is given to achieving targets through voluntary instruments that are not binding.

PROBLEMS WITH VOLUNTARY APPROACHES

There are some serious problems with the voluntary approach, which are discussed below.

PROBLEM 1: LIMITS OF THE MARKETPLACE

Even though voluntary instruments are more flexible and efficient to use than regulation is, there are limits to the level of targets that can be set in a voluntary instrument, especially when the instrument is developed within the confines and demands of the commercial market. This is exemplified in a paper published by the OECD in 1998, which argues that the ability to design effective voluntary instruments ends when economic efficiency is maximized. The paper goes on to state that many social and environmental standards lie beyond the economic boundary.[18]

The implementation record of several voluntary instruments in a competitive environment clearly supports this argument. The corporation meets costs incurred in reducing or eliminating pollution, for example. Increased costs must be recovered through greater sales and therefore an increase in market share. As a result, a corporation will not develop a code that will increase its costs at the expense of market share and hence profits. Many codes of conduct are specifically designed not really to raise a given standard any higher, except if the party that designs the code is forced to do so due to regulatory threat or market competition.

BOX 18.1 THE NGO TASK FORCE ON BUSINESS AND INDUSTRY[23]

The NGO Task Force on Business and Industry (ToBI) is a coalition of concerned NGOs around the world who work together to promote the concept and implementation of corporate accountability within government, business and civil society. This coalition first began as an idea which emerged from an ANPED workshop on NGO strategies on TNCs, held in April 1996. The idea was to produce an NGO statement focusing international attention on the issue of corporate accountability, especially its role in sustainable development, to be presented at the UN General Assembly Special Session's five-year review of progress on Agenda 21 since the Earth Summit.

In the autumn of 1997, ToBI agreed to solicit NGO input on the topic of 'responsible entrepreneurship' for the major groups' dialogue on industry and sustainable development at CSD-6. After various outreach efforts, 30 NGOs from around the world contributed substantive inputs on the topic, with special attention to the question of corporate voluntary approaches in contrast to stronger regulatory frameworks. The resulting discussion paper, 'NGO Perspectives and Recommendations on Responsible Entrepreneurship' was published by the CSD and circulated, along with parallel papers from trade union and business and industry groups, to government delegations.[24,25,26] In particular, the NGO paper made a number of recommendations, including a multistakeholder review of the effectiveness of voluntary initiatives.

In the chairman's summary, the CSD noted: 'that more work was necessary to clearly define terms and concepts related to voluntary initiatives and to develop appropriate mechanisms for evaluating the effectiveness and successful characteristics of those initiatives'.[27] The chair acknowledged that: 'Representatives of non-governmental organizations, with support from trade unions, proposed a review by all major groups of voluntary initiatives undertaken by industry. The major groups planned to meet to consider the elements and goals of such a review' (paragraph 22).[28]

Later, in the UN document 'Decisions of the General Assembly and Commission on Sustainable Development, Decision 6/2: Industry and Sustainable Development', the UN General Assembly took note of the above-mentioned chairman's summary. In the section on 'Future Work' (paragraph 68), the assembly recommended that 'the Commission should, in cooperation with other relevant intergovernmental bodies, industry, trade unions, non-governmental organizations and other major groups, establish a process to review the effectiveness of voluntary initiatives intended to promote sustainable and equitable business practices'. This was the successful fruit of months of lobbying.

After CSD-6, when the mandate was given to set up a multistakeholder process – later called the Multistakeholder Steering Committee – ToBI, the International Confederation of Free Trade Unions (ICFTU), the International Chamber of Commerce (ICC) and the CSD had to develop a way of talking and making decisions. There was no rulebook and various assumptions held by one group about the appropriate procedures had to be challenged and reconstructed by one of the other groups.

Much of the Multistakeholder Steering Committee's discussions over the months had been in preparation for a meeting of practitioners and experts on voluntary initiatives and agreements (VIAs) that was held in Toronto. The point of the Toronto meeting was not to try to review and evaluate VIAs, but rather to have a series of presentations on a number of different types of VIAs as catalysts for discussions on the key elements that should be part of a review process. Initiatives selected for this catalyst process included, among others, the Mitsubishi-Rainforest Action Network agreement, the ICC Business Charter and the Responsible Care initiative.

One question that kept arising is that there are already many reviews, evaluations and studies of voluntary approaches; why begin another one at the CSD? First of all, academic research is not enough, even if it targets the specific issues and questions of the CSD. A multistakeholder process allows the key stakeholders – industry, trade unions and NGOs – an opportunity to ask whether the academic research and available information adequately address their main concerns and questions. For governments to have the best understanding of whether and how a particular voluntary initiative or agreement might contribute to policy decisions on sustainable agriculture, deforestation, energy and climate change and other challenges, they also need to have a clear understanding of what stakeholders think.

These were some initial points made in the ToBI introductory speech to the Toronto Multistakeholder Consultation meeting (10–12 March 1999), which brought together delegations from NGOs (organized by ToBI), business and industry (organized by the ICC) and trade unions (organized by the ICFTU), along with speakers from OECD, UNEP, ILO and consultants specializing in this area. The CSD chairman's summary of the Toronto consultative meeting is now available on the UN website.[29] Other information on the multistakeholder review process is also available on this site.[30]

From the discussions at this meeting, participants identified 'nine elements that would need to be considered in a review':

1   impetus and context;
2   purpose and design of the voluntary initiative or agreement;
3   multistakeholder participation;
4   commitment to sustain the voluntary initiative or agreement;
5   mutual trust and respect;
6   monitoring and assessment;
7   verification;
8   communication;
9   replication and capacity-building.

In addition to helping move the process towards the construction of this list, ToBI raised another key point during the Toronto meeting. The concept of voluntary initiatives is new in the developing world and there is a need to explore how – or if – voluntary initiatives can contribute to sustainable development in these countries. This point was reiterated in the VIA report by the secretary-general, stressing that 'more study is needed on the possible use and impact of VIAs in developing countries, particularly where regulation and compliance mechanisms are still at a formative stage'.

PROBLEM 2: DEMOCRATIC ACCOUNTABILITY

There are questions of democracy and accountability involved in this discussion. If a policy objective or a standard is made voluntary, what redress through the courts do those affected have if the instrument is not implemented and damage is done?

PROBLEM 3: CREDIBILITY AND IMPLEMENTATION

Voluntary instruments suffer from a general lack of credibility. They are often paraded as a substitute for regulations, which causes a natural suspicion about them within the general public. Who is to say that the actual targets set in the voluntary instruments are high enough to address issues related to sustainability, for example? The fact that an initiative is voluntary is enough of a signal that leads to credibility concerns. There are concerns raised as to whether a code is used as a smokescreen to cover up real issues of concern to the public. The major question is: how do we know that a code is working? Voluntary codes of conduct, therefore, need to be evaluated according to certain criteria in order to establish their credibility.

According to a growing amount of research on voluntary codes of conduct, there is sometimes little motivation to implement them. Research points to the fact that, in some cases, the motivation to design voluntary codes of conduct is mainly to use them to lobby against regulations. According to a study on the implementation of Responsible Care®, which is a code of conduct for the chemical industry, codes that are designed for operations not intended for the public eye are adhered to less within the programme; codes, on the other hand, which deal with external relations are better implemented.[19] There seems to be a lack of motivation to implement these instruments. This reinforces the thought that many such codes exist mainly to pacify the public, and therefore to circumvent rather than complement regulations.[20]

HOW CAN CODES BE EFFECTIVE?

Codes become credible only if they conform to certain credibility criteria. The more parties (NGOs, trade unions, governments, business associations, community groups) that are involved in the design, implementation and evaluation of a given code, the higher the chances are for establishing such credibility.[21] When designing new, and reviewing old, codes the challenge is to set the standards as high as possible; to instil a sense of ownership in those affected and involved; and to pay close attention to incentives for implementation. Ideally, parliamentarians should have a say in the final phase in order to ensure that a democratic process supports the targets. The groups mentioned should be involved fully in order to ensure a high-quality code. Moreover, a voluntary agreement that is legally binding and that can be enforced through a strong regulatory system is one that will be the most credible.

Appropriate incentives (government procurement policies, export-credit systems, publicity of wrongdoings as well as of good adherence) need to be in place to ensure that TNCs implement guidelines. Without incentives, corporations will most probably not take voluntary codes of conducts seriously enough. Governments and other stakeholders should work together to clearly determine what these incentives should be.

Finally, to aid in the development of appropriate standards, the actual impact of such a code needs to be measured. Any code should require stakeholders to report on its environmental and social performance through an independent monitoring and evaluation system, which is based on a set of independently set and independently verified indicators. Compliance can then be measured. If the set standards have not achieved the intended result, the code of conduct should be reviewed and adjusted, for example by making measures binding.[22]

THE WAY FORWARD

It is necessary to move ahead. Sustainability can only be achieved through action. Integrating trade policies into social and environmental ones, and addressing the power questions involved with titanic TNCs, both need creative and integrated solutions. The example in Box 18.1 of the multistakeholder process which began in 1997 at the CSD shows the potential of new inclusive approaches.

FROM DUALISM TO INTEGRATION

Governments have a primary responsibility that all concerns and needs of society are addressed equitably. Governments are currently responsible for the dualism that exists between, on the one hand, the weaker international regulatory frameworks on environment and development and, on the other hand, the stronger international regulatory frameworks on trade and investment. Governments are also responsible for creating freedom of movement for TNCs. Lastly, governments are primarily responsible for the situation where there is a clear lack of accountability regarding the environment, human rights and social development.

A first step for governments is to prioritize sustainability issues. Trade and investment are not ends in themselves, but means (or tools) to achieve sustainable development. Treaties that liberalize trade or investment should not be allowed to override treaties that protect the environment, or ensure equitable social development. Decisions by governments taken to achieve inter- and intragenerational equity, or in other words those decisions that protect ecological and human rights concerns, should actually gain priority over those measures that serve only a few.

Governments need to move away from the dogma of the market as the cure-all. As was shown in our discussion of voluntary initiatives, the market has serious limitations. Governments have a role to play, and this role must be as far reaching as is needed to achieve sustainability. A truly inclusive participatory approach to decision-making will aid governments in setting those priorities highest that most benefit all members of society.

THE FREEDOM AND POWER OF TNCs

Making society's needs subject to the voluntary whims of TNCs is unacceptable. We live in a society where the concept of accountability has not been adequately integrated within our day-to-day affairs. Societies where all actors are accountable and act responsibly will ultimately help us move towards achieving sustainable development. Through multistakeholder research, this role can be better defined and translated into workable practices that will complement sustainable development. ToBI, in its report 'Minding our Business', has listed several steps towards corporate accountability and responsibility.[31] The first step is to ensure that the UN and its member states acknowledge the fact that 'corporate accountability is an element of sustainable development'. To this effect, then, governments should ensure that TNCs are accountable to society. This should be done through government- and citizen-based mechanisms.

Another important step, also part of the ToBI agenda, is that citizens and governments should have adequate access to information about TNCs and their production products so that they can make informed choices which support sustainability. Governments are perhaps the only actors powerful enough to ensure the availability of such information from TNCs in order to achieve accountability, and to set in place 'community right-to-know' laws, universal product-labelling legislation and other legal tools to break the information barrier that currently exists between TNCs and civil society. Access to information is a fundamental human right and should be upheld and enforced by governments. The struggle of the Ogoni community against Shell is one case where community's access to information might have made the fight much easier and probably would have saved lives as well. There are many TNCs operating in Kenya, for example, that boast voluntary codes that go beyond the Kenya labour law. However, workers in these corporations have absolutely no idea about what these codes of conduct are and what they are out to achieve. Access to information can aid the transition to a sustainable society. Withholding information will stop that transition. Given this very unequal allocation of resources globally, it is the moral duty of governments to empower communities and not just TNCs.

NETWORKING AMONG CIVIL SOCIETY GROUPS

Caucusing and coalition-building within the NGO sector and other civil-society sectors, such as trade unions and academic research institutions – with a view to an open exchange of information and ideas – can help increase the informational power of civil society. A strong and well-informed NGO coalition, for example, can easily and quickly gather the strength and the strategies needed to offset unwilling TNCs and governments. We live in an age where ownership and understanding of information gives power. It is this power that makes it possible to balance the economic might wielded by TNCs.

NOTES

1 Jagjit Plahe is from Kenya. She is an independent researcher on trade and human rights
2 Pieter van der Gaag is Executive Director of ANPED, the Northern Alliance for Sustainability based in The Netherlands
3 UN (1999) 1999 World Investment Report, United Nations Publications
4 Nyberg, M (1998) *The Green Capitalists*, Goteborg: Friends of the Earth, Sweden, pp14–15
5 Economies of scale are the reductions in the average cost of producing a commodity in the long run as the output of the commodity increases
6 UN (1997) *1997 World Investment Report*, United Nations Publications, pxv
7 UN (1998) *World Investment Report, 1998: Trends and Determinants*, United Nations Publications, pxvii
8 The physical investment of resources and capital through the establishment or take-over of a production facility or of an office in the services sector

9   UN (1997) op cit Note 6, pxv

10   Ibid, pxv

11   UN (1998) op cit Note 7

12   Charkiewicz, E (1998) 'Impacts of Economic Globalisation and Changes in Consumption and Production Patterns in Central and Eastern Europe and Other Countries in Transition', CEECAP Report, June 1998 pp35–38

13   Consumer Unity and Trust Society (1997) 'Globalising Liberalisation Without Regulations', Consumer Unity and Trust Society, Briefing Paper, No 6, July, p1

14   Dual is used here in the traditional sense. In some societies development occurred through a conscious effort by governments to extend privileges and rights to only a certain few members of society, usually found living in cities. Returns of economic gains, and the right to establish corporations, were given to them. On the other side, a large sector of society, usually found in the rural areas, was not able or even allowed to profit from these developments. Its role was to provide the agricultural and resource base for the society in the city. In these societies a conscious dualism was established

15   These seven points have been quoted from a briefing paper by the Consumer Unity Trust Society, India, entitled 'Competition Policy In a Globalising and Liberalising World Economy', No 4, May 1996, p5

16   A convention between the EU and the African, Caribbean and Pacific countries; the current negotiations on a future regional agreement are being based on WTO compatibility by the EU

17   Barde, J P (1998) 'Voluntary Approaches for Environmental Policy in OECD Countries' (ENV/EPOC/GEEI (98) 30), Paris: OECD, pp16–25

18   Ibid, p17. This paper concludes that corporations will reach targets short of those that are required for sustainable development

19   Howard, J, Nash, J and Ehrenfield, J (1998) 'Responses to Uncertainty in an Institutional Environment: Responsible Care Adoption by Chemical Companies', paper, Massachusetts Institute for Technology, May

20   For more details on regulatory capture, see OECD (1998) 'Voluntary Approaches for Environmental Policy in OECD Countries', paper, Paris: OECD, p25

21   Van Tulder, K et al (1998) SCOPE Research, Rotterdam: Erasmus University

22   The criteria mentioned in this paragraph – namely, multistakeholder participation, verification and monitoring, continuous improvement, and incentives (ensuring commitment) – were also considered the main indicators for a successful voluntary instrument by a workshop of experts from governments, business, trade unions and NGOs organized by the CSD. A full report can be found under the following title: 'Voluntary Initiatives and Agreements: report of the Secretary-General', New York: Commission on Sustainable Development, 5 April 1999, E/CN 17/1999/12

23   The following report has been synthesised from the progress report on the NGO Taskforce on Business and Industry: Barber, J (1999) Integrative Strategies Forum for ANPED and VRO, August

24   For more details on this paper, see Section 4: 'Reporting on Progress'

25 For the discussion papers on responsible entrepreneurship produced by the trade unions (ICFTU) and business and industry (ICC), see http://www.un.org/esa/sustdev/indu3.htm

26 The paper can be found on gopher://gopher.un.org:70/00/esc/cn17/1998/background/BGPAP3.TXT. However, note that 'NGO steering committee' is listed after the title and ToBI (the author) is not mentioned anywhere except at the very end of the document

27 See paragraph 6 of the chairman's summary of the industry segment at CSD-6, at http://www.un.org/esa/ sustdev/volini98.htm

28 The chair also noted that: 'Concerns were expressed that one of the weaknesses of current corporate reporting was the absence of information that would permit an assessment of the contribution of voluntary initiatives towards achieving sustainability' (paragraph 10). This question of reporting and verification has turned out to be one of the key issues in the voluntary initiatives debate

29 See http://www.un.org/esa/sustdev/vi-sum-fin.htm

30 See http://www.un.org/esa/sustdev/via.htm

31 Barber, J (1997) 'Minding our Business: The Role of Corporate Accountability in Sustainable Development', an independent assessment to the CSD, submitted by the NGO Taskforce on Business and Industry, 12 February, pp 3–8

19

Getting Health in a Handbasket

Chip Lindner

INTRODUCTION

I would like to begin my analysis of the post-Rio process with a short comment on the name that was originally proposed for the event in 2002: 'Earth Summit III'. Why a concern about names? The fact remains that the official name of the Rio conference, the United Nations Conference on Environment and Development, was not the United Nations Conference on Sustainable Development. This seemingly simple choice of words affected much of the thinking and political positioning around the conference's agenda and had an effect on its outcome. The choice of name was also not coincidental, since leaving the words 'sustainable development' out of the title opened the door to leaving equity and poverty issues to the side.

With regard to the proposed 'Earth Summit III', I found the name to have a strange ring to it even though the first conference was widely, if not universally, referred to as the Earth Summit. I suppose my unease arose from the fact that virtually no one knows that there was an Earth Summit II, much less what transpired during it! As to the revised name, Earth Summit 2002, I accept that the word 'summit' implies heads of government and that that is the level at which issues related to sustainable development must continue to be addressed.

Regardless of the nomenclature used, however, I believe it is incumbent upon all of us to add our support and efforts to a rethink, and creation, of a renewed governmental and public commitment to sustainable development and Agenda 21.

BRINGING SUSTAINABLE DEVELOPMENT CENTRE STAGE

Rio was special – very special, indeed; but it was neither intended to, nor did it, solve every problem or aberration of sustainable development faced by the world's people in 1992. It began the journey to a sustainable world, but turned the job of continuing the search for sustainable development over to the world's governments and the major groups working through the mechanism of the CSD. With the tenth anniversary of Rio fast approaching, it is certainly timely and appropriate for us to examine closely the progress that has been made since Rio, identify the areas where greater effort is needed and agree the mechanism of implementation to address those issues.

For those of us who were very involved in the preparations for Rio, it requires quite a step back from the present, or a step out of our current affairs, to obtain an objective and fair perspective of how far we have come along the road to sustainable development since Rio. The agenda there was so broad and complex, the issues so intersectoral and interdisciplinary, and the multilateral initiatives taken so numerous that this is not surprising. At times, it seems to all of us that there has been enormous progress and at other moments it seems as if the global community is still discussing the same issues for the last quarter of a century, without much change. In fact, with regard to different issues, both perspectives are correct – although overall I would opt for a very positive perspective.

Why? Before the Brundtland Commission and Rio there was little knowledge, much less acceptance, of the concept of sustainable development. Furthermore, there were no climate or biodiversity conventions, nor was there an intergovernmental panel on forests, or a world commission on oceans, water and dams. Persistent organic pollutants (POPs) had hardly made it into the public consciousness and biotechnology was just turning its development corner. The Uruguay round had not yet finished and there was no World Trade Organization (WTO). And the Cairo, Beijing and Copenhagen conferences had not yet been held.

Less than 15 years after the Brundtland Report (WCED, 1987) and eight years after Rio, much has changed and significant progress has been made on numerous fronts. The climate convention is on track to make a significant difference by introducing emissions reductions – notwithstanding the stance of the US and Middle Eastern countries. The WTO is up and running (for better or for worse). But everyone would agree that trade negotiations without consideration of environmental and social dimensions is simply a non-starter. Recognizing the need to properly and sustainably manage water, fisheries, oceans and natural resources has never been stronger. And with the Jubilee 2000 initiative, we may even be on the threshold of a major transition in the debt load of the developing countries. There are, of course, other significant changes for the better – many discussed in this book. The fact is that we have made some very real progress and have every reason to be proud at having done so. And this progress is attributable both to governments, as well as to NGOs and the private sector.

But there are also aspects of sustainable development where progress has been lacking, and several of these are health related. One of the most serious and threatening concerns is HIV/AIDS; with respect to what has happened since the Brundtland Report and Rio, most of it, unfortunately, has been negative.

THE HIV/AIDS PANDEMIC

When discussing this book with UNED Forum, I was asked and agreed to write a chapter on health. I decided, however, to restrict my attention to HIV/AIDS for various reasons. Firstly, since a chapter on health and the post-Rio agenda was already being written by Gro Harlem Brundtland (see Chapter 20), and my credentials as a doctor were non-existent, I felt it inappropriate to take on 'health' per se. Secondly, and probably most significantly, I opted to address HIV/AIDS because I carry the virus myself and have done so for many years now. It is much easier, therefore, for me to relate to the fears, anxieties, doubts, stigmatization and psychological pain of those infected and – since I have four children, with each of whom I have a close relationship – those 'affected' by the disease.

Furthermore, serving as senior adviser to the chairman and executive secretary of the 12th World AIDS Conference held in Geneva in July 1998 opened my eyes to many aspects of the pandemic that were formerly non-existent for me. The experience of working with AIDS researchers and NGOs from around the world, government agencies from many countries, and international institutions (including UNAIDS, the International AIDS Vaccine Initiative (IAVI), the EU, WHO and UNDP) gave me a much broader insight into the challenges confronting all of those engaged in the fight against this horrific disease.

Finally, I feel very strongly, as I did during both the Brundtland and Rio processes, that priorities need to be established by the international community when facing an agenda as wide and diverse as sustainable development. The need to set priorities is also as important in the field of health as it is for sustainable development.

We should have learned by now that to attempt to do everything at the same time may just as likely result in achieving nothing significant at any time! Both the Brundtland and Rio processes suffered from this tendency to want to do it all – right away; and both processes could

Table 19.1 *Global summary of the HIV/AIDS epidemic in 1998 (millions)*

	Adults	(Women) <15 years	Children	Total
People newly infected with HIV in 1998	5.2	(2.1)	0.6	5.8
Number of people living with HIV/AIDS	32.2	(13.8)	1.2	33.4
AIDS deaths in 1998	2.0	(0.9)	0.5	2.5
Total number of AIDS deaths since the beginning of the epidemic	10.7	(4.7)	3.2	13.9

Source: UN AIDS Epidemic Update, December 1998, UN AIDS and WHO

have perhaps achieved much greater results if, as difficult as it would have been, they had established priorities with respect to the goals they wished to achieve and had established specific time frames for addressing them.

In light of my remarks above, I think it is therefore not surprising that I look at HIV/AIDS as a priority health and sustainable development issue. Why others do not, I find hard to comprehend – given the statistics related to this pandemic. And it with these statistics that I would like to begin my analysis. Many, if not most of you, are already familiar with them, yet the situation continues to worsen. Millions of ordinary people (most of them from the developing world and increasingly women and children) continue to die painful and undignified deaths while medications sit on shelves in the hospitals and pharmacies of industrialized countries.

One has to ask why? Yes, the figures are mind numbing (see Tables 19.1 and 19.2), both those related to the number of people infected and those related to the costs of treatment. But these mind-numbing figures are not sufficient justification for the failure of the global community to make significant advances in ensuring that fair and equitable access to treatment for everyone infected is available. Is it because so many of those infected (32 million of the world total of 34 million) live in the non-industrialized countries? Why should this make a difference in a world of open trade and markets? Or does an explanation lie in the mistakenly held view that the disease is a 'gay' disease and therefore definitive responses to it are less urgent. I hope this is not the case, since most global infections of HIV are heterosexually passed, notwithstanding widely held perceptions – even held by many Northern AIDS NGOs – to the contrary. (This is the subject of another

Table 19.2 *Regional HIV/AIDS statistics and features, 1998*

Region	Epidemic started	Adults and children living with HIV/AIDS (millions)	Adults and children newly infected with HIV (millions)	Adult prevalence rate (%)	Percent of HIV-positive adults who are women (%)	Main mode(s) of transmission for adults living with HIV/AIDS
Sub-Saharan Africa	late 1970s –early 1980s	22.5	4.0	8.0	50	Hetero
North Africa & Middle East	late 1980s	0.21	0.019	0.13	20	IDU, Hetero
South & South East Asia	late 1980s	6.7	1.2	0.69	25	Hetero
East Asia & Pacific	late 1980s	0.56	0.2	0.068	15	IDU, Hetero, MSM
Latin America	late 1970s– early 1980s	1.4	0.16	0.57	20	MSM, IDU, Hetero
Caribbean	late 1970s– early 1980s	0.33	0.045	1.96	35	Hetero, MSM
Eastern Europe & Central Asia	early 1990s	0.27	0.08	0.14	20	IDU, MSM
Western Europe	late 1970s– early 1980s	0.5	0.03	0.25	20	MSM, IDU
North America	late 1970s– early 1980s	0.89	0.044	0.56	20	MSM, IDU, Hetero
Australia & New Zealand	late 1970s– early 1980s	0.012	0.0006	0.1	5	MSM, IDU
Total		33.4	5.8	1.1	43	

Note: MSM = sexual transmission among men who have sex with men; IDU = transmission through injecting drug use; Hetero = heterosexual transmission

Source: UN AIDS Epidemic Update, December 1998, UN AIDS and WHO

chapter in another book!) Suffice it to say that lack of a serious commitment to equitable treatment options on the grounds of sexual preference would be both shortsighted and grossly immoral!

So what are these statistics? Since Rio, more than 35 million people have been infected with the virus and more than 13 million have died. A summary of the epidemic and regional statistics for the epidemic, as of December 1998, are set out in Tables 19.1 and 19.2.

A quick glance shows that the numbers are both staggering and geographically imbalanced, with more than 90 per cent of the total located in the non-industrialized countries and 70 per cent of the total located in Africa. It is hard to believe, but true, that without an effective vaccine against the virus, these numbers will certainly become much worse between now and 2020. Already, India has four million cases of HIV infection and the infection rate in Russia has doubled in the last year.

With infection rates running this high, for many it is inconceivable to learn that while billions of dollars are invested by governments, foundations and the private sector in treatment regimes (including the successful tri-therapies announced in Vancouver during the 11th World AIDS Conference, which are so expensive and sophisticated to monitor that they are virtually useless to the 32 million people infected in the developing countries), only several hundred million dollars have been invested in vaccine development. Furthermore, the vaccine figure has only reached the level of hundreds of millions of dollars in the last year! At the time of Rio the figure was in the tens of millions.

Why is a vaccine so important? To answer that essential question we need to look at the cost of treatment for HIV infection. Currently the cost of tri-therapy (a combination of three drugs which acts on various stages of HIV viral replication) differs from country to country, but on average it is generally not less than US$10,000 per annum. At present rates of infection, this means that the world community will need to find US$310 billion per annum to treat everyone infected or US$1.9 trillion during the 'no less than five years' it is anticipated it will take to discover an effective vaccine. Obviously, these costs were not known, understood or appreciated at Rio, since the cost of implementing Agenda 21 in its entirety was estimated in 1992 at US$561 billion per annum. Moreover, UNAIDS, the joint UN Programme on HIV/AIDS which was created after Rio, has an annual budget of only US$60 million. It certainly does not bode well for HIV-infected persons that only a tiny percentage of the funds necessary for universal treatment has been forthcoming, that vaccine funding is still extraordinarily difficult to obtain, and that UNAIDS is so remarkably underfunded. Even WHO's budget, the principal health agency within the UN, is grossly underfunded to adequately handle the health and development issues faced by our changing world.

Indeed, finding funds at the level of US$1.9 trillion to treat a single disease is not only impossible but fantastical – particularly when one considers that most countries in the developing world have at their disposal for all medical interventions somewhere in the neighbour-hood of US$30 – US$50 per person per annum maximum! In Guatemala, this has meant 187 people receiving tri-therapy out of total number of over 50,000 infected individuals. For Guatemala to treat everyone infected at current market costs of US$10,000 would require US$500 million per annum – or if the price could be lowered to US$4000 per person, which is the price paid by Brazil for tri-therapies, this would amount to US$200 million per annum. Brazil is one of the few countries which by law has guaranteed access to tri-therapy and it has used bulk purchasing price from the pharmaceuticals to lower the cost. Note, however, that the full story of Brazil's approach to provid-ing treatment to all is controversial, but not a subject for this chapter. It will need to be examined, however, in the context of whatever policy decisions are taken at Earth Summit 2002 in order to benefit from its experiences.

To reach the goal of 'access for all' will require a Herculean effort and an unprecedented level of participation and compromise on the part of the private sector: no government or multilateral institution will ever have the funds necessary to cover the costs referred to above.

In my view, priority must given by governments, science and the private sector to finding a vaccine as quickly as possible, while chang-ing pricing policies for current drugs so that they are made available to everyone who needs and wants them. With political will and commit-ment, this should be achievable, particularly given the numbers involved and the returns those numbers would translate into if the pharmaceutical companies rose to the occasion.

Consider, for instance, tri-therapy being made available to all infected people in developing countries at US$100 per person per annum (400 times less than current cost). This may strike one as 'pie in the sky' talk, but I do not understand why, given the dimensions of the problem and the level of financial return such a gesture would generate: an additional US$3.1 billion of revenue per annum to the pharmaceuticals or US$15.5 billion during the five years of vaccine research at a time when their return from developing countries on HIV anti-retroviral drugs is virtually nil!

Given the return the pharmaceuticals receive on their sales in industrialized countries and the fact that they plan on no income stream to speak of from developing countries, would this or should this not be enough to mobilize the industry? If it is not, then how much would be? We must move forward, and to do so we must have a fair and trustworthy set of revenue stream figures which the private pharmaceutical sector requires – and here I really do want to emphasize the words 'fair and trustworthy'. The lives of tens of millions of people demand agreement on such figures – and quickly. Those lives also demand the response of government in providing the necessary legal and trading framework and medical infrastructures within which such an initiative could be launched and carried out.

Having the pharmaceutical sector take primary responsibility for access to treatment will leave the public, governmental and foundation sectors free to fund vaccine development on a much more aggressive and generous basis. This is not an untoward demand given the profits they have already received on their AIDS drug marketing. Indeed, one can envisage funding for that research increasing to more than US$1 billion per annum.

Additional or alternative mechanisms which could also be tried as a means of addressing the issue of equitable access for all is 'compulsory licensing' and parallel importing. Compulsory licensing, which derives from WTO's TRIPS Agreement, makes it possible for a country, under certain conditions, to issue a compulsory licence against the will of the patent holder. For example, for a country with high HIV seroprevalence, a government could decide that it is in the best interests of the public to ensure that appropriate drugs are manufactured locally and made available at a cheaper price than is currently the case. Many countries, however, are under strong pressure from others, such as the US and the pharmaceutical industry, to avoid issuing any such licences, threatening trade boycotts if they do!

Parallel importing consists of purchasing drugs covered by patents from third parties in another country, rather than directly from the manufacturer, and taking advantage of the fact that pharmaceutical companies sometimes charge significantly lower prices in one country than in another. Were parallel importing permitted, companies could shop around and get better prices using market forces to lower national expenditures on a range of goods, including pharmaceuticals. As an example, a 1998 study by the Consumer Project on Technology found that prices for SmithKline Beechman's version of Amoxil were US$8 in Pakistan, US$14 in Canada, US$16 in Italy, US$22 in New Zealand, US$29 in the Philippines, US$36 in Malaysia, US$40 in Indonesia, and US$60 in Germany.

Both of these mechanisms carry very real possibilities for greater access to drugs, and they should be much more aggressively pursued than has been the case in the past.

Unfortunately, none of the above developments have any chance of success without renewed public pressure and political will. Earth Summit 2002 must provide that motivation; and in the area of health it must make securing access for all (whether through concessional funding, compulsory licensing or parallel importing), and finding a vaccine for HIV/AIDS, central priorities for the first decade of the 21st century. Without such a renewed commitment, the judgement of history will fall heavily upon the shoulders of today's government and business leaders.

REFERENCES

This chapter relied heavily upon the following sources:

AIDS/HIV Briefings (1997–1999) London and Washington, DC: Panos

The AIDS International Economics Newsletter (1996–1999) International AIDS Economic Network

Duckett, M (1999) *Compulsory Licensing and Parallel Importing*, Toronto: International Council of Aids Servicing Organization

Earth Negotiations Bulletin (1996–1999), New York: IISD

UN AIDS (1998) *The UN AIDS Report 1998*

UN AIDS (1999) *The UN AIDS Report 1999*

UNDP (1997) *Human Development Report 1997*, New York: Oxford University Press

UNDP (1998) *Human Development Report 1998*, New York: Oxford University Press

UNDP (1999) *Human Development Report 1999*, New York: Oxford University Press

WCED (1987) *Our Common Future*, Oxford: Oxford University Press

WHO (1999) *World Health Report 1999: Making a Difference*, Geneva: World Health Organization

The World Bank (1997) *Confronting AIDS*, Washington, DC: The World Bank

20

Our Common Future and Ten Years after Rio: How Far Have We Come and Where Should We Be Going?[1]

Gro Harlem Brundtland

'Our souls are too long for this short life.'

Goethe

The issues of the relationship between humankind and planet Earth exist because our souls are too long for this short life. As far as we know, we are the only species that has the capacity to look beyond ourselves – to care about our posterity and to think in intergenerational terms. We have probably had this capacity for thousands of years.

Millions of fellow human beings face a much more cruel choice than do those of us who live in industrialized countries. That choice is between surviving in our lifetime alone, and disregarding the future, knowing that we limit future choices. It is human, under such unfortunate conditions, to choose life. But few would be comfortable with such a situation. We feel an obligation which goes beyond ourselves. What is new to our generation is that we also have the knowledge and technical capacity – for the first time – to choose to leave, for posterity, an inhabitable planet. Our challenge today is to organize our knowledge, and our tremendous scientific and technological potential, and address the survival issues of our times.

The planet and its environment are complex mechanisms. But our knowledge is sufficient to realize a lot of what is needed and what

must be avoided. The question remains: do we have the political ability
to organize and to change what we need to change?

Before looking ahead, let us look briefly to the past. The urgency
of the situation became apparent in the decades that lie behind us.
The 1960s, 1970s and 1980s brought immense volumes of new knowledge about pollution and the overuse of natural resources. Political
movements, particularly in Western countries, focused on environmental issues and became formidable green forces to be reckoned
with. They were able to articulate what many of the established political parties had neglected.

We remember the disasters of the 1970s. Seveso, shipwrecks,
shores and seabirds smeared with crude oil – all over the evening
news. Then came the disasters of the 1980s: Bhopal, killing thousands;
Sandoz, sending its lethal injection into the artery of Europe – the
Rhine; Three Mile Island and Chernobyl. Chernobyl happened in May
1986. Reagan and Gorbachev met in Reykjavik five months later, when
they almost agreed to scrap all nuclear weapons. But what really made
the wealthy segments of Western populations listen were the threats
to the ozone layer and the prospects of cancer. Then we truly knew
that money can offer little refuge, and that we are all in the same boat.
These threats were truly democratic ones.

But there was more. Concerned people pointed to less explosive
issues. 'Do not forget', they said, 'life that might perish – not with a
bang but with a whimper': the loss of species, of topsoil, groundwater,
the gradual change of the climate. And while we, all over the world,
reacted to this new knowledge, the World Commission on
Environment and Development (WCED) was working: studying causes
and effects, scientific reports, voluntary groups' and NGOs' submissions; listening, studying, deliberating and producing a report entitled
Our Common Future.[2]

Environment and development became inextricably linked.
'Poverty is the greatest polluter,' said Indira Ghandi. She did not blame
the poor. She pointed to the obvious: as long as people are poor the
immediate issue is survival. Caring for the future is a luxury. Climate
change, biodiversity, desertification and water depletion are all cancer-
ous threats to the future which can be ignored one day at a time
without visible repercussions.

The WCED made a difference. Although I am not totally unbiased,
having chaired the commission at the request of the UN secretary-
general, I believe it did move the world more than an inch forward. It
proposed Rio, and Rio – the Earth Summit – happened. The commission proposed in 1987 that an international conference be held five
years after the launch of its report to review progress made and to
promote follow-up arrangements, to set benchmarks and maintain
human progress.

There was much hyperbole around the Earth Summit, the biggest international conference ever, and in the end phase of preparations, most countries poured in their experts to ensure that there was a minimum rocking of boats at one's own expense. Responding to popular demands at the time, a number of countries seemed to favour environmental protection measures that would not disrupt domestic production lines or established patterns of employment. Saving the rainforests is a good example. While in itself important, saving forests as sinks for carbon dioxide could have the effect of diverting attention from the burning of fossil fuels in OECD countries.

Norway introduced new carbon taxes ahead of Rio. I experienced, during these years, that political leaders in other oil-producing countries plainly could not believe it. Did they hear correctly? Had Norway, in fact, introduced a special tax on CO_2, and did we recommend such measures to other countries? Yes, we did – and our experiences have been positive.

Some countries have done more than just listen – but many more should take this challenge seriously. Such taxes are among the tools we have in order to conduct public policies to respond to very public needs – to get the market to function well and channel the impressive imaginative potential of industry. But if these measures are to work we need a broader framework than the national scene. We need a level playing field – one which pushes towards a higher standard of performance, not to a lower level of environmental excellence.

So what came out of Rio? First of all, there was a global learning process which cannot be undone. Rio was a giant leap for mankind, measured in the knowledge increase and the number of people involved. What more came out of Rio? There was Agenda 21, which is a giant programme of work; the Rio declaration on legal principles for sustainable development; and two framework conventions on climate and biodiversity. People got involved: civil society, parliaments and business. This gathering would probably not have happened without Rio. None of that can be undone.

Some results from Rio were good but not optimal. The climate convention and the biodiversity conventions are useful tools which we are fortunate to have. They are reluctant steps in a necessary direction. They came to be that way – watered down – because in a world run by consensus, those who want the least change have a stronger say than those who want more. There are volumes of environmental law being developed, building on the Rio declaration. We are getting equipped to react against industrial practices which cause immediate damage. But we still lack the long-term approach to addressing the intergenerational problems generated by parallel activities of large numbers of individuals and industries.

What did not come out of Rio? There were no concrete, measurable commitments in areas in need of action, nor were there additional resources for development – with a few honourable exceptions.

Since Rio the rich countries have been through a steady process of growth. The Uruguay round created the World Trade Organization (WTO). We saw the North Atlantic Free Trade Agreement (NAFTA) created. The EU expanded in size and mandate. The North Atlantic Treaty Organization (NATO) expanded.

Countries in central and eastern Europe hunger to join the prospering Western economy. Perhaps the greatest environmental achievement was in Europe with the closing down of outdated industries in former communist countries. Vaclav Havel said it aptly in his famous New Year's address ten years ago: 'You have not elected me to this office so that I should lie to you. Our country is not blooming.' But today, Poland and the Czech Republic are more important to the economy of Germany than are Russia, Sweden and Norway. This is part of globalization. And not all of that is detrimental to the environment. Effective production and distribution is definitely not detrimental, if we get more out of less.

To many companies, the global market is like a local market. While so much happened in the wake of the fall of the Berlin Wall, industrial countries gradually turned their backs to the very modest commitment of allocating 0.7 per cent of GDP for development assistance. Only four countries – Denmark, The Netherlands, Norway and Sweden – live up to that pledge, while the OECD average is stumbling around 0.2 per cent.

This shameful state of affairs contradicts important values within each of our home countries, such as equity and justice – and, I would add, common sense. There is a lack of good development projects, some say – and this proves that their eyes and ears have fatal defects. I see that so very clearly from the position of world health, where we can list many concrete interventions which would make a huge difference for the lives and perspectives of billions, ranging from immunizing half the children of Africa who do not get the vaccines, to providing bed nets to the millions of children who are living in acute danger from the malaria mosquito. If we do this, poverty will go down. Societies will develop. And ultimately new markets will open.

What have we learned since Rio? I came into the environment and development agenda from a background in public health. The WCED's work was human-centred. Health was, of course, central to our work. Some antagonists believed that the environment and development agenda was too focused on reducing population growth, which was not true. We all know that on average a person in a rich country consumes about 100 times the amount of non-renewable resources than does a person in a very poor country. We also know that there are very rich people in very poor countries, and very poor people in very rich countries, and that this poses enormous challenges. The health statistics provide the most telling evidence.

Implementing the sustainable development agenda means investing in people. This means giving them the opportunity to grow up, to get an education – especially for young girls. It also means giving individuals an opportunity to pursue happiness and giving them a life expectancy and a surplus of hope – this is the only way to ensure that people all over the world will have the opportunity to realize how their 'souls are too long for this short life'. It is basically an organizational problem. We seem to be too confined in our thinking and too restrained in our imagination to be guided by phenomena we cannot see quite close to our own lives.

What amount of crisis do we need to understand? How close must people be for most of us to react and to understand? Recent disasters such as Hurricane Mitch and Hurricane George are ruining entire health systems and the economies needed to support them. The Honduras and neighbouring Nicaragua are now rife with cholera, malaria, dengue fever and respiratory diseases. Floods in China and Bangladesh have had devastating effects on the health of millions. I saw with my own eyes the extensive burden put on China in protecting against emerging diseases and epidemics following floods – weeks after the water had receded.

But what does it take to change the wider global trends? Since Rio, the number of people living in absolute poverty has increased. They number today some 1300 million people who live on less than US$1 per day. If we go up to US$2 a day, the number rises to half of the world's population – to three billion fellow human beings.

So far the war on poverty has failed. This degrades and threatens us. It looms as a threat to the environment – not only that of the poor but of all of us. Since Rio we have had frequent lessons of global interdependence. A changing climate is one. Global contamination is another. Disease spreads with people on the move, be they the 1 per cent of the world's population – 50 million – who are uprooted and forced to move, heavily exposed to disease, or be they the 1.4 billion yearly air passengers – up from 2 million 50 years ago.

In November 1999 a Norwegian died of multidrug-resistant tuberculosis in Trondheim. In August of that year a German photographer died of yellow fever here in Berlin – the first such case in this country since 1946. We count malaria incidents in Geneva and Brussels. The growth of tuberculosis cases in the former Soviet Union is stronger than in Africa. The message is as with the environment: the poverty trap is fatal. Poverty breeds ill health. But it also works the other way; ill health breeds poverty.

What more can we qualify as new knowledge since Rio? Let me mention just a few examples. Did you know that arsenic contaminates water not only in Bangladesh but also in Finland? The occurrence of arsenic in drinking water has recently caught the headlines because of the severe exposure and escalating consequences among the population of Bangladesh. It has been called the largest mass contamination in history. It was an unintentional side effect of a programme originally intended to assist in providing safe drinking water. The problem is readily solved in large, centralized water supply systems. But this is of little help at the village well. There are four million such wells in Bangladesh. The surprise is that the problem also occurs in Finland. We didn't know that in Rio.

Food-borne diseases have emerged as a major public health issue, also in industrialized countries. Food-borne diseases are annually affecting up to 10 per cent of the population. The mishandling of food during its preparation by domestic food handlers, including care-givers of small children, is prevalent. We can all be affected. We saw four billion cases of diarrhoea last year from food. Food-borne diseases thrive on trade and tourism. And the use of credit cards will not exempt us!

Did you know that one of the most damaging environmental hazards is indoor air pollution? An example of this is the woman bending over her oven, inhaling hazardous smoke from the wood she is burning, her child suffering as she sits on her mother's back. Its impact in developing countries is much greater than that of ambient air pollution. And imagine how little it would take to change all of this by cheap improvements in cleaner forms of cooking and heating.

Did you know that work-related injuries and diseases are responsible for the death of over one million people every year? At least 250 million accidents and 160 million new cases of work-related diseases occur every year. The cost to the economy has been estimated at 4 per cent of the world's gross national product.

Did you know that the spread of chemicals, such as dioxins and PCBs, impairs the intellectual development of children, reducing their level of IQ? Before Rio, we used to read about the discovery of such substances in polar bears and other forms of Arctic life. This was interesting, but possibly a red herring considering the close-up problems of modern society.

We have learned – at least in theory – that the world would be better off if the developing world did not have to commit the same errors as the developed countries. There is no way the rich world can say: 'Sorry, we filled up the waste baskets, there is no more space left for you.' What it can say is: 'Learn from our experience, use our technology, leapfrog the polluting steps on the ladder.' This needs to be said. A child in the developed world consumes and pollutes 30 to

50 times as much as a child in the developing world. Just imagine the trend as the poor countries prosper.

It needs to be said and acted upon, but we see how hard it is. If the poor countries are to grow, they need to export. And if they are to succeed, they need markets. But what they often experience – such as Bangladesh with its textiles, or South Africa with its wine production – is that the rich world closes the gates. And as the millennium round of trade talks that began in Seattle last year demonstrated, health and environment risk becoming bouncing balls in a struggle to protect not necessarily health or environment, but market shares.

There is a global market. Industry can reap some tremendous benefits from that market. But gradually people see that this global market needs rules and some order. Beyond that, the interdependence of people and the environment requires that we are more ready to invest in the development of others. It will not just happen. And I believe it cannot simply be forced. It is a process which needs to be driven by new awareness and by growing consensus and mechanisms which also enable companies to make investments in what I would call global public goods: health, environment and education.

Since Rio we have seen it happen in some areas where government and the private sector have charted courses together with due respect for complementary roles. A range of service industries contribute extensively and positively to public health. Effective water supply and sanitation services underpin long-established health gains in industrialized countries, and are proven interventions with large-scale health benefits when deployed in the developing world.

Since the publication of *Our Common Future*, there has been a radical reappraisal of the role of the public and private sectors in providing these services. A radical change in management is continuing, while the role and profile of both domestic and international companies are developing rapidly. But what we often see is that critical private-sector management skills and investment are drawn into the system of supplying wealthy neighbourhoods, rather than extending supply to the poor. We tend to end up with ''all for some' rather than 'some for all'.

We have heard it said that the market is always right. Of course it is not. The prime minister of India said a couple of years ago that he saw no multinational companies willing to invest in educating the children of India, or immunizing them and helping them to grow up. Those organizations who are dependent upon tomorrow's consumers – the multinationals – are betting on governments providing healthy enough and wealthy enough populations.

I now move to the role of the business sector in the context of current and future trends. Of course the stock market, which has the ability to 'react' or to be 'sensible' to certain trends, will have a hard time perceiving ethical dimensions. The individual human being – operating within certain confines – will not. But the experience of ethical perceptions, as a motivating factor, may not always point in the same direction as other motivating factors, such as career perspectives, prestige and personal profit.

The best thing we can do is to explore where several of these factors can be made to work together for health and sustainable development. People are generally not insensitive to ethical dilemmas. Companies may adopt an ethical code or its equivalent. And such a code may or may not comprise sustainable development. We have seen many such examples in recent years.

Business will have an important role and responsibility in helping to:

- curb the use of non-renewable fuels;
- promote a reduction of the generation of wastes; and
- reduce transboundary pollution and help to minimize global environmental change.

Business, in fact, does many of these things. The construction and engineering sector, for example, has an enormous impact on upgrading the human environment through environmental engineering for health-risk reduction and management. Many of the achievements in a broader common understanding of sustainable development cannot be rolled back. They need to be further built upon.

Looking ahead, I believe we need to focus on incentives for investments in global public goods. Health and the environment are such goods. The public sector needs to innovate. Beyond paying national taxes, there is little likelihood that industry will pour profits into unspecified funds for vague development. We need to be concrete – and we can be concrete. With the mining industry, WHO has developed a cooperative scheme where we draw up programmes for community health development in areas in which industry engages. Industry has a self-interest of investing in these programmes – and communities at large benefit.

We have gone several steps further and invited the private sector to join in supporting a major effort to provide vaccination to all children. The Global Alliance for Vaccinations and Immunizations brings together WHO, UNICEF, the World Bank, industry and foundations. The purpose is simple: to support development of new vaccines and help spread new and existing ones to countries who can hardly afford to buy them. Bill Gates has decided to support this initiative with US$150 million a year for the next five years. Others are invited to follow – not only the aid agencies but also industries.

Or take malaria – which is on the rise because environmental changes provide new breeding grounds for mosquitoes, making malaria one of the two leading killers in sub-Saharan Africa. It kills 3000 children every day, ravaging societies and economies. There are no vaccines and medication is poor. Industry says: 'There is no market and no incentive to develop these drugs.' So we have to say: 'Can these incentives be developed?' Recently, WHO and the pharmaceutical industry launched the Medicines for Malaria Venture. It is a new approach. A venture fund financed by aid agencies and other donors will invite ideas for research proposals – and fund the best ones. The interest has been overwhelming and our target is to produce a new viable medicine every five years.

These are some examples. We need similar schemes to engage key stakeholders in the struggle to halt and combat the AIDS pandemic. The idea is clear: we need private–public interaction. We need to address the challenges and tailor the solutions into projects that can be funded – technologies that can be developed and local capacities that can respond. For decades WHO has led the campaign to eradicate polio, much as we did away with smallpox 20 years ago. We may only be months away from succeeding – wiping another disease off the face of the Earth, saving billions in vaccination costs, and – not least – saving future generations from this crippling disease.

I know this can be a motivating contribution in a company: to say that we make a contribution to saving lives and developing the economies of Africa by giving every child an impregnated bed net against malaria. Bed nets cost US$4 a piece. But our studies tell us that the average family in Africa cannot afford to pay more than half that price. So let us mobilize to fund the missing US$2.

And let us be very clear when industry's behaviour runs against health, the environment and ethics. There are such cases – and in some of these WHO has no choice but to speak out. One example is tobacco. Let me share the crude figures with you. This year four million people will die from smoking. People who you know are probably going to be among them. These numbers are expected to rise to ten million into the next century, with all the growth coming in the developing world – adding yet another burden onto the shoulders of health systems which are already overstretched. Tobacco is about to climb to the very top of the podium of leading causes of premature death and disease. So we need to act.

Late last year, WHO and its member states began to work on the first international public health convention on tobacco control, inspired and modelled on the conventions coming out of Rio. It will provide basic global standards for tobacco control and will address transnational issues such as global advertising and promotion bans, smuggling, product regulation and trade. While we continue to do this, the tobacco industry is not happy. It talks about freedom of choice. But look at the facts. Globally, between 82,000 and 99,000 young people start smoking every day. It is no surprise, knowing that the tobacco industry targets their huge commercial machine specifically on adolescents. They know what they do, because habits start in youth. Eight out of ten smokers say they started before they were 18. When they got addicted, they were often 14, 15, or 16 years' old. That is no freedom of choice! Civilized nations protect their people under 18 – they don't let them play around with a product which statistically kills one out of two of its permanent users.

Tobacco is bad for health. But what about the economy? We let the World Bank answer on the basis of a major study. The answer is clear: tobacco costs huge sums for any economy. And it is bad for the environment because it is bad for the soil, because what the world needs is food growing on those fields – not killing leaves turning tobacco plants into killing fields. It is a sad legacy how an industry has been able to work relatively unchecked for decades, passing on the costs of health and lives to taxpayers and to social insurance.

The skill of the tobacco industry's lawyers is known. Their practices at hiding facts and diverting science are now public knowledge – available on the worldwide web after the US court trials. It is not pretty reading. Governments should act, and more and more governments do. WHO has decided to act. And the private sector – representing the broad industrial core of development – should also speak out, and at least not be protective of an abusive industry. I believe it is a matter of time in OECD countries. The battleground will be in the new emerging economies and developing countries.

Industrial history is replete with examples of political struggles over health and environmental impacts of industry. Imperial Germany favoured improved working conditions to improve the standards of their young soldiers. Women were the victims of the match industry and the struggle to outlaw white sulphur.

A dramatic century has also just closed, which gave so much at such a high cost. The world population passed six billion just before the end of that century – up a billion since 1987. It may reach nine billion in 2050. This is, in fact, not too bad news – it is perceived to be manageable compared to what was feared a few years ago. But management cannot wait. It has to start now. We have the evidence. We have the technology. But is the will there?

We know that future generations will examine carefully how we acted with all of this knowledge. Most of us will not be around when the first half of the next century passes. But think about it. Roughly half of the people alive today will be alive in 2050. Many of the children of today's decision-makers will be around to see how we coped with an extra three billion. So although attention may temporarily be swinging away from the survival issues – away from Rio – and onto the latest figures from the DOW industrial or the exchange rate of the Euro versus the US dollar, let us not lose the vision. There is a lot to do for many and I urge you to move ahead.

George Bernard Shaw said that the only thing we learn from experience is that we do not learn anything from experience. He was a playwright, not a scientist. We have learned much from experience. I believe we can learn even more, and move on to prove that Shaw was wrong.

NOTES

1   This chapter has been adapted from an address by Dr Gro Harlem Brundtland to the World Business Council on Sustainable Development in Berlin on 4 November 1999
2   WCED (1987) *Our Common Future*, Oxford: Oxford University Press

21

Sustainable Consumption and Production

Laurie Michaelis

INTRODUCTION

Chapter 4 of Agenda 21 sets out the need to promote patterns of consumption and production that reduce environmental stress and meet the basic needs of humanity. It also draws attention to the need to develop both a better understanding of the role of consumption and the means by which more sustainable consumption patterns can be achieved. Broadly, it identifies two areas for action:

- improving the efficiency of production and developing and deploying cleaner technologies;
- developing new concepts of prosperity and reinforcing the values that would foster more sustainable production and consumption.

The first of these can be seen as a technological and institutional challenge, which has been taken up by the business and government community with growing efforts for eco-efficiency, sustainable product design and pollution prevention. The second area is challenging, as it involves asking fundamental questions about the relationships among culture, the economy and the environment. Ultimately, it may involve questioning our concepts of human nature and of community. While these issues are researched and debated in the academic community, there has been little progress in developing the kind of coherent and shared understanding that could form the basis for concerted action.

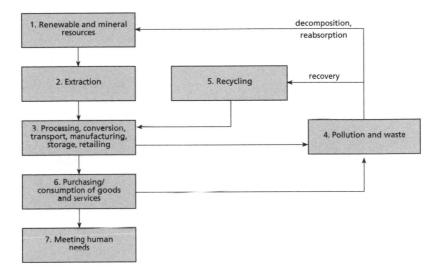

Figure 21.1 *A material-flow perspective on production and consumption*

The diversity of viewpoints has deterred serious discussion in policy circles, although several international workshops have begun to explore the theory and practice of sustainable consumption.

INCREASING RESOURCE EFFICIENCY

The concept of eco-efficiency has been developed and promoted by both businesses and governments. The World Business Council for Sustainable Development (WBCSD) describes eco-efficiency as being 'reached by the delivery of competitively priced goods and services that satisfy human needs and bring quality of life, while progressively reducing ecological impacts and resource intensity throughout the life cycle to a level at least in line with the earth's estimated carrying capacity'.[1] This is an ambitious statement. It suggests that the business community is working to find 'win–win' solutions, hitting the 'triple bottom line'. The economic dimension of sustainable development is addressed by producing competitively priced goods; the social dimension by satisfying human needs and bringing quality of life; and the environmental dimension by reducing ecological impacts and resource intensity.

Eco-efficiency is mostly interpreted more simply. OECD defines it as 'the efficiency with which ecological resources are used to meet human needs'.[2] It is often summarized as 'doing more with less'.

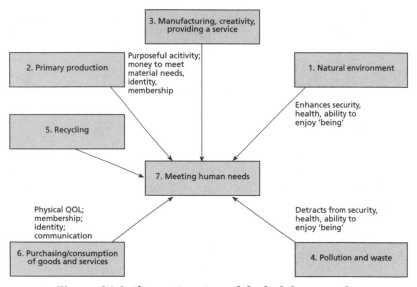

Figure 21.2 *Alternative view of the link between the production/consumption system and meeting human needs*

Current efforts to improve eco-efficiency are focused on making technologies and practices both cheaper and less resource intensive. This focus is too narrow: we need to pay much more attention to the cultural dimension of technological change, and to the role of the system of production and consumption in meeting human needs.

Figure 21.1 offers a picture of the world view that underlies eco-efficiency thinking. This is essentially a techno-economic or engineering perspective in which scarce natural resources are converted by the economy into goods and services that meet a given set of human needs. The economy generates waste and pollution. Eco-efficiency aims to maximize the 'meeting human needs' output, while minimizing the input of resources and generation of pollution and waste.

While the picture is useful for thinking about the physical system of production and consumption, it does not help much with thinking about human needs and values. The connection between the physical and economic system and the fulfilment of human needs are much more complex.

Adults in modern market economies spend most of their waking time either producing or consuming commercial goods and services. Our identities are increasingly defined by the work we do, our possessions, the shops and restaurants we frequent, our mode of transport and the products and forms of entertainment that we enjoy. Other sources of meaning in our lives, such as our families and communities, are still important to us but our engagement with them is shaped by our patterns of work and consumption. As illustrated in Figure 21.2, each element of the system of production and consumption is related in one way or another to meeting somebody's needs.

CONSUMPTION PATTERNS AND CONCEPTS OF PROSPERITY

Looking harder at human needs and welfare leads to a number of questions about the nature of prosperity and the sustainability of consumption trends. In addition to the widely acknowledged challenge of reducing the environmental impacts of consumption, we need to consider how growing material prosperity contributes to our quality of life.

Firstly, we need to consider whose needs are being addressed by the system of production and consumption. The current competitive market system seems to foster inequality, and perhaps even to thrive on it. The economist Joseph Schumpeter described the role of 'creative destruction' in the market in bringing about progress in technology and institutions. Drawing on biological models of evolution, many analysts have noted the importance of failure (of inefficient firms, production processes, technologies, institutions) in enabling progress to take place. Within many economies in the North, such models have been extended to people: the holes in the social safety nets have been enlarged in the belief that a real threat of destitution is needed to motivate the unemployed to find work. The model is also applied to whole economies: all countries, whatever their institutional and technological capacity, are urged to open their borders to free trade and to undergo 'structural adjustment', accepting the anticipated social costs in return for long-term economic benefits.

Secondly, many types of human need are best met in ways that are only tenuously connected with material consumption. Examples include our need for tranquillity, love, community, spiritual development, learning, and excitement. Indeed, material consumption sometimes inhibits us from addressing these needs by absorbing our time in the 'work and spend' cycle. It may even encourage us to look in the wrong direction in our efforts for fulfilment. Few of us really believe, as implied in many TV commercials, that driving a particular brand of car will bring us peace or a loving relationship, but the culture of the market encourages us to look for material solutions to existential problems.

Thirdly, we must acknowledge that the system of production and consumption may have a negative effect on cultural stability and diversity, and on the coherence of communities. People trapped in the work-and-spend cycle have little time to participate in civic or community activities, weakening social solidarity. This trend is reinforced by the ethics of the market, which promote a view that human beings are, and should be, egocentric, competitive and materialistic. Meanwhile, the increasing interconnectedness of markets is reducing the distinctions between the consumption patterns and cultures of different regions and countries.

Despite efforts to develop an agenda for sustainable consumption, a huge gap remains in current policy thinking on the underlying values and the social, ethical and institutional changes that might be involved.

TRENDS IN THE SUSTAINABILITY OF PRODUCTION AND CONSUMPTION

A first step towards understanding the types of change that might be needed is to look at current trends. Many efforts have been made to construct sustainability indicators. The UN Department of Economic and Social Affairs has identified a candidate set of core indicators of the sustainability of production and consumption; the OECD has also identified candidate indicators of progress towards sustainable consumption and has gathered data for a core set.[3,4]

Both of these proposed indicator sets focus mainly on the environmental and economic dimensions of consumption and production, and pay little attention to the social dimension. The near omission of social indicators is not surprising. It is easy enough to quantify the resource use and many of the environmental impacts associated with production and consumption using existing published statistics. Good statistics are also available on the quantities and financial values of goods and services produced and consumed. Social indicators, on the other hand, are often subjective and qualitative, and changes are difficult to ascribe to specific causes.

CONSUMPTION TRENDS

Between 1970 and 1995, global income per capita increased by nearly a third. Increasing incomes and falling production costs have meant that people in most world regions consume more food and energy, travel more and live in larger homes.

In industrialized countries, rapid growth in the use of consumer credit and a decline in personal savings have enabled consumption to grow faster than income. At the same time, there has been a shift in the breakdown of household spending, with less growth in spending on food and clothing, and more growth in spending on housing, transport, recreation and medical care.

One of the most environmentally significant trends is the continuing rapid growth in road and air traffic. The global motor vehicle fleet multiplied by 2.6 between 1970 and 1995. Air traffic grew sixfold in the same period. 81 per cent of the road vehicle fleet and 87 per cent of the car fleet were in OECD countries in 1995, although vehicle ownership is growing very rapidly in developing countries. Industrialized country airlines accounted for 80 per cent of air traffic in 1995 although, again, the developing country contribution is growing rapidly.

Energy consumption is also continuing to grow rapidly: electricity consumption per capita in developing countries more than doubled between 1980 and 1985, although remaining at only a tenth of consumption levels in industrialized countries. Increases in the least-developed countries were marginal.

Water shortages have become more acute as demand for irrigation and municipal supplies continues to grow. There has also been continued growth in demand for minerals and forest products. Meat consumption has more than doubled since 1970; fish consumption has increased even more rapidly.

An important recent trend is the rapid growth in communication technology. Ownership of radios doubled in developing countries between 1980 and 1995, while television ownership more than quadrupled. Recent years have seen rapid growth of mobile telephone networks and the Internet.

ENVIRONMENTAL TRENDS

Globally, many of the environmental and resource impacts of production and consumption have worsened in the last 25 years. However, there has been a shift in the character of production and consumption, and hence in environmental trends, in recent years.

Perhaps the most important trend, especially visible in the industrialized countries, is that environmental problems are increasingly linked to consumption rather than production patterns. Many forms of industrial pollution have been effectively regulated. Industry in many countries has made substantial reductions in its wastage of energy, water and materials. These trends, along with the continuing shift in the economy towards services, mean that more resource use and pollution are caused by activities in the transport, residential and commercial sectors. Also, whereas regulatory incentives and technological solutions have been very effective in reducing the environmental impacts of industry, such measures have had little impact on energy and material use by consumers.

Partly because of the growing transport sector, and partly because of increasing electricity use in buildings, energy demand has continued to rise. This has resulted in a 50 per cent increase in emissions of CO_2 between 1971 and 1995. While there have been some signs of a levelling off in consumption of energy and materials in some industrialized countries, commodity prices have declined in recent years, stimulating ongoing increases in demand.

On the other hand, there have been some notable successes. Emissions of ozone-depleting substances have declined as a result of internationally agreed controls. Industrialized countries have achieved substantial reductions in atmospheric emissions of SO_x, carbon monoxide and heavy metals, and in applications of phosphate fertilizers. Developing countries are beginning to install state-of-the-art pollution controls in many new power plants and industrial facilities. However, if we are to address the full range of environmental challenges linked to the system of production and consumption, we will have to find ways to address trends in individual consumption.

RESOURCE EFFICIENCY TRENDS

Table 21.1 illustrates a number of trends in resource efficiency. It shows that, in the period 1971–1995, while the world economy was growing by an average 2.8 per cent per year, the energy intensity of the economy fell by only 1 per cent per year. Energy efficiency improvements followed the long-term trend recorded in industrial economies. Massive efforts to reduce energy intensity following the oil price rises of the 1970s have had little long-term effect except perhaps in the industry sector.

There are exceptions to this slow pace of change. Some countries have achieved rapid efficiency improvements by adopting existing technology and practices from overseas. Certain sectors have also made rapid progress – the aviation industry achieved nearly 4 per cent per year energy-intensity reduction during the high oil price years. However, this rate of change was slow compared with its rate of labour productivity increase, and was not maintained when the oil price fell. The fuel economy of US cars also improved rapidly during the 1970s, but little or no progress was made from 1982 as the average size, weight and power of personal vehicles increased.

In the few countries for which statistics exist on total material use, the material intensity of the economy is improving a little more rapidly. In mature industrial economies, material intensity is falling roughly at the same pace as GDP is rising, so that aggregate material use is more or less stable. However, the picture with regard to material use is very complicated. Some sectors such as telecommunications are achieving very rapid 'dematerialization' but are also undergoing very rapid growth. Others are achieving relatively little change. Trends vary

Table 21.1 *Historical increases in a range of productivity indicators*

Sector/ technology	Region	Productivity indicator	Period	Annual productivity change (%)
Whole economy	World	GDP/primary energy	1971–1995	+1.0
Whole economy	OECD	GDP/primary energy	1971–1995	+1.27
Whole economy	UK	GDP/primary energy	1890–1995	+0.9
Whole economy	China	GDP/primary energy	1977–1995	+4.9
Whole economy	Japan	GDP/material use	1975–1994	+2.0
Whole economy	US	GDP/material use	1975–1994	+2.5
Industry	OECD	Industrial production/ energy	1971–1995	+2.5
Industry	OECD	Industrial production/ oil use	1974–1986	+8.0
New cars/ light trucks	US	Vehicle fuel economy	1972–1982	+7.0
New cars/ light trucks	US	Vehicle fuel economy	1982–1992	+0.0
Commercial aviation	World	Tonne-km/ energy	1974–1988	+3.8
Commercial aviation	World	Tonne-km/ energy	1988–1995	+0.3
Commercial aviation	World	Tonne-km/ labour	1974–1995	+5.6
Whole economy	16 OECD countries	GDP/hours work	1820–1992	+2.4
Whole economy	Japan	GDP/hours work	1950–1973	+7.7
Telephone cables	Transatlantic	Telephone calls/mass	1914–1994	+25.0

Source: OECD (1998)[5]

considerably between different types of material, with rapid growth in the use of paper, plastic and composites, and declining demand for some traditional materials.

IMPACTS OF PRODUCTION AND CONSUMPTION ON QUALITY OF LIFE

Quality of life can be defined in many different ways. Perhaps one of the most widely accepted indicators is the Human Development Index (HDI), developed by the UNDP. The HDI is used to rank countries based on their income per capita, average life expectancy, educational participation and literacy levels.

On the whole, economic growth means that the basic human needs are being better addressed, as reflected in the components of the HDI. Since 1960, life expectancy in developing countries has increased from 46 to 62, years although some countries have seen setbacks due to the spread of HIV/AIDS. The global average daily per capita supply of calories increased from 2340 in 1970 to 2700 in 1995 and protein intake increased by 25 per cent. However, in the least-developed countries, where per capita income declined in this period, food supply was stationary at about 2100 calories per day, about 10 per cent below normal requirements. In industrialized countries, obesity is a growing problem: food intake is about one third in excess of normal requirements and still rising. On the other hand, cigarette smoking in industrialized countries fell by 10 per cent between 1970 and 1995. In the same period, cigarette smoking in developing countries increased by 60 per cent.

Educational participation is also improving. Personal freedom and access to information continues to improve with the growing publication of books and ownership of radios and televisions.

Indicators based on broader definitions of quality of life give a more mixed message. Several new indicators of human welfare have been developed. The Index of Sustainable Economic Welfare (ISEW) includes corrections to GDP, such as a reduction related to income inequality, benefits from unwaged labour, and costs associated with pollution, resource depletion and some types of medical care. Such indicators have been developed for several countries, and typically show that welfare improved with GDP until some time in the 1970s, but then stagnated or declined despite continuing GDP growth.[6]

At the same time, collective activity declined – cinema attendance declined in most countries in the same period.[7] Other indicators of cultural participation and diversity are difficult to assess: UNESCO has gathered recent statistics for many countries – for example, on the publication of books, attendance at artistic performances, and numbers of speakers of different languages – but trend data are not available.

Communication networks are important mechanisms for change. The membership and esteem function of consumption has been altered by the spread of television, portraying disproportionately affluent lifestyles.[8] Those who watch large amounts of television increasingly take such lifestyles as benchmarks for themselves, resulting in an escalation of desired levels of consumption. The implication is that changes in television programming, to present sustainable lifestyles more often and more positively in drama and documentaries, could contribute to changing consumption patterns.

Globalization and increasing interconnectedness are also contributing to consumption trends.[9] The availability of high-quality transport and communications networks permits the development of highly dispersed communities, which feeds back into escalating demand for transport systems. The growing pressure of meeting the demands of multiple communities (work, social, family) further contributes to the rise in car use and restricting the time available for cooking or other housekeeping activities, encouraging the growth in demand for convenience goods and services.

MOVING TOWARDS MORE SUSTAINABLE PRODUCTION AND CONSUMPTION

In 1994 the Factor 10 Club called for a tenfold improvement in material and energy productivity in industrialized countries over the next 30 to 50 years. It said that this would halve total resource use while allowing for a doubling of worldwide economic activity and an improvement in international equity.

Several governments have taken up the Factor 10 concept as a useful benchmark, but such aims will not be achieved easily. A tenfold efficiency improvement over 30 to 50 years represents a 4 to 8 per cent sustained annual improvement. Historically, as noted above, such rates of change have only been maintained in very special circumstances and for short periods in particular countries or sectors. This does not mean that a societal change on this level is not possible; but it would require radical changes throughout the system of production and consumption and, indeed, in the underlying culture, ethics, social structures and institutions. While it might not be possible or necessary for our fundamental values to alter, there is a need to reconsider which of our values we express in our economic activity and how we interpret them.

On a practical level, rapid technological change can occur for a variety of reasons and may require a combination of different stimuli. Influences contributing to rapid productivity improvements in the past have included large price increases, new competitive pressures, strong regulatory incentives, absolute constraints on resources, and, more generally, a good climate for innovation. All of these stimuli are likely to be needed, and we should continue to pursue the standard policy recommendations for subsidy reform, environmental cost internalization, and support for new technology. However, these should form only a small part of a strategy to foster an evolutionary, learning approach in the system of production and consumption, and to promote creativity. The OECD emphasizes that:

> *'Faced with a very complex set of goals, interests and interrelationships in the economy, government strategies are more likely to succeed if they are: broadly based and coherent, using a mix of instruments; inclusive of stakeholders in policy design and implementation; tolerant of experimentation and occasional failure; and adaptive, using monitoring and feedback mechanisms to adjust measures when necessary.'* [10]

Such strategies might include the following:

1 Establish environmental, economic and social goals, criteria, and indicators. Public and stakeholder processes may be required to establish shared goals and robust targets. If the targets are to be credible, governments must show leadership and consistency in their own actions.
2 Adapt the economic, regulatory and physical infrastructure so that it supports the pursuit of those goals. In addition to reforming subsidies and introducing ecotaxes, governments might consider establishing legal responsibilities to conserve the environment and natural resources, and changing urban and transport planning guidelines to support the development of more sustainable lifestyles.
3 Provide support for basic research and for experimentation with new technologies, practices and institutions. Many forms of support are possible, ranging from direct funding of research to government procurement schemes and awards for green technology.
4 Support the development of best practice schemes and networks to encourage information-sharing and the replication of successful innovations.
5 Reinforce the values that support sustainable development and encouraging a better understanding of environmental and social issues among consumers and small firms. This may require new education and training programmes and the cooperation of the media.

Perhaps the most difficult challenge, both for improving resource efficiency and for developing more sustainable consumption patterns, is the last of these five points. Much of the mainstream debate over consumption patterns has focused on relatively well-understood influences. These include market circumstances, especially prices, technology development, infrastructure design, and demographic trends such as urbanization, migration and ageing. While economic and physical circumstances help to shape consumption, they do not explain why people consume. A more difficult discussion relates to the role of culture, values and individual psychology in motivating and shaping consumption. These influences are hard, if not impossible, to quantify and demonstrate. Yet they will have to be addressed if progress is to be made, even in implementing the most widely advocated policies of subsidy and tax reform.

Our current concepts of prosperity relate mainly to material well-being. But many studies have found that people's reported happiness or satisfaction depends most heavily on their health and on family and other relationships. Having a 'meaning' in life is of fundamental importance.[11] Financial security is also a high priority, but this is rather different from having high levels of consumption.

Few people who have experienced modern levels of hygiene and comfort want to return to a pre-industrial standard of living. On the other hand, many wealthy people long for meaning and for a stronger sense of community. They are torn between the social compulsion to continue to work long hours and accumulate wealth, and spending valuable time with their family and friends. Having made accumulation of wealth, their main source of meaning, they are confronted with the emptiness of what they have achieved.

Most of the world's cultures are based on ethics supporting the family and personal relationships, and discouraging excessive materialism. It is often observed that Western consumerist culture is based on an ethic of individual freedom and the aim of maximizing personal material wealth; but the foundations of Western economic development are built on traditions that emphasize community and generosity. Indeed, Western democracies have long cherished three core values: personal freedom, equal rights and community or solidarity. They were expressed in the French Revolution's rallying cry as 'liberté, égalité, fraternité'. The first two of these values sit uneasily together. Personal freedom, the watchword of the market, often leads to an unequal distribution of wealth and power; enforcing equal rights challenges personal freedom. The two can only be reconciled when people choose to exercise their freedom and rights for the good of other community members: solidarity is the required foundation. Solidarity – with current and future generations and with other species – is also one of the most fundamental values underlying sustainable development.

To support sustainability, and to help us to meet our own needs, our concepts of prosperity do need to change in three ways:

1   Revive the concept of 'sufficiency' to know when we have enough.
2   Re-emphasize sources of real satisfaction such as human relation-
    ships.
3   Value the search for meaning, whether in personal growth, social
    development, or spirituality.

This is not something that governments can do, or at least, not alone.
There are many diverse influences on our values and ethics. The
most important are our direct contacts with other people, especially
family and friends. The most effective sources of societal change are
likely to be those that involve repeated personal interaction, for
example in schools, work places and religious institutions.
Consumption patterns are also strongly influenced by retailers and
other service providers.

Among the most controversial influences on consumption patterns
are those of mass communication. Narrative and symbol carried by the
mass media form a large part of the means through which ideas,
arguments and values are transferred from the public to the private
sphere, and ultimately may be integrated within individuals' consciousness and identity. Studies have found that consumption choices
respond strongly to personal morals or ethics, which are shaped partly
by the public debate and narrative.

Advertising is perhaps the most obvious mechanism by which the
mass media may influence consumption patterns, although perversely
this influence is disputed by the advertising industry. The power of
advertising almost certainly does not lie in its ability to persuade
people to make rational choices to behave differently, but in the
frequent repetition of symbols and value statements so that they gradually become integral parts of mainstream culture and thought. Other
important cultural mediums include television and other drama, political debate, popular music, the visual arts and novels.

Alliances among powerful groups can play a dominant role in
determining societal norms through both narrative and symbol.
Governments, transnational companies, financial institutions, the
media represented the main power alliance in the late 20th century.
One example of an alliance supporting a specific interest is the 'road
lobby'. This coalition of business interests, professions, government
departments and citizens' groups played a strong role in the early
development of roads and road-based transport. In recent years, the
strength of the coalition has made it difficult for alternatives to the car
to flourish.

Alliances may also be the route to a change in our concepts of
prosperity, and in the values and ethics that shape our life styles and
communities. A new alliance working for change might include
schools, universities, religious institutions, community groups and

local governments. Ideally it would also draw in national government, the media, and the business community.

I believe that the central task of that alliance would be to develop a new story or myth to describe where we are going as a society. Maybe it can be based on a synthesis of traditional myth. Or maybe it should be made up of true stories of individuals and communities who have achieved the transformation we are looking for. The alliance should embody the values of sustainability in words, symbols and actions.

Perhaps the greatest contribution we can make is by doing it ourselves.

NOTES

1   BCSD (1993) *Getting Eco-Efficient*, Report of the Business Council for Sustainable Development, First Antwerp Eco-Efficiency Workshop, November, Geneva: Business Council for Sustainable Development

2   OECD (1998) *Eco-Efficiency*, Paris: Organisation for Economic Co-operation and Development

3   United Nations (1998) *Measuring Changes in Consumption and Production Patterns: A Set of Indicators*, New York: United Nations

4   OECD (1999) *Towards More Sustainable Household Consumption Patterns: Indicators to Measure Progress*, OECD Series on Environmental Indicators, ENV/EPOC/SE(98)2/FINAL, Paris: Organisation for Economic Co-operation and Development

5   OECD (1998) op cit Note 2

6   UK Friends of the Earth have an interactive tool on their website, http://www.foe.co.uk/progress/index.html, so that the public can experiment with different weightings on the terms in the ISEW

7   UNESCO (1998) *World Culture Report: Culture, Creativity and Markets*, Paris: UNESCO Publishing

8   Schor, J (1998) *The Overspent American*, New York: Basic Books

9   Mulgan, G (1997) *Connexity: How to Live in a Connected World*, Boston, MA: Harvard Business School Press

10 OECD (1998) op cit Note 2

11 Argyle, M (1987) *The Psychology of Happiness*, London: Routledge

22

Fish Forever

John Gummer

It was once thought that the sea was an inexhaustible source of food. 'The harvest of the sea' was a wonder of the natural world even within the lifetime of most of us. In the standard geography lessons which dealt with the trawlers and the drifters, the Dogger Bank and the Grand Banks of Canada were seen as places where fish abounded and only the weather and the wind made their capture a hazardous pursuit.

In his 19th-century autobiography *From Cabin Boy to Archbishop*, the Archbishop Ullathorne of Birmingham reminisced about his early life on the ships that ran from Hull to Scandinavia. He wrote of one voyage to the Baltic, 'we have been held here in port for three days so thick have been the shoals of fish, we cannot leave the harbour'. There could be no starker contrast with the experience today. Nor is this change confined to Northern waters. Far off in the South Atlantic, Korean and Taiwanese, Spanish and South American boats compete in a fishery which is already dangerously near overexploitation and where some species face extinction. In the South China Sea, all the way down the coast of Africa, even in Australasia, the story is much the same. Bigger and bigger boats from countries increasingly far away seek fish which is no longer plentiful in their own waters. Sir Crispin Tickell, chairman of the UK government's high-level advisory group on sustainable development, warned in his very first annual report five years ago that the collapse of the world's fishing stocks was perhaps the most imminent ecological disaster.

Yet, the global nature of this situation points to something more than just a common threat. The reason for the depredation of far-flung resources from Ecuador to Indonesia lies in the growing demand for fish in the developed and developing world alike. The recognition of its place in a balanced diet among the increasingly health-conscious rich, and the dependence upon fish of so many of the world's poor, present unparalleled pressures upon the stocks.

However, it is science and technology that has made the crucial difference. The developments in radar, which wars have fostered, have meant that fish can be located with relative ease. Subsequently, the conquest of space brought the ability to fix a boat's position within a hair's breadth. So the relative positions of hunter and hunted were irremediably changed. Fish no longer had a chance. Better boats, better engines, better nets, and better gear made their contribution but it was refrigeration which proved the greatest boon. From the 1950s, factory ships which could freeze huge quantities of product, together with their equivalent on-shore installations, have provided a market for the increased catches which these new techniques have made possible.

So, it is a new world for the fisherman and yet his image in many countries has remained remarkably constant. Say 'fisherman' in the UK and the picture which is conjured up is of the bronzed, weather-beaten young man with deep blue eyes and a sinewy frame, looking into the distance with a suitably romantic and far-away look. He is a man battered by wind and weather who 'goes down to the sea in ships' and battles to 'do his business in great waters'. Those long-repeated words give a hint of the way that fishermen have entered the folklore of England. It is no wonder that when Margaret Thatcher was ennobled, she chose a fisherman rather than a heraldic beast to be one of the supporters of her arms. It was her way of celebrating 'the fishermen of England'. What is true of England holds for Scotland and Denmark, the Faroes and The Netherlands, Spain and Portugal, even Germany and France. Fishermen are held in a regard which is far greater than their economic importance and reflects much more their place in history.

Even so, as a major renewable resource, fisheries provide a livelihood for hundreds of thousands of people around the world, sustaining coastal communities and representing a valuable source of income to the global economy. Beyond Europe, the role of fishermen is crucial in the lives of many a community. They provide almost the only source of protein for very large numbers. They fish almost as they have always fished and their production is to satisfy local needs. These are the fishermen who increasingly will be squeezed by the voracious appetites of the large operators who come in search of new stocks as they exhaust the old. This is to repeat an old story. It has been the greed of the rich world that has produced the shortages and it will be the wealth of the rich world which will buy what fish are left even though it is essential to the very existence of the poor.

For fish has rarely been so popular. The Americans ate a record 1.9 billion kilogrammes in 1994. China's consumption has doubled in the last decade. In many countries, there are new and successful chains of seafood restaurants. Seafood choices, partly for health reasons, and a fall in consumer confidence in meat, are increasingly common on restaurant menus throughout the developed world. It may be true that people shy away from using fish in home cooking; but now that one in four meals even in Britain are taken outside the home, the catering trade has taken up the challenge of serving fish with great success.

In developing countries seafood is a vital source of protein. Indeed the FAO reports that fish provides 29 per cent of total animal protein in Asia, 19 per cent in Africa, and 8 per cent in Latin America. The International Centre for Asian Development has estimated that over a billion people in Asia alone depend upon fish and seafood as their major source of animal protein. These are the people who are at risk from the increasing depredation of the world's fish stocks. It is these vulnerable communities who will be outbid by the rich when their present sources are fished out.

The future of the marine industry and the lives and livelihoods which it sustains are threatened. The FAO in 1996 reported that of the top 200 important commercial fish species, 35 per cent were in the senescent phase with declining landings, 25 per cent were in the mature phase with a high level of exploitation, and 40 per cent were still being developed. Perhaps the most important conclusion drawn by FAO from its report is that 60 per cent of fish stocks were in urgent need of management. Put more starkly, FAO says the great majority of the world's fish stocks were fully fished, overexploited, depleted, or slowly recovering. FAO's more recent reports contain nothing which makes the picture less depressing.

In addition to overfishing, it is the discarding of fish which has so damaging an effect upon stocks. Nearly a quarter of all that is caught at sea for human consumption is thrown back, dead or dying. This serious situation is the result of bad resource management. Countries which seek to control fisheries often have the opposite effect. By insisting upon minimum landing sizes and imposing quotas, they make discarding a way of life for their fishermen who wish to maximize their quotas in terms of the saleability of the fish they land. Of course, it is not an easy matter as fish do not observe national boundaries. There are many places where the fishery is shared between different countries, each one jealous of the rights of its own fishermen and sure that if it has an effective conservation system, others will take advantage of its reticence. Fish migrate in patterns which change and put further pressure upon fishing regimes, and the friction between fisherman from different ports and groups is a continuing feature in almost all parts of the world.

The complexity of these management problems should not be underestimated. Fishery management is an inexact science and, therefore, even where the expertise is available, it is often unwelcome and contested by fishermen. They often present anecdotal evidence to gainsay the scientists. On the very eve of the collapse of the fisheries on the Canadian Grand Banks, fishermen were still claiming that there were shoals out there for the taking. Scientists too can be very wrong. We just do not know enough about the reproduction cycle of many species. The effect of even small changes in the temperature of the ocean and the impact of changes in land use, extraction and pollution are not properly understood. As a result, neither fisherman nor scientist is ever entirely right, and it is perfectly understandable that the hunter tends to refute evidence that would restrict his operations and clings to that which favours further exploitation.

Nor are fisheries simple. There are often several species with different characteristics in the same fishery, caught by different fishermen of several countries and an even larger number of communities, using different types of boats and gear. Management in these circumstances is bound to be difficult and, even if successful, is complex to explain and enforce. Many resources are highly migratory and under different jurisdictions for different times of their journeying. International management regimes often lack enforcement authority and expertise, and management systems that are based on the best of intentions often end up by rewarding the worst of behaviour. Nor is it surprising that the worst features of domestic management are often compounded in an international setting where there is much illegal conduct and little sense of ownership of the resource.

And it was ever thus. The competition among hunters; the sharing of fisheries; and the pursuit of migratory species led constantly to conflict and sometimes to bloodshed. Yet, when there was plenty of fish, there was little effect on the stocks. It is only now when fishermen are so much more effective that the lack of effective management begins to threaten the world's supply, rather than merely to affect fishermen and their immediate communities.

It is this that has led to the emergence of a consensus that these problems should be addressed. We cannot collectively afford to allow the situation to deteriorate to a point at which a major source of protein is unavailable to the world or, indeed, out of the reach of those indigenous communities who depend upon it for their lives and livelihood. Nor should we forget that countries such as Norway, Iceland and Denmark depend significantly upon their fishing industry's products as major contributors to their GNP.

Marine fishing, by its very nature, is not one of the more visible ecological issues. The effects of the depleting ozone layer, of climate change, of acid rain, and factory pollution are all readily appreciated by large numbers of people. It is less easy for people to be engaged in what is going on beneath the seas. So the fact that the collapse of the world's fishing stocks is one of the most harmful ecological threats of all goes relatively unmentioned. Fish may not be cuddly but they matter nonetheless. Were we to lose these once abundant stocks, we would deprive our children of an inestimable benefit.

Although management of fish stocks is so difficult it is still possible for systems to produce sustainable fisheries. Nonetheless, they are constantly faced with challenges, not least from those who see little advantage to present fishermen in the marketplace. Promising a continuing fishery for future fishermen is not always attractive enough bait when compared with the certainty of greater short-term profit in a less restricted fishery. Clearly, innovative approaches must be found to make the good management systems more attractive. Only in such ways will we be able to turn chronic overfishing and discarding into fisheries which will recover in a sustainable way. In particular, we need to harness the power of the market in order to add to the attraction of successful and effective regulatory systems. This is not to challenge national or international policies, but to make it easier for them to do their job because the market is pulling in their direction and not in a contrary way.

Not that this will be easy. After all, this is a problem which has so far defeated all who have tried to find an answer. Even as far back as 1756, Henry Fielding recognized the immensity of the problem. In his *Journal of a Voyage to Lisbon* he wrote: 'While a fisherman can break through the strongest meshes of an Act of Parliament, we may be assured that he will learn so as to contrive his own meshes that the smallest fry will not be able to swim through them'. Even then, when fishing was so much less complex a business, Fielding recognized that it was in the nature of a hunter to seek his prey in the most effective way possible and with a great unwillingness to accept the dictates of others. Indeed, Fielding showed an immense capacity to understand the very problem with which we are faced today:

> *'Of all the animal foods with which man is furnished there are none so plenty as fish. If this be true of rivers, it is much truer of the sea shores which abound with such immense variety of fish that the curious fisherman, after he has made his draft, often culls only the daintiest part and leaves the rest of his prey to perish on the shore.'*

What could be more contemporary than that? Over 250 years ago, Fielding described our greed as we render that huge variety of species increasingly rare and squander the wealth of the sea. All that has changed is the scale. More fish, bigger boats, more certain catching, further and further away – that is what is new. Yet even in the 18th century, the danger was recognized and Fielding saw the passage through the British parliament of an Act for the Effectual Preservation and Improvement of the Spawn and Fry of Fish in the River Thames and the Waters of the Medway. It failed as every Act has since.

So, we face an ancient problem exacerbated by modern technology. We have never found an achievable solution even in the waters which are well policed and cared for and within the jurisdiction of a single effective government. Nor will we help to find a way through unless we admit that this stricture applies to ourselves here in the UK as much as to others in the rest of Europe and beyond. Let us accept from the beginning that it is impossible to ensure that every fisherman in the north-east of the UK keeps to the rules imposed by the national and EU authorities. What is true nationally is even more so when we think of waters shared by different nations and competing fishermen.

A common fisheries policy for the EU is crucial because member nations share so many of the fisheries. Even within the 12-mile (19-kilometre) limit off the coast of Britain there are historic rights for Belgian, Dutch and French fishermen. Once beyond that limit, the whole area is shared by even more countries of the EU. Any suggestion that there should be a repatriation of fisheries policy to the individual nations makes no sense either practically or environmentally. It is not the commonness of the EU policy that has caused difficulties; it is the policy which is wrong and needs to be radically revised.

The problems of the Common Fisheries Policy (CFP) afflict all efforts to manage fisheries on an international basis. There is little special about the fundamental difficulty. Every minister who sits round that council table is there as the representative of his national fishermen. It is his job to ensure that they get as large a share as possible of the fish that are to be divided out. Even if the fish are not really there, he has to obtain his quota. It is not surprising that conservation takes a back seat. Every year scientists produce figures for the catch which would be sensible, given the condition of the stocks. Every year that translates into an unacceptable share-out for each of the nations concerned. So every year the levels are set higher than they ought to be in order to make the agreement politically acceptable. Ministers return home and all too often connive at public statements that suggest that the real fault lies with someone else, with another country or with the EU in general. It just is not politically acceptable to admit the truth.

There is too much fishing in European waters, too much capacity and a great deal too much hypocrisy. This is a universal truth which is exemplified in the UK as elsewhere. Even when, at last, the ministers agreed in 1999 to cut quotas very significantly, it was still not as much as was really necessary. Many opposition politicians sought to make capital out of the cuts – not on the basis that they were environmentally insufficient, but that they were too divergent and that somehow the government or the EU were to blame. In truth, of course, it was the unwillingness of successive governments to reduce the size of the British catching capacity by an effective buyout scheme and proper help for the communities that were thus affected. Parsimony does not explain it all. The electoral effect of the votes of fishing communities was a great influence and there was always the fear that others, with whom the UK shares the resource, would cut their fleets less or enforce the rules more leniently. There was a history of fraud and ineffectiveness in the administration of an earlier UK decommissioning scheme. Above all, there was an unwillingness to face up to the fact that technical advances meant that we could no longer support the same fishing effort as before.

What is true in the UK is, to a greater or lesser extent, true in the rest of Europe too and can be mirrored in the arguments wherever fisheries are shared between nations. Nor should we underestimate their strength. Fishermen are hardy, worthwhile and valued members of society. They uphold communities in distant places. Their livelihood is very often the only means of living for whole villages and therefore the issue is not just about fish and fishermen but about regions and history.

We recognize that by the importance attached to the fishing industry, even in a country such as the UK where less than 50,000 people are supported by it. We have five government ministers to look after an industry which directly employs fewer individuals than work for the supermarket chain Asda. That is because the public sees the industry as different. If that is true in Britain, then it is even truer in Spain or Portugal where the industry's proportionate importance is so much greater. It is therefore not surprising that we have failed to produce a policy which puts conservation first when the parties involved carry so much political baggage to the negotiating table. That doesn't mean that we can find a unilateral way through. The shared fisheries make that impossible.

Indeed, even at home there are competing interests between Scotland and England, Wales and Northern Ireland which make solutions difficult. Nor does it stop there: the east and west of Scotland are fiercely divided over many questions and unite only to see off any threat from the south-west of England, which itself will argue strongly against views held in Lowestoft.

We therefore need something which will support the best intentions of governments not only in the EU but all over the world. For that we have to go back to consider the problem. We have accepted that fishermen are hunters and therefore will seek to catch fish wherever they are. We have seen, too, that it is the efficacy of fishing which has brought about the crisis. What needs to be emphasized is that it is the market which has made both so acutely dangerous. Fishermen can sell their fish in abundance. The greater the shortage, the more that is true. This is a worldwide business, so the supplies will be drawn to the best prices. Thus do the rich possess the protein of the poor. It is the market that causes the problem and it is the market which must provide the solution. There is no way forward through an international extension of the governance systems which have so far failed nationally and in the EU. Somewhere, therefore, within the power of the market we have to find an answer that will give strength to the regulators and make conservation measures effective.

The problem is simply that the market is about today and tomorrow and maybe next week, but certainly not about ten years' time. The market needs the fourth dimension – time. It needs to take into account what it requires in the future as well as what it needs now. That is why we must provide a premium for permanence. Those who contract to supply now and next year, and then again the year after, must be rewarded over those who merely produce for today. That is in the interests of buyers, sellers and consumers alike. Yet the market cannot satisfy these needs without some outside help.

It is in appreciating this need that conservationists and industrialists alike saw that they had a common interest in changing the terms of the market. At the moment, every packet of fish fingers could truthfully carry a second sell-by date reminding purchasers not when those fish fingers should be eaten, but when – at the present rate of exploitation – the last fish finger will be eaten. The raw material upon which huge businesses round the world depend is rapidly being exhausted.

Where the individual fisherman or even the whole of a particular fishery can ignore the warning signs or trust to anecdotal evidence, Unilever cannot. Where the corner shop can expect someone, somewhere, to sort out the supplies of anchovies and tuna, Sainsbury's – Britain's biggest fishmonger – can't leave it all to chance. So what the conservationists were warning of, and the politicians were struggling with, became a matter for the market. It was that simple fact that gave the Marine Stewardship Council (MSC) life. Because there was money in fish, there was money in the future of fish.

Now, of course, this was a concept which came strangely to many. The fish producers, the processors, even the supermarkets had been seen by environmentalists as part of the problem. They made the overfishing profitable. They were, therefore, the cause of the depredation. To turn that on its head and see instead that business could become the means of saving the stock was psychologically not easy. What was also difficult was coming to terms with the idea of conserving a depleted resource rather than saving an endangered species.

That was an unfamiliar concept for many who are alive to environmental needs. Yet, it was precisely this realization which was so important a change in the thinking of all involved.

There is a moral imperative at the heart of any concept of stewardship. Religious or philosophical in origin, it says that it is wrong to destroy what cannot be replaced. It defines something about the nature of human beings: that we should not plunder and rape but enhance and respect; that a generation should not deprive the future of what it received from the past; that the world is not ours but our children's and their children's. When applied to endangered species, that moral case is simple and overwhelming. Save the whale or protect the panda – everyone can see the point. But fish? The logic is fine, the attraction much more limited. It is not just that fish aren't cuddly; it's that the preservation is not only to keep. It is to cull.

The successful protection of the whale or the elephant always presents the conservationist with a fundamental dilemma. Now that the species is no longer under threat, should controlled and responsible culling be allowed? The instincts and emotions, roused in fighting extinction, are not readily turned to support even a controlled cull. It is a wholly different set of ideas which explains that creatures are properly for humankind's use or that individuals have a place in the predatory chain which makes it necessary for them to keep animal populations under control. No wonder it has proved so hard to deal with the damage done by too many elephants in Southern Africa, or the Norwegian demand for a resumption of whaling.

Fish conservation faces that issue from the start as, less acutely, does forestry stewardship. We are not saving the fish for them to die at a ripe old age. Our concern for biodiversity is coupled with our interest in fish as a resource. 'Fish forever' is not only about avoiding extinction, it is about a continuous supply of food. It is therefore perfectly proper that both interests should come together in achieving their common goal. Resource management may not be the stuff of high-profile popular campaigns but it is going, increasingly, to be at the top of our environmental agenda. The moral imperative is joined with practical concern.

This conjunction is growing in importance. Polluting the atmosphere ought always to have been recognized as a matter of man's morality; it now has also to be seen as a matter of man's survival. At Kyoto, therefore, we recognized not just a duty but a need. When it comes to fish, that need is much more easily identified with financial interests. Climate change has no such clear identification. Governments have to act if the problem is to be addressed at all. Yet, the slow and painful pace of progress – even when the world is faced with disaster – reminds us just how hard it is for governments to face up to global challenges. It ought, therefore, not to surprise us that, despite years of effort, governments haven't succeeded yet in dealing with the worldwide decline in fisheries.

Nor should this be a matter of shame. It is very hard to reconcile real differences in a region or a country, let alone those that straddle nations and even continents. It is worth remembering that when the last fish was caught off the Canadian Grand Banks, it was within one of the most regulated fisheries in the world and confined to the jurisdiction of one government. It should therefore not surprise us that we have been so unsuccessful where fisheries are shared between nations deeply suspicious of each other's motives.

So, if governments, the EU, and the UN-FAO have found it hard to find a way to prevent the increasingly certain destruction of the world's fish stocks, it was essential to seek another method. Not a competitive method, but one which might make more sense of regulatory regimes throughout the world. If the financial interests of those involved could be linked with the manifest necessity for conservation, then the industry could put the power of the market behind the efforts of the regulators.

That was the understanding which Unilever and the World Wide Fund For Nature (WWF) brought to the creation of the Marine Stewardship Council. Both had a crucial interest in saving the world's fish and were sufficiently far-sighted to overcome the suspicion which has historically attended the relationships between businessmen and conservationists. The result has been quite remarkable. The two organizations have not just created the MSC, but have had the sense to allow it to become independent of them. What they created was an organization which produces market incentives to encourage sustainable fisheries and reward responsible fishery practices.

This will be achieved by certifying fisheries which harvest the sea in a sustainable way. The MSC logo will be carried by the products of those fisheries and is supported by all the big retailing names in the UK and many more in the rest of Europe and the US. Processors and many of the leading manufacturers have also come in to support the initiative and during 2000, fisheries in the UK, Australia and the US will be among the first to be certified. The logo will be a sign to consumer and producer alike that fish is not just for now but forever. Processors and retailers will increasingly choose to buy from sources which guarantee continuity of supply. So, fisheries which do not sacrifice tomorrow for today will benefit from a premium price and a long-term market. Increasingly, those who source elsewhere will properly be marginalized as the market protects its future.

Not that this is the only initiative which gives real hope for the future of fisheries. The effective campaign in the US to highlight the threat to the swordfish; the growing consumer understanding of the seriousness of the problem of overfishing; and the heightened interest in the media all across the world have begun to turn the tide. Governments and international organizations have been affected by a new urgency in their efforts to find a solution. The FAO, the CSD, even the World Trade Organization (WTO), have moved fisheries much higher up their priorities. The development of ITQs – individual transferable quotas – is just one more example of the innovation and imagination which is being brought to bear on the issue. Fishermen and their organizations are becoming much more concerned and, as a result, the swingeing 2000 quota restrictions introduced by the EU were accepted much more readily than could have been imagined even five years ago.

There is still a very long way to go before universally better management will enable us to guarantee a future for the world's fisheries. The fact that such management could, according to the FAO, enable an additional 10 to 20 million tonnes of fish to be taken annually shows just how positive effective control can be. Indeed, the recovery of stocks could herald the recovery of an industry that has for so long been in decline. Without it that decline will be terminal.

So, it is all to aim for. The present prognosis is pretty dire, but at last the interests that imagined they were opposed have begun to understand that they have a common goal. Fishermen and processors, manufacturers and retailers, conservationists and governments, international organizations and regional trading blocks – all of them need to safeguard fish for the future. It is still very early days but the intention is now there. The necessary institutions are in place – whether it's the Straddling Stocks Convention or the Marine Stewardship Council. What we need is the vision and tenacity to make them work. Only that will give us and our children fish forever.

23

Freshwater: A Global Crisis of Water Security and Basic Water Provision*

Rosalie Gardiner

In March 2000, the Ministerial Declaration of the Second World Water Forum in the Hague, The Netherlands, set water security as a principal concern for sustainable development in the 21st century. The global statistics speak for themselves. Approximately one in three people live in regions of moderate to high water stress and it is estimated that two thirds of people will live in water stressed conditions by 2025 (WBGU, 1999; UNEP, 1999). Human demand for and the misuse of water resources continue to grow. Intensive irrigation is placing steadily increasing pressure on aquifers and their ability to recharge, and reported incidences of groundwater and surface water contamination continue to rise. In large cities, total municipal and industrial uses of water have grown by 24 times in the last century and urban populations are expected to grow to 5 billion people by 2025. Some large-scale water infrastructure projects, and an intensification and greater frequency of natural threats, such as flooding and droughts, are having a devastating impact on people's livelihood and access to water. These pressures are also placing freshwater ecosystems and their associated species under enormous strain. The critical issues for water security, in terms of the causes and the resultant

* This chapter was peer-reviewed by individuals from different stakeholder groups. Particular thanks go to Danielle Morley, Lyn Billman-Golemme, Pierre Najlis, Frank van Steenberger and the various members of the Towards Earth Summit 2002 project International Advisory Board for their contributions.

Table 23.1 *Regional issues related to global water insecurity*

	Key issues
Asia & Pacific	• *Critical health problems:* In Asia, 1 in 3 people lacks access to safe drinking water; 500,000 infants die each year from diarrhoeal diseases related to a lack of adequate WSS. • *Water pollution:* In many countries bacterial waste from human sources exceeds levels recommended in OECD guidelines by ten times. • *Overuse:* Agriculture accounts for 90 per cent of freshwater withdrawals in South Asia. Aquifer depletion in Asia has led to a drop in water availability per capita from 10,000 m^3 in 1950 to 4200 m^3 in the 1990s. West Asia faces particular pressure on groundwater resources, where withdrawals far exceed natural recharge rates.
Africa	• *Poverty and water scarcity:* 25 countries will face water stress or scarcity by 2025. Over 300 million people lack access to safe water supply. Nearly 51 per cent of people in sub-Saharan countries lack access to safe supply and 41 per cent lack adequate sanitation. Fourteen countries are already experiencing water stress. The number is expected to rise to 25 countries by 2025. Approximately 16 per cent of the continent's 230 million people will be subject to water scarcity in 2025. • *Uneven distribution of water resources:* Natural variation and a lack of regional basin level planning are exacerbating uneven distribution. • *Overuse:* Lack of groundwater protection from agricultural uses, which makes up 88 per cent of total water use. • *Lack of risk preparedness and mitigation:* Flooding, droughts and storms displace human settlements and have chronic health effects. For example, in Mozambique over 1 million people were displaced by the floods in 1999/2000 and an unknown number killed.
Europe & Central Asia	• *Lack of access to drinking water:* Many parts of Eastern Europe and Central Asia lack access to safe drinking water. • *Increasing water consumption:* Demand has grown from 100 km^3 1950 to 560 km^3 in early 1990s. Agriculture accounts for 60 per cent of water use in the Mediterranean and a further 90 per cent in Central Asia. More than half Europe's cities are overexploiting groundwater reserves. Industrial and urban uses are 55 per cent of total water use and current levels are expected to double by 2025. • *Declining water quality:* Many countries report groundwater pollution (nitrates, pesticides, heavy metals and hydrocarbons) impacting watersheds, aquifers and

associated biota, eg Mediterranean, Aral Sea, Scandinavian lakes. Nitrate levels in many parts of western and central Europe exceed max. admissible human consumption (EU Drinking Water Directive).

Latin America & Caribbean	• *Groundwater contamination and depletion:* Release of heavy metals, nutrients, chemicals and hazardous wastes from mining, agriculture and industry are growing. Sanitation: Only 2 per cent of all sewage produced in Latin America receives treatment with considerable health and environmental risks, eg cholera and typhoid outbreaks.
	• *Conflict over access and use of water:* many national water policies fail to incorporate integrated approach to management environmental limits or rights of access to water, and lack coordination between regulatory agencies.
North America	• *Aquifer depletion:* demand on water resources, especially from fossil stores, has steadily increased due to population growth, municipal, expansion of irrigation and industry, eg cotton farming in Texas and New Mexico have reduced water supplies. Canada and the US are the world's largest per capita users of water globally.
	• *Water pollution:* agrochemical runoff and non-point sources of water pollutants have contaminated many ground and surface waters. Detection of Mercury, PCBs, DDT found in fish from water pollution have led to warnings about fish consumption.

Notes: Adequate access: 20 litres per person per day from a source located within 1 km of users' dwelling. Water stress: less than 1700 m³ per capita per year (OECD 1999)
Sources: WBGU, 1999; UNEP, 1999; ECOSOC, 2000

impacts, are particular to each locality and region of the world (see Table 23.1).

For developing countries, the most pressing issue for water security is in meeting basic provision of water supply and sanitation (WSS). Twenty per cent of the world's population still lack access to safe drinking water and 50 per cent lack adequate sanitation, a statistic that has not improved since the end of the eighties international WSS decade. The UN Secretary-General's report to the 8th session of the UN Commission for Sustainable Development (CSD) on the *Progress Made in Providing Safe Water Supply and Sanitation for All During the 1990s* (ECOSOC, 2000) paints a bleak picture of the present status of WSS provision. Latin America, Asia and Africa are facing the greatest difficulties (see Figure 23.1).

Over the last ten years, rural sanitation provision in Africa has decreased by 2 per cent, and the low levels of urban water supply and sanitation have hardly improved. Urban water supply in Asia has also

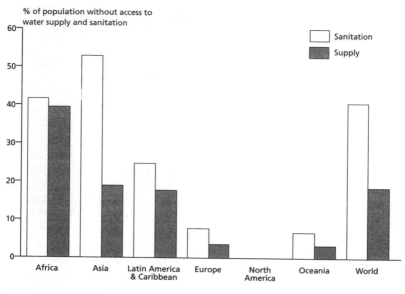

Source: ECOSOC, 2000

Figure 23.1 *Lack of access to water supply and sanitation
by region, 2000*

fallen since 1990 (see Figure 23.2). In Latin America, sanitation in rural areas has remained low. Arid and semi-arid areas, especially in West Asia and North Africa, are likely to be most affected by increasing water stress. Underlying many of these problems is the fact that water is a fixed resource, faced with increasing demand and pressure from competing water uses.

The Secretary-General's report outlines some key areas of reform, especially towards better WSS coverage and water resource allocation. Some of these aspects are discussed below with reference to previous meetings, future international process and the drivers for directing water strategies towards more sustainable economic activities and poverty eradication.

DECENTRALIZATION OF GOVERNANCE

*'without the fullest participation of people at all levels
of society the goal of full coverage (of WSS) is unlikely to
be obtained'* Secretary General Report to UN CSD, 2000

In 1992, at the Dublin Freshwater Conference, and at numerous subsequent meetings, the principle of subsidiary has been advocated, where

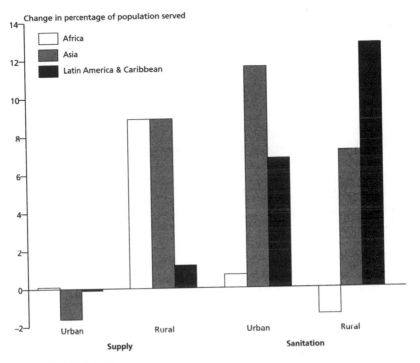

Source: ECOSOC, 2000

Figure 23.2 *Change in water supply and sanitation for Africa, Asia and Latin America and Caribbean, 1999–2000*

management of public water supply, irrigation and water resources should occur at the lowest appropriate level. The Hague Declaration indicated further ministerial support for devolution of governance, enhancing the role of local authorities, industries, NGOs and individual citizens in water regulation, monitoring and planning. Crucially, the government's role is not reduced, and remains pivotal in supporting local inclusion (eg education and capacity-building), monitoring and producing enforceable regulations, as well as supporting transboundary collaboration between regions and other states. Local authorities can encourage community involvement, for example through consultative processes and public meetings, with planning incorporated into a wider water and land use context. Industry has an increasingly vital role in water and sanitation provision, technical and productive efficiency and support of local communities via employment, income generation projects and developing partnerships with public and water projects. Voluntary codes of practice and initiatives can enable industry to take a more proactive position, going beyond the minimum legislative requirements in support of sustainable water practice. NGOs' traditional role for community support can be greatly developed through, for example: supporting innovative mechanisms for local financing of water projects; capacity-building; promoting blue funds; awareness-building in general; promoting good research through social venture capital; reality checks on water data; and through participation in decision-making at a variety of levels.

COMMUNITY EMPOWERMENT

At the 6th session of the CSD (CSD-6) in 1998 it was agreed that governments need to formulate goals for involving communities in water management. Rights, responsibilities and roles need to be defined within a broad institutional framework for participatory planning and management at all levels and across all sectors. Furthermore, to increase community effectiveness as 'agents for change', strategies are required for enhancing awareness, technical, managerial and administrative capacity via training, education and publicity campaigns. Governments, NGOs and other public and private bodies will all have a role in supporting greater community involvement in WSS strategies. International task masters UNESCO, DESA, as well as UNEP, OECD and other international organizations were identified as critical for raising global awareness on the importance of WSS.

The importance of gender was raised at the UN General Assembly's Special Session (UNGASS, 1997) and the Second World Water Forum (SWWF, 2000) where it was recognized that particular attention should be paid to the role, skills and needs of women (along with indigenous communities) as critical actors in safeguarding and monitoring water resources. WSS programmes show links between greater female participation to higher coverage, better management and lower incidence of water-related diseases. There is therefore a need to enhance WSS programmes with gender focused capacity-building, education and training in administration, management strategies, as well as developing mechanisms and indicators for gender participation in decision-making.

SERVICE PROVISION: RURAL AND URBAN CHALLENGES

Requirements for water to better sustain people's livelihoods clearly differs between rural and urban areas. However, central to better distribution and provision, alongside devolved governance, is the increased recognition of the importance of water as a productive element. In addition to supporting basic needs, it plays a key role in sustaining development. Not only in socioeconomic terms, with the production of food (cereal, fisheries) and a whole range of other goods and services (manufacturing, power generation, textiles etc), but also in supporting ecosystem functioning and species (WWC, 2000).

Governments and local authorities need to ensure that policy targets and programmes meet all these ends, towards maximizing development aims. This means not only in terms of upgrading infrastructures to improve operation and maintenance for basic WSS, but also through better internalization of social and environmental externalities from other water uses, eg regulating production inefficiencies and improved cost recovery. Private enterprise may assist this process with the adoption of water efficient technology, administration and management practices. Traditional and small-scale water use practices may be more sustainable, cost effective and efficient than new, mammoth installations or 'technocratic' approaches, therefore public/private planning, implementation and management processes need to take place in open consultation with local water users to weigh up the costs and benefits of alternative approaches. Authorities need to ensure that the poorest are fully reflected in decision-making through the better definition and communication of rights of access and frameworks for community involvement.

INFORMATION MANAGEMENT

Six years after the 1994 Ministerial Conference on Drinking Water and Environmental Sanitation held in Noordwijk, The Netherlands, there is still a notable lack of assessment and up-to-date baseline data about the status of WSS provision and water resources, including identification of problems and constraints to provision. Nationally, governments have a role in collating and promoting good practice, supporting ongoing research and monitoring programmes. Monitoring and modelling of water resources assists more targeted policy decisions by developing baseline data about the physical status of surface and groundwater, identifying those areas where water resources are critically threatened or may be at risk from human conflict or natural pressure. Further research is needed into the causal links between water provision and poverty to assist more targeted poverty elevation strategies. Internationally and regionally, a number of monitoring and information provision programmes exist, such as the International Hydrology Programme (UNESCO), Joint Water Supply and Sanitation Monitoring Programme (WHO, UNDP, UNICEF) and Global Programme of Action for the Protection of the Marine Environment from Land-Based Activities (UNEP). Much of this work could be collated and reviewed in a biennial World Water Development Report produced by the UN Administrative Committee on Coordination (ACC) Subcommittee on Water Resources (SWWF, 2000).

EDUCATION

At the 1998 International Conference on Water and Sustainable Development in Paris, ministers agreed to improve knowledge and information exchange through technology transfer, education and training, particularly to enable the involvement of poor, disadvantaged, indigenous communities, youth, local authorities and NGOs. Education in hygiene, and more generally, is an essential prerequisite to better health and sanitation. Education and better access to information are also important components for empowering people to take greater responsibility over their water use, giving people the skills to self regulate and monitor water resources. This should cover formal and informal mechanisms, including all levels of schooling and via the media. At a local level, authorities can work with and support local community surveillance networks (eg water user associations and river associations).

FINANCIAL AND ECONOMIC MECHANISMS

The World Bank recently estimated that US$600 billion investment in WSS infrastructure implementation would be necessary to reach full coverage. The World Summit on Social Development in 1995 stated that 20 per cent of public expenditure and 20 per cent of national aid budgets should be allocated for provision of basic services. Governments remain the principle financial source for WSS provision. Current global estimates of annual expenditure for WSS is US$50 billion from governments, US$15 billion from the private sector, US$9 billion from international donors and US$4 billion from foreign direct investment (Cosgrove and Rijsberman, 2000). Economic and legislative instruments can produce additional finances, however appropriate and effective regulation, monitoring and better cost recovery by authorities is necessary to ensure that these funds are reinvested into WSS and water-related programmes. Foreign and domestic private organizations and donors should be encouraged to support and supplement these activities. The GEF Water Programme (under UNDP, UNEP and World Bank) plans to inject US$0.5 billion over the next five years for international waters projects in developing countries and economies-in-transition. Such programmes need to ensure aid is linked into strategies for poverty eradication and sustainable water consumption.

INTEGRATED WATER RESOURCE MANAGEMENT

Since the 1977 UN Water Conference held in Mar del Plata, Argentina, integrated water resource management (IWRM) has been advocated widely as the most sustainable means to incorporate the multiple competing and conflicting uses of water resources. Governments are to develop and implement national strategies for sustainable development (NSSDs) by 2005. NSSDs should clearly include integrated plans, at the watershed level, for sustainable water resource use and management. Local participation, cross-border collaboration over shared water courses and linkage of strategies to land use management are also vital elements of IWRM. All of which require adequate provision for financial, technical and human support, along with political will (UNGASS, 1997). For several countries these strategies will need international support to develop effective management tools for more integrated approaches. One of the institutions involved in the Second World Water Forum was the Global Water Partnership (GWP). The Framework for Action Unit of the GWP aims to develop toolkits along with regional and national Technical Advisory Committees working towards achieving IWRM. Such activities should incorporate approaches from different sectors (environmental, technical, community, financial, legal, collation and dissemination of information, advocacy) that are relevant to the specific needs of different regions and localities.

THE WAY FORWARD

There are a number of positive regional examples of movement towards better WSS and water resource management (see Table 23.2). Regionally, Asia and Africa will need far greater international support to meet even basic levels of water provision and poverty elevation. Not only in terms of developing long-term management frameworks but also to implement strategies for reducing water stress.

Transitional countries in Europe and Central Asia will need support in the adoption and enforcement of EU water directives, particularly regarding pollution control and water demand management in urban areas. More generally in Europe there is a need to develop and strengthen green taxation of water pollution, reduce perverse subsidies and build enterprise capacity for environmental management systems.

Latin America and Caribbean need to further develop economic instruments to meet the funding gaps that exist to enable the implementation of national water legislation, regulatory institutions and monitoring systems, including legal instruments to overcome land

Table 23.2 *Examples of regional action*

Region	Actions
Asia & Pacific	• *International commitment:* Signature of CBD >75 per cent of countries; CCD and Basel >50 per cent; Ramsar <50 per cent. • *Shared water resources:* Mekong River Commission (Cambodia, Lao People's Democratic Republic, Thailand, Vietnam and China observing) coordinates the use and development of the lower watershed and an environmental support unit monitors the area. • *Participation:* Local people and NGOs more widely consulted in national environmental action plans, eg Thailand government, Indian government Environmental Monitoring System Network collects, analyses and disseminates environmental data, including freshwater resources.
Africa	• *International commitment:* Signature of CCD >75 per cent of countries; Ramsar >50 per cent; Basel <50 per cent. • *Economics:* 22 per cent of GEF goes to Africa, 38 per cent of this to water programmes. ODA is declining • *Shared resources:* Interagency land/water programmes are developing, eg South African Development Community (SADC) protocol for shared water course systems aims to ensure better equity and resource sharing between riparian states (to be ratified). African ministerial Conference on Environment (Cairo 1985) set up a committee for river and lake basins. • *Participation:* SADC's environmental education centre in Umgeni Valley (South Africa) undertakes education and training programmes for communities.
Europe & Central Asia	• *International commitment:* Signature of CBD, UNFCCC and Ramsar >75 per cent of countries; CCD > 50 per cent. • *Economics:* EU cohesion fund includes water sanitation, nature conservation and waste water treatment elements for countries of GDP less than 90 per cent average. • *Operations and maintenance:* Regulation of water pollution, eg EC Urban Waste Water Treatment Directive (91/271/EEC), Nitrates Directive (91/676/EEC). • *Shared resources:* eg Convention of the Rhine against Chemical pollution, Helsinki Convention on the Protection and use of Transboundary Watercourses and International Lakes. • *Participation:* Wider legislation and infrastructure have developed in many Eastern European countries, eg in Poland, Hungary, Czech Republic, Slovenia.

Latin America & Caribbean	• *International commitment:* Signature of CBD = 100 per cent of countries; CCD and Basel >75 per cent; Ramsar <75 per cent. • *Economics:* Mexico, Colombia, Uruguay and most Caribbean countries charge for effluent discharge and drinking to encourage better quality and quantity control. • *Shared resources:* Regional agreement on the Transboundary Movement of Hazardous Wastes (Panama, 1992), La Plata River Basin Treaty (Brasilia, 1978). • *Governance and participation:* Brazil has a National Law of Hydraulic Resources which includes watershed committees and agencies to ensure integrated water policies with public participation. Chile has a national system for releasing environmental information (1994).
North America	• *International commitment:* Signature of CBD, CCD, Basel and Ramsar by Canada; US has signed Ramsar. • *Ecosystem protection:* Canada has an Accelerated Reduction/Elimination of Toxics programme to reduce persistent, bio-accumulative and toxic substances by 90 per cent. • *Shared resource:* Canada–USA Agreement on Transboundary movement of Hazardous Waste (1986). • *Participation:* US Clean Water Action Plan (1998) supports the participation of local communities.

Note: Basel = Basel Convention on the Control of the Transboundary Movements of Hazardous Wastes and Their Disposal; CBD = Convention on Biological Diversity; CCD = Convention to Combat Desertification; Ramsar = Convention on Wetlands of International Importance especially as Waterfowl Habitat; UNFCCC = United Nations Framework Convention on Climate Change.
Source: UNEP, 1999

tenure issues at the community level. With better 'ring fencing' of such approaches, WSS and water management infrastructures can be further developed and education and information strategies developed.

In North America excessive water use from inefficient practices will require greater institutional accountability at all levels. The US has fairly extensive national laws but these may need to be better linked to other regulations, and it still has not signed international agreements on control of hazardous wastes and biodiversity. The challenges are considerable and each sector will have to face greater roles and responsibilities to meet those challenges (see Table 23.3).

At the Second World Water Forum, ministers agreed an international process with regards to target-setting for WSS and sustainable water practice. Governments will need to develop the financial, technical, human and legislatory drivers for meeting these targets. The progress of national programmes for the implementation of IWRM

Table 23.3 *Institutional roles and responsibilities*

Institution	Examples of key activities
Local authority	With a move to decentralized decision-making, authorities will take an increasingly important role as implementers of water strategies. This brings with it greater responsibility, not only to ensure adequate and equitable WSS provision and water resource allocation but also enabling community involvement to produce more integrated, accountable and realisable plans.
Private sector	The private sector has a direct role to play, in terms of contracted, private or public limited service provision and indirectly, as a major water user. Key responsibilities of the sector will be to maintain accountable and transparent practices (not only to regulators, shareholders and consumers but also to public as a whole), as well as incorporate sustainable principles of water management (eg implementation of environment management systems, strategies for social corporate responsibility).
NGO	The roles of NGOs cross local to international realms, acting as advocates, calling institutions to account but also in the development of solutions for more integrated water strategies. Their key responsibilities lie in relaying information to and from communities and relevant groups, ensuring that such groups are able to understand policy implications so that they are better equipped to actively participate at all levels of decision-making.
Government	At a national level, governments should regulate and facilitate the process of devolved WSS provision and water resource management. It will be their responsibility to provide the enabling environment for local implementation (legislative, financial, human and technical capacities), as well as to develop and implement frameworks and regulatory mechanisms in support of participatory and integrated processes across departments and regions. Internationally, governments need to take responsibility for linking water with wider priorities. This includes enacting transboundary watershed agreements and related environmental conventions, exchange of information and technology, as well as (human, financial, technical) support for those countries less able to adopt sustainable water strategies.
International institutions	Roles of the UN, Bretton Woods and other institutions range from technical/financial support, monitoring, conflict resolution, information dissemination and facilitation in formulating national IWRM and sustainability strategies. It is a crucial responsibility to pool together the activities of different institutions in a way

that lessons can be shared and improved upon, eg through the ACC Subcommittee on Water Resources, whose member organizations include DESA, ECA ECE, ECLAC, ESCAP, ESCWA, FAO, UNCHS (Habitat), IAEA, the Secretariats of UNCBD UNCCD, UNFCCC, and IDNDR, UNDP, UNEP, UNESCO, UNHCR,UNICEF, UNIDO, UNU,WHO,WMO and World Bank.

Sources: WWV, 2000; GWP, 2000; ECOSOC, 2000

practices will be presented at the International Water Conference in Bonn in December 2001 (Dublin +10). NSSDs should be completed by Earth Summit 2002. These should include strategies for how countries will improve water resource use and practice. The UN ACC Subcommittee on Water Resources is likely to play a key role in monitoring the progress of all these processes through the first World Water Development Report (to be produced for Bonn). Utilizing sustainability indicators for water, such as those defined at CSD-6, would assist monitoring the use of these drivers and progress towards meeting targets (see Table 23.4).

The two overarching objectives of sustainable development – poverty eradication and sustainable production and consumption – are clearly not being met in terms of freshwater priorities, especially in relation to WSS. Without identifying and implementing more joined-up strategies towards poverty reduction and WSS provision, an ever growing number of people from developing countries will be subject to increasing hardship and ecosystems subject to increasing water stress. For more developed countries, widespread adoption and support for mechanisms to reduce polluting production and overcon-sumption of water resources requires greater political will to develop incentives for better use.

Water is an element that is fundamental to so many aspects of life and of the natural environment. The fact that it cuts across so many areas relating to sustainable development poses considerable challenges. Institutions and individuals will need to look more collec-tively at these critical issues, through international, regional, national and local water strategies, so that when they come together at Earth Summit 2002, it is with a fuller understanding and a commitment to thinking ahead, ready to take the next steps towards the sustainable achievement of global water priorities.

Table 23.4 *Sustainability indicators for freshwater*

	Type	Example indicators
Economic	Expenditure	Public and private expenditure on water abstraction, treatment and distribution, health services, planning, management, regulation, review.
	Investment	Level of investment (from ODA, FDI, GEF, domestic public and private sources) in income generation programmes and water infrastructure development, especially directed towards marginalized communities.
	Institutional	Resources invested in cost recovery, enforcement and penalization for water regulation. Reinvestment of taxation into water sector.
Environment	Quality	Concentration of faecal coliform bacteria in freshwater, biochemical oxygen demand in water bodies. National implementation of multilateral environment agreements, eg CBD, Ramsar and Basel conventions.
	Consumption and efficiency	Level of water consumption by sector, domestic consumption of water per capita, foreign and domestic technology transfer. Groundwater reserves; annual withdrawals of ground and surface water
	Institutional	Transnational, national and sub-national river basin action plans
Social	WSS provision	% population with access to safe water, adequate sanitation, health services (including health education).
	Poverty	% population without access to WSS living below poverty line in rural/ urban areas.
	Institutional	Degree of local level water resource management, capacity-building/ education, participation in policy and legislation.

Sources: UNCED, 1992; World Bank, 1998; ECOSOC, 1998

References

Cosgrove, W J and Rijsberman, F R, for the World Water Council (2000) *World Water Vision: Making Water Everybody's Business*, London: Earthscan Publications Ltd

ECOSOC (1998) *Commission on Sustainable Development: Report on the Sixth Session*, E/CN.17/1998/20 – E/1998/29, ECOSOC Official Records, Supplement No 9, New York: United Nations

ECOSOC (2000) *Progress Made in Providing Safe Water Supply and Sanitation for All During the 1990s: Report of the Secretary-General*. Available at http://www.un.org/esa/sustdev/csd8/wss4rep.pdf

GWP (2000) *Towards Water Security: A Framework for Action*, Stockholm: Global Water Partnership

SWWF (2000) *Ministerial Declaration of the Hague on Water Security. Second World Water Forum, March 2000*. Available at http://www.world-waterforum.org/Conference/declaration.html

UNCED (1992) Agenda 21, Earth Summit 2002, Chapter 18. Available at http://www.un.org/esa/sustdev/agenda21chapter18.htm

UNEP (1999) *Global Environment Outlook 2000*, London: Earthscan Publications Ltd. Available at http://www.unep.org/geo2000/

UNGASS (1997) United Nations General Assembly 19th Special Session New York, 23–27 June 1997 Resolution A/RES/S-19/2 19 September 1997 S/19-2. Programme for the Further Implementation of Agenda 21 Freshwater 34

World Bank (1998) *World Development Indicators 1998*, Washington, DC: World Bank

WWC (2000) *A Vision of Water for Food and Rural Development*. Final Version, February 2000. Part of the Global Vision on Water, Life and the Environment in the 21st century. Marseille: World Water Council. Available at http://www.worldwatercouncil.org/vision/documents/water-forfoodvisiondraft2.pdf

WBGU (German Advisory Council on Global Change) (1999) *World in Transition. Ways Towards Sustainable Management of Freshwater Resources. Annual Report 1997*, Berlin: Springer Verlag

Related Conventions

Basel Convention on the Control of the Transboundary Movements of Hazardous Wastes and Their Disposal: http://www.unep.ch/basel/

Convention to Combat Desertification (CCD): http://www.unccd.de

Convention on Biological Diversity (CBD): http://www.biodiv.org

Convention on Wetlands of International Importance especially as Waterfowl Habitat (Ramsar Convention): http://www.ramsar.org

UN Framework Convention on Climate Change (UNFCCC): http://www.unfccc.de/

KEY ORGANIZATIONS

Global Water Partnership (GWP) Secretariat: c/o Sida, Stockholm, Sveavägen 24-26, 7th floor, S–105 25, Sweden. Tel/fax: +46 8 698 5000/5627; http://www.gwpforum.org

UN Administrative Committee on Coordination (ACC) Subcommittee on Water Resources: Mr Manuel Dengo, Secretary, ACC Subcommittee on Water Resources, DSD/DESA, United Nations Headquarters, Room DC1-864, New York, NY 10017, USA. Tel/fax: +1 (212) 963-4208/4340; email: dengo@un.org

UN Commission on Sustainable Development (CSD) Secretariat: UN Division for Sustainable Development (UNDSD) New York, NY 10017 ,USA. Tel: + 1 212 963 3170; email: aydin@un.org; http://www.un.org/esa/sustdev/water

Water Supply and Sanitation Collaborative Council (WSSCC): c/o World Health Organization, 1211 Geneva 27, Switzerland. Tel/fax:+ 41 22 791 3544/4847; http://www.wsscc.org

World Water Council (WWC) Secretariat: 10, place de la Joliette, Atrium 10.3 13304, Marseille, Cedex 2, France. Tel/fax: +33 4 91994100/101; http://www.worldwatercouncil.org

24

Energy: Fuel for Sustainable Development

Jürgen Maier

When sustainability is discussed among all the relevant groups and players, it is relatively easy for an agreement to be reached on the principles. However, there is often much resistance when it comes to moving from talk to action. Many political conflicts, from fuel price protests or the BSE ('mad cow disease') crisis in Europe to popular resistance against huge dams or pipeline projects in developing countries, are in fact conflicts about sustainable development – with huge vested interests trying to prevent moves towards sustainability while paying lip service to it. A major part of such conflicts about implementing sustainability is in fact related to energy. Energy is not only the fuel for economic development, its unsustainable use is also the main cause for many of the environmental problems associated with traditional economic development: from air pollution and global warming to oil spill disasters and nuclear waste. Within the last 200 years, the large-scale combustion of fossil fuels has already caused the highest atmospheric CO_2 level in 160,000 years and the highest global average temperatures since measurements began. Conflicts about unsustainable energy policies gave birth to a major part of the environmental movements, and the question whether we will continue to use energy unsustainably will probably decide the future of the Kyoto Protocol and thus perhaps the entire Rio process.

It is therefore no surprise that energy was such a hot topic at the Earth Summit in Rio that governments preferred to avoid it almost entirely. There is no energy chapter in Agenda 21, and apart from the International Atomic Energy Agency (IAEA), a relic from a distant past, there is no UN organization or convention that deals with energy in a comprehensive way. There have been various UN reports about energy, the latest being the interagency report *World Energy Assessment*, but these were produced by UN staff without much involvement of the governments of the member states. The first time that a UN commission dealt with energy policy was CSD-9 in 2001. However, this meeting was deeply stuck in entrenched antagonisms between industrialized and developing countries and among countries within these groups alike. Of paramount importance to the energy issue for sustainable development is the absence of an institution in the UN dealing with energy in a comprehensive way. The stalemate that exists within the international discussions on energy clearly underline the need for Heads of Government to address this issue at Earth Summit 2002 and cut through the Gordian knot in energy policy that holds so many international negotiations hostage.

THE CURRENT ENERGY SYSTEM IS UNSUSTAINABLE EVEN IN THE SHORT TERM

Industrial nations, that is, OECD member countries, in 1995 consumed about 54 per cent of the world's primary energy. Fossil fuels amounted to roughly 75 per cent of the world's energy consumption, while the average for industrialized nations is about 90 per cent. Oil and coal continue to be the backbone of many economies.

The current oil consumption is 67 million barrels globally, every day. About 900 billion barrels of oil have already been used up; about the same amount still remains in the earth. The remaining stock of fossil fuels – oil, coal, natural gas – is the equivalent of a mere 11 days of sunshine. Even assuming that industrialized nations stabilize their demand for oil, meeting the demands of the developing world (if they simply 'develop' the way industrial nations so far have been 'developing') would require a tripling of global oil output. China in 1994 became a net oil importer – the significance of this fact so far has been more or less completely ignored. Production capacity, however, can hardly be expanded any more, and most serious projections predict that the world will reach the peak of oil production within this decade. With ever growing demand, the era of inexpensive oil is definitely gone forever, and at the same the power of the oil cartel the Organization of the Petroleum Exporting Countries (OPEC) is going to rise again because non-OPEC oil is being depleted at a much faster rate than OPEC oil.

The International Energy Agency (IEA) has calculated that in a business-as-usual scenario, we will see 65 per cent growth of global energy demand, increasing global CO_2 emissions by 70 per cent –

unless new policies are put into place. Two thirds of this growth will happen in developing countries, and 95 per cent of this increased demand will come from fossil fuels.

At the same time, the modern energy system bypasses about 2 billion people who have no access to either 'modern' fuels or electricity, and another 2 billion cannot afford such energy amenities as refrigeration or hot water. The richest 20 per cent of humanity consumes 58 per cent of the energy, while the poorest fifth ends up with less than 4 per cent. People in rich countries have become accustomed to the idea that access to abundant, inexpensive energy is some kind of constitutional right. But the facts are crystal clear: continuing present policies, business as usual, simply is not an option. The task is nothing less than a complete reinvention of the energy system.

THE ENERGY SECTOR: RIGGED IN FAVOUR OF UNSUSTAINABLE DEVELOPMENT

The energy sector in many nations continues to be one of the most distorted markets, with deeply entrenched market interventions in place which no antitrust or cartel authority would tolerate in any other sector. Governments are deeply involved in the energy sectors, frequently as owners or majority shareholders of energy companies, as guarantors of monopoly positions of certain companies or as providers of massive subsidies, research-and-development money, etc. The energy sector is characterized by large, centralized companies that have traditionally been following the logic of Lenin rather than Adam Smith. Competition is often effectively shut out by state-guaranteed monopolies or de facto oligopolies. While in markets there is every incentive to minimize fixed investment costs, for the energy sector monopolies the opposite has been true as high investment costs were passed on to the consumer and rewarded by a certain percentage of profits on investment. As in medieval societies, control over resources gives such companies vast economic and political power, and government-owned utilities often display every feature of utility-controlled energy policies.

The Worldwatch Institute has estimated that by 1992, when the climate convention was adopted in Rio, global subsidies for fossil fuels amounted to nothing less than US$200 billion. More recent estimates put that figure at US$240 billion – money that keeps outdated and uncompetitive production in existence, that artificially rigs markets against renewable energies and that prevents consumers from even knowing the true price of energy and thus wasting it needlessly. The bulk of these subsidies undermines sustainable development in almost every aspect. Only about US$10 billion goes to renewable energies or energy conservation. About 80 per cent goes to fossil fuels.

The most uncompetitive white elephant in energy markets, nuclear energy, currently receives about US\$16 billion annually in subsidies and was pushed into existence and kept operating with almost Soviet-style disregard for basic principles of market economies – a fact that only became obvious when nuclear power turned out to be the first casualty of liberalized markets in many countries. In industrial nations, production subsidies that keep production costs artificially low (mostly as tax subsidies or as the provision of infrastructure and complimentary services whose costs are not fully recovered from the users, but also as direct subsidies) are the predominant form of energy subsidies. In developing nations, consumer subsidies are commonplace – subsidies that keep the price of certain forms of energy below world market prices, and which therefore support domestic consumption and often drain foreign exchange reserves. The benefits from such subsidized cheap energy are rarely enjoyed by the poor but mostly by the middle and upper classes who consume far more of the subsidized energy such as electricity or petrol.

While the OECD countries are certainly rich enough to afford such subsidies, they still account for only roughly US\$90 billion or about 40 per cent of global energy subsidies, about half of it going into sectoral support for ailing coal mines. Non-OECD countries spend their subsidies predominantly on consumer subsidies for gas and oil. However, the poor often pay for inefficient, 'dirty' energy such as from kerosene, candle wax and batteries. Indeed, they often pay a far greater percentage of their income for energy, and even in absolute terms more per kilowatt for electricity than do middle-class, urban households or wealthy farmers who benefit from heavily subsidized grid electricity or car owners from subsidized petrol. To help the poor, the best solutions are targeted subsidies for the very poorest that are not linked to energy consumption.

There is ample literature on the economic impact of subsidies, yet it is difficult finding even one study which can seriously show that subsidies in any sector are benefiting an economy as a whole. Eliminating both producer and consumer subsidies would allow markets to give the right price signals for energy use, thus providing better and more efficient resource allocation, while at the same time lifting a sometimes quite heavy burden from taxpayers and government budgets. The major losers of such a comprehensive global elimination of energy subsidies would be all those who earn money from selling energy in distorted markets; apart from fossil-fuel companies this also includes countries exporting oil and coal. OECD studies figure the loss of the real income for such countries at 5 per cent annually. Developing countries dependent on energy imports, on the other hand, would benefit handsomely, as experience with energy subsidy reform in Indonesia, Ghana, Colombia, Turkey and Zimbabwe shows. A very good example is China, where the gradual transformation from a socialist command-and-control economy to a market economy was accompanied by phasing out many price controls (ie subsidies) typical for socialist countries. Subsidies to coal have been reduced to less than a third of its original level, and the result was a fall in energy intensity by about 30 per cent since the mid-1980s.

World Bank and OECD calculations show that global energy subsidy removal could reduce CO_2 emissions by about 10 per cent worldwide and, combined with a reform of the tax system in line with ecological criteria, 15 per cent in the OECD. Clearly, countries with very low energy efficiency such as the US, Canada or Australia would stand to gain most of these emissions reductions. The *OECD Environmental Outlook 2001* found that the removal of harmful subsidies and an energy tax linked to the carbon content of fuels alone would reduce the OECD's total CO_2 emissions by 15 per cent by 2020 – with almost no difference to the GDP compared to the business-as-usual scenario.

Despite all the differences, rigged energy markets are a common and uniting feature of industrialized and developing countries alike. However, access to affordable energy is an issue of far greater importance to people in poor nations than to saturated auto drivers in rich countries. The rising petroleum prices on the world market are a much greater burden to the vast majority of developing countries than for the OECD nations. Unlike fossil fuels, which are concentrated in a rather small number of countries, renewable energies are domestic sources of energy everywhere.

POWER TO THE PEOPLE: THE FUTURE IS DECENTRALIZED

A sustainable future for the energy sector will inevitably lead to decentralized markets, where government interventions are generally limited to a few subsidies for emerging technologies for a specific timeframe, and where the market distortions of today caused by political interventions will have to be phased out rapidly. Independent power producers (IPPs) have turned into serious competitors where markets have been liberalized and historic monopolies abolished. In many developing countries established state-owned utilities were so obviously unable to meet the demands of the population that now IPPs are growing rapidly, particularly in Latin America and Asia.

Fossil fuels have displayed an almost natural tendency to centralization of the technical infrastructure and the political power. They do not occur everywhere, so those who sit on the resources or the import channels control the energy flow. In stark contrast, renewable energies occur naturally everywhere and are difficult to centralize, and thus their commercial use is often opposed vigorously by the established power companies. This is particularly important for developing countries: most of them are far better endowed with renewable energy sources than with fossil fuels.

Some scientists have argued that the seriousness of climate change requires a huge concerted international effort comparable to the Apollo programme to introduce new technologies on a large scale. The experience with government-designed programmes in energy (and many other sectors) shows that the opposite is far more likely to be true. If governments get out of the business of rigging energy markets in the wrong direction, and make sure every form of energy is charged as much as possible with its external costs according to the polluter-pays principle, new and old energy companies and billions of consumers would do their best to quickly make a sustainable energy future a reality. So far, I know of no example where the logic of central planning has been superior to the logic of creating the right framework for millions of people competing for the best way to do the job.

Gas-fired turbines and increasingly fuel cells of any size herald the age of decentralized power production, usually co-producing heat and electricity. They will increasingly replace ageing giant power plants, and the whole notion of an electricity company may turn into more of a power broker than a power producer. The market for small-scale generation in poor countries could be huge, because the demand for reliable power is intense. Political risk as well as economic necessity also favour small-scale generation. Big, in other words, is vulnerable. The big-is-better philosophy will be increasingly at odds with the economic realities. An increasing and significant proportion of new power will come from small generators: as much capacity will be built in the next 25 years as in the whole of the 20th century.

FINANCING FOR UNSUSTAINABLE DEVELOPMENT

Government intervention is again largely responsible for delaying this transformation. Development aid is still all too often aiding and abetting old patterns of development that have clearly been shown to be unsustainable in (mis)'developed' nations. There are vast numbers of conflicts about development money helping uneconomical fossil fuel extraction projects to become profitable, from the Chad–Cameroon pipeline to Colombian oil wells in the Amazon jungle. The World Bank and other international financial institutions continue to pour billions into completely destructive fossil fuel projects, prompted by corrupt host nation governments standing to gain considerable personal wealth as well as by multinational companies in the North. At the Earth Summit, World Bank officials vowed to take the lead in investing for a 'green' future. Since 1992, however, the bank has promoted US$13.9 billion worth of fossil fuel projects. Over the next 20 to 50 years, *The Ecologist* estimates, these projects will produce some 37.5 billion tons of CO_2 – 1.3 times the approximate CO_2 emissions of the entire industrial world in 1995. 'We must ensure that the policies and operations of the World Bank and other IFIs [international finance institutions] take full account of climate change.' This statement was issued by the G-8 Environment Ministers and endorsed by the G-8 leaders in their final communiqué after the G-8 Summit held in Birmingham on 17 May 1998. Not much has changed since then.

The World Bank Group devotes a significant share of its portfolio to extractive sectors. Oil, gas, and mining embody an unsustainable model of economic development that has failed the world's poor in the 20th century. There is no reason for any institution using public money to finance these sectors in the 21st century. Such projects need not be prohibited. Rather, what should be prohibited is the public funding (= subsidization) of such projects; those wishing to carry out such projects can go to commercial banks and should have no direct or indirect export credit guarantees from governments. It is safe to say that a large share of these projects will immediately be cancelled under such conditions that are nothing less than (theoretically) normal market conditions.

A shift is necessary, away from the grandiose energy-related projects supported by aid donors that are all too often unsustainable both in ecological as well as economic terms, and now can only be pushed through in conditions without democracy and without functioning markets. In the past, central planners not only in the former Soviet Union but worldwide have lavished vast sums on large dams and nuclear or coal-fired power plants. Such projects, usually completed late and at greatly increased expense than projected, had a much greater social impact than expected and turned out to be far less efficient than promised.

Many countries would be better off without such projects. Indeed, for many oil-producing countries the 'black stuff' is more of a curse than a blessing. More often than not, oil is greasing corruption and fuelling wars. Without oil, places like Iraq, Nigeria, Angola or Indonesia would be better off, with much less corruption, war and foreign debt. Renewable energies, on the other hand, (with the exception of large hydro) occur in such a decentralized way that it is difficult to imagine a war over control of thousands of windmills or the income generated by homeowners with solar panels injecting a strong dose of corruption into an economy. It is unsurprising that many vested interests, not only in developed but also in developing countries, are so opposed to any concrete steps towards sustainable development.

ENERGY IN THE UN

In spite of the UN's tedious repetition of mantras heard so many times, the energy discussion at CSD-9 still managed to display something that was rather revealing: when it came to energy subsidies, the need for a radical liberation of the energy sector from politically motivated market distortions became fully obvious – but likewise so did the political resistance to openly discuss the issue. Among the represented major groups, NGOs, scientists, even trade unions denounced distorting subsidies for fossil fuels, yet businesses (supposed to be for free markets, right?) did their best to ignore the issue or come up with such ridiculous demands as to link subsidy removal with energy tax removal. Most governments simply preferred to remain silent on the issue.

Simultaneously, UNEP and the IEA held a side event at which they presented the results of regional workshops on energy subsidies. Government officials who participated in them unanimously reported that energy subsidies in their countries cause large fiscal drains, lead to overconsumption and inefficient energy use, do not benefit those that need them most but rather the rich and middle classes and that sometimes the subsidized fuel only became available for the poor when the subsidy was removed (because it then became unattractive for alternative, unintended commercial use). An Indonesian government official reported that his country spends literally 25 per cent of its routine expenditure on fuel subsidies, and if that money went instead to the poor there would be no poor people in Indonesia any more. Unfortunately, people like him had no influence or even interaction with their diplomats at the CSD, and so it was impossible to get any meaningful language on energy subsidies in the CSD decision which was meant to be the first comprehensive UN text on energy.

The CSD, however, is only a sideshow. Other fora where binding decisions are adopted also suffer from similar paralysis when it comes to energy. The unwillingness to take any concrete steps away from the deeply entrenched unsustainable energy policies of the last century is responsible for the stalemate in the negotiations over the Kyoto Protocol. When 154 nations signed the UN Framework Convention on Climate Change (UNFCCC), which entered into force in March 1994, they accepted the obligation, for instance, to adopt national programmes containing measures to stabilize greenhouse gas emissions at a level preventing dangerous human intervention with the climate system, and promote public awareness programmes on climate change.

Yet no government took the obligation seriously (and maybe for that reason the UNFCCC sailed more or less unchallenged even through the US Senate). The consequence of no-action was that in 1997, when the Kyoto Protocol to the Convention was supposed to move towards concrete action, emissions in many countries had already gone up considerably compared to 1990, and so governments became quite unambitious. Years of no-action followed, and it becomes increasingly difficult to reach the Kyoto targets. The discussion of 'policies and measures' in the early years of the climate negotiations, the key to action and a cornerstone of the whole endeavour, has now become something like a dirty word that is best not mentioned, or even negotiated, and yet without policies and measures, emissions inevitably will go up. All the sophisticated talk about emissions trading that has replaced policies and measures is thus basically in vain, as there will be no emission right on the market because everybody will need them for themselves and nobody will sell.

Likewise, with all the trade disputes in WTO dispute settlement bodies, there so far seems to be a kind of silent agreement that trade distortion by energy subsidies is not to be challenged in the WTO. Why does no coal exporter challenge the massive coal subsidies of Germany or Spain that have the declared intention to deny South African or Australian coal market shares? Why does no oil exporter challenge the US's massive subsidies to oil drilling that have the declared aim of denying foreign oil market shares? Compared to the money involved here, trade disputes about bananas or hormone-treated beef are indeed negligible.

WHAT COULD HAPPEN IN JOHANNESBURG

Earth Summit 2002 in Johannesburg will not have much chance of success if it pits industrial nations with an eco-agenda versus developing nations with a development agenda. We have to link the two, not with sophisticated semantic gymnastics, but with concrete proposals. Phasing out energy subsidies is probably the biggest win-win option currently imaginable. Industrial countries stand to win a lot from it, and a substantial percentage of the saved government expenditure should be invested in technology transfer for renewable energies and energy efficiency. Coupled with massive shifts in the energy portfolios of multilateral funding institutions such as the World Bank, this could give many developing countries substantial boosts for leapfrogging into a sustainable energy future, reducing foreign exchange needs for importing oil, producing energy from decentralized domestic sources, allowing the establishment of domestic production of windmills and similar equipment, and injecting new economic life into rural areas. Such programmes, however, should in any case be linked to reducing fossil energy subsidies in the developing country concerned, not only because market distortions against renewables and energy efficiency are serious roadblocks for the success of such programmes, but also to create ownership by insisting on financial participation by funds generated from such subsidy removal.

Removing energy subsidies could be done jointly by countries in the North and South, or independently by groups of like-minded countries. Any country would benefit, regardless of whether or not other nations follow suit. In OECD countries, tax reforms are particularly urgent to remove the various tax breaks that encourage fossil energy production. Price protection policies should be eliminated – they do not exist in almost any other sector – and further liberalization of the energy sector pursued jointly with progressive cost internalization of external costs which so far have been covered by the general taxpayer. Governments in developing countries and economies in transition should gradually phase out consumer subsidies, but at the same time use part of the revenues to finance targeted direct support programmes for the poor, regardless of whether they consume fossil fuels or not. It would be a vast job for international aid donors to co-finance such schemes which would be extremely important in allowing developing countries to avoid the fossil-fuel addiction that characterizes today's industrial countries. Any serious energy subsidy reform in developing countries should also be supported by donors through enhanced technology transfer in renewables and energy efficiency. Countries participating in such a partnership stand to win a great deal and will lose almost nothing.

There could be a resolution to apply the WTO's Subsidy Agreement rigorously against any fossil fuel subsidy. In fact, political agreement to phase out fossil energy subsidies would be a shining example where environmental measures actually improve free trade rather than impede it. There could be other forms, such as a global register of energy subsidies.

I am not suggesting that governments subsidize us into the renewable age. Even if the money were available, this would be a poor solution. If water is being lost through a hole in a bucket, it is better to plug the hole rather than constantly refill the bucket. Similarly, it would make most sense to phase out all the direct and indirect subsidies to fossil and nuclear energies. It seems likely that governments have one key task with regard to the transition to a sustainable energy future. They should stop delaying it by funding unsustainable energy, and get the prices right by comprehensive application of the polluter-pays principle. The money saved by such subsidy removals could easily dwarf the most radical tax cut proposals currently discussed.

A coalition of like-minded countries in the North and South could announce in Johannesburg that they clearly commit themselves to such steps. The fossil lobby of OPEC and the US and a number of other countries will most likely prevent any meaningful agreement of all nations at the summit. It is therefore essential for more countries to refuse to be stopped by a minority that is stuck too deep in its fossil-fuel addiction. They will quickly become attractive models for other nations. Energy is too important for sustainable development to let the discussion stop at the current miserable state of affairs, and where it inevitably will be when we seek consensus among all nations.

REFERENCES

André de Moor (2001) 'Towards a Grand Deal on Subsidies and Climate Change', *Natural Resources Forum: A United Nations Journal*, vol 25, no 2

Brown, L and Flavin, C (1999) *State of the World 1999: A Worldwatch Institute Report on Progress Toward a Sustainable Society*, London: Earthscan Publications

IEA (1998) *World Energy Outlook 1998*, Paris: International Energy Agency

OECD (2001) *OECD Environmental Outlook 2001*, Washington, DC: OECD Washington Center

UNDP, DESA and World Energy Council (2000) *World Energy Assessment*, New York: United Nations Development Programme. Available at http://www.undp.org/seed/eap/activities/wea

Part V

Overview

25

Reforming the International Institutions

Felix Dodds

INTRODUCTION

*'To practise tolerance and live together in peace with
one another as good neighbours.'*
Charter of the United Nations[1]

One of the key challenges that will be facing us as we prepare for Earth
Summit 2002 is: will governments seriously address what kind of international machinery we need to guide us through the first decades of
the 21st century?

This chapter will try to review where we have come from, where
we are, and offer some ideas of where we might go. It will not try to
identify one idea but give a series of approaches that should all be
considered for 2002.

WHERE HAVE WE COME FROM?

The UN was originally set up when 50 countries met in San Francisco
in June 1945. By October 1999 the UN membership had expanded to
185 countries.

UN reform, it must be said, is hardly thought to be the most interesting subject, but the design of any system can have an enormous
impact on the ability of the system to deliver. Not only are there many
more countries than there were in 1945, but there is a considerable

amount of intergovernmental fora. There are now more than 1000 international institutions that have been set up and the need for some form of streamlining is well overdue. If you add to this the growth and influence of the 'non-governmental sector', here meaning all stakeholder groups, then it can easily be seen how much more complicated the intergovernmental process has become in the past 55 years.

The 1990s saw a proliferation of UN summits and conferences, starting with the Rio Summit in 1992. After taking an overview at Rio the following summits dealt with aspects of Agenda 21 in more depth:

- 1994 UN Conference on Population and Development (Cairo);
- 1994 Conference on Small Island Developing States (Barbados);
- 1995 World Summit on Social Development (Copenhagen);
- 1995 Fourth Conference on Women and Development (Beijing);
- 1996 Habitat II – Conference on Human Settlements (Istanbul);
- 1996 Food Summit (Vienna);
- 1997 UN General Assembly to Review Implementation of Agenda 21;
- 1999 UN General Assembly Review of Cairo;
- 1999 UN General Assembly Review of Barbados Plan of Action.

Most of the conferences had a five-year review built in and the relevant UN commission looked at the implementation on a year-by-year basis.

The Rio Earth Summit set the scope for the active involvement of NGOs in the UN conferences and summits. This will be dealt with later in the chapter. Here, I would just mention the importance of chapters 24 and 32 of Agenda 21 which deal with 'major groups' – this includes youth, women, farmers, NGOs, local government, business, academics, indigenous people and trade unions.

With so much going on, the ability of the UN, governments and NGOs to be able to implement, monitor or, more importantly, create 'joined-up thinking' between the processes has been greatly challenged. Sometimes there just seems to be too much noise and it is difficult to know which meeting or set of meetings it is best to focus on. People are used to working in their particular area, and now we are asking them to, as Gary Lawrence – previously an adviser to the US President's Council on Sustainable Development – says, 'embrace complexity': not an easy thing to do.

WHERE ARE WE?

The world has changed enormously since the 1992 summit. We have seen globalization come to the forefront, and we have experienced the outcome of the changes in eastern Europe, as well as the increased role of multinational companies, to mention but a few changes. For us to address these, Earth Summit 2002 needs not only to rekindle the fire of the Rio accord but to address the very serious challenges we are now facing and to create the international machinery that will do this appropriately.

The UN was set up to recognize the supremacy of the nation state; it now needs to factor in the impact of globalization on the system. In the last ten years there has been an increased role for other players, such as multinational corporations, NGOs, women, local government, trade unions and other stakeholders. At the same time, there has been a move towards some lower levels of government – closer to the people where many of these groups have direct experience of the impacts of globalization.

Integrating environment and development within the UN and governmental processes has not been easy in the eight years since Rio. Joined-up thinking in the UN, in governments and in the stakeholder groups has caused a lot of problems.

Three of the key institutions that have been working on implementing, monitoring and developing Agenda 21 have been the UNEP, the CSD and the Inter-Agency Committee on Sustainable Development (IACSD).

UNITED NATIONS ENVIRONMENT PROGRAMME (UNEP)

Since the first UN Environment Conference in 1972 we have seen the creation of the UN Environment Programme – a direct result of the Stockholm Conference. It was set up in 1973 in order to 'provide leadership and encourage partnerships in caring for the environment by inspiring, informing and enabling nations and people to improve their quality of life without compromising that of future generations'.

UNEP's MISSION STATEMENT

UNEP has had a mixed history. The annual budget of the organization is around US$60 million, which makes some NGOs appear bigger in financial and staff terms. UNEP is not a delivery agency; rather, it is an institution that has created much of the international law that we now use. This includes the Vienna Convention on Ozone Depletion, the Basel Convention on the Control of Transboundary Movements of Hazardous Wastes and their Disposal, CITES and the Convention on Migratory Species (CMS).

UNEP provides the secretariat for these conventions. In addition, UNEP has rendered considerable support to negotiating, adopting and implementing the Convention to Combat Desertification and the UN Framework Convention on Climate Change. UNEP and the FAO are now in the process of catalysing negotiations for the elaboration of a Convention on the Information Exchange on International Trade in the Field of Toxic Chemicals.

The conventions set up since 1972 now cover a wide range of topics, but all have separate staff and are housed around the world, from Montreal to Bonn and Nairobi – making coordination difficult to say the least.

THE UN COMMISSION ON SUSTAINABLE DEVELOPMENT (CSD)

As the Earth Summit dealt with issues of environment and development it was obvious who should have responsibility for ensuring that Agenda 21 was monitored and implemented. Agenda 21 set out a whole set of changes to the institutional agenda in an attempt to ensure that the work agreed at Rio would be monitored and implemented. Chapter 38 identifies the setting up of the CSD; it states:

> *'In order to ensure the effective follow-up of the conference, as well as to enhance international cooperation and rationalization, the intergovernmental decision-making capacity for the integration of environment and development issues and to examine the progress of the implementation of Agenda 21 at the national, regional and international levels, a high-level Commission on Sustainable Development should be established in accordance with Article 68 of the Charter of the UN.'*[2]

The UN General Assembly met in the autumn of 1992 to debate the setting up of the commission. It resolved the following:

- The UN Economic and Social Council (EcoSoc) has been requested to establish a high-level commission as a functional council body.
- Representatives of 53 states have been elected by the council for up to three-year terms.
- The commission will meet once a year for two or three weeks. It is a functional EcoSoc commission with a full-time secretariat based in New York. Care has been taken to ensure that the secretariat has a clear identity within the UN system.
- Relevant intergovernmental organizations and specialized agencies, including financial institutions, are invited to designate representatives to advise and assist the commission, and also to

serve as focal points for the members and secretariat of the commission between sessions.

In creating the mandate for the commission, governments recognized the important role that major groups would have in the realization of Agenda 21. There is no question that the CSD gives the major groups the greatest involvement in the work of any UN commission. The CSD's mandate is to:

- Monitor progress on the implementation of Agenda 21 and activities related to the integration of environmental and developmental goals by governments, NGOs and other UN bodies. This includes monitoring progress towards the target of 0.7 per cent GNP from developed countries for overseas development assistance (ODA).
- Review the adequacy of financing and the transfer of technologies as outlined in Agenda 21.
- Receive and analyse relevant information from competent NGOs in the context of Agenda 21 implementation.
- Enhance dialogue with NGOs, the independent sector and other entities outside the UN system, within the UN framework.
- Provide recommendations to the UN EcoSoc.

During the first seven years of its existence it has been seen as a pioneer in many areas. It is important to note that there are very good reasons for this:

- It is the most recently set up UN commission and therefore the structures it developed encompassed the approach taken for Rio.
- The CSD is a 'political' forum. Each year it gets between 40 and 60 ministers of environment, development, finance, tourism, and forests to attend out of a membership of 53 countries. The chair of the CSD is usually a minister or former minister.
- It has the active involvement of 200–600 representatives of major groups.
- It has the active, positive involvement of industry.

Some of the key successes of the CSD are a result of the fact that it:

- recommended there should be a legally binding status of the prior informed consent procedure (1994);
- called for greater cooperation of the CSD with the governing bodies of the Bretton Woods institutes and the WTO (1994); introduced national reporting to the CSD; and started an integrated indicators programme (1994);

- established an Intergovernmental Panel on Forests (1995) and an International Forum on Forests (1997);
- set up a work programme on sustainable consumption and production (1995);
- supported the Washington Global Plan of Action on protecting the marine environment from land-based activities (1996);
- agreed the replenishment of the GEF (1997);
- agreed the new work programme for the CSD (1997);
- informally highlighted to governments the problems of the Multilateral Agreement on Investment (1997);
- prepared governments for the negotiations on climate change (1997);
- set a firm date of 2002 for governments to produce their national sustainable development strategies (1997);
- instituted the multistakeholder dialogue sessions (1998);
- set up a multistakeholder group under the Department for Economic and Social Affairs (DESA) to look at voluntary agreements in industry (1998);
- set up a new process in the UN General Assembly to discuss oceans (1999);
- agreed new consumer guidelines to include sustainable development (1999);
- discussed tourism for the first time, bringing the issue within the Rio process (1999);
- developed an International Work Programme on Sustainable Tourism (1999).

These are some of the successes that the CSD has managed to achieve since its first substantive meeting in 1994. One of the key lessons has been that in order to achieve change time is needed. In addition to the two-week CSD and the two-week preparatory meeting, there have been hundreds of government- and major group-hosted intersessional meetings over the past seven years. These meetings have been crucial to developing the successes of the CSD.

THE INTER-AGENCY COMMITTEE ON SUSTAINABLE DEVELOPMENT (IACSD)

The setting up of the IACSD was a direct result of Rio. In Agenda 21, it is stated:

> 'To ensure effective monitoring, coordination and super-
> vision of the involvement of the United Nations system
> in the follow up to the conference, there is a need for a

coordination mechanism under the direct leadership of the Secretary-General. This task should be given to the Administrative Committee on Coordination (ACC) headed by the Secretary-General.[3]

The IACSD is a subsidiary body of the UN Administrative Committee on Coordination (ACC), which in turn acts as the 'cabinet' for the Secretary-General. The IACSD is chaired by Undersecretary-General Nitin Desai and is made up of senior-level officials from nine core members of the ACC: the FAO; International Atomic Energy Agency (IAEA); International Labour Organization (ILO); UNDP; UNEP; UNESCO; WHO; the World Bank; and World Meteorological Organization (WMO). Officials from other UN bodies, intergovernmental agencies and representatives from major groups are able to attend by invitation. The IACSD was set up in the aftermath of Rio and was asked by the ACC to focus on four areas:

1　Streamline the existing interagency coordination machinery.
2　Allocate and share responsibilities for Agenda 21 implementation by the UN system.
3　Monitor the new financial requirements of UN system organizations that relate to Agenda 21.
4　Assess reporting requirements that are related to the implementation of Agenda 21 and make recommendations on streamlining.

The IACSD has two sub-committees which report through it: the ACC Sub-Committee on Oceans and Coastal Areas and the ACC Sub-Committee on Water Resources.

Commenting in 1998, Joke Waller Hunter, director of the division on sustainable development, said:

'In many ways, the interagency coordination system, working with the task manager, has not created a threat to those agencies (such as UNEP) at all. By not sending someone from the outside to investigate their agency, but instead inviting them to report to the CSD themselves, we have not questioned or challenged agency policies nor mandates of agencies.'[4]

The IACSD set up a task manager system for every chapter of Agenda 21. This ensured that there was transparency in who was coordinating the follow-up process. As Joke Waller Hunter indicates, the involvement of UN agencies as task managers of the different chapters that their work covered ensured a more cooperative approach to reviewing the work of their agency. The CSD does offer one of the few places

where there is a chance to review the work of different agencies out of
their own governing bodies.

In 1997, the UN General Assembly Special Session to review
Agenda 21 recognized that the IACSD had done a good job, and it was
agreed to:

> '...strengthen the ACC-IACSD and its system of task
> managers, with a view to further enhancing system-
> wide intersectoral cooperation and coordination for the
> implementation of Agenda 21 and for the follow-up to
> the major United Nations conferences in the area of
> sustainable development.'[5]

The IACSD has proved a good model of how to integrate the work of
different UN agencies in the follow-up to a UN conference. Although
there has been success, there has also been opposition where some
UN bodies take a less than positive attitude towards the CSD, making
suggestions about the work they should be engaged in or producing
work programmes for them. Sometimes their attitude has been hostile;
to quote one UNESCO official: 'We have our own governing bodies.'
Although this is true, the nature of Rio in particular was to ensure that
we had a more integrated approach to sustainable development. It
does raise the serious question: if the UN General Assembly (GA)
endorses the CSD decision, which it does each year, should a UN
agency be able to just disregard a decision of the GA?

OTHER UN CONFERENCES

This chapter does not discuss this in detail; however, needless to say,
the UN conferences from 1994 to 1996 filled in gaps and emphasized
parts of Agenda 21, in this way developing particular areas. Although
population was dealt with by Chapter 5 of Agenda 21 ('Demographic
Dynamics and Sustainability'), the Cairo Conference on Population
and Development was able to set out more clearly how we might
approach the stabilization of population. The Copenhagen World
Summit on Social Development did the same, particularly for poverty
(Chapter 3 of Agenda 21), and the Beijing Fourth World Conference
on Women: Action for Equity, Development and Peace did the same
for nearly all chapters of Agenda 21. The habitat conference developed
the human settlements area (Agenda 21, Chapter 7). These conferences also dealt with subjects not discussed in Agenda 21.

The implementation of these conferences was then reviewed by
the relevant UN commissions on a five-year cycle. The time has come
to draw these threads back together and to decide how to integrate

them with each other.
   Where are we going?

ARCHITECTURE FOR THE FUTURE

One of the discussions before the Rio Summit in 1992 concerned the institutional architecture that would oversee the implementation of Agenda 21. Three of the main ideas were:

1 utilizing the Trusteeship Council;
2 creating a Committee on Sustainable Development under the General Assembly;
3 creating a Functional Commission on Sustainable Development under EcoSoc.

As we start the discussion for 2002, perhaps we now need to look at a broader reform agenda.

UN CHARTER CHANGE TO PROMOTE SUSTAINABLE DEVELOPMENT

Perhaps one of the easiest ideas would be to change the Charter of the United Nations so that the body as a whole is able to promote sustainable development throughout its work. Like any constitution, the ability to amend one is taken very seriously and the idea of amending the charter may become an outcome of the UN Millennium Assembly. It has gained support from many stakeholder groups and some governments. If not, the summit in 2002 should address this as an important issue.

UTILIZING THE SECURITY COUNCIL

Under the charter, the functions and powers of the UN Security Council allow it 'to maintain international peace and security in accordance with the principles and purpose of the United Nations'.[6]
   The World Resources Institute (WRI) argued that this allows for issues of environmental security to be brought to the UN Security Council. WRI went further by suggesting that under Articles 22 and 29 of the UN charter a standing committee on environment and development should be created; as one of its tasks it would raise issues of environment and development that undermine international peace and security. It is only relatively recently that the issue of environmental security has moved further up the political agenda. UNEP's Global

Environment Outlook 2000 report (GEO-2000) registered, for the first time, that there are more environmental refugees than refugees caused by conflict. GEO-2000 also showed other issues that might cause conflict in the future, when we will see two-thirds of the world's population by the year 2020 living in water-stressed areas. NATO and other bodies are now seriously looking at environmental security issues – so should the Security Council.

The Security Council has dealt with development crisis issues and called on NGOs such as Oxfam to address the council. This approach should be expanded in a coordinated way.

REALIGNING THE BRETTON WOODS INSTITUTIONS

One of the key questions that needs to be addressed at Earth Summit 2002 by developed countries is: are they committed to 'democratic governance and transparency within the UN system'? The 1990s have seen a shift among developing countries and the former Soviet bloc to democratic regimes. This has happened at the same time as there has been a move away from the UN towards the Bretton Woods institutions for discussions on finance, trade and even poverty. The result of this is that the developed countries now have a greater control of the agenda through Bretton Woods institutions. The integration of the Bretton Woods institutions within the UN should be on the agenda for 2002.

One reason why the Bretton Woods institutions have moved ahead is that they use the fact that there is an unequal decision-making structure where the richer countries who 'pay the bills' have more influence. Understanding in the donor countries about the impact of the Bretton Woods institutions has been highlighted very well by the late president of Tanzania, Julius Nyerere :

> 'I was in Washington last year. At the World Bank the first question they asked me was: "How did you fail?" I responded that we took over a country with 85 per cent of the adult population illiterate. The British ruled us for 43 years. When they left, there were 2 trained engineers and 12 doctors. This is the country we inherited.
>
> When I stepped down there was 91 per cent literacy and nearly every child was in school. We trained thousands of engineers, doctors and teachers.
>
> In 1988 Tanzania's per capita income was US$280. Now [1998] it is US$140. So I asked the World Bank people what went wrong. Because for the last ten years Tanzania has been signing on the dotted line and doing everything the IMF and World Bank wanted. Enrolment

> *in school has plummeted to 63 per cent and conditions*
> *in health and other social services have deteriorated. I*
> *asked them again: "What went wrong?" These people just*
> *sat there looking at me. Then they asked: What could*
> *they do? I said: "Have some humility".* '7

EcoSoc has been conducting a series of 'dialogues' with the Bretton Woods institutions. It is too early to say where these are going, but the hope is that they will start to bring the institutions into a more focused and accountable relationship with EcoSoc. One of the issues here is not only related to the World Bank but also to what impact a decision by EcoSoc or the UN General Assembly has on UN agencies and programmes.

TRUSTEESHIP COUNCIL

The Trusteeship Council is one of the United Nation's six principal organs and has played a vital role in the process of decolonization and overseeing the progress of trust territories to independence and self-government. One of the recommendations from the Commission on Global Governance was that: 'The Trusteeship Council should be given a new mandate: to exercise trusteeship over the global commons.'[8]

One of the strengths of this idea is that the council would be a body acting on the behalf of all nations. It would give due recognition to the importance of the environment. Its functions would, according to the Commission on Global Governance, 'include the administration of environmental treaties in such fields as climate change, biodiversity, outer space and the Law of the Sea. It would refer, as appropriate, any economic or security issues arising from these matters to the Economic and Social Council or the Security Council.'[9]

Putting this recommendation into practice would have a drastic impact on UNEP and the CSD; it could cause the discussion of 'sustainable development' to be taken apart – with economic and social issues being referred to the proposed Economic Security Council or to the present Economic and Social Council, and environmental issues going to the Trusteeship Council.

Another possible way of approaching the Trusteeship Council is to have it take the place of the CSD and address the soft and hard areas of sustainable development but at a higher level within the UN. This would ensure the necessary integrated approach to sustainable development. If the practice of how the CSD operates and the active involvement of capitals could be retained, then it would take away the need for the CSD recommendations to go to EcoSoc and to the GA. If sustainable development is taken in its broadest sense, then it could include the work of other functioning commissions of EcoSoc such as the Social Development Commission.

WORLD ENVIRONMENT ORGANIZATION (WEO)

In the preparation for UNGASS (Earth Summit II), the issue of the need to create a counterbalance to the World Trade Organization became more and more obvious. In the period since 1992, UNEP had become weaker. At the Earth Council event in Rio in March 1997 the then executive director of UNEP, Elizabeth Dowdeswell, told Inter Press Service that she felt that 1997, the 25th anniversary of the Stockholm Conference on Environment, was the year in which her organization would be able to meet the new challenges of globalization:

> *'I think people are worried about globalization, and they want an international organization that is strong enough and that has the authority to be a counterweight to the World Trade Organization ... The challenges of globalization in the era of the WTO are such that nations' laws to protect the environment can be superceded if they are deemed to interfere with free trade.'*[10]

UNEP unsuccessfully pushed for the creation of a stronger World Environment Organization (WEO). Other UN officials also saw the need for an environmental check against free-trade rules. James Gustave Speth, administrator of UNDP, told the Rio forum that there is a need for:

> *'...an effective partner at the international level to work with the WTO and other new entities. The United Nations is the logical location for such an institution, and it could be built from an entirely rebuilt, expanded and renamed UNEP. The proposed World Environmental Organization should be capable of developing and monitoring international environmental agreements and promoting international environmental protection and cooperation.'*[11]

The discussion on the WEO was brought to the 1997 Special Session of the General Assembly by Germany, with the support of South Africa, Singapore and Brazil. Former Chancellor Helmut Kohl of the Federal Republic of Germany told the Special Session at New York on 23 June 1997 that:

> '...*global environment protection and sustainable development need a clearly audible voice at the United Nations. Therefore, in the short term, I think it is important that cooperation among the various environmental organizations be significantly improved. In the medium term this should lead to the creation of a global umbrella organization for environmental issues, with the United Nations Environment Programme as a major pillar.*'[12]

The discussion fell on deaf ears as there had been little preparation and the financial situation in the world did not allow for the creation of such a body.

One suggestion for the WEO is to collect together under one organization the conventions and the GEF. By doing so, this would enable the environment conventions to have the financial mechanisms to deliver the convention built into the same institution. There are some interesting issues that must be addressed if this approach is to be taken. These include the following questions.

*   Should the body be set up with a universal membership?
*   How can the issue that different countries have ratified different conventions be addressed?
*   What relationship will this body have to the UN as a whole and to the WTO?
*   What relationship will it have to the CSD?

If these questions can be answered adequately, then the WEO will also have to answer the issue of focusing on environment and not sustainable development. This will greatly strengthen the environmental axis; but where does that put the interplay between the environment and development agendas that Rio brought about?

A different suggestion concerning how one might construct a WEO has come from the Yale Environmental Governance Dialogue. It suggests that some of the key problems that need to be addressed are:

*   There is fragmentation of the present environmental regime (UNEP, CSD, UNDP, WMO, IOC, FAO, UNESCO and treaty organizations) and this hampers efforts on coordination.
*   The organizations that we depend upon internationally to deal with environmental issues have narrow mandates and small budgets.
*   What should be the location of UNEP (Kenya)?

The present global environmental governance structure is dated and needs restructuring. The Yale dialogue also proposed some suggestions of the way forward. It suggests that a global environmental organization should have the capacity to:

- Gather data and monitor environmental indicators.
- Provide an early warning system to forecast and identify environmental disasters and societies at risk.
- Promote information and technology exchange.
- Serve as a catalytic force to focus the world community on emerging global-scale pollution and resource management issues.
- Act as a convening authority to coordinate global responses to environmental challenges (engaging not only governments but also civil society at large, including business and NGOs).
- Offer a forum for dispute resolution.
- Establish policy guidelines to promote global responses to environmental challenges.

The Yale dialogue argues that, in the short term, institutional coordination might be achieved through a new UN 'development and environment group' chaired jointly by the heads of UNEP, UNDP and the World Bank. It also suggests that the new global environment organization should have a three-level structure. The core function should be an 'effective international response to inherently global issues'. Moreover, it proposes the following:

> 'At the centre of this entity, we recommend that organizations responsible for the global commons – UNEP, WMO, the International Oceanographic Commission (IOC) and the International Hydrological Programme (IHP) of UNESCO be merged.'[13]

The dialogue suggests that a second level would consist of coordinating the conventions without compromising the legal character of the COP.

The third level would be permanent consultation links with CSD, UNDP, FAO, WHO and UNESCO and the multilateral economic and development agencies, as well as stakeholders working in the field of environment.

What is clear is that the discussion on a WEO is now being addressed seriously by NGOs, think tanks and governments. There is a rich agenda of ideas on the way forward which will make it more likely that there will be progress.

STRENGTHENING UNEP

Following the 1997 UN General Assembly Special Session to review

Rio, the Secretary-General Kofi Annan established a task force on environment and human settlements under the new UNEP Executive Director Klaus Töpfer to draft recommendations for improving the work of the UN in the area of environment and human settlements.

One of the key areas it was to look at was the coordination of the UN conventions in the area of environment. It had become increasingly clear that many of the conventions cover common areas and the need to have them work together has become more important. The report made suggestions for better coordination:

> '*The task force recommends that, in addition to integrating convention secretariats and convention-related issues in the work of the Environmental Management Group (EMG)...the executive director of UNEP should continue to sponsor joint meetings of heads of secretariats of global and regional conventions and use this forum to recommend actions to ensure that the work programmes established by the Conferences of Parties to the conventions, together with substantive support offered by UNEP, are complementary, fill gaps and take advantage of synergy, and avoid overlap and duplication. Recommendations from these meetings should be presented to the Conferences of Parties by the respective secretariats...with respect to existing conventions, approaches should include promoting cooperation among the secretariats with a view to their eventual co-location and possible fusion into a single secretariat; and in the longer term, the negotiation of umbrella conventions covering each cluster.*'[14]

The problems with achieving better coordination at times come down to the lack of political will or vested interests, or a real framework in which they might happen. For Earth Summit 2002 these problems need to be faced. One way of doing this is to bring all the conventions together in one place and under one administrative system. Creating the conditions where staff involved in one convention can work with those involved in another, but dealing with the same area, is crucial to ensuring that there is better coordination; this will help to ensure that governments and others will have a clear idea of what is actually being achieved. Another idea is to suggest that convention meetings happen at the same time, in the same place and that there is a common agenda. Joined-up thinking requires some attempt to bring people together who do not usually meet.

A COMMITTEE OF THE UN GENERAL ASSEMBLY

One of the suggestions before the Rio Conference was that a sustainable development committee of the UN General Assembly should be established. Discussions then were of a UN standing committee similar to the Committee on New and Renewable Sources of Energy which was created after the 1982 UN Energy Conference. One of the results of the 1997 Special Session was to take responsibility for this area, which had been inadequately dealt with by the standing committee.

A more adventurous idea would be for one of the General Assembly committees – parts of the second combined with parts of the third – to become the sustainable development GA committee. This would require governments to commit funds to ensure that the discussion was supported adequately by capital experts in the issues and not just by representatives from government missions in New York. It would also require an opening of the system to allow major groups a more effective involvement along the lines that the CSD has pioneered. The result, though, would be a 'higher-level' discussion on sustainable development with all countries taking part, not just 53 as is the case with the CSD.

UNDP AND OTHER UN AGENCIES

Agenda 21 was full of recommendations for the UN agencies and programmes.[15] One of the problems has been to try to ensure that these recommendations place sustainable development and Agenda 21 at the heart of their work. There has been some good work by people in several UN agencies and programmes, but it is hard to see a real concerted and strategic approach being carried out from Rio. Some of the ways this might be approached beyond 2002 include the following:

- The IACSD should produce a yearly report on implementing Earth Summit 2002 for the CSD and for governments. This will make UN agencies and programmes answerable for their decisions in a forum other than their own governing council.
- The UN Development Group (UNDG) should be empowered to produce reports on implementation at the national level.
- The UNDP should make poverty eradication the key to their contribution to sustainable development.
- All relevant UN agencies and programmes should make the follow-up to Earth Summit 2002 an item on their governing councils' agendas, up to the year 2012.

CSD: MOVING THE ENVELOPE FORWARD

Originally, the Rio Conference in 1992 did not intend to implement a follow-up mechanism. The conference was, in effect, created by a coalition of progressive Northern and Southern governments and NGOs. In opposition were the US, UK, China, India, Brazil and Kenya. Many of these countries have become great supporters of the CSD since it was formed.

The CSD has supported the involvement of major groups and, as was mentioned before, it has managed to set itself up as a political forum with a high level of involvement from ministers.

For the period beyond 2002, there is a need for more joined-up thinking between the CSD and the other UN commissions that are actively involved in monitoring aspects of Agenda 21 and whatever comes out of Earth Summit 2002.

The UN EcoSoc has four commissions which cover areas that could work together more. These are the commissions on social development, the status of women, sustainable development and population and development. All of these commissions are serviced by the UN Department for Economic and Social Affairs (DESA). In the next phase of work, these commissions – including the Commission on Human Settlement, which is a standing committee – could work for a set of common meetings.

This approach would have some very important side effects. It would not only ensure more coordination between the UN divisions responsible for servicing the UN commissions, but it would also force government departments to coordinate among themselves. This should ensure that there is better implementation. Table 25.1 tries to give some idea of what an integrated approach might look like.

REGIONAL COMMISSIONS: MONITORING IMPLEMENTATIONS

Post-Earth Summit 2002, there will still need to be a review of governments and other stakeholders' implementation of Agenda 21. This could be devolved to the UN regional commissions. The commissions were under threat in the 1980s from countries who saw them as unnecessary institutions.

If financed adequately, regional commissions can be very effective at monitoring and implementation. The countries that are members of these commissions tend to have much more in common than at a global level in the area of economic development. Many face similar environmental problems; and a structured review at the regional level, with built-in multistakeholder dialogue processes, timetables and targets to implement the agreed outcomes, should ensure that devel-

Table 25.1 *Possible work programme of the CSD, 2003–2007*

Year	Sectoral themes	Key bodies	Cross-cutting issues	Enablers	Dialogue session
2003	Health: AIDS/HIV	WHO; UNEP; UN	Consumption and production; Poverty	Trade; Technology transfer; Capacity-building; Finance; Governance; Education	AIDS/HIV; Development finance
	Population	Commission on Population and Development; UN AIDS; International financial institutions		Trade; Technology transfer; Capacity-building; Finance; Governance; Education	
2004	Tourism; Freshwater	Commission on the Status of Women; UNEP; UNDP; IFIs; WTO	Finance; Consumption and production	Trade; Technology transfer; Capacity-building; Finance; Governance; Education	Tourism
2005	Poverty; Agriculture	Commission on Social Development; UNDP; World Bank and IMF; FAO	Trade; Consumption, and production	Trade; Technology transfer; Capacity-building; Finance; Governance; Education	Poverty; Environment
2006	Urbanization/LA21	Commission on Human Settlement; UNDP; UNCHS; UNEP; World Bank	Finance; Consumption and production	Trade; Technology transfer; Capacity-building; Finance; Governance; Education	Trade
2007	Summit of the Regions				

Table 25.2 *Possible work programme for UN regional commissions*

Year	Sectoral themes to review	Key bodies	Cross-cutting issues	Dialogue session
2003	Transport; Energy	UNEP; WHO; UNDP; WHO; FAO; UNCTAD; IFIs	Poverty; Technological transfer; Capacity-building; Finance	Air pollution
2004	Freshwater; Forests	UNEP; UNDP; WHO; FAO; UNCTAD; IFIs	Poverty; Technological transfer; Capacity-building; Finance	Freshwater
2005	Agriculture; Forests	UNDP; FAO; IFAD; UNEP; IFIs	Poverty; Technological transfer; Capacity-building; Finance	Forests
2006	Oceans	IOC; FAO; Regional fisheries bodies; UNEP; IMO	Poverty; Technological transfer; Capacity-building; Finance	Fisheries
2002	Summit of the Regions			

oping countries will see the required funds, technological transfer and capacity-building released.

The UN Economic Commission for Europe has been an effective law-maker across eastern and western Europe in areas such as air pollution. Other UN regions have yet to go down this path, but they could. A convention on transboundary air pollution within the area of the UN Commission for South-East Asia has been considered. There could be a coordinated approach between the different UN commissions where each would also work to an agreed multiyear thematic programme of work. Table 25.2 attempts to produce a possible five-year work programme of regional law.

To support this institutionally, the Inter-Agency Committee on Sustainable Development should convene a yearly meeting of high-level representatives from the regional commissions and relevant UN agencies, including the Bretton Woods institutions, in order to oversee coordination. This could lead to a 'summit of the regions' five years after Earth Summit 2002, which would share the experiences of implementation and development of a framework of regional law.

THE ROLE OF STAKEHOLDERS

The CSD has been a very important arena in which major groups can develop their relationships with the UN and among themselves. The CSD has been one of the key places where stakeholders' involvement in the UN has been developed.

In 1993 the CSD asked that the NGOs, including all major UN groups who had been accredited to Rio, should be allowed to be accredited to EcoSoc. This started a three-year dispute where the more conservative members of the UN rejected the CSD agreement on NGOs when it went to the UN General Assembly. In 1996 it was finally agreed that the NGOs would be written to, asking if they wanted to become fully accredited NGOs. In the end, 123 NGOs joined together, bypassing the normal NGO accreditation process.

The CSD has enabled major groups at its annual sessions to increase their involvement. This has included the following:

- being let into informal and formal meetings and then invited to speak (1993);
- asking their governments questions in front of their peer group in national presentations (1994);
- the introduction of 'a day on a major group' (1995);
- the introduction of the dialogue sessions as a series of five half-day 'major group' presentations (1997);
- developing the dialogues as an interactive two-day discussion among governments and certain stakeholder groups on a specific topic (1998);
- setting up the first multistakeholder process to follow up a CSD decision (on voluntary agreements and initiatives on industry) (1998);
- giving the outcomes of the dialogues higher status and putting them on the table with the ministerial discussion and CSD intersessional document for the CSD chair's consideration (1999);
- setting up the second multistakeholder process to follow up a CSD decision (on tourism) (1999).

The CSD has seen quite a large involvement of major groups in its work. Each commission meeting has had around 200 to 300 major group representatives attending at some point throughout the three-week period. In the 1999 CSD this grew to over 600. The CSD has pioneered a greater involvement of major groups in the sessions of the commission. None of the sessions are now closed; even the small working groups are held open for major group representatives to attend and in many cases speak.

The increased involvement of major groups in implementing the UN conference agreements has seen a higher participation in the framing of the agreements. Perhaps the Habitat II Conference expanded the involvement to where the norm should be. At this conference and its preparatory meetings, NGOs were allowed to enter suggestions of text amendments. To do this they were asked to organize themselves into a negotiating block; the UN then brought the NGO amendments out as an official UN document: A/Conf.165/INF/8. This was the first time this had happened.

The Habitat II process also had another first, Committee 2. In Committee 2 in Istanbul there was a series of half-day dialogues between stakeholder groups. The reality was that as the negotiations were going on in Committee 1, the level of participation was low and there was no input within the negotiations. The idea of the dialogues was taken up by the CSD NGO steering committee, who wrote to the Undersecretary-General Nitin Desai in August 1996 requesting his support for the introduction of dialogues at the CSD in 1997. The UN General Assembly agreed in November 1996 and asked each of the major groups to prepare for half-day dialogue sessions on the role they had taken in implementing Agenda 21.

The CSD dialogues in 1997 were held at the same time as the negotiations and were in most cases poorly attended. They were written into the five-year work programme of the CSD. The topic for the dialogues during 1998 was agreed to be industry, and the then director of the UN division on sustainable development, Joke Waller Hunter, brought together the International Chamber of Commerce and the World Business Council on Sustainable Development (for industry), the International Confederation of Free Trade Unions (for trade unions), and the CSD NGO steering committee (for NGOs). Under her leadership a new formula was agreed. This included the breakthrough that the negotiations would not take place during the dialogues. Each stakeholder group was to consult and produce a starting paper on the sub-themes of:

- Responsible entrepreneurship;
- Corporate management tools;
- Technology cooperation and assessment;
- Industry and freshwater.

These papers were to be given out as UN background papers before the CSD intersessional in March; governments would have the opportunity to reflect upon them as they discussed the issues for the first time. One of the very important by-products of this approach by all stakeholders was that it caused 'peer group' review inside the stakeholder group. Another important outcome was that comments, which in the past were made by a group to governments in the corridors, now could be made in a 'creative' forum where governments could hear the reasons for and against and – as a result – challenge them.

When the dialogues started at the CSD, some governments were unhappy about the idea that they had to listen to stakeholder groups and saw this as an encroachment on governmental space. The success of the dialogues in part was due to the chairing by the then Philippines Minister of the Environment Cielito Habito, who challenged the stakeholder groups on what they were saying and caused peer group review between stakeholder groups and with governments. This caused the birth of the first really dynamic model for engaging the different stakeholders in a UN ongoing process.

The third-year dialogue session was on tourism; in order to focus better on the issues, the NGO CSD steering committee suggested that the papers should be four pages long and structured by the following themes:

- Problems;
- Solutions;
- Institutional responsibilities;
- Possible partnerships.

The active involvement of Simon Upton, the then New Zealand minister for the environment, saw the dialogues succeed again during the preparatory process. Through his office a meeting was convened in London under the chairing of David Taylor (New Zealand government), where representatives of all the stakeholder groups were brought together at the end of March to see what might be agreed upon. This was followed by a meeting chaired by David Taylor, on behalf of Simon Upton, the night before the CSD to see if the agreements would hold.

The outcome of the CSD dialogue sessions was important in two areas:

1   A multistakeholder group was set up under the World Tourism Organization (WTO) to look at financial leakages in the tourism industry and to make recommendations the following year; this group would prepare a joint initiative to improve information availability and capacity-building for participation in tourism.
2   The agreements that came out of the two days were then used with the CSD intersessional document, and the outcomes of tourism

Table 25.3 *A review of proposals and their requirement for the UN charter amendment and major group involvement*[16]

Proposal	Charter amendment	Ability for involvement of major groups	Binding decision
UN Charter Change to Promote Sustainable Development	Yes	Not applicable	No
Utilizing the Security Council	No	Possibly as experts	Yes
Realigning the Bretton Woods Institutions	No	Possibly	Yes
Trusteeship Council	Yes	Possibly	Yes
World Environment Organization	Yes	Probably	Yes
Committee of the General Assembly	No	Probably	Yes
Strengthening UNEP	No	Yes	No
UNDP and other UN Agencies	No	Yes	No
CSD: Moving the Envelope Forward	No	Yes	No
Regional Commissions: Monitoring Implementations	No	Yes	No

from the high-level ministerial were used to develop the final text of the international work programme on sustainable tourism.

This was an enormous leap in major group involvement in the UN. Instead of the work and expertise of the major groups being part of a side show, or having to work exclusively in the corridors, we are now seeing the work incorporated within the negotiations.

A recommendation has been made to UNEP that it should replicate the dialogue process for the next UNEP governing council in 2001. Other UN bodies and the WTO should look seriously at the approach the CSD has taken, since it offers a good way to involve relevant stakeholders and to ensure better-informed decisions.

IMPLICATION OF THE PROPOSALS

The suggestions above in certain cases require some charter amendments; as a result, Table 25.3 looks at the possible implications of the suggestions in this chapter for charter amendments, the involvement of major groups, and if what is being proposed would create binding decisions.

CONCLUSION

This chapter has tried to outline some of the options for moving forward the international machinery; however, alone this will not achieve the implementation of any of the global plans of action agreed upon by countries. What is needed to achieve this is a 'new realistic deal' between developed and developing countries to which both will adhere. This deal will also require a newly found responsibility by other stakeholder groups regarding their role in implementing any agreement. It will require some vision and, most importantly, some trust.

NOTES

1   The Charter of the United Nations was signed on 26 June 1945, in San Francisco, at the conclusion of the United Nations Conference on International Organization, and came into force on 24 October 1945. The full text can be accessed at the United Nations website: http://www.un.org/aboutun/charter/
2   UNCED (1992) Agenda 21, Chapter 38: 'Institutional Structure', Section 3, London: the Regency Press, p231
3   Ibid
4   Osborn, D and Bigg, T and (1998) *Earth Summit II: Outcomes and Analysis*, London: Earthscan Publications Ltd, p64
5   United Nations (1997) *Report of the UN General Assembly Special Session Programme for the Further Implementation of Agenda 21*, New York: UN
6   Charter of the United Nations op cit Note 1
7   Nyerere, J (1999) 'The Heart of Africa', *New Internationalist*, London, No 309, pp12–15
8   Commission on Global Governance (1995) 'Summary of Proposals in Reforming the United Nations', *The Report of the Commission on Global Governance*, Oxford: Oxford University Press, p301
9   Ibid
10 Dowdeswell, E (1997) 'Momentum Builds for Successor to UNEP', interview by Farhan Haq for Inter Press Service, Rio
11 Speth, J G (1997) 'Momentum Builds for Successor to UNEP', interview by Farhan Haq for Inter Press Service, Rio
12 Kohl, H (1997) Chancellor of the Federal Republic of Germany, speech to the UN Special Session of the General Assembly of the United Nations, New York, 23 June
13 Esty, D (1998) *Strengthening Global Environmental Governance*, New York: Yale Environmental Governance Dialogue
14 UN Task Force on Environment and Human Settlements (1998) *1998 Report*, Nairobi: UN Task Force on Environment and Human Settlements
15 UNCED (1992) op cit Note 2
16 Tampier M (1996) Concept adapted from 'The UN and Environmental Conflict', thesis, Brussels: Vrije Universiteit

Appendix 1

List of Acronyms and Abbreviations

ACC	Administrative Committee on Co-ordination
AIDS	acquired immune deficiency syndrome
ANPED	Northern Alliance for Sustainability (The Netherlands)
AOSIS	Alliance of Small Island States
ASTIMWR	application of space techniques to the integrated management of a river-basin water resources
BSE	bovine spongiform encephalopathy
CAN	Climate Action Network
CBD	Convention on Biological Diversity
CCAMLR	Commission for the Conservation of Antarctic Marine Living Resources
CCD	Convention to Combat Desertification
CEC	Commission of the European Communities
CEDAW	Committee for the Elimination of Discrimination Against Women
CEE	central and eastern European countries
CEO	chief executive officer
CEREAL YES	Cereal Yield Estimation System
CFP	Common Fisheries Policy
CGIAR	Consultative Group on International Agricultural Research
CHS	(UN) Commission on Human Settlements
CITES	Convention on International Trade in Endangered Species of Wild Fauna and Flora
C&I	certification and indicators
CLC	Convention on Civil Liability
CMS	Convention on Migratory Species
CO_2	carbon dioxide
COFI	(FAO) Committee on Fisheries
COP	Conference of the Parties
COP-n	nth Meeting of the COP
CPD	(UN) Commission on Population and Development
C Soc Dev	(UN) Commission on Social Development
CSC	Convention for Safe Containers
CSD	(UN) Commission on Sustainable Development

CSD-*n*	*n*th Session of the CSD
CSD NGO SC	(UN) CSD NGO Steering Committee
CSW	(UN) Commission on the Status of Women
CTE	(WTO) Committee on Trade and Environment
CTP	Common Transport Policy
DAC	(OECD) Development Assistance Committee
DAW	Division for the Advancement of Women
DESA	(UN) Department for Economic and Social Affairs
DETR	(UK) Department for the Environment, Transport and the Regions
DSD	(UN) Division on Sustainable Development
Earth Summit II	see UNGASS
EC	European Commission
ECA	(UN) Economic Commission for Africa
EC DG XI	European Commission Directorate General XI (Environment and Nuclear Safety)
ECE	(UN) Economic Commission for Europe
ECLAC	(UN) Economic Commission for Latin America and the Caribbean
EcoSoc	(UN) Economic and Social Council
EEC	European Economic Community
EFITA	European Federation of Information Technology in Agriculture
EFP	ecological footprint
EFTA	European Free Trade Association
EIA	environmental impact assessment
EMG	Environmental Management Group
EPOTFA	Eastern Pacific Ocean Tuna Fishery Association
ESCAP	(UN) Economic and Social Commission for Asia and the Pacific
ESCWA	(UN) Economic and Social Commission for Western Asia
EU	European Union
FAL	Facilitation of International Maritime Traffic
FAO	(UN) Food and Agriculture Organization
FCCC	see UNFCCC
FDI	foreign direct investment
FFA	Forum Fisheries Association
FoE	Friends of the Earth
FSC	Forest Stewardship Council
G8	Group of eight leading industralized nations
Group of 77	Group of developing nations (now over 140)
GA	(UN) General Assembly
GATS	General Agreement on Trade in Services
GATT	General Agreement on Tariffs and Trade
GC	governing council
GCOS	Global Climate Observing System
GDP	gross domestic product
GEF	Global Environment Facility
GEO	Global Environment Outlook (UNEP report)
GESAMP	Group of Experts on Environmental Aspects of Marine Environmental Protection
GFPP	Global Forestry Policy Project

GHG	greenhouse gas
GNP	gross national product
GPA	Global Programme of Action
GRI	Global Reporting Initiative
GSP	(EC) generalized system of preferences
GTI	Global Toxics Institute
GWP	Global Water Partnership
HDI	Human Development Index
HDR	Human Development Report
HIPC	highly indebted poorer countries
IACSD	Inter-Agency Committee on Sustainable Development
IACWGE	ACC Inter-Agency Committee on Women and Gender Equality
IAEA	International Atomic Energy Agency
IATTC	Inter-American Tropical Tuna Commission
IAVI	International AIDS Vaccine Initiative
ICC	International Chamber of Commerce
ICCAT	International Convention for the Conservation of Atlantic Tunas
ICFTU	International Confederation of Free Trade Unions
ICLEI	International Council for Local Environmental Initiatives
ICPD	International Conference on Population and Development
ICSEAF	International Commission for the South-East Atlantic Fisheries
ICSU	International Council for Science
IDT	international development target
IEA	International Energy Agency
IGO	intergovernmental organization
IFAD	International Fund and Agricultural Development
IFAP	International Federation of Agricultural Producers
IFF	Intergovernmental Forum on Forests
IFI	international financial institution
IFIR	International Forest Industries Round Table
IHP	International Hydrological Programme
IIED	International Institute for Environmental Development
ILO	International Labour Organization
IMF	International Monetary Fund
IMO	International Maritime Organization
IOC	International Oceanographic Commission
IOTC	Indian Ocean Tuna Commission
IPCC	Intergovernmental Panel on Climate Change
IPF	Intergovernmental Panel on Forests
IPP	independent power producer
IPRs	intellectual property rights
IRPUD	Institute of Spatial Planning University of Dortmund
ISA	International Seabed Authority
ISEA	Institute for Social and Ethical Accountability
ISEW	Index of Sustainable Economic Welfare
ISO	International Standards Organization
ITDP	Institute for Transport and Development Policy
ITFF	Interagency Task Force on Forests
ITQ	individual transferable quotas

ITTO	International Tropical Timber Organization
IUCN	International Council for the Conservation of Nature
IULA	International Union of Local Authorities
IWC	International Whaling Commission
IWRM	integrated water resource management
IWSA	International Water Services Association
LA21	Local Agenda 21
LDC	least-developed country
LEAD	Leadership for Environment and Development
MAFF	(UK) Ministry of Fisheries and Food
MAI	Multilateral Agreement on Investment
MAP	Mediterranean Action Plan
MARPOL	International Convention for the Protection of Pollution from Ships
MDB	multilateral development banks
MEA	multilateral environmental agreement
MNC	multinational corporation
MOU	memorandum of understanding
MSC	Marine Stewardship Council
NAFTA	North Atlantic Free Trade Agreement
NAFO	North-West Atlantic Fisheries Organization
NATO	North Atlantic Treaty Organization
NEF	New Economics Foundation
NFP	national forest programme
NGO	non-governmental organization
NIS	Newly Independent States (of the former Soviet Union)
NOP	National Opinion Poll
NPRP	National Poverty Reduction Programme, Ghana
NSSD	national strategy for sustainable development
NZODA	New Zealand Overseas Development Aid
ODA	official development assistance
ODS	(UN) Optical Disk Service
OECD	Organization for Economic Co-operation and Development
OEEC	Organization for European Economic Co-operation
OPRC-1990	International Convention on Oil Pollution Preparedness Response and Co-operation – 1990
OSCE	Organization of Security and Co-operation in Europe
PCB	polychlorinated biphenyl
POPs	persistent organic pollutants
POJA	programme of joint action
QCPTA	Queensland Cleaner Production Task Force Association
RSPB	Royal Society for the Protection of Birds
SACTRA	Standing Advisory Council on Trunk Road Assessment
SADC	Southern African Development Community
SAR	Maritime Search and Rescue
SEA	strategic environmental assessment
SFM	sustainable forest management
SIDS	small island developing states
SO_x	sulphuric oxide
SOLAS	(IMO) International Convention for the Safety of Life at Sea

SPACE	Special Trade Passenger Ships Agreement
SPREP	South-Pacific Regional Environment Programme
SRM	self-regulated mechanism
STCW	Standards of Training, Certification and Watchkeeping
SVF	Safety of Fishing Vessels
TBC	to be confirmed
TEN	Trans-European Network
TINA	Transport Infrastructure Needs Assessment Programme
TNC	transnational corporation
ToBI	Task Force on Business and Industry
TRIPS	Trade-Related Aspects of Intellectual Property Rights Agreement
TUAC	Trade Union Advisory Committee
TWG	technical working group
UCCEE	UNEP Collaboration Centre on Energy and Environment
UNA-UK	United Nations Association – UK
UNAIDS	United Nations Programme on HIV/AIDS
UNCED	United Nations Conference on Environment and Development (known as Earth Summit)
UNCHS	United Nations Centre for Human Settlements
UNCLOS	United Nations Convention on the Law of the Seas
UNCTAD	United Nations Conference on Trade and Development
UNDESA	United Nations Department on Economic and Social Affairs
UNDG	United Nations Development Group
UNDP	United Nations Development Programme
UNDSD	United Nations Division for Sustainable Development
UNEP	United Nations Environment Programme
UNESCO	United Nations Educational, Scientific and Cultural Organization
UNESCO-IOC	UNESCO Intergovernmental Oceanographic Commission
UNED-UK	United Nations Environment and Development – UK Committee
UNFCCC	United Nations Framework Convention on Climate Change
UNGASS	United Nations General Assembly Special Session (known as Earth Summit II)
VIAs	voluntary initiatives and agreements
WB	World Bank
WBGU	German Advisory Council on Global Change
WBCSD	World Business Council for Sustainable Development
WCEC	World Clean Energy Conference
WCED	World Comission on Environment and Development (known as the Brundtland Commission)
WDR	World Development Report
WEDO	Women's Environment and Development Organization
WEO	World Environment Organization
WFS	World Food Security
WHO	World Health Organization
WICE	World Industry Council for the Environment
WCFSD	World Commission on Forests and Sustainable Development
WMO	World Meteorological Organization

WRI   World Resources Institute
WSS   water supply and sanitation
WSSD   World Summit for Social Development
WTO   World Tourism Organization
WTO   World Trade Organization
WTTC   World Travel and Tourism Council
WWF   World Wide Fund For Nature

ABBREVIATIONS IN FIGURE 1.1 AND BOX 1.1

Abidjan   Convention for the Cooperation in the Protection
                   and Development of the Marine and Coastal
                   Environment of the West and Central African Region
Anadromous Stocks Convention for the Conservation of Anadromous
                   Stocks in the North Pacific Ocean
Atlantic Treaty '59 Northeast Atlantic Fisheries Convention
Baltic '92   Convention on the Protection of the Marine
                   Environment of the Baltic Sea Area
BAMOKO   Convention on the Ban of Imports into Africa and
                   the Control of Transboundary Movement and
                   Managements of Hazardous Wastes Within Africa
Basel   Basel Convention on the Control and Movement of
                   Hazardous Wastes and their Disposal
Bering Sea   Convention on the Conservation and Management
                   of Pollock Resources in the Central Bering Sea
BLU   Code of Practice for the Safe Loading and Unloading
                   of Bulk Carriers
Bonn '79   Amendment to the Convention on International
                   Trade in Endangered Species
Cargo   Relating to Numerous IMO Cargo Codes
Carriage of Nuclear Convention relating to Civil Liability in the Field of
Materials '71   Maritime Carriage of Nuclear Materials
Cartagena   Convention for the Protection and Development of
                   the Marine Environment of the Wider Caribbean
                   Region
CCAMLR '80   Convention on the Conservation of Atlantic Marine
                   Living Resources
CLC   Convention on Civil Liability for Oil Pollution
                   Damage
Conserve HS   Convention on Fishing and Conservation of the
                   Living Resources of the High Seas
CS   Convention on the Continental Shelf
CSV   International Convention for Safe Containers
CTU   Guidelines for the Packing of Cargo Transport Units
FAL   IMO Convention on Facilitation of International
                   Maritime Traffic
FAO IPOA   Food and Agriculture Organisation International
                   Plan of Action
FFA   FAO South Pacific Forum Fisheries Agency

FUND '92	International Oil Compensation Fund Convention
Geneva Convs	Geneva Conventions
HNS	Hazardous and Noxious Substances
HS	Convention on the High Seas
HSC	High Speed Craft
IATTC	International American Tuna Commission
IBC	IMP International Code for the Construction and Equipment of Ships Carrying Dangerous Chemicals in Bulk
ICCAT	International Convention for the Conservation of Atlantic Tuna
ICES	The International Council for the Exploitation of the Sea
ICSEAF	International Commission for the Southeast Atlantic Fisheries
IGC	IMO International Code for the Construction and Equipment of Ships Carrying Liquefied Gases in Bulk
ILO 147	International Labour Organisation Merchant Shipping (Minimum Standards) Convention 1976
IMDG	IMO International Maritime Dangerous Goods Code
IMO	International Maritime Organisation
INF Code	Code for the Safe Carriage of Irradiated Nuclear Fuels, Plutonium and High Level Radioactive Waste in Flask Aboard Ships
Int Grain	International Code for the Safe Carriage of Grain in Bulk
Intervention '69	International Convention Relating to Intervention on High-Seas Cases of Oil Pollution Casualties
IOTC	FAO Indian Ocean Tuna Commission
ISA	International Standards Authority
ISM	IMP International Safety Management Code
IWC	International Convention for the Regulation of Whaling
Load Lines	International Convention on Load Lines
London Dumping	Convention on the Prevention of Marine Pollution by Dumping of Wastes and Other Materials
LSA	IMP Life Saving Appliances Code
MARPOL	IMP International Convention for the Prevention of Pollution from Ships
MOU	IMP Memorandum of Understanding on Port State Control in the Region...
NAFO	North West Atlantic Fisheries Organisation
Nairobi	Convention for the Protection, Management and Development of the Marine and Coastal Environment of the East African Region
North Atlantic Salmon '82	Convention for the Conservation of Salmon in the North Atlantic Ocean
North West Atlantic '78	Convention on Future Multi-lateral Co-operation in the North West Atlantic Fisheries

NOWPAP	UNEP Regional Seas Programme for the North West Pacific Area
Oil Pollution re Seabed Resources	Convention on Civil Liability for Oil Pollution Damage Resulting from Exploitation for and Exploitation of Seabed Mineral Resources
OPRC	International Convention on Oil Pollution Prepardness, Response and Co-operation
Oslo	Convention for the Preservation of Marine Pollution by Dumping from Ships and Aircraft
PAL	Athens Convention Relating to the Carriage of Passengers and their Luggage at Sea
Paris	Convention on the Prevention of Marine Pollution from Land Based Sources
ROPME	UNEP Regional Seas Programme for the Red Sea and Gulf of Aden
SACEP	UNEP Global Plan of Action for the South Asian Co-operative Environment Programme
SALVAGE	IMO International Convention on Salvage
SAR	International Convention on Maritime Search and Rescue
SFV	The Torremolinos International Convention for the Safety of Fishing Vessels
SOLAS	IMO International Convention for the Safety of Life at Sea
SPACE	International Conference on Space Requirements for Special Trade Passenger Ships
SPREP	UNEP Global Plan of Action for the South Pacific Regional Environment Programme
STCW	International Convention on Standards of Training, Certification and Watch-keeping for Seafarers
Timber Deck	Code of Safe Practice for Ships Carrying Timber Deck Cargoes
Tonnage	IMO International Convention on Tonnage Measure of Ships
TS-CZ	Convention on the Territorial Sea of the Contiguous Zone
WAIGANI	Convention to Ban the Importation into Forum Island Countries of Hazardous and Radioactive Wastes and to Control the Transboundary Movement and Management of Hazardous Wastes within the South Pacific Region
Washington Declaration GPA	Washington Declaration on the Protection of the Marine Environment from Land Based Sources

Appendix 2

Addresses of Contributors

Minister Cletus A Avoka
Ministry of Environment, Science and
Technology
PO Box M 232
Accra, Ghana
+23 321 666049
+23 321 666828

Mr Stephen M J Bass
International Institute for Environment
and Development (IIED)
3 Endsleigh Street
London, WC1H 0DD, UK
+44 (0) 20 73882117
+44 (0) 20 73882826
www.iied.org
mailbox@iied.org

Ms Barbara J Bramble
National Wildlife Federation
1400 16th Street NW
Washington, DC 20036, USA
+1 202 7976800
+1 202 7975486
www.nwf.org
bramble@nwf.org

Mr Jeb Brugman (Secretary-General)
International Council for Local
Environmental Initiatives (ICLEI)
City Hall, West Tower, 16th Floor
Toronto, Ontario, M5H 2N2, Canada
+1 416 3921462
+1 416 3921478
www.iclei.org
sec.gen@iclei.org

Dr Gro Harlem Brundtland
World Health Organization
20 Avenue Appia
1211 Geneva 27, Switzerland
+41 227 912111
+41 227 910746
www.who.org
postmaster@who.ch

**Ms Margret Brusasco-Mackenzie
(Vice-Chair)**
UNED Forum
3 Whitehall Court
London, SW1A 2EL, UK
+32 276 79342
+44 (0) 20 79305893
www.uned-uk.org
brusascomackenzie@compuserve.com

**Mr Nitin Desai (Undersecretary-
General)**
Department of Economic and Social
Affairs
United Nations
DC2-2320
New York, NY 10017, US
+1 212 9635958
+1 212 9630443
www.un.org/esa/desa
esa@un.org

Mr Felix Dodds
UNED Forum
3 Whitehall Court
London, SW1A 2EL, UK
+44 (0) 20 78391784
+44 (0) 20 79305893
www.uned-uk.org
fdodds@earthsummit2002.org

Ms Victoria Elias
Centre for Environment and Sustainable
Development
ECO-Accord
pr. Mira, 36
129010 Moscow, Russia
+7 (095) 2804779
+7 (095) 2804779
www.accord.cis.lead.org
victoria@aivaschenko.home.bio.msu.ru

Mr Pieter van der Gaag (Executive Director)
ANPED, The Northern Alliance for
Sustainability
PO Box 59030
1040 KA Amsterdam, The Netherlands
+31 204 751742
+31 204 751743
www.antenna.nl/anped/
anped@anped.antenna.nl
Visiting address: Amaliastraat 5, 1052
GM Amsterdam

Rosalie Gardiner
UNEP Forum
3 Whitehall Court
London, SW1A 2EL, UK
+44 (0) 20 78391784
+44 (0) 20 79305893
www.uned-uk.org
rgardiner@earthsummit2002.org

Mr Winston Gereluk
International Confederation of Free
Trade Unions (ICFTU)
5 Boulevard du Roi Albert II, Bte 1
1210 Brussels, Belgium
+32 2 2240211
+32 2 2015815
www.icftu.org
internetpo@icftu.org

Mr Herbie Girardet (Chairman, Schumacher Society)
Visiting Professor
Middlesex University
93 Cambridge Gardens
London, W10 6JE, UK
+44 (0) 20 89696375
+44 (0) 20 89602202
herbie@easynet.co.uk

Mr Hon John Gummer MP (Chairman)
Marine Stewardship Council (MSC)
119 Altenburg Gardens
London, SW11 1JQ, UK
+44 (0) 20 73504000
+44 (0) 20 73501231
www.msc.org
Secretariat@msc.org

Dr Minu Hemmati
UNED Forum
3 Whitehall Court
London, SW1A 2EL, UK
+44 (0) 20 78391784
+44 (0) 20 79305893
www.uned-uk.org
mhemmati@earthsummit2002.org

Mr Maximo Kalaw
The Earth Council
Apartado 2323-1002
San Jose, Costa Rica
+50 625 61611
+50 625 52197
www.ecouncil.ac.cr
eci@terra.ecouncil.ac.cr

Mr Rob Lake (Director of Policy)
Traidcraft Exchange
Suite 308
16 Baldwin's Gardens
London, EC1N 7RJ, UK
+44 (0) 20 72423955
+44 (0) 20 72426173
www.traidcraft.co.uk
robl@traidcraft.co.uk

Jürgen Maier (Director)
German NGO Forum Environment &
Development
Am Michaelshof 8–10
D-53177 Bonn
+49 228 359704
+49 228 359096
www.forumue.de
chef@forumue.de

Mr Warren (Chip) Lindner
Chalet le Fort
30933 Route de la Barliette
74300 Carroz, France
+33 450 903612
+33 450 900321
101376.3300@compuserve.com

Mr Frans de Man (Director)
Retour Foundation
PO Box 1570
6501 BN Nijmegen, The Netherlands
+31 243 606224
+31 243 606224
www.retourfoundation.nl
frans@retourfoundation.nl

Dr Lauric Michaelis (Director)
Research Commission on Sustainable
Consumption
Oxford Centre for the Environment,
Ethics & Society
Mansfield College
Oxford, OX1 3TF, UK
+44 (0) 1865 282903
+44 (0) 1865 270886
http://users.ox.ac.uk/~ocees/
laurie.michaelis@mansf.ox.ac.uk

Mr Derek Osborn
UNED Forum (Chairman)
48 Talbot Road
London, N6 4QP, UK
+44 (0) 20 83407560
+44 (0) 20 83407560
www.uned-uk.org
derek_osborn@csi.com

Ms Delke Peters
Institute for Transportation &
Development Policy
115 West 30th Street
Suite 1205
New York, NY10001, US
+1 212 6298001
+1 212 6298033
Mobility@igc.org

**Ms Jagjit Kaur Plahe (Southern
Coordinator)**
NGO Task Force on Business and
Industry
30 Chapel Street
Glen Waverley
Melbourne, VIC 3150, Australia
+ 61 398 844176
jplahe@cheerful.com

Ms Nina Rao
University of Delhi + EQUATIONS
J-152 Saket
New Delhi-110017, India
+91 116 962376
+91 114 365180
theraos@vsnl.com

Mr Lucien Royer
Health, Safety and Environment Coordinator
International Confederation of Free
Trade Unions (ICFTU)
and Trade Union Advisory Committee to
OECD (TUAC)
+331 47 634263
+331 47 549828
www.ICFTU.org
www.TUAC.org
LRoyer@Compuserve.com

**Mr Andrew Simms (Global Economy
Programme)**
New Economics Foundation
6–8 Cole Street
London, SE1 4YH, UK
+44 (0) 20 74077447
+44 (0) 20 74076473
www.neweconomics.org
info@neweconomics.org

Rt Hon Simon D Upton MP
National Party
Parliament Buildings
Wellington, New Zealand
+64 447 19704
+64 447 30469
adrienne.frew@parliament.govt.nz
www.arcadia.co.nz

Appendix 3

UNED Forum

The United Nations Environment and Development Forum (UNED Forum) is a multistakeholder NGO that has been working to further the implementation of the sustainable development agenda since 1992. The organization operates at the national, regional and international level by providing space for dialogue and policy development between all groups. This includes: local government, trade unions, industry, NGOs, women's groups and academics. In addition, we work closely with UN agencies, addressing environment and development issues by facilitating access to their processes and raising awareness of their work in civil society. These agencies principally include: the UN Commission on Sustainable Development (UN CSD); the UN Environment Programme (UNEP); the UN Development Programme (UNDP); and the UN Centre for Human Settlements (UNCHS).

In its capacity as the current co-chair of the UN CSD NGO steering committee, the UNED Forum acts as an adviser to the global NGO community. In addition, the organization has increasingly extended this role to all sectors involved in the UN, including those working with the International Chamber of Commerce, the International Confederation of Free Trade Unions and the international local government associations.

At the European regional level, the UNED Forum, in 1998, was one of the founding members of the European Sustainable Development Network. This is an informal network of organizations equivalent to UNED Forum from The Netherlands, Germany, Norway, Denmark and Ireland. The network meets to coordinate the domestic and regional activities of its members, feeding into the international agenda on a range of environment and development issues. Part of the network's current role is in preparing for Earth Summit 2002.

To complement the present work, the UNED Forum will be active at the international level in the run-up to Earth Summit 2002. This will involve engaging stakeholders from all regions into the debate. We will ensure that this spotlight on Earth Summit 2002 spreads through all our activities at regional and domestic levels, as well as for our partners. Our role will be to continue to provide space for others, at all levels, in support of better coordination for Earth Summit 2002. It is hoped that through these activities, and by expanding the networks of communication, the UNED Forum can help to provide wholehearted yet realistic opportunities to carry the sustainable development agenda forward, beyond the summit and into the new millennium.

Index